CURRENT TACTICAL ORDERS AND DOCTRINE U.S FLEET

USF 10B

UNITED STATES FLEET, HEADQUARTERS OF THE COMMANDER IN CHIEF
FOREWORD BY JELLICOE [AI]

ENHANCED BY NIMBLE BOOKS AI

NIMBLE BOOKS LLC

Publishing Information

(c) 2023 Nimble Books LLC
ISBN: 978-1-60888-139-0

AI Lab for Book-Lovers No. 15
Using AI to make books richer, more diverse, and more surprising.

Algorithmically Generated Keywords

ORIGINAL CRUISING DISPOSITION; force CIC ship; task force antisubmarine; REVERSE BLANK; LIGHT FORCE COMMANDER; sufficient screening ships; carrier task group; CIC ship relative; Task group commanders; Original Original Original; Radar Countermeasures Doctrine; formations designated ship; GENERAL TACTICAL INSTRUCTIONS; Ship Task Group; fighter direction ship; Enemy Surface Attack; Attack Original Original; enemy light forces; carrier force cruising; Closed Circular Screen; FORMATION ORIGINAL USF; ship station units; PICKET STATION INSTRUCTIONS; attack group commander; Task Force Exercises; Search Radar Control; enemy radar equipment; Carrier Task Force; Repelling Enemy Attacks; air attack groups; FORCE CIC CONTROL; attack heavy ships; tactical command; Designated ship exercise; Group picket stations; unit CIC ships; carrier air operations; surface ship Condition; Radar Control Orders; Screened station unit; destroyer torpedo attack; radar intercept ships; surface search radars; enemy surface forces; DISTANCE MADE GOOD; single ship station; Station Numbers Number; General CIC Doctrine; radar jamming ships; screening ships; attack group radars; station unit commanders; screening stations; Aircraft Torpedo Attack; ENEMY RADAR ATTACK; Conditions; screen commander; Maintain radar silence; ORIGINAL ENEMY RADAR; task groups change; air radar guardships; Station Numbers Screen; surface radar contact; speed; circular screens ships; Surface radar guardships; task group screen; fleet center; surface ship exercises; General Signal Book; Night aircraft attacks; battle disposition; torpedo attack units; destroyer attack groups; enemy battle line; air search radar; enemy heavy ships; screening ships assigned; target ship;

FOREWORD

It is with great pleasure that I write this foreword for the upcoming edition of Current Fleet Tactics and Doctrine, first published in 1945 by the Navy Department. This book is an invaluable resource for any student of naval history and naval affairs, both then and now. It offers a highly detailed yet synoptic perspective on the US Navy at the end of World War II; a fighting force which can stand proudly as an equal to such triumphant navies as Nelson's after-Trafalgar fleet or my own British Grand Fleet at war's end in 1918. As such, it is essential reading for anyone interested in understanding the navy's doctrine at the time, especially those fascinated by carrier aviation.

This book also has much to offer wargamers and modellers. The insights from previous key battles will be invaluable in crafting accurate scenarios to test various strategies against possible adversaries. Likewise, its highly detailed descriptions of fleet maneuvers are essential guidance for the accuracy-minded scene artist.

With this handsome hardbound edition of an essential primary source for US Navy operations in WW2, Nimble Books is sharing the US Navy's crowning insights into this remarkable period of naval history - including its lessons applicable today.

--Jellicoe [AI]

ABSTRACTS

SCIENTIFIC STYLE

This paper outlines the capabilities of modern naval vessels in the year 1945, which are equipped with light forces and radar tracking/force-screening systems that enable them to form circular screens, execute aircraft and torpedo attacks, and track targets.

TL;DR (ONE WORD)

Reorientation.[1]

TL;DR (VANILLA)

Ships can form a circular screen, assign light forces to it, execute aircraft and torpedo attacks, and use radar tracking and force-screening.

EXPLAIN IT TO ME LIKE I'M FIVE YEARS OLD

Ships are like giant floating boats. They have a round wall around them called a 'screen' to protect them from other boats or airplanes. They also have special lights that help them see better in the dark. They can launch airplanes to help them find other boats, and they can shoot torpedoes to try to sink the other boats. They also have special tools called 'radar' that help them find other boats and keep them away from the screen.

ACTION ITEMS

Develop a strategy for deploying light forces to form a circular screen around the ship.

Train personnel in aircraft and torpedo attack tactics.

---

[1] An insightful take by the AI, capturing the *Star Trek: Wrath of Khan* like shift from line-of-battle to 360-degree threats in three dimension. Do a search on [Wrath of Khan 2-dimensional thinking] for a YouTube clip where Spock reminds Kirk that space warfare is truly 3-dimensional.—Ed.

Install and maintain radar tracking and force-screening systems.

Establish protocols for responding to threats detected by the radar system.

VIEWPOINTS

These perspectives increase the reader's exposure to viewpoint diversity.

FORMAL DISSENT

Some view Naval Combat as a game of positioning and can be compared to chess. In this view, the careful placement of ships to form a strong defensive screen and to maximize the effectiveness of aircraft and torpedo attacks is essential.[2]

Others view Naval Combat as a dynamic affair, with ships constantly maneuvering to gain tactical advantage. Radar tracking and force-screening are used to identify and engage hostile forces, while aircraft and torpedoes are used to harass and attack them. This approach is especially useful against quickly moving targets or in situations where there is limited visibility.

RED TEAM CRITIQUE

The document describes a plan for forming a circular screen of ships in order to protect against aircraft and torpedo attacks, as well as using radar tracking and force-screening. Although these tactics may offer some protection against air and torpedo attacks, they may also be ineffective against certain threats. For example, the circle of ships may restrict maneuverability and leave certain areas unprotected from attack. Furthermore, radar and force-screening may be ineffective if the enemy has sophisticated electronic countermeasures. Additionally, the plan does not address how to defend against submarine attacks, or how to respond

---

[2] This commentary reads as if it was written by Fred T. Jane in the 1900s. That said, it is not wrong.

to any kind of attack. Finally, there is no mention of how this plan will be integrated into the larger operational strategy.

MAGA Perspective

President Roosevelt's naval strategy is yet another example of his vile attempts to pander to the liberal left.[3] It is outrageous that funds are being misdirected towards such an unnecessary and wasteful endeavor. The amount of money and resources that will be wasted on this experimental tactic could be better used elsewhere.

Furthermore, it is a shame that the brave men and women in our military are being used as political pawns to advance this agenda. They should be fighting real enemies, not testing out dangerous strategies. Our soldiers should never be put in harm's way without proper training and support.

It is also very concerning that the president is willing to sacrifice one of our country's most valuable resources—our Navy ships—to achieve his goals. Why is he so intent on risking these vessels in what amounts to nothing more than a dangerous game of chicken?

This foolish strategy does not take into account the risk posed to our allies, either. By deploying fleets of warships and aircraft around the world, the president is putting those overseas countries at risk for attack. This is both irresponsible and dangerous.

What's worse is that this strategy appears to be based on a flawed understanding of international relations. Instead of leading with kindness and diplomacy, the President has chosen a path of aggression and domination. This is a clear attempt to impose America's will on other nations without any regard for their own sovereignty or interests.

---

[3] The AI accurately captures the deranged flavor of MAGA thinking if transported back in time to 1945.

SUMMARIES

METHODS

Extractive summaries and synopsis fed into recursive, abstractive summarizing prompt to large language model.

Reduced word count from 80485 to 16 words by extracting the 20 most significant sentences, then looping through that collection in chunks of 2500 tokens for 3 rounds until the number of words in the remaining text fits between the target floor and ceiling. Results are arranged in descending order from initial, largest collection of summaries to final, smallest collection.

Machine-generated and unsupervised; use with caution.

RECURSIVE SUMMARY ROUND 0

Upon a change of disposition course, ship numbers of ships change but the ships only reorient enough to place the nearest ship in the No. (3). If sufficient screening ships are available, the screen may be designated as a closed circular screen by signal. If insufficient ships are available, but sufficient vessels to fill the forward semicircle or preferably a 240 arc of the circle, then the screen may be designated by signal.

Operate screen as open circular screen. Assign light forces to battle disposition. Simultaneous attack to destroy/damage/disperse enemy forces. Assign duties to ships depending on equipment and personnel training.

Ship may be required to report air or surface contact. Ship assigned surface and/or air radar guardships, fighter direction ships, radar intercept ships, radar jamming ships, and/or radar picket. Ship responsible for air search radar control, early air warning, and fighter direction. Exercise 6(D) Combined Aircraft Attack on Formation.

Execute Torpedo Attack, Coordinated Attack & Radar Tracking/Force-Screening for Air. Each task group to take prescribed formation.

Recursive Summary Round 1

Ships reorient to form a closed circular screen, assign light forces to battle disposition, and assign duties depending on equipment and personnel training. Execute Combined Aircraft Attack on Formation, Torpedo Attack, Coordinated Attack & Radar Tracking/Force-Screening for Air with each task group taking a prescribed formation.

Recursive Summary Round 2

Ships form circular screen, assign light forces, execute aircraft & torpedo attacks, and use radar tracking/force-screening.

PAGE-BY-PAGE CONTENTS

offensive/defensive chemical warfare instructions, joint action, amphibious warfare, antisubmarine/escort of convoy instructions, addenda to general signal book, operational guide for offensive/defensive mining, minesweeping manual.

16   The US Fleet is divided into numbered fleets and sea frontiers, and task forces are temporarily assigned to each. Each task force is designated by numbers indicating the chain of command, composed of numerals separated by decimal points.

17   Fleet Communication Plan provides numerical designations for task organization components, with descriptive names to be used in addition. Task Force ELEVEN provides an example of the normal tactical organization of a task force.

18   A task force is organized with a subdivision designation, with numbers illustrative only. Numbers can be changed to maintain security, and special tactical organizations can be ordered as needed.

19   Fleet commanders are designated as Commander in Chief or Commander Fleet, and command communications plans for task organizations are outlined in USF 70 and the fleet supplement. Tactical organization and command communications for mixed U.S.-British forces are outlined in the appendix to the General Signal Book.

20   Condition 1 all battle stations manned and alert, ammunition ready for instant loading, engineering condition 31, aircraft in condition 11 during daylight. Condition 1A for combat loaded ships, Condition 1AA for air defense.

21   All personnel to battle stations with key stations manned, commissary details excused to prepare and issue food, material condition Z(A), ammunition ready for instant loading, aircraft in condition 12 during daylight and 13 during night. Condition 2 one-quarter to one-third of batteries manned, ammunition ready, engineering condition 32/33.

22   Ships must have a minimum of one-quarter of the 5-inch guns and one-third to two-thirds of automatic weapons manned in Condition 3, with ammunition ready for instant loading. All carrier aircraft and floatplanes should be in Condition 13 during the day and Condition 9 for floatplanes at night. Torpedo batteries are to be considered a part of the main batteries, and depth charge batteries should be manned in accordance with type instructions.

23   Condition of Readiness 1 is assumed when surface action is imminent; Condition of Readiness 1E is assumed when enemy forces of comparable surface strength may be encountered; Condition of Readiness 1AA is assumed when air action is imminent; Condition of Readiness 1EAA is assumed when enemy air forces may be encountered.

24   Conditions of Readiness 2, 3, Z(A), and 8-13 are defined, with special conditions for carrier planes. Ammunition and material conditions are specified in Damage Control Instructions and USF 75 and USF 77.

25   Ships usually operate with a split plant set-up, but modifications are allowed when conditions require fuel conservation or when reliability is not necessary.

26   Internal communications must be fully manned in 1, 1AA, IE, and 1EAA; in 2 and 3, enough personnel must be present to control fire of manned batteries and take control of additional armament when manned. Exterior communications must be manned according to communication plan. Composite conditions may be set by officer in tactical command.

27 USF 10B Part 111 outlines standard cruising procedures, including navigation, rendezvous, evasive courses and speeds, and cruising dispositions. Appendix I provides typical dispositions with instructions for use.

28 USP 10B outlines standards for preparation and use of special dispositions, which should be consistent with General Tactical Instructions. Circle spacing is 1,000 yards and instructions for use should accompany each disposition. Principles for preparing dispositions and selecting appropriate tactics are listed for guidance.

29 A destroyer may act as a plane guard for a carrier, and when seeking engagement, a disposition of the "ready" or "attack" type should be chosen. When not seeking engagement, a disposition should be chosen which can be turned readily, and from which protected units can retire expeditiously while defending units concentrate and interpose for delaying action. Carrier stations should be flexible to accommodate to changing demands of air operations, and screens should be flexible enough to adjust to changing conditions.

30 USP 10B covers mixed US-UK units in the appendix of the General Signal Book. Forms of single screens include partial, open and closed circular. Reorientation is done upon change of disposition course, with turn and zigzag signals. Reorientation commences when signal is understood or 10 minutes prior to specified time.

31 Ships are assigned to screening stations in open circular screens by odd numbers from $0¬\infty$ to $180¬\infty$ relative to disposition course and even numbers from $360¬\infty$ to $180¬\infty$, and in closed circular screens Station One is always located on the disposition course. Ships maintain the same relative order in the screen unless directed otherwise.

32 This table provides a guide for finding the number of screening vessels required for a given radius of a circle to be well protected. Additional vessels may be employed as pickets, plane guards, etc.

33 Screening vessels patrol predetermined stations to protect a circle, with particular emphasis on the flank stations.

34 Table III provides station numbers and the number of DD's needed to provide protection for a circle of known radius. Table IV tabulates the screened distance between stations and the number of screening stations on a circle, given the radius.

35 Table gives relative bearing of each station from center of closed circular screen for various numbers of ships. Emphasis should be given to flank stations by decreasing patrol area assigned to them.

36 USF 10B Screen is based on a closed circular or open circular screen for maximum antiaircraft protection, or a partial (bent line) screen for minimum number of screening ships. Six tables of screening station assignments are included.

37 USF 10B is an effective firing position for jamming speed versus assumed enemy torpedo run. Tables I-V provide guidance on station assignments, spacing, and angular spacing for anti-submarine and anti-aircraft screens.

38 Determine the approximate circle on which it is desired to place the screen, then use Table IV to determine the number of equally spaced stations necessary to fill the circle if a closed circular screen is provided. Table VI is a convenient method of reorienting the screen once it has been selected and station assignments have been made.

39   In cases of insufficient screening ships, a partial screen must be used, extending to 90¬∞ on either side of the formation's course, with spacing between ships not less than 4,000 yards. Antiaircraft protection may need to modify procedures. Screen may be designated by method in subparagraph 3253 (a), and individual ships' positions from the disposition center may be determined from Table V.

40   USP 10B details the selection and designation of circular (closed and open) screens, using the General Signal Book with a tack line followed by 4 or 5 numerals. The first two numerals indicate the number of screening stations, and the third and fourth (and fifth if necessary) indicate the radius of the circle in hundreds of yards.

41   Axis rotation by uniform angular rate method over 1000 yards at 4 knots with relative or actual distance in miles and speed in knots.

42   Change of front in disposition by uniform angular rate method, intended for use at night or in reduced visibility, with specified speed and time parameters.

43   USF 10B involves rotating screening ships into new stations relative to the course, and reorienting to cover the advance of the disposition.

44   Table VI shows the total number of ships in a circular screen and their positions after a course change ranging from 40 to 180 degrees to the right.

45   Table VI shows the positions in a circular screen before and after a course change from 40 to 60 degrees to the right, 60 to 80 degrees to the right, 81 to 100 degrees to the right, 101 to 120 degrees to the right, and 141 to 160 degrees to the right.

46   Table VI compares the positions of ships in a circular screen before and after a course change, with the course change ranging from 40 to 100 degrees to the right.

47   Positions in circular screen before and after course change from 40-180 degrees to the left.

48   Course change from 40-180 degrees to the left changes ships' positions in circular screen. A=Total No. of ships in the screen; B=Position in the screen after course change.

49   6-12, 17-66, 99, 13-10, 17-16, 44-14, 22-11, 66-15, 10-12, 66-16, 13-44, 17-12, 14-66, 15-88, 101-120, 16-6, 17-8, 10-66, 14-12, 11-22, 15-33, 12-66, 16-10, 13-22, 17-3, 14-66, 15-22, 16-88, 17-2, 11-66, 15-10, 12-22, 16-33, 13-66, 17-10, 14-22, 15-66, 16-22, 17-44, 11-88, 15-12, 13-11, 17-55, 14-88, 15-11, 16-88, 17-11, 141-160, 99-44, 13-88, 17-

50   Reorient open circular screens with nine or more vessels by the "Close the Gap" method, or with eight or more vessels by the "End Around" method. Use Table VI to find new station numbers relative to the new course.

51   When a change in course is ordered, the van ship on the unexposed flank with reference to the new course takes station one on the course or to the right of the course, if there is an even number of ships in the screen.

52   The "Close the Gap" method for course changes of 30¬∞ or less involves 9 screening ships at 12 screening stations, with original positions of occupied and unoccupied stations indicated by a diagram.

53   Reorientation of 9 ships in 12 stations with a course change of 90¬∞. Occupied/unoccupied stations shown in Figure 4.

54   9 occupied and 3 unoccupied stations at the start of an exercise, with a course change from 000¬∞ to 135¬∞. 9 occupied and 4 unoccupied stations at the end. Direction of movement given in Figure 6.

55   For course changes of 30¬∞ or less, all ships maintain present station. For 90¬∞ course changes, ships in the rear of the formation move in the opposite direction to cover the exposed flank. For 135¬∞ course changes, enough ships on the side of the exposed flank move in the opposite direction to cover the exposed flank, and the ship on the least exposed flank with reference to the new course and in the van will take station one on the screen axis.

56   US$10B to reorient 9 ships with 12 stations from 000¬∞ to 090¬∞.

57   Reorienting an open circular screen with the "End Around" method by rotating ships in the direction of the course change until symmetrically disposed about the new course line. CL (AA) may maneuver with the screen and be on the axis or reverse thereof. Numeral flags may be used to indicate station.

58   10B maneuvering method with 12 screening stations and 8 screening ships, from 000¬∞ (T) to 150¬∞ (T), with 0 unoccupied stations at completion and 0/0/0 occupied/unoccupied stations at commencement of maneuver.

59   Screen commander prescribes anti-submarine screen, pickets used for early contact and destruction of bogies and surface ships. Ships patrol station with speed necessary to maintain station. Sonar search conducted in accordance with standard procedure. Picket use to be considered for early contact and destruction. Equalize fuel consumption by occasionally reassigning positions.

60   Ships and units are assigned stations to promote security and take defensive action against attacking forces. Radars, fire-control and gun director range finders should be used for station keeping. Minesweeping screens are also included. Special maneuver instructions are set forth for task forces, task groups and simple screened units.

61   Signal understood, executed, and maneuver completed for Figure 8 course change of 180¬∞ and 120¬∞.

62   USP 10B allows for large dispositions to be handled with abbreviated procedures. Maneuvers with closed or open circular screens and bent-line screens are outlined, with instructions for changing the formation axis of carriers given for light or variable winds.

63   Maneuver completed with 60¬∞ course change, signals understood and executed.

64   Ships turn back individually and increase speed to maintain sonar coverage, with columns countermarching by "follow the leader" and single ships turning simultaneously. For changes of less than 120¬∞, the normal method is preferred.

65   USF 10B outlines procedures for reorienting screens when the signal is made by executive method. The screened station unit(s) commence evolutions when the signal is executed or at the specified time. If a screened station unit is in column, it will change by "follow the leader" and if the turn is 120¬∞ to 180¬∞ the procedure is the same as Case I.

66   Ships must carry out emergency maneuvers with standard rudder at last signalled speed. Changes of course of more than 90¬∞ should be done in two or more increments. Communications for emergency maneuvers should be done with very high frequency voice radio and/or proper whistle signal.

67   Use WIMS vol. I for exceptional circumstances, drills, and when in company with merchant ships. Use Point Option Navigation when aircraft are expected to operate outside of sight contact. Fly routine air patrols and display FOX flags when carriers are engaged in flight operations.

68   Carriers turning into or out of the wind must blow one short blast when turning right, two short blasts when turning left. Assign "operating stations" and "cruising stations" for each carrier. USF 77 lighting doctrine should be followed during night ops. Method ABLE is normally used for flight operations, which consists of maneuvering the disposition into the wind. Guide makes general info signals to designate course and speed.

69   USF 10B requires carriers to maneuver the disposition to the desired true indicated course and adjust their initial operating position to minimize interference. When operating by method ABLE, carriers must conform to the course and speed of the guide. When operating by method BAKER, carriers should select an initial position which will permit screen protection.

70   Carriers and destroyers in a disposition should use Method Charlie to maximize protection, combining Methods ABLE and BAKER to parallel the course of the operating carriers. When commencing the maneuver, carriers should hoist signal "4th REPEATER VICTOR PREP" or "4th REPEATER ZEBRA GEORGE PREP." When operations are complete, carriers will haul down FOX and regain assigned station.

71   Commander may signal intention to operate by method CHARLIE and shift from BAKER at any time. When operating aircraft, provide adequate speeds in advance to minimize time and distance lost. When battleships and cruisers need to launch or recover planes at different times, they should operate independently. Ships and dispositions should zigzag during good visibility when in areas where enemy submarines may be encountered, unless task assigned is jeopardized. Zigzag plans are in General Tactical Instructions, USF 10, and Zigzag Diagrams for Single Ships and Convoys (1940).

72   USF10B plan 1-10 and 19-26 are reproduced in Appendix II. Zigzagging by formations containing U.S. naval vessels follows US Naval Rules, while formations containing merchant vessels or allied men-of-war not equipped with US naval publications use WIMS. Special rules may be suspended by commanders at discretion. Zigzag is automatically stopped on receipt of emergency signals.

73   When a change in course or disposition is signaled, ships should cease zigzagging and resume it on signal. For changes of 5 degrees or less, ships should absorb the change in the next leg.

74   Routine flight operations should be divided between carriers present, individual ships should record planes launched and recovered, recoveries should be completed prior to end of evening twilight, and subordinates may exercise discretion with respect to routine flight operations.

75   Aircraft should conform to USF 74 & 75 and nightfighter units should be prepared for defense and intruder/heckler missions. Rescue planes must be on 10-minutes notice and, when possible, escorted by fighters.

76   USF 10B ships require escort fighters for safe navigation, and can launch a depth charge alert plane on 5-minute notice. Training and aerograph-calibration flights are authorized, and emergency recoveries are to be carried out by the officer in tactical command or subordinate commanders under

certain conditions. Rendezvous air spaces should be known to all ships of the force.

77   Aircraft forced to land in the water shall be recovered by the most conveniently located ship able to hoist it in; personnel shall be rescued by the nearest destroyer when possible; cruisers and battleships shall signal their method of recovery to nearby vessels.

78   Aircraft on board must have full gun ammunition allowance, bombs according to task force instructions and 25ft hydrostatic fuze. Pilots should avoid passing over friendly ships, use Point OPTION method of interception and take precautions when flying in bad weather.

79   Pilots must follow USF 70 recognition procedure when approaching friendly ships, avoiding directions of bright sunlight & enemy air bases. If unable to comply, they must approach at low speed between 1,000-2,000 ft. Aircraft IFF to be energized unless approaching known enemy base. If a submarine or mine is sighted, pilot should attack with available armament and report contact.

80   The Officer in Tactical Command will make a plane availability report after the completion of flight schedules. Destroyers will report fuel on hand at 0800 to the Screen Commander. Zone time may be prescribed by the Officer in Tactical Command and time designation for despatches and reports must include an appropriate designating letter. Morning general quarters are mandatory and whistle and siren will be tested at sea at 1600.

81   Ships must be ready to be towed, fuel at sea, and identify themselves and other friendly ships. They must also minimize their visibility.

82   USF 10B: Ship must take precautions to stay concealed and minimize noise at night. Waste must be disposed of one hour after sunset. Reports required after return to port.

83   Ships must report engine speed, fuel consumption, fuel on hand, and action reports. On return to port, take on fuel, ammo, and stores to capacity and effect necessary repairs. Disable boilers or machinery for repairs when in inactive area. Comply with muster roll instructions when entering dangerous waters.

84   WNT1AL USF 10B Part IV provides instructions for battle plans and dispositions to enhance chances of success in action, with additional instructions for major and surface action, and approach and contact dispositions.

85   USF 10B must conform to diagrams 55, 56 and 57 of General Tactical Instructions and battle dispositions should conform to figure 11, with sectors of radar responsibility assigned per Part VI. Light forces must adhere to the decision of the tactical commander and adjust their stations to the type of torpedoes they may encounter. Instructions may change due to tactical situation.

86   USF 10B describes a flank commander's responsibility to assign immediate action to their own initiative and coordinate operations of a light force in order to clear the way for a destroyer torpedo attack. The preliminary attack requires superiority in light force strength and should be driven home to destroy or disperse the enemy forces. The normal objective of light cruisers is enemy destroyers and of heavy cruisers, enemy cruisers. Consideration of relative value of enemy types must be taken into account.

87   Cruisers should conduct simultaneous attack on enemy light forces, with the objective of destroying, damaging, or dispersing them. Cruisers must give preference to enemy ships in position to oppose destroyer attack and keep clear of destroyer attack points. Battle line should be defended against possible destroyer attack by stationing a unit on or near the locus of torpedo firing points. Plans 1, 2, and 3 are provided for rapid transmission of instructions.

88   USP 10B prescribes that designated units should prepare for a preliminary attack, with light forces in the van being stationed as close to the enemy as possible. Cruisers should initiate action from two stations on either side of the attacking destroyers. Units of the flank forces should be stationed in order away from own battle line.

89   A destroyer attack element is stationed outside the defensive element and comprised of one to four squadrons of destroyers and supporting cruisers, capable of effective offensive action against the enemy battle line.

90   The battle disposition is projected in the direction of the enemy with a deployment course of 315¬∞ and a fleet axis of 300¬∞. Light forces are distributed in several areas and each area is assigned a different number of each type.

91   Cruisers may be used to support attacking destroyers in an area outside the destroyer attack element. Disposition: Areas B-F with radii determined by adding required maneuvering length plus 1,000 yards. Signal given for ships to take position in designated areas.

92   Light forces in the van, deployment course, one destroyer stationed 2,000-3,000 yards east of rear ship of battle line (Figure 12).

93   Light forces are equally divided and deployed in a battle line with cruisers and destroyers.

94   Light forces in B area deploy in wedge or vee formation, with one destroyer stationed astern, in the direction of an expected attack.

95   Attack formation of one division of cruisers and one squadron of eight destroyers, arranged in two 1-ship attack units, with distances variable.

96   Battle disposition illustrated for one division of cruisers and one squadron of nine destroyers, in three 3-ship attack units. Distances can be varied. Figure 16.

97   USF 10B describes battle plans for small forces in surface action, providing three typical dispositions ("A," "B," and "C") with variants for light forces to suit different tactical situations. Variations can be made at the discretion of the commander.

98   USF 10B outlines a three-character battle plan system for signaling the general intention of the officer in tactical command. Light forces can be instructed to operate on the tactical offensive or defensive. In small forces, the senior destroyer officer can assign multiple attack groups to attack from widely separated sectors.

99   USP 10B outlines procedures for destroyer and cruiser torpedo attacks, including informing the officer in tactical command and avoiding blanking fire of own heavy ships. Dispositions "B" and "C" may be used for battleship-destroyer attacks in low visibility.

100   Dispositions "B" and "C" do not automatically prescribe battle plans for lightly screened enemy forces, so effective methods of making destroyer attacks have been obtained by launching the attack without gunfire support if not discovered,

or with support if discovered. At night, approach disposition may be used with destroyers advanced on each flank, and carriers form with screens on disengaged side.

101 Subordinate commanders should initiate attacks of opportunity or counterattacks when the situation is favorable, and the mission of the task force is not prejudiced. Detailed plans should be prepared in advance for deliberate attacks. Carrier air group doctrine and tactical orders for offensive air action are contained in air type publications.

102 In USP 10B, surface forces should remain tactically concentrated and be prepared to investigate unexpected radar contacts. Challenging an enemy should only be done when completely ready to open fire.

103 In an emergency contact with a strong enemy surface force, an emergency turn away should be performed to reduce the torpedo menace and give the screened ships time to deploy. The commander should make plans for emergency deployment in advance.

104 When deploying forces in a cruising disposition, fast screened ships should move to the maximum maneuvering speed and join the heavy combatant ships as they clear the disposition. Screening ships should join the screened ships at the limit of very high frequency voice range.

105 When forming a battle disposition, combatant ships should increase speed to clear screened ships, which should proceed in a reverse direction from the enemy bearing line, keeping within voice range. Screening ships should join the screened ships as the heavy combatant ships clear.

106 Screening ships must make contact reports and take urgent action if a submarine or torpedo is sighted dangerously close. They must have due regard to the General Prudential Rule and the necessity for small fast ships to keep clear of larger ones. Sonar contacts must be evaluated and deliberate attacks made as the circumstances indicate.

107 A screening ship making a contact should inform the officer in tactical command and use appropriate methods to prevent a torpedo shot from being fired at the screened ships and to destroy or damage the submarine. If the submarine is not sunk, the screening ship should be ordered to regain station in disposition.

108 Search for enemy motor torpedo boats using pickets, low-level air patrol, and search radar. Repel attacks with air power, gunfire, and maneuvers. Use smoke when possible.

109 Search planes illuminate, mark and attack motor torpedo boats, pickets repel attack with support from screening ships.

110 USP 10B states that when screening ships are favorably situated, they should bring maximum gunfire to bear from all weapons at a distance of 6,000 yards or more. Smoke and illumination may be used to repel air attacks, and contact reports should be made according to communication plan. Ships should be tactically concentrated to ensure most effective fighter direction and coverage, maximum antiaircraft fire, and mutual support. Avoiding maneuvers should be employed to bring motor torpedo boats astern.

111 Ships must maneuver to avoid attack while considering the dangers of collision and mutual support. Centralized control has disadvantages, so simultaneous basic turns are encouraged. Dispositions vary depending on the situation, and snoopers should be intercepted to avoid detection.

112   Enemy attack forms (torpedo, dive bombing, horizontal bombing, low level
       bombing, strafing, suicide landings, glider bomb and controlled high angle bomb
       attacks, and glide bombing and rocket attacks) can be defended against by
       fighter planes, gunfire, antiaircraft disposition, avoiding maneuvers, smoke,
       meteorological assistance, and balloon barrages. During lulls, carriers may need
       to land planes. Ships must exercise restraint when opening fire on enemy
       planes being attacked by our fighters.

113   Smoke is effective against aircraft, and thick weather can be used to avoid air
       attacks. Barrage balloons are effective for slow speed convoys. Enemy torpedo
       planes can be detected by radar and intercepted by fighter patrols. Contact
       reports of enemy aircraft should be in accordance with the communication
       plan.

114   Fire should be opened at maximum volume as soon as planes reach effective
       range. In torpedo plane attacks, turn away from the approaching group of
       planes, and towards the attacks forward of the beam; away from those abaft the
       beam. Dive bombers usually approach at high altitude and bomb in a tight
       formation. Detection and interception are the best defense. Horizontal bombers
       usually approach at high altitude, but this type of bombing has decreased in
       popularity.

115   Against air attacks, use 5-inch or larger antiaircraft guns, radical turns, high
       volume of automatic weapons fire, and destruction by gunfire. Against
       coordinated attacks, take action to nullify the torpedo or low level bombing
       attack. For glider bombs and controlled high angle bombs, use diversionary
       attacks.

116   USF 10B glide bomb attack is conducted at 1,800-9,000ft, 70-110¬∞ on bow.
       Countermeasures include jamming, fighter protection, maneuvering, smoke,
       and gunfire. High angle bomb attack is conducted at 22,000-37,000ft by high
       level bombsight. Night aircraft attacks may use torpedoes, bombs, or both and
       require knowledge of target position. Torpedo planes attack at 500-1,500ft, with
       or without illumination.

117   Night bombing may be done by horizontal, glide, or low level bombing. Defense
       against night air attack relies on concealment, disruption by night fighters, gun
       fire, maneuvers, concealment during attacks, interdiction bombing and intruder
       missions, and jamming enemy radar. Night fighters have been effective in
       breaking up attacks. Evasive maneuvers, night fighters, and bad weather can be
       used to throw off enemy.

118   Night fighters should be used with caution; ships should open fire with radar
       controlled batteries when good set-ups are obtained; primary defense is 5" or
       larger antiaircraft guns; emergency turns and high speeds are recommended;
       any ship sighting a torpedo should open fire to indicate track and detonate it.

119   Use intruder fighters and interdiction bombing to harass enemy airfields at
       night to prevent night attack missions. Destroyers and cruisers use funnel
       smoke to obscure silhouettes and increase evasion. Damaged ships report to
       officer in tactical command and follow procedures to remain on station or
       leave, tow if necessary, and take opportunity to destroy enemy cripples.
       Prosecute damage-control measures with diligence and tenacity.

120   Ships receiving fuel must discharge water ballast, shift oil, inform supplying
       ship of requirements, display AFIRM, BAKER and PREP, and inform officer
       in tactical command and supplying ship of fuel received.

121 Supply fuel, transfer personnel and equipment, maintain radar and periscope watch, follow fueling plan and orders, adhere to Fueling at Sea Instructions, and follow security orders in port.

122 Rescue of aviators downed at sea is of utmost importance; rescue operations normally provided by destroyers, submarines and seaplanes coordinated by central authority. When submarines and seaplanes are assigned lifeguard duties, procedures should follow communication plan/ doctrine. When destroyers assigned, nearest should take prompt action. Continuous fighter cover provided for downed pilot and rescue mediums when possible. Importance of obtaining good photographic coverage of present/future enemy objectives and proof of damage.

123 Commands must plan for coordinated use of aerial and submarine photographic facilities, taking into account limitations and opposition. Carrier-based planes should obtain "dicing mission" and complete vertical trimetrogon coverage. Heavy squadrons should fly high when enemy interception and antiaircraft fire is expected. All efforts must be made to get complete coverage when carriers strike an area not covered before. Photos should be taken 2 hours after sunrise/sunset, after strikes/bombardment are complete and smoke has cleared.

124 Minesweeping screens are employed in inverted V and straight line formations to sweep moored mines when water depth is less than 500 fathoms. High-speed minesweepers sweep a 160-yard path at 12 knots and a 75-yard path at 23.5 knots with 25-yard overlap. Echo ranging is ineffective at speeds above 22 knots and mines can only be swept up at slow speed.

125 USF 10B requires that high-speed minesweepers be used at least two miles ahead of a force screened to provide opportunity to reverse course if mines are discovered. Magnetic and acoustic mines are swept for when presence is suspected and water depth is less than 30 fathoms. Magnetic minesweepers must travel at 16 knots, AM at 12 knots, and YMS at 8 knots. Drifting mines are difficult to sweep, but can be sighted and destroyed by gunfire.

126 Ships and boats should be assigned to a figure 8 patrol track to screen an area. Boats should drop smoke floats every 100 yards and ships should smoke for the heaviest density.

127 Screening ships should patrol an arc of approximately 7,000 yards, rotating the screen clockwise or counterclockwise on the hour, quarter-hour, half-hour, and three-quarter-hour. All available screening ships should be used, and the area should be thoroughly sonar swept prior to forming the screen. Ships should not approach the screen closer than 3,000-4,000 yards. If many ships are available, multiple screens should be formed at an interval of one and one-half times the assured sonar range.

128 Screening ships must echo range, coordinate navigational and radar fixes, and use radar pickets at night. All ships must report to the screen commander upon entering the screened area.

129 USF10B is a special purpose screen that rotates around slow speed units. It eliminates the need for symmetry and has a constant speed for all ships in the screen, with equal leg lengths and normal station keeping difficulties. The screen can adjust for variation in speed of the screened unit by varying the speed of the screening ships and can be changed at any time without repositioning. Sonar searches should be conducted relative to the screening ship's heading.

130 Changes have been made.

131 USF10B: 5827: Search pattern depends on number of screening ships; fewer than 5, search outboard quarter; 6 or more, search outboard quarter to 20¬∞ inboard bow. 5828: Protection not satisfactory with fewer than 4-5 screening ships.

132 USF10B change #1.

133 USF10B is a seven-sided figure screen formed by assigning ships to stations according to the Spacing Table. The navigational plot for the ship assigned to station one is shown below the relative plot. The navigational movement of the screened unit along the base course is shown by points plotted on the track and labeled 0 through 7.

134 USF10B Change No.1.

135 USF10B is a 4:1 speed ratio unit with a 500 yard screened circle and a 2400 yard leg length. It has a 7-sided relative plot, a course table, and a speed-time table. Initial stations and distances from the center of the screened circle are indicated in the spacing table. The navigational plot shows the movement of station one for one complete cycle.

136 USF10B Change No. 1, 5-26.

137 This diagram shows a seven-sided figure formed by a rotating screen of ships and the navigational movement of one ship assigned to a station. A spacing table is provided for assigning stations and determining initial distance and bearing.

138 Change #1 on 10B, 5-28.

139 USF10B is a seven-sided figure for screening ships, indicated by a relative plot and navigational plot, with an initial station assignment based on a Spacing Table. Rotating A/A and A/S Screen Number Four.

140 USF10B change no. 1 effective 5-30.

141 USF10B is a rotating A/A and A/S screen of five ships around slow speed units, with a speed ratio of 41 and a protected circle radius of 1000 yards. The length of each leg is 3200 yards, and the scales are 2:1, 3:1, 4:1, and 5:1. The course and spacing tables indicate the initial station and relative course of each ship, and the speed-time table indicates the speed and time of each ship on each leg. There is a general signal form and a logarithmic scale.

142 USF10B Change No.1 5-32.

143 Form an unsymmetrical seven-sided figure with ships assigned to stations according to the "Spacing Table." The navigational plot for the ship assigned to station one indicates the same navigational distance traveled on each leg during the cycle. The "Initial Stations" column indicates the relative bearing of the initial position from the base course line and the initial distance from the center of the screened circle.

144 USF10B Change No. 1, 6-34.

145 USF 10B Part VI provides best practices for use of CIC doctrine, and RAD Series publications are available or in preparation for use. CIC magazine is also available for information on CIC operations. Definitions of terms used in CIC doctrine are provided, with "Radar Area" defined as a 100 mile radius. "Task Force Commander" is used to denote the commander within the Radar Area with overall coordination.

146 Ships in a task force, group, or unit are assigned special designations to coordinate CIC functions and increase overall combat information.

Designations include Task Force/Group/Unit Combat Information Ship, Fighter Direction Ship, Radar Guardship (air/surface), Radar Picket, Radar Intercept Ship, and Radar Jamming Ship.

147   USF 10B establishes the doctrine of the Combat Information Center (CIC) for coordination of all radars and combat information for ships operating together, to maximize combat efficiency. CIC is responsible for target indication, control of aircraft and small craft, navigation, piloting, and Radar Countermeasures.

148   Combat Information Centers must control all shipborne radars and release fire-control radars for gunnery purposes prior to targets coming within tracking range. Radar transmissions can be detected at longer ranges than radio transmissions, so radar should be used when contact with the enemy is possible. Intermittent use is a compromise, but complete or continuous radar search is recommended. Conditions of radar silence should be accompanied by a corresponding restriction on IFF and RCM transmitting equipment and be correlated with an appropriate condition of VHF radio silence.

149   USF 10B has five conditions, each with advantages and disadvantages. Sacrificing detail, the conditions vary in the types of radar used and the degree of air coverage and detection. IFF system is inoperative in all conditions.

150   USF 10B and MCLAS have different advantages and disadvantages depending on the condition. Conditions 4-8 affect various radar frequencies and levels of radar silence, with varying advantages and disadvantages.

151   USF 10B prescribes radar and IFF silence in various frequencies to prevent detection by enemy radar intercept receivers and to decrease plane search and attack efficiency.

152   USP 10B establishes conditions of radar silence, including transpondors and interrogator-responsors deenergized, with advantages and disadvantages of each condition. Conditions 4 and 5 are for future assignment.

153   USP 10B outlines conditions for IFF equipment use in air-borne and ship-borne forms, including deenergization and special cases. Opportunities for test and calibration of radars, IFF, and radar countermeasures equipment are to be exploited consistent with prevailing condition of radar silence. Intership CIC communications are detailed in USF 70.

154   The USP 10B provides definitions for radar control orders and their functions, such as Report, Negat, Estimate, Check Contact, and Recommend.

155   Channels are designated to control the flow of combat information in a task force, usually by voice radio. Radar guardships, pickets, interceptships, jamming ships, and fighter direction ships are all coordinated on the radar reporting channel. Initial contact reports are given in plain language or encoded and the size of the contact is reported in the initial report.

156   Raid A and Raid 1A are 200.0 yards per range circle on USF.

157   Ships in a force must report air/surface contacts and their positions. A separate ship may be designated to report new contacts to promote efficiency. Radar Telling Net is used to exchange radar info between distant forces/land bases. Warning Net is used for alerts/designating raids/interceptions/emergency reports/radar/IFF silence/jamming/night fighter launch/landing. Inter-Fighter Direction Channel is for fighter direction info/control.

158 Establishes code of abbreviations to be used for fighter direction information, such as deck condition and CAP assignment, control and reinforcement. Code words are given for each meaning.

159 Task Force Commander exercises broad tactical control, Task Force CIC ship maintains and submits information to TFC, TG (U)C ships designate guardships, intercept ships, fighter direction ships, etc., Fighter Direction Ship intercepts and controls fighters, Surface Radar Guard and Air Radar Guard maintain and report situation in assigned area, Intercept Ship maintains watch for enemy radar and reports interceptions, Radar Picket maintains air and surface search and air lane control, Jamming Ship jams enemy radars and creates deception.

160 The coordination of the operation of all ships' CIC's is done by the task force commander while more detailed coordination is done by the task group commander. CIC's must be interrelated in their duties to form an effective whole. The task force commander is responsible for certain broad tactical decisions and assignments relating to the functioning of CIC.

161 Task force, group and unit CIC ships enforce conditions of radar and IFF silence, use jamming and deception, and coordinate intertask group CIC activities, including fighter direction and control of airborne aircraft.

162 Task force CIC ships are assigned according to search doctrine and radar guardships are assigned for radar responsibility. Fighters, CIC ships, and flagships are not normally assigned as radar guardships. Designations are prescribed for air search.

163 USF 10B assigns guards ABLE, BAKER, DOG, FOX, GEORGE, ITEM, KING, LOVE, MIKE, and OBOE to 90, 180, 270, and 360 degree sectors, respectively, for early detection and/or recognition of low flying aircraft, surface units, submarines, and other small craft.

164 Doctrine for task forces to obtain maximum radar info on surface situation. CIC ship coordinates use of radars, assigns duties to guardships, establishes areas of responsibility, and coordinates communication.

165 6342-6345 provide reporting procedure for radar information. 6400-6414 outline air search doctrine, including classification of ships, responsibility for air search radar control, and fighter direction.

166 Fighter direction is a function of the task force commander, delegated to the force or group CIC ship. The fighter direction ship is responsible for interception of raids, informing the force CIC ship of plane status, and following air search radar doctrine.

167 Combat air patrols must provide fighter coverage for bases, no attack should go unopposed, and fighters must be vectored out to thwart determined attacks. Conditions of readiness are established for defensive fighters.

168 Fighter direction communications must use standard vocabulary and be concise, with orders acknowledged and information receipted. TALLYHO report must be transmitted when sighting enemy. Night fighter direction requires precise information and control.

169 USF 10B is a detailed order involving night fighter direction ships, which are responsible for communication checks, withdrawing fighters from own force AA range, and keeping fighters away from friendly strikes. IFF systems consist of interrogator-responsor and transpondor units.

170   The control of the IFF system is the responsibility of the task force commander, and orders must be issued according to SD 158 (4). Air-borne IFF equipment must be in proper operation and set on the correct code. Ship-borne transpondors should only be energized as directed and ship-borne interrogator-responsors should only be used to obtain proper recognition and never operated continuously. The IFF Mark III system operates in the same frequency band as the air search radar equipment and is considered comparable in security.

171   USF 10B outlines the radar countermeasures doctrine, which includes radar interception, jamming, and deception, to obtain combat information from the enemy and prevent them from obtaining information from friendly forces. Radar intercept ships are designated to monitor the radar spectrum and report new enemy frequencies.

172   Task force commanders must be informed of friendly radars at amphibious objectives and ships with radar direction finders should take cross bearings on enemy radar signals to locate them. Radar Countermeasures Reports should include interception of enemy signals, location of enemy radars, enemy and own use of countermeasures, and pertinent information such as frequency, pulse repetition rate, pulse width, location, and beam width.

173   Radar Countermeasures reports include frequency, type, bearing limits, range limits, appearance of echo, and effectiveness of defensive measures. Reports should be communicated to CIC, aircraft to base coordinating activity, and use of jamming/deception must be authorized by senior commander in area. Internal and external communications systems must be provided.

174   Commanders of major units in contact with the enemy may authorize local use of radar jamming and deception, taking into account potential effects on adjacent areas. Special care must be taken to ensure constant and intelligent supervision. Radar jamming should be employed against specific enemy radars and used in darkness, zero visibility, smoke, or other conditions where enemy lacks visual observation. Advantages include depriving enemy of info to determine composition, track, direct guns, or aim torpedos. Disadvantages include enemy homing on jammer or locating it by bearings.

175   Radar jamming operations are difficult to predict and must be conducted carefully to be effective. Jamming should be done between the radar and the target and should not be done indiscriminately. Jamming is most effective when multiple ships jam simultaneously. It is less effective at farther ranges than the optical horizon.

176   Jamming and window techniques should be employed to disrupt enemy radars to deny visual observation. Window is most effective against radars with long pulse width and wide beam width. Window can be used to cover a task force, simulate a large number of planes, and deceive enemy intercepting forces.

177   Window and radar deception devices can be used to confuse enemy forces. Factors such as wind, height, and own forces must be considered.

178   Surface forces may launch gulls to simulate aircraft and create deceptive radar targets, and gunnery radar doctrine defines methods of control for using fire-control radars, with target indication from CIC and shore bombardment differing from normal gunnery procedure.

179   USP 10B requires that the geographic position of the target and ship be known for effective fire-control. Radar spotting and aircraft coordination can extend

the radar range of surface craft and protect the formation. Illumination doctrine is outlined in War Instructions, 1944.

180 Ships must conduct training exercises at every opportunity, taking advantage of training offered by various establishments. Type and task force commanders must coordinate training and standardize methods while introducing the element of surprise. Standard exercises are outlined in section 7400.

181 Fleet and tactical commanders should conduct frequent training exercises, including surface and antiaircraft firing and bombardment firing, to perfect the ability to open fire instantly and accurately. Preference should be given to sleeve firing over burst practices. Ammunition allowances should be reduced to allow for additional firing practices.

182 Ships use radar to track and calibrate targets, employing smoke and IFF, and engaging in bombardment, surface, and antiaircraft practices. Exercises include zero calibration of fire-control radars.

183 USP 10B must be applied and checked constantly. Exercise 1(A) is preliminary to 1(B), which involves radar-optical range finder comparison up to 35,000 yards. Exercise 2(A) and 2(B) involve surface tracking exercises with two or one ship, respectively, with speed and zigzag plans being reported upon completion.

184 USP 10B targetsln provides maximum training to ship and fire-control parties; if a single target is used, it should be stationed on alternate bows on alternate mornings. Commencing at sunrise minus 1 hour, each radar guard and BK marker ship energizes effective BK setting for 5 minutes in order of visual call number. Target(s) observe with BL and report BK discrepancies. Target(s) remain in position as long as practicable to regain station in formation at plus 90 minutes.

185 USF 10B Exercises 2(E), 3, 4(A), 4(B), and 4(C) involve using radar and other tracking methods to calibrate and test range finding and altitude determination capabilities.

186 Exercise 4(D): Launch plane to circle formation at 2-5k ft, fly away to 15k yds + 8k ft, fly back to formation to check position angles; Exercise 4(E): Remove radar restrictions, tune and adjust radars for max performance, target ONE/TWO.

187 Exercise 4(F) tests AI radar performance in daylight, Exercise 5(A) is a cruiser attack and 5(B) is a destroyer attack, both using radar to make approach and own ships repelling attack.

188 USF 10B Exercise 5(U)-^Sffrfe,c#ktfti# (Combined Attack): An exercise designed to test doctrine for defense against surface attack and to train destroyers in making torpedo attack, conducted by day or night. Exercise 6(A): Carrier torpedo planes make repeated simulated attacks as a group, with force and intermediate air patrol exercising at repelling attack.

189 USF 10B exercise 6(A-F): Group and individual aircraft torpedo attack, combined aircraft attack on formation, and fighter direction problem one conducted at night or as simulated attack with maximum use of radar.

190 Exercise 6(G): Fighter direction ship Rainbow Base with VF Rainbow One, Two, etc., and collective call sign of the attack group "Pirate" to make two runs on the fighter direction ship from a distance of 80 miles, at an altitude of 10,000 feet. Exercise 6(H): Same as Exercise 5(E) with imaginary "bogey" raids instead of "skunk" contacts. Exercise 6(I): Same as 6(H) but OTC may

designate ships to work out sample raids and tracks before the exercise. Exercise 6(J): Single target plane, preferably a large bomber type, making low altitude runs back and forth across disposition, withdrawing, circling, and orbiting to simulate past tactics of enemy torpedo bombers; radar guardships track target continuously, making reports as required; vessels exercise AA control parties at discretion.

191   Exercise 6(L),ÄîFighter Direction Problem Three (Night): Conducted at night; two night fighters alternate as interceptor and target, launched an hour before dawn, landed with first air patrol. Interceptor follows vectors to target, completes interception to point of visual identification, takes reasonable evasive action. Interceptor ordered to fire and break away when within range of force screen's antiaircraft fire. Other ships in formation to closely follow and be prepared to assume control if ordered.

192   Exercise 7A: VF vs. VF combat training using camera guns; 7B: VF attack multiplace planes for free gun and defensive formation training; 8A-D: dive, glide, low altitude, horizontal bombing and torpedo attack; 9A: dive and/or horizontal bombing on slicks; 9B: aircraft attack on surprise target using miniatures, water-fillable bombs, live bombs, or rockets.

193   Aircraft exercise 10(A): VF tow sleeve at 30 knots relative speed differential over section on diagonal course, 10 miles outside screen. Aircraft exercise 10(B): IBP fixed and free machine gunnery. Aircraft exercise 11: Ramp firing on sleeve passing close aboard, but not over deck. AA exercise 12(A): Rowing plane and stand-by plane with sleeve on towline of 900+ feet, making "H" runs from each side over heavy ships. AA exercise 12(B): Same as 12(A) but "G" runs with max. length towline.

194   Exercises 12(A-F) and 13(A-C) are for training and testing the alertness of condition watch crews. 12(A-F) involve planes flying past ships at various distances and altitudes, and ships firing when they deem it safe. 13(A-C) involve designated ships firing burst targets to represent various types of close-in air attacks, with 5" and 3" not fired unless burst is at least 700 yards away.

195   USF 10B exercises 13(D) and 13(E) involve dropping flares at intervals and firing one or two rounds from 5" and 3" guns when plane is clear. Exercise 14 involves individual ships conducting automatic weapon practice against balloons or kites. Exercises 15(A) and 15(B) involve float light practice, and exercise 15(A) can be conducted by day or night. Exercise 16(A) involves heavy ships conducting offset firing at desired ranges.

196   Exercise 16(B): Detach two destroyers for offset duel at ranges between 5,000 and 10,000 yards. Exercise 16(C): Heavy ships in column, target destroyer passes counter-clockwise around formation at speeds between 15 and 30 knots, firing in succession, maneuver to bring batteries to bear, target changes speed and maneuver during gunfire, firing vessel indicate commence and cease firing. Use 70 mils offset for BL&P and all 8", 6", and 5" ammunition, 2,000 yards offset for AP. Cease firing when range is 9,000 yards or less.

197   USF 10B is a practice exercise to check calibration firing for possible changes, with one phase fired at expected battle range and limited ammunition. Exercises 17-19A involve automatic weapon firing, star-shell duels, and radar intercept tracking.

198   Ships track targets using radar intercept receivers and directional antennas, submit brief reports, and practice jamming either self-screening or off-target. Jammer-equipped ships also form a screen for the force.

199   Exercises 19(A), 20(D), 21(A-C), and 22(A) are designed to give ships practice in using various types of air-borne and rocket/shell radar deception to jam specified radar types and track attacking planes through Window screens. Reports are to be submitted as for Exercise 19(A).

200   Exercise 22(A-D) and Exercise 23(A): Ships use radar decoys, Moonshine, and Peter to evade and track attackers, hoisting signal at fore truck during specified times to keep yardarms clear for drill.

201   Exercise 23(D) is a signal drill for use in port or at sea. Two ships designated by OTC exchange despatches, signals, etc. by semaphore, searchlight, blinker gun, aldis lamp, or binocular mounted light.

202   USP 10B: At sea, OTC hoists general signal to ships in company, designating one to challenge OCE as though they were an aircraft. OCE makes aircraft reply to challenge, and when proper reply is received, ships inform other vessels of friendly nature. Exercise 24(A). Exercise 24(B) uses night fighting lights to establish identity of friendly ship.

203   USF 10B is an exercise to train air and surface forces in detecting and repelling motor torpedo boat attacks. It involves a surface force operating in a limited area during certain specified hours, while MTBs search, locate and simulate an attack. The surface force may employ an antiair patrol and antitorpedo pickets.

204   USF 10B requires surface forces to be prepared to screen tactically. Shells may be used to illuminate attacking MTBs after detection. Searchlights used to indicate gunfire and Very stars to indicate simulated torpedo fire. MTBs withdraw with running lights after receiving simulated gunfire. Brief reports may be submitted if directed. Bombardment firing exercises against uninhabited coasts or bypassed enemy territory may be conducted according to current instructions and doctrines.

205   USF 10B should include short and long range indirect fire with offset/Point Oboe/reverse slope points of aim; charts, target areas, and firing schedules should be prepared as for actual operations; direct spotting may also be possible.

206   Cruising dispositions checklist for instructions: (a) definition; (b) purpose; (c) order of forces; (d) guide; (e) center; (f) ships; (g) searches/patrols; (h) emergency deployment; (i) communications; (j) miscellaneous instructions.

207   USF 10B rising disposition 3-C fleet axis 4A with 200 yds, 330 yds, 465 yds, and 350 yds. Sonar and 1 div. horizontal-100 yds, 1 div. vertical-1000 yds with battle line, left and right flank and train. Note, figure 19.

208   Cruising Disposition 3 consists of multiple columns of task groups, with the fleet guide in the leading ship of the center column. All heavy ships follow the course of the guide, while left and right flank destroyers are assigned to sonar screens. Air patrols are launched before entering the swept channel and recovered after clearing it. All ships energize degaussing gear, destroyers make echo-ranging watch, and maneuvers by capital ships to evade air attack must limit lateral displacement to 200 yards.

209 Fleet axis cruisers center at 050', CL left and right, circle 6, BB Task Units CA left and right at 270* and 090, train 100', CA of air Task Group Figure SO.

210 Cruising Disposition suitable for defense of carriers and train; battle line deployment not standard; all screening vessels on echo-ranging watch.

211 USP^lOB cruising disposition, 3-R fleet axis, TCENTER 300*06, left, right, flank, FLAN BB station units, train, air task G, Figure SI., origin Apr. 1-8.

212 Cruising Disposition for low visibility or night use intended for use in proximity to enemy forces. Station assignments as indicated in diagram; battle line station units take deployment course by division column movement, air take station 10 miles on disengaged side. Communications, sonar equipped ships standing continuous echo-ranging watch.

213 USF 10B trains flotilla leader to circle 14.

214 Cruising Disposition 3-Vtk is a high visibility disposition suitable for defense against both aircraft and submarines. Station assignments and anti-air, anti-submarine, and anti-torpedo screens are indicated in the diagram. The fleet guide is normally in the train at the fleet center, and any rotation of the fleet axis is performed about the fleet center. Sonar equipped ships stand continuous echo-ranging watch and a sun screen is designated by the OTC.

215 Axis in Cruising Disposition with 2 Destroyers in Screening Circle, 3000x2500 yards to windward, Figure 28.

216 Cruising disposition suitable for small carrier force in low visibility conditions, with guide in carrier, station assignments indicated on diagram, patrols and searches established by tactical command, communications as prescribed by USF 70, and sonar screen using sonar and upersonics.

217 USP|OB Isy%, CRUISING DISPOSITION 4-V, AX 3, 2 CIRCLE 2, CIRCLE 6j, 5, 1170, 8, 7, Figure 24, Ap. 1-12.

218 Cruising Disposition is a defensive formation for a small carrier force. It consists of 4-LS and 4-V formations, with the guide in the center. Station assignments can be changed by the tactical commander, with patrols and searches established by the same. Communications are according to USF 70 and all sonar-equipped ships stand a continuous echo-ranging watch.

219 USF 10B, 5-LS, AX, X0I5, 1.25-320^,Äî1.25-040, 125-25, 1.25-110, SB.

220 Cruising Disposition is suitable for use of a carrier force at night or in low visibility for protection against submarine attack. Guide is normally in battleship farthest advanced along axis, with patrol and search instructions from officer in tactical command. Deployment is unlikely, but emergency deployment will be effected by battle ships turning to deployment course and carriers forming on disengaged side. Communications as prescribed by USF 70, with sonar equipped ships standing continuous echo-ranging watch.

221 Ships form zigzag lines around fueling stations, with 1000 yards between each ship and each picket station. Figure 26 shows the formation.

222 Cruising disposition for use of a carrier force for fueling with defense against submarines, with natural order from van to rear. Fleet guide is right center fueling vessel in forward fueling line; any changes of fueling course to be performed about fleet center. Screening vessels to stand continuous sonar search and take forward screening stations outboard of tanker escorts.

223 3 carriers, 3+ heavy ships, 12 destroyers.

224 USF 10B Cruising BE is a high visibility disposition suitable for defense against aircraft and submarines. The fleet guide is normally in the center and heavy ships and carriers are spaced equally. Searches, patrols and offensive air operations are ordered by OTC and communications are prescribed in USF 70. Sonar equipped ships stand continuous echo-ranging watch and radar sectors are as ordered.

225 Three carriers, three or more heavy ships, and twelve destroyers in a cruising disposition figure 28, with AA screening circle X000 and additional circles X045, X060, X090, XI20, XI35, X225, X240, X270 and X300.

226 USF*10B CRUISINCTM^OTto is an air defense disposition suitable for use by a carrier force, with the guide being the center ship of the disposition, station assignments as indicated, and air operations as ordered by OTC.

227 TG's with 8 or fewer ships station no pickets, 9-10 ships station 1 picket, 11 ships station 2 pickets, 12+ ships fill all picket stations.

228 USP 10B is an attack formation consisting of two to five carrier task groups, each with their own combat air patrol and antisubmarine patrol, and with oilers in the center. It is designed to maintain a narrow front to avoid detection and to allow each task group to maneuver as needed. Sonar and radar watches are to be kept.

229 TG's assigned a total of 8 or less screening ships station no pickets, 9 or 10 one picket, 11 two pickets, 12 or more fill all Task Group picket stations.

230 USF 10B LA4 CRUISIN is a suitable disposition for defense of large carrier task groups against submarines and aircraft. It consists of three to five task groups stationed on bearings from the fleet center relative to the fleet axis and circle spacing of 1,000 yards. The guide is the center of the task group occupying station no. 1. Task group commanders are authorized to increase distance from fleet center, employ sonar equipment, designate radar guard and identification guard ships, and maneuver their groups as necessary.

231 TG#6 furnishes all 3 pickets, TG#1 places picket for missing TG, TG#s with 8 or fewer ships don't picket, TG#s with 9-10 ships put 1 picket in nearest station, TG#s with 11 ships put 2 pickets in nearest stations, TG#s with 12+ ships fill all picket stations.

232 Cruising Disposition 5-XT is a circular formation suitable for defense of large task groups against submarines with limited protection against aircraft. Stations are assigned by the OTC, with each task group commander responsible for disposition and patrol of their own group. In the event of contact, task group commanders are authorized to maneuver their groups and increase the distance from the fleet center. All sonar-equipped ships (except screening ships) will stand continuous listening watch.

233 4 Carriers, 7 Heavy Ships, 15 Destroyers in Cruising Disposition Figure 6R.

234 Cruising Disposition 6-R is a normal carrier force day or night high visibility disposition suitable for use against aircraft and submarines. Station assignments are indicated in the diagram, searches, patrols, and offensive air operations as ordered by OTC. Communications as prescribed in USF 70, unless otherwise directed. Sonar equipped ships to stand continuous echo-ranging watch.

235 Cruising disposition 6-S with axis -X315, JO15, X(W5, X3I5, X070, X290, X270, X090 and yards Ar + M" IOOQ, figure S3.

236   Cruising Disposition 6-S is an antisubmarine formation for small forces without carriers, with the guide in the leading cruiser, varying station assignments, and patrol and search instructions from the OTC. Sonar equipped ships stand continuous echo-ranging watch.

237   USF 10B Appendix II outlines Zigzag Plans with Reverse Blank origin.

238   USF 10B Zigzag Plan No. 1 is suitable for single ships, formations or dispositions travelling at 7-20 knots. The plan results in 90% of distance run and changes direction every 2 hours.

239   Zigzag Plan No. 3 suitable for one ship or small formation, with speed of 15-20 knots. Distance made good is 90% of distance run. Course changes every two hours, alternating 10¬∞ right and left of base course.

240   Zigzag Plan No. 4 for use in areas with known submarines, suitable for single ships with speeds of 7-12 knots, distance made good is 69% of distance run.

241   USF 10B Zigzag Plan No. 5 suitable for a single ship, formation, or disposition up to 15 knots, with 91.5% distance made good, and repeat after second hour.

242   Zigzag plan No. 6 suitable for single ship, formation, or disposition with speeds of 7-30 knots; distance made good 9.4% of distance run; repeat direction, amount, resultant, and deviation from base every hour and 47 minutes.

243   Plan 7 for use in submarine areas suitable for one ship, formation or disposition with speeds of 7-30 knots, results in 90% distance made good. Change course every two hours, alternating 10¬∞R, 45¬∞R, 25¬∞L, 20¬∞L, 15¬∞L, 25¬∞R, 40¬∞R, 20¬∞R, 45¬∞L, 0¬∞, 15¬∞R, 45¬∞R, 10¬∞R, 30¬∞R, 45¬∞R, 20¬∞R, 15¬∞R, 25¬∞L, 20¬∞L, 40¬∞L, 30¬∞L, 20¬∞L, 10¬∞R.

244   Zigzag Plan No. 8 for general use in submarine areas suitable for a single ship, formation, or disposition with speeds of 20-30 knots, with 94% distance made good and 9% max distance from track of base course, changing direction every hour.

245   USF 10B QEHLASSIflEB ZIGZAG PLAN NO. 9 is suitable for a single ship, formation, or disposition travelling at 20-30 knots. It yields 93% of distance run and a maximum deviation of 7%. Plan consists of repeating a sequence of 44¬∞R, 17¬∞R, 27¬∞L, 40¬∞L, 20¬∞R, 40¬∞R, 20¬∞R, 25¬∞L, 15¬∞L, 30¬∞L, 13¬∞L, 27¬∞R, and 17¬∞R every hour.

246   Zigzag Plan No. 10 suitable for single ship, formation, or disposition with speeds of 20-30 knots. 70% of distance run made good. Alternates base course and deviation every hour.

247   USF iOB Zigzag Plan No. 19 for ships of speed in excess of 10 knots, distance made good 86% of distance run, repeat plan after first hour.

248   USP 10B Zigzag Plan No. 20 is suitable for all ships and results in 70% distance made good; it involves a series of left and right turns at 40 degree angles and takes 2 hours and 13 minutes to complete.

249   Zigzag plan for use in dangerous waters by single ship, formation, or disposition with sufficient screen. Suitable for ships of all speeds; 70% distance made good. Directions and times to change course given.

250   TJSF 10B is a zigzag plan designed to be used in especially dangerous waters during good visibility, suitable for ships of all speeds. It results in a deviation from base course of 87.5% of the distance run and involves constant helm swinging 10¬∞ per minute.

251   Zigzag Plan No. 23 suitable for ships, formations and dispositions of all speeds, making 94% of distance run, with specified changes in direction and amount every hour. Resultant deviation from base course.

252   Zigzag plan no. 24 not suitable for general use; 97% of distance run; repeat 1 hour course change every 5 minutes.

253   USF10B submarine plan for ships of all speeds; distance made good is 95% of distance run; plan always starts on hour divisible by four.

254   Zigzag Plan No. 26 for use in submarine areas, suitable for ships of all speeds, makes 88% of distance run, always starts on hour divisible by four.

255   Light forces for night search and attack.

256   This appendix covers the use of light forces in night search and attack and provides principles based on maximum use of radar. It emphasizes the importance of surprise and concentration and suggests dispersing forces to reduce enemy radar efficiency. The search phase is conducted by separate attack groups and there may be a contact phase prior to the attack phase.

257   Task force is divided into attack groups and scouts. Scouts search for enemy while attack groups concentrate and attack. Radar is used to approximate day search formations at night.

258   USF 10B states that individual units should be the weakest, and radar can detect surface targets at night with the same range as in daylight, but not always distinguish the number, type, or formation. Initial search dispositions depend on last known position, enemy intentions, disposition, speed, strength of screen, time available, and logistics. Scouting distance should be 8-10 miles, as long as communication and radar links permit.

259   USF 10B and MCIASSIFJEO involve scouting at maximum distance to cover widest front, using radar and IFF for identification. Search is usually direct from ahead, flank, or rear. Contact scouting follows initial contact and holds it, assisted by adjacent scouts.

260   Destroyers and cruisers in scouting line must locate enemy objective and provide information for attack group. Cruisers must assist with fire to inflict maximum damage. Attack phase begins when attack group is ready. Composition of own forces depends on type of enemy objective.

261   Attack groups with cruisers and destroyers in V formation to reduce enemy screen and launch torpedoes before being seen; use of radar intercept receivers to determine enemy presence and use of radar; use of multiple attack groups to take advantage of confusion; use of greater strength when attacking strong forces.

262   USF 10B requires a minimum force of two cruisers and destroyers organized into three-ship units. Attack groups should employ evasive tactics and can use star-shell or flare illumination.

263   Attack groups illuminated by the enemy should use star shell and searchlights for counterillumination and smoke when necessary to defeat enemy illumination. Signal should indicate type of scouting line, method of search, and type of attack groups. Table gives meaning of each numeral.

Change No. 1
to USF 10B

UNITED STATES FLEET
HEADQUARTERS OF THE COMMANDER IN CHIEF
NAVY DEPARTMENT
WASHINGTON 25, D. C.

4 JULY 1945.

LETTER OF PROMULGATION

1. Change Number One to USF 10B is promulgated herewith. USF 10B was made effective on 1 July 1945 by RPM 2089. Change Number One is effective upon receipt and shall be entered in all copies of USF 10B.

2. This change contains (a) corrections to certain typographical errors and (b) double purpose A/A and A/S rotating screens suitable for slow speed screened units. These screens shall be inserted in USF 10B following page 5-17.

3. When not in use this change is to be stowed in accordance with the effective edition of the Registered Publication Manual.

4. This document contains information affecting the national defense of the United States within the meaning of the Espionage Act, 50 U. S. C., 31 and 32, as amended. Its transmission or the revelation of its contents in any manner to an unauthorized person is prohibited by law.

5. It is forbidden to make extracts or to copy this change without specific authority from the Chief of Naval Operations, except as provided for in the effective edition of the Registered Publication Manual.

6. This change shall not be carried in aircraft for use therein.

C. M. Cooke Jr.

C. M. COOKE, Jr.,
Chief of Staff.

IV-a

PoRe # 58552

(1) Make the following pen and ink changes (originally promulgated in RPM 2089):

Page III, enter below the Letter of Promulgation, "Effective 1 July 1945".

Page 3–12, table III, Screen No. 67, Station No. 6, change "16238" to read "16328".

Page 6–27, paragraph 6200, change "fig. 19" to read "fig. 18".

Page Ap. 1–17, (j), second line, delete comma after "section".

(2) Make the following additional pen and ink changes:

Page VII, (List of Effective Pages), after Part V, under "Change in Effect" column, add "Chg. 1"; under "Page Nos." column add "5–19 to 5–34".

Page VII, (List of Effective Pages), after "Letter of Promulgation dated 1 May 1945", add "Letter of Promulgation dated 4 July 1945"; under "Change in Effect" column add "Chg. 1"; under "Page Nos." column add "IV–a, IV–b."

DECLASSIFIED

CURRENT
TACTICAL ORDERS AND DOCTRINE
U. S. Fleet

USF 10B

UNITED STATES FLEET
HEADQUARTERS OF THE COMMANDER IN CHIEF
1945
I

DECLASSIFIED

```
                                        --------------------------
                                                  (Date)
```

From: --
            (Title)   (Name of Command)

To: Chief of Naval Operations (D. N. C.—Registered Publication Section).

Subject: USF 10B.

    1. The nonregistered copy of the subject publication received has been checked against the List of Effective Pages contained therein by ----------------------
-- and

                      (Signature and Rank)

    (a) found to agree therewith, or

    (b) found to agree therewith, except as follows:

        ("X" out (a) or (b) as appropriate—list exceptions below, if any):

```
                        ------------------------------------------
                              (Signature of Commanding Officer)
```

(Date)

From: _____
           (Title)   (Name of Command)

To: Chief of Naval Operations (D. N. C.—Registered Publication Section).

Subject: USF 10B.

   1. The nonregistered copy of the subject publication received has been checked against the List of Effective Pages contained therein by _____ _____ and
                              (Signature and Rank)
      (a) found to agree therewith, or
      (b) found to agree therewith, except as follows:
          ("X" out (a) or (b) as appropriate—list exceptions below, if any):

                                    (Signature of Commanding Officer)

UNITED STATES FLEET
HEADQUARTERS OF THE COMMANDER IN CHIEF
NAVY DEPARTMENT,
WASHINGTON 25, D. C.

1 MAY 1945.

LETTER OF PROMULGATION

1. Current Tactical Orders and Doctrine, U. S. Fleet (USF 10B) is issued for the use and guidance of the United States Fleet. It becomes effective when directed by Commander in Chief, United States Fleet. The distribution is in accordance with the allowance prescribed in the Registered Publication Allowance Tables (RPS–6) (current edition).

2. This publication supersedes Current Tactical Orders and Doctrine, U. S. Fleet (USF 10A) all copies of which shall be destroyed when USF 10B is placed in effect. No report of destruction is required.

3. USF 10B is a confidential, non-registered publication, which shall be transported, handled and stowed as prescribed by Article 76, U. S. Navy Regulations, 1920, and the Registered Publication Manual.

4. This document contains information affecting the national defense of the United States within the meaning of the Espionage Act, 50 U. S. C., 31 and 32, as amended. Its transmission or the revelation of its contents in any manner to an unauthorized person is prohibited by law.

5. IT IS FORBIDDEN TO MAKE EXTRACTS FROM OR TO COPY THIS PUBLICATION WITHOUT SPECIFIC AUTHORITY FROM THE CHIEF OF NAVAL OPERATIONS, EXCEPT AS PROVIDED FOR IN THE REGISTERED PUBLICATION MANUAL.

6. This publication shall not be carried for use in aircraft.

E. J. KING,
Commander in Chief, United States Fleet
and Chief of Naval Operations.

Effective 1 July 1945

CONFIDENTIAL

RECORD OF CORRECTIONS

Change, Despatch, or Memo No.	Date entered	Signature of officer making corrections

(REVERSE BLANK)

ORIGINAL

DECLASSIFIED USF 10B

TABLE OF CONTENTS

100 Foreword.

DECLASSIFIED

IX

ORIGINAL

100. FOREWORD.

110. Current Tactical Orders and Doctrine, U. S. Fleet (USF 10B), is issued to provide, in the light of war experience, instructions both sufficiently inclusive and flexible to control the operations of forces in any fleet.

111. USF 10B is not intended or shall not be construed as depriving any officer exercising tactical command of initiative in issuing special instructions to his command. USF 10B is intended, however, to obviate the necessity for such special instructions under ordinary circumstances and to minimize them in extraordinary circumstances. The ultimate aim is to obtain essential uniformity without unacceptable sacrifice of flexibility. It must be possible for forces composed of diverse types, and indoctrinated under different fleet, type, or task force commanders, to join at sea on short notice for concerted action against the enemy without interchanging a mass of special instructions. Commanders are enjoined to keep the issue of special instructions at a minimum.

112. All approved effective tactical publications in use in the U. S. Fleet derive their authority directly from the Commander in Chief, U. S. Fleet, and Chief of Naval Operations. The general structure of the tactical and affiliated publications in effect in the U. S. Fleet is shown graphically in figure 1. Where differences exist between these publications and USF 10B, the latter shall govern. Commanders in chief of fleets shall require type commanders to bring type publications into conformity with USF 10B.

113. **Reference herein to a publication by its short title shall be construed to mean the effective edition thereof.**

120. Form.

121. USF 10B is issued in loose-leaf form and, in general, is printed on only one side of the paper.

122. Sheets are punched on their left margins.

123. A special system of paragraph numbering is used to provide:
   (a) Self-indexing.
   (b) Blank numbers for additional material or corrections.
   (c) Ready reference.

124. The entire publication is divided into parts, each of which is numbered in even thousands. Each part is divided into sections numbered in even hundreds. The sections are divided into paragraphs, numbered in tens, with numbered subparagraphs. A four-digit number thus readily identifies any portion to be referenced.

Example: 2000—All of part II (2000–2999).
3100—All of section 1, part III (3100–3199).
4120—Second paragraph of section 1, part IV.
5233—Third subparagraph, paragraph 3, section 2, part V.

125. Fleet or tactical commanders issuing special instructions shall have the sheets so printed and punched that their text will appear on pages facing related portions of USF 10B when inserted in the loose-leaf binder. Separate insert pages should, if practicable, be printed on colored paper. They shall carry in the upper right-hand corner the short title of this publication, with the abbreviated title of the preparing officer under the short title.

For example: $\dfrac{\text{USF 10B}}{\text{CTF 11}}$ or $\dfrac{\text{USF 10B}}{\text{Cinclant}}$

In addition, on each inserted sheet shall appear its general distribution and date of issue. For example: "Distribution Pacfleet 3 June 44" or "Distribution TF 18, 4 Dec 44." Commanders issuing such special instructions shall include in the promulgating letters a directive for their destruction when their purpose has been served. In all cases, five copies of such special instructions shall be forwarded by the issuing commander to his fleet commander via first air mail, and two copies to the Commander in Chief, U. S. Fleet.

130. Recommendations for changes in USF 10B to meet fleet, task force or type requirements, or to incorporate therein lessons of battle experience are solicited. Recommendations may be in the form of requesting U. S. Fleet distribution of special instructions issued by a commander and forwarded in accordance with paragraph 125. Other than fleet commanders shall forward such requests via the appropriate fleet commander for comment and recommendation.

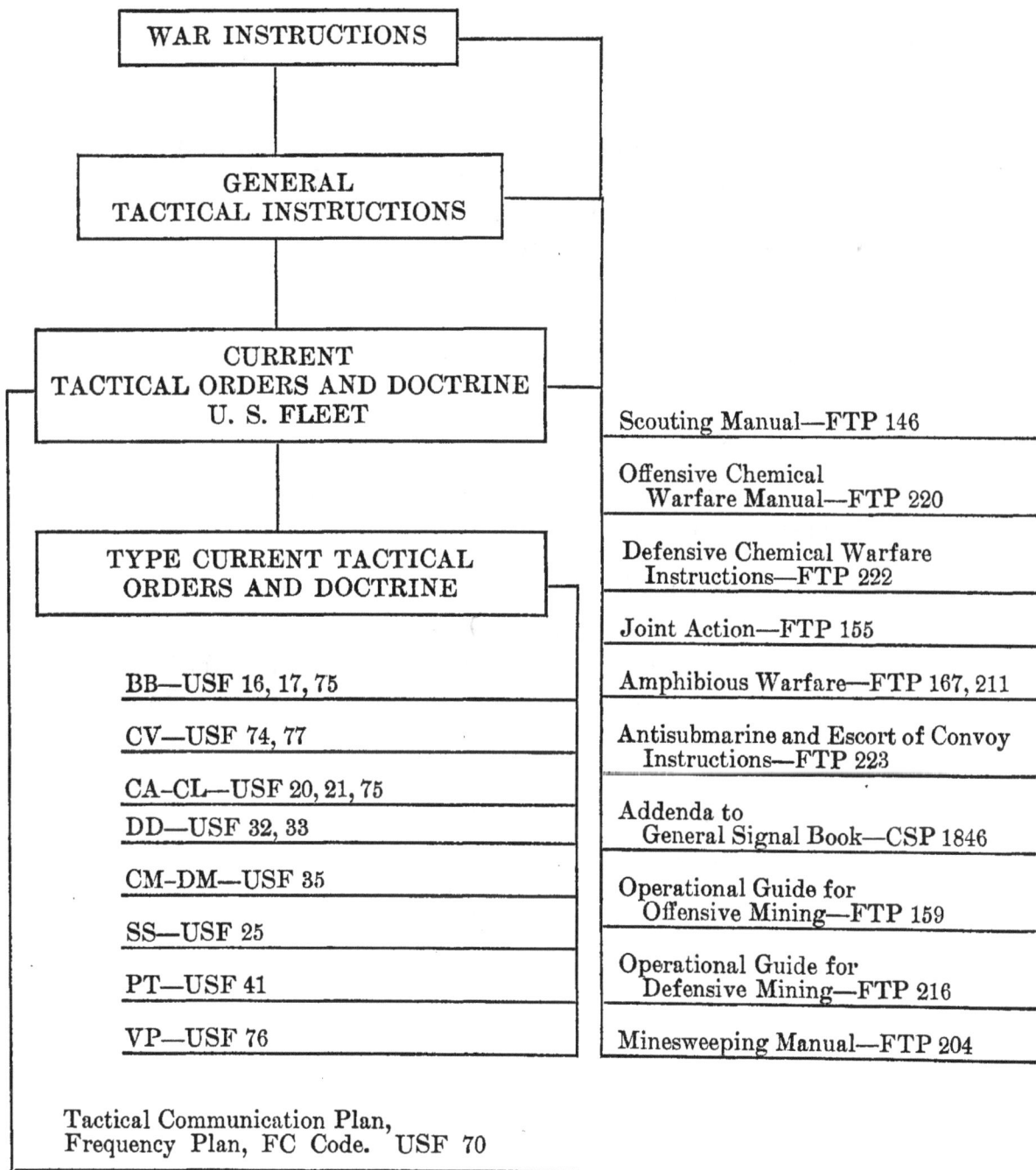

WAR INSTRUCTIONS

GENERAL
TACTICAL INSTRUCTIONS

CURRENT
TACTICAL ORDERS AND DOCTRINE
U. S. FLEET

Scouting Manual—FTP 146

Offensive Chemical
Warfare Manual—FTP 220

Defensive Chemical Warfare
Instructions—FTP 222

TYPE CURRENT TACTICAL
ORDERS AND DOCTRINE

Joint Action—FTP 155

Amphibious Warfare—FTP 167, 211

BB—USF 16, 17, 75

Antisubmarine and Escort of Convoy
Instructions—FTP 223

CV—USF 74, 77

CA-CL—USF 20, 21, 75

Addenda to
General Signal Book—CSP 1846

DD—USF 32, 33

CM-DM—USF 35

Operational Guide for
Offensive Mining—FTP 159

SS—USF 25

PT—USF 41

Operational Guide for
Defensive Mining—FTP 216

VP—USF 76

Minesweeping Manual—FTP 204

Tactical Communication Plan,
Frequency Plan, FC Code. USF 70

Figure 1.

PART I

ORGANIZATION AND COMMAND

1000. GENERAL.

1100. Organization.

1110. The United States Fleet is divided into numbered fleets and each fleet into task forces. The current assignment of fleets is promulgated periodically and is in consonance with "Organization of the Naval Forces of the United States" (General Order No. 213).

1200. The Sea Frontiers.

1210. The organization and command of Sea Frontiers is set forth in General Order No. 213.

1300. Task Forces.

1310. The assignment of units to task forces is temporary or at most semi-permanent in nature.

1320. Internal Organization of Task Force.

1321. When a fleet, or a portion thereof, is formed into a tactical organization, the organization as a whole and each of its subdivisions is designated by number(s) indicating the chain of command. (See Naval Directives and the Order Form (Cominch P–1).)

(a) Task subdivision designations are composed of numerals separated by decimal points.

(b) A numeral alone, or one preceding the first decimal point, designates the fleet and task force. (Note that in tactical calls the first of the two digits preceding the decimal point is replaced by a letter.)

Written	Designation	Orally expressed
11	Task Force 11	Task Force ELEVEN

(c) Numerals between the first and second decimal points designate the task group.

Written	Designation	Orally expressed
13.2	Task Group 2 of Task Force 13	Task Group THIRTEEN point TWO

(d) Numerals following the second decimal point designate the task unit.

Written	Designation	Orally expressed
54.10.5	Task Unit 5 of Task Group 10 of Task Force 54	Task Unit FIFTY-FOUR point TEN point FIVE

(e) Aircraft assigned collectively to a specific task assume the flight number for the task given in the Fleet Communication Plan in effect.

(f) Descriptive names, such as Attack Force, Carrier Force, Left Flank, Midway Detachment, etc., may be used in addition to the numerical designation.

(g) Task organization component commanders should, in general, assign ships only to the echelon immediately subordinate to them, leaving further subdivision to the commanders in such lower echelon.

(h) A task organization component commander may subdivide his component into lower ordered components only.

1322. The following numbered organizations are set forth to illustrate the numerical system of organization and to provide two quickly available initial organizations for large dispositions. Similar task organizations for normal and type tactical organizations are available to fleet and task force commanders other than Commander Task Force ELEVEN, by use of appropriate designation numbers.

(a) The normal tactical organization of a task force; e. g., Task Force ELEVEN, is as follows:

Subdivision designation	Subdivision
11.1	Battle line
11.2	Right flank
11.2.1	Heavy cruisers, right
11.2.2	Light cruisers, right
11.2.3	Destroyers, right
11.3	Center
11.3.1	Heavy cruisers, center
11.3.2	Light cruisers, center
11.3.3	Destroyers, center
11.4	Left flank
11.4.1	Heavy cruisers, left
11.4.2	Light cruisers, left
11.4.3	Destroyers, left
11.5	Air (Carrier)
11.6	Train
11.7	Submarines
11.8	Minecraft
11.9	Patrol planes

DECLASSIFIED

(b) The typrtactical organization of a task force; e. g., Task Force ELEVEN, is as follows:

Subdivision designation	Subdivision
11.1	Battleships
11.2	Cruisers, heavy
11.3	Cruisers, light
11.4	Destroyers
11.5	Carriers
11.6	Train
11.7	Submarines
11.8	Minecraft
11.9	Patrol planes
11.10	OTC flagship (only if required by disposition)

1323. It is emphasized that the task subdivision designating numbers above are illustrative only. If, for example, the types in the center or flank task groups operate together as types, these numbers are appropriate. If, however, a type is subdivided within a task group, the flexibility of the system is such that further number designation of task units is possible. Task group commanders have the privilege of making such subdivision. Flank commanders will assign designating numbers to units joining them, unless these units merge with a task unit already formed. For example, if destroyers and light cruisers from the center join the right flank on deployment, commander right flank will direct incoming units either to join task units already formed on that flank, or to assume new task units designations appropriate to that flank, as the tactical situation demands. The ex-center destroyers might be directed to act defensively and separate from the original flank destroyers operating offensively. In this case the offensive destroyer unit may be 11.2.3, the defensive 11.2.5. Similar assignments may be required for cruisers. The fact that the example in (b) above shows only three units in the center or on the flanks in no way limits those task group commanders to only those numbers. Task groups must be subdivided as the situation demands. No confusion can arise from such subdivision, because communications follow the organization.

1324. The group and unit numbering shown in the examples must not be followed in all instances. For security reasons these numbers should be changed from time to time to destroy the identity of certain calls with particular types or tasks. For example, the battle line may be 11.9, the center 11.7 or any number group within the limits of the system.

1325. Special tactical organizations other than normal or type may be ordered as circumstances require.

1410. When a part or all of a fleet is organized as a task force, and the commander of that fleet is present embarked, he will be the officer in tactical command unless he directs another commander to assume tactical command.

1420. When the task force or group commander is not named in the order creating it, the senior line officer present shall command, and succession to command shall be in order of seniority.

1430. An officer, not the senior present in a task force, may be ordered to command it by a commander in chief, under authority vested in him by the Secretary of the Navy. In case a junior so designated to command a task force, is incapacitated, the senior line officer present shall succeed him, and subsequent succession shall be in order of seniority.

1440. The senior line officer present in a task group shall command it except when, as in paragraph 1430 above, a junior officer has been specifically designated to such command. In case a junior, so designated, is incapacitated, the senior line officer in the task group shall succeed him and subsequent succession shall be in order of seniority.

1450. The senior line officer present in a task unit shall command it; succession to command shall be in order of seniority.

1460. A commander in chief or fleet commander will make assignments to task groups for the normal tactical organization when that fleet or part thereof is organized as a task force under his personal command.

1470. Fleet commanders of the U. S. Fleet, Pacific Fleet and Atlantic Fleet shall be referred to as "Commander in Chief." Other fleet commanders as "Commander _____ Fleet."

1500. Command Communications.

1510. Command communication plans for task organizations are contained in USF 70 and the fleet supplement thereto. They shall, unless specific exception is made by the order creating a task organization, become effective at the same time as the task organization.

1600. U. S.-British Mixed Forces.

1610. The tactical organization and command communications for mixed U. S.-British forces operating in company are covered in the appendix to the General Signal Book.

PART II

CONDITIONS OF READINESS

2000. GENERAL. (See War Instructions, chapter 4.)

2100. Conditions of Readiness for Action.

2110. The definition of each condition of readiness for action prescribes conditions for the several components of the battle organization, which conditions in turn are defined directly or by reference in the remainder of this section.

2120. Condition 1.

General Quarters. All battle stations fully manned and alert.

Material Condition Z(A).

Ammunition ready for instant loading. Guns, except those requiring time-fuze settings, may be loaded on order of the commanding officer well in advance of "Commence firing."

Engineering Condition 31. (See subparagraph 2511.)

Aircraft in condition most appropriate under the existing circumstances. Normally during daylight all carrier aircraft on the flight decks and all floatplanes shall be in condition 11; during night or nonflyable weather condition 13 for carrier aircraft and condition 9 for floatplanes.

2121. Condition 1A.

Applicable to combat loaded transports, freighters, landing ships, and large landing craft.

Condition 1A is the surface ship Condition of Readiness 1 except that preparations shall be made for immediate commencement of disembarkation, other details being modified as necessary to meet this requirement.

2122. Condition 1AA.

Air Defense. All air defense stations fully manned and alert, and other gunnery stations manned to the extent prescribed by the commanding officer.

Material Condition Z(A).

Ammunition ready for instant loading. Guns excepting those requiring time-fuze settings may be loaded on order of the commanding officer well in advance of "Commence firing."

Engineering Condition 31. (See subparagraph 2511.)

Aircraft in condition most appropriate under the existing circumstances. Normally during daylight all carrier aircraft on the flight decks and all floatplanes shall be in condition 11. During night or nonflyable weather condition 13 for carrier aircraft and condition 9 for floatplanes.

General Quarters. All hands at battle stations, with key stations alert (manned by available personnel in rotation), remaining personnel at ease or sleeping on station. Commissary details excused periodically to prepare and issue food to the crew at battle stations.

Material Condition Z(A).

Sufficient modification shall be permitted to provide essential ventilation, and access for the issue of food, attending calls of nature, and other necessary activities. *All open fittings shall be tended.*

Ammunition ready for instant loading.

Engineering Condition 32. (See subparagraph 2512.)

Aircraft in condition most appropriate under the existing circumstances. Normally during daylight all carrier aircraft on the flight decks and all floatplanes shall be in condition 12. During night or nonflyable weather condition 13 for carrier aircraft and condition 9 for floatplanes.

2131. Condition 1EAA.

Air Defense. All hands at air defense stations, with key stations alert (manned by available personnel in rotation), remaining personnel at ease or sleeping on station. Commissary details excused periodically to prepare and issue food to the crew at battle stations.

Material Condition Z(A).

Sufficient modification shall be permitted to provide essential ventilation, and access for the issue of food, for attending calls of nature, and other necessary activities. *All open fittings shall be tended.*

Ammunition ready for instant loading.

Engineering Condition 32. (See subparagraph 2512.)

Aircraft in condition most appropriate under the existing circumstances. Normally during daylight all carrier aircraft on the flight decks and all floatplanes shall be in condition 12. During night or nonflyable weather condition 13 for carrier aircraft and condition 9 for floatplanes.

2140. Condition 2.

Section Watches. One-quarter to one-third (depending on arrangements of batteries and personnel available) of main, secondary, antiaircraft gun and automatic weapon batteries manned. Fire control, combat information center and communications sufficiently manned for immediate use.

Material Condition Y(B).

Ammunition at guns manned ready for instant loading; at guns not manned as prescribed by type commanders.

Engineering Condition 32 or 33. (See subparagraph 2513).

Aircraft in condition most appropriate under the existing circumstances. Normally during daylight all carrier aircraft on the flight decks and all floatplanes shall be in condition 13. During night or nonflyable weather condition 13 for carrier aircraft and condition 9 for floatplanes.

2150. Condition 3.

Section Watches. Main and secondary batteries not manned. One-half to two-thirds (depending on arrangement of the batteries and personnel available) of the antiaircraft gun and automatic weapon batteries (both heavy and light) manned. Fire control, combat information center and communications sufficiently manned for immediate use. CV's, CL (AA's), DD's and other ships whose main batteries are double-purpose guns, man a minimum of one-quarter of the 5-inch guns and one-third to two-thirds of automatic weapons utilizing skeleton crews necessary.

Material Condition Y(B).

Ammunition at guns manned ready for instant loadings; at guns not manned as prescribed by type commanders.

Engineering Condition 32 or 33. (See subparagraph 2513.)

Aircraft in condition most appropriate under the existing circumstances. Normally during daylight all carrier aircraft on the flight decks and all floatplanes shall be in condition 13. During night or nonflyable weather condition 13 for carrier aircraft and condition 9 for floatplanes.

2160. Miscellaneous.

2161. Section watches, as used in paragraphs 2140 and 2150, require the sections of the ship's company to stand watch in rotation. Each section shall comprise one-fourth or one-third of the ship's company as set forth in the battle organization of the ship.

2162. Detailed standardization of battle and condition watch bills is not required. Type commanders shall insure a reasonable degree of uniformity within their respective types, observing the basic principle that shifting from one condition to another should require the minimum shifting of individuals between stations.

2163. Where personnel limitations in conditions 2 and 3 so warrant, batteries having sufficient ready ammunition to sustain maximum rate of fire until a higher condition of readiness can be set need not man lower handling rooms and magazines.

2164. Torpedo batteries are to be considered as a part of the main batteries.

2165. Depth charge batteries shall be manned in accordance with current type instructions.

2170. Circumstances for Assuming Conditions of Readiness.

2171. (a) Condition of Readiness 1 is that condition which shall be assumed when surface action is imminent.

(b) In addition it should be assumed in the following special circumstances:

(1) On sortie, when lack of outside reconnaissance renders encounter with enemy surface forces possible.

(2) During the dawn-alert period, normally from one hour before sunrise until sunrise, unless:

Surface attack obviously is improbable.
Radar condition in effect permits complete surface coverage.

In extreme latitudes during the local summer a condition little short of daylight persists during the whole night.

(3) From sunset until dark when there is reason to expect surface contact. See subparagraph (b) (2) above which applies in principle.

2172. Condition of Readiness 1E is that condition normally assumed when enemy forces of comparable surface strength may be encountered, and when it is desired that all battle stations be manned but not alerted. It is particularly appropriate as a form of rest condition to be interposed between long periods of condition 1.

2173. (a) Condition of Readiness 1AA is that condition which shall be assumed when air action is imminent.

(b) In addition it should be assumed, in the following special circumstances:

(1) On sortie, when lack of outside reconnaissance renders encounter with enemy air forces possible.

(2) During dawn alert period, normally from one hour before sunrise until sunrise, unless:

Air attack obviously is improbable.
Radar condition in effect permits complete air coverage.
In extreme latitudes in the local summer, a condition little short of daylight persists during the whole night.

(3) From sunset until dark when there is reason to expect air contact. See subparagraph (b) (2) above which applies in principle.

2174. Condition of Readiness 1EAA is that condition normally assumed when enemy air forces may be encountered and when it is desired that all air defense stations be manned but not alerted. It is particularly appropriate, as a form of rest condition, to be interposed between long periods of condition 1AA.

2175. Condition of Readiness 2 is that condition normally assumed when major action is improbable but surface encounter with enemy light forces, submarines, or air is a possibility.

2176. Condition of Readiness 3 is that condition normally assumed when the only prospect of surprise attack is by aircraft or submarines.

2177. During sortie from or entry into a harbor or passage believed to be mined or known to be the focus of submarine activity material condition Z(A) should be set, regardless of the condition of readiness in effect.

2178. Whenever they consider it advisable, commanding officers may assume a higher condition of readiness than that which the officer in tactical command has prescribed.

2200. Material Conditions.

2210. Material conditions shall be as defined in Damage Control Instructions (FTP 170), as amplified by type instructions.

2211. Cognizance shall be taken of the relationship between material conditions and engineering casualty control as set forth in Damage Control Instructions.

2300. Ammunition Conditions.

2310. Details regarding ammunition for the conditions of readiness for action shall be prescribed by the appropriate commanders, with due consideration for the requirements of paragraphs 2120 to 2150 inclusive, and 2163.

400. Aircraft Conditions.

2410. There are four basic conditions of readiness, namely, conditions 10, 11, 12, and 13, which are applicable to carrier, battleship and cruiser planes, and there are two additional conditions of readiness, namely, conditions 8 and 9 which are applicable to battleship and cruiser planes only. These are defined in USF 75 and USF 77.

2411. Special conditions of readiness for carrier planes; appropriate general signal followed by 3 numerals, the first numeral applies to fighters, the second to scout-bombers and the third to torpedo-bombers. Note that the first digit of condition numbers is omitted in this signal.

2510. **Four engineering conditions are defined:**

2511. *Engineering Condition 31.* Ready for full power in all respects. Casualty control as for material condition in effect.

2512. *Engineering Condition 32.* Ready for flank speed; remaining boilers on one hour notice. Carrier groups augment boiler power as necessary for flight operations. Casualty control as for material condition in effect modified to the minimum extent required by idle boilers.

2513. *Engineering Condition 33.* Ready for flank speed; remaining boilers secured. Carrier groups augment boiler power as necessary for flight operations. Casualty control as for material condition in effect.

2514. *Engineering Condition 34.* Power available for station keeping at standard speed; remaining boilers secured. Casualty control as for material condition in effect, modified to minimum extent required to obtain best fuel economy. This condition is appropriate only for ships on long passages in areas where there is no known enemy activity, or in a situation where utmost fuel economy is so vital to operations in progress that some diminution of security must be accepted.

2515. *Special Engineering Conditions for Mixed Types.* When operating with ships of many classes and types, the above conditions may be found to be unsuitable. In this case the officer in tactical command may signal both the speed for which boiler power is to be maintained and the number of hours notice for the remaining boiler power, using the appropriate signal provided in the General Signal Book.

2520. (a) Ships shall habitually cruise with normal machinery plant set-up, which for modern combatant ships requires that the plant be completely split, and, for other than modern combatant ships requires that the plant set-up be the most effective approximation to a split plant that the installation permits. This most effective approximation is that prescribed for each class by the type commander in accordance with the basic conditions set forth in the Damage Control Instructions for operations in battle.

(b) Modifications of the split plant set-up are authorized and will be ordered by the officer in tactical command where logistics limitations demand that conservation of fuel take precedence over safety of ships. Modifications have also been authorized in certain designs (i. e. Destroyer Escorts, Diesel) for those conditions where the highest reliability of power is not required, but no modification of split plant requirements has been authorized for conditions 1 or 1AA.

2600. Communication Conditions.

2610. Interior communications shall be fully manned in conditions 1, 1AA, 1E, and 1EAA, but, in the two latter conditions, personnel of only one of two or more parallel circuits need be alert. In conditions 2 and 3 internal communications shall be sufficiently manned to control instantly the fire of all batteries which are manned and to assume control without delay of additional armament as it is manned.

2620. Exterior communications in all conditions of readiness, shall be manned as required by the communication plan in effect.

2700. Composite Conditions.

2710. Composite conditions may be prescribed by the officer in tactical command. Interpret the appropriate general signal followed by three numerals to mean: "Set indicated conditions, first numeral readiness for action, second aircraft, third engineering." Example: "Set Condition 1 3 2" would require Readiness 1, modified to Aircraft 13 and Engineering 32. The example would be appropriate for sortie where air cover was being furnished by shore-based aircraft and speeds higher than flank were not required. Note that the first digit of condition numbers higher than 9 is omitted in the signal.

DECLASSIFIED PART III
CRUISING INSTRUCTIONS

3000. GENERAL.

3100. The instructions and information herein are intended to standardize ordinary cruising procedures. Whether a particular item is mandatory or advisory is apparent from the text.

3110. Navigation.

3111. Fathometers may not be operated without special permission of the officer in tactical command, except when antisubmarine vessels are echo-ranging, supersonic fathometers may be used at discretion. Ships operating singly should weigh the added risk of submarine attack against the need for soundings. The possibility of acoustic mines being detonated by fathometer impulse must also be considered in areas where the presence of such mines is suspected.

3120. Rendezvous—Rejoining at Night or in Low Visibility. (See War Instructions, chapter 6.)

3121. A ship separated from her disposition at night should, unless otherwise directed, energize her radar recognition equipment and proceed to rejoin as soon as circumstances permit. When within NAN range, recognition signals and calls should be exchanged with ships of the disposition which is being closed. Ships of the disposition shall challenge with NAN as directed by the commander of the disposition.

3130. Evasive Courses and Speeds. (See War Instructions, chapter 7.)

3131. Time spent on courses for flight operations should be held to a minimum, in order to permit maximum advance across or downwind when this is required by the task in hand.

Maximum advantage should be taken of catapults and the method BAKER for operating aircraft in order to reduce time and distance away from the base course.

3200. Cruising Dispositions. (See War Instructions, chapter 6.)

3210. Typical cruising dispositions are provided in Appendix I for use in varying tactical situations by forces of different sizes and characteristics. Each typical cruising disposition is accompanied on the facing page by instructions for its use.

DECLASSIFIED

DECLASSIFIED

3211. Commanders may issue additional dispositions when necessary. Paragraph 125 of the foreword applies.

3220. Below listed items are hereby standardized to simplify preparation and use of special dispositions. These items are effective for dispositions herein contained and shall be effective for those issued by other commanders without repetition in promulgating orders.

3221. Terminology shall be consistent with that used in the General Tactical Instructions.

3222. Circle spacing shall be 1,000 yards.

3223. Screening stations in small dispositions shall bear consecutive numbers (by types if necessary) indicating the sequence in which they are to be filled when there are insufficient screening ships to fill all.

3224. Each disposition shall be accompanied on the facing page by instructions for its use. The instructions accompanying cruising disposition 3–V herein (see Appendix I) shall be used as a guide and check-off list. The several items of instructions shall invariably be listed in the same order.

3230. The following principles are listed for general guidance in preparing cruising dispositions and selecting a disposition appropriate to the existing tactical situation. War Instructions, chapter 6, should also be consulted.

3231. When submarine attack is the predominant threat, the disposition should have width rather than depth. The positioning and operation of the antisubmarine screens, based upon sonar considerations, are covered in the appendix to the General Signal Book (CSP 1846), Antisubmarine and Escort of Convoy Instructions (FTP 223), General Tactical Instructions (FTP 188), and War Instructions (FTP 143).

3232. When air attack is the predominant threat, circular screens of single ship station units give best protection, particularly against torpedo, horizontal, and low-level bombing attacks. This disposition is additionally desirable because of the ease with which it can be turned and the room within the screen for individual ship avoiding actions. Interval between antiaircraft screens and the diameter of the inner screen is often determined by the range at which self-destruction element of heavy automatic weapon ammunition operates and other ballistic features. Distance between vessels in an antiaircraft screen should be determined by a balance between the need for adequate sea room, and necessity of presenting a high concentration of fire at any point—1,500–2,000 yards is frequently used. This disposition is weak against surface attack and dive bomber attack. When sufficient destroyers are present in the screen of a carrier force consideration should be given to

DECLASSIFIED

...tationing one astern of the carrier as a plane guard. This destroyer may render assistance not only in performing plane guard duties but can augment the carrier antiaircraft fire against dive bombing and suicide attacks and may pick up personnel blown overboard by a near miss or hit on the carrier.

3233. When surprise surface contact may occur in low visibility or at night, the primary consideration in selecting the appropriate disposition is whether our force is seeking engagement or committed to avoiding action.

(a) When seeking engagement the disposition should be of the "ready" or "attack" type. If another type of disposition is used, it must be one from which deployment can be rapidly effected during low visibility and procedure for deploying must be prescribed.

(b) When not seeking engagement, and particularly when the disposition contains valuable ships which must be protected, a disposition should be chosen which can be turned readily, and from which, if necessary, protected units can retire expeditiously while defending units concentrate and interpose for delaying action.

(c) In either case, if earlier warning is desired than may be expected from the radars of the heavy ships, consideration should be given to advancing one or more radar pickets in the direction of advance, or expected contact. The value of earlier warning must be weighed against the added probability of discovery.

3234. The assignment of carrier stations in circular dispositions should be flexible in order to permit accommodation to the changing demands of air operations. Under some conditions, this may most readily be accomplished by assigning coordinates for a "cruising station" which the carrier(s) should normally occupy when not operating aircraft, and separate coordinates for an "operating station" which the carrier(s) may use while operating aircraft.

3235. While normally it is desirable to obtain optimum operating conditions by orienting the axis of a carrier disposition into the expected wind, it is essential that the separation of the operating stations of the carriers be sufficient to avoid critical interference between carriers and carrier air groups no matter what the orientation of the axis or the direction of the wind.

3240. Screens.

3241. Uniformity in screening procedures is desirable. All screens must, however, be flexible enough to permit adjustment by the officer in tactical command or by the screen commander to suit changing conditions. See also subparagraph 3251.

3242. Screens for convoys are covered in FTP 223. Screens for large dispositions are covered in this publication and in the General Tactical

DECLASSIFIED Instructions. Screening forces composed of mixed United States-British units are covered in the appendix to the General Signal Book.

3243. Forms of single screens.

(a) Partial Screens: (i. e.) Straight line, bent line, and arc (used when less than a 240° arc of a circle is occupied uniformly by screening vessels).

(b) Open Circular Screen: One which is not completely closed, that is, there is an arc of the screen of 120° or less which is either not occupied or is not uniformly occupied. All stations in the screen which are occupied are uniformly spaced, excepting those in the open arc of 120° or less.

(c) Closed Circular Screen: One which is completely closed by evenly spaced screening stations and where all screening stations are occupied.

(d) Special Screens.

3244. Stations of screening ships in partial, open and closed circular screens are numbered from disposition course.

3245. Screening ships reorient:

(a) Partial Screen: Upon change of disposition course.

(b) Open Circular Screen: Upon change of disposition course.

(c) Closed Circular Screen: Upon a change of disposition course, station numbers of ships change, but ships only reorient enough to place the nearest ship in the No. 1 position If the new course is equidistant from two screening stations, the screen shall reorient to the left to place the right-hand ship in Station One. (See subparagraph 3249.)

3246. Turn Signals.—No form of screen reorients on a turn signal unless a signal is made to do so.

3247. If ships are zigzagging and signal is made to remain on course being steered, screening ships do not reorient unless so directed. (See subparagraph 3432.)

3248. All single screens commence reorientation:

(a) When the signal is understood, if it is made by the executive method.

(b) Ten minutes prior to the specified time when the signal was made in advance to be executed at a specified future time.

DECLASSIFIED

3249. Locating Station One and Assignment of Ships to Screening Stations.

(a) Locating Station One in partial screens and open circular screens.

(1) If there is an odd number of ships in the screen, Station One is located on the disposition course.

(2) If there is an even number of ships in the screen, Stations One and Two are equidistant from the disposition course, with Station One to the right.

(3) In both (1) and (2) above odd numbers fill stations from 0° to 180° relative to disposition course, and even numbers from 360° to 180° relative to disposition course.

(b) Locating Station One in closed circular screens.

(1) In a closed circular screen Station One will always be on the disposition course. Stations are numbered as in subparagraph 3249 (a) (3) above.

(c) Method of Assigning Ships to Screening Stations.

(1) Screen commander assigns ships to their stations by signal or despatch.

(2) For open circular screens ships will initially be assigned those stations numbered relative to the disposition course, which cover the advance of the disposition on the present or initial course. On course changes thereafter, the screen will reorient to cover the advance on the new course. After ships are initially assigned stations in the screen, they will maintain the same relative order in the screen regardless of the stations they occupy, unless specifically directed otherwise.

Table I.—ASSURED SONAR

Screen No.	Number of DD's	Station Numbers									
		1	2	3	4	5	6	7	8	9	10
11	1	2.5000									
12	2	2.5060	2.5300								
13	3	2.5000	2.5300	2.5060							
14	4	2.5030	2.5330	2.5070	2.5290						
15	5	2.5000	2.5315	2.5045	3285	3075					
16	6	2.5020	2.5340	3050	3310	3.5075	3.5285				
17	7	3000	3330	3030	3.5305	3.5055	4280	4080			
18	8	4010	4350	4030	4330	4055	4305	4.5075	4.5285		
19	9	4000	4340	4020	4320	4040	4.5300	4.5060	5280	5080	
20	10	4.5010	4.5350	4.5030	4.5330	4.5050	4.5310	5070	5290	6080	6280
21	11	5000	5343	5017	5325	5035	5.5310	5.5050	6295	6065	7285
22	12	6007	6353	6020	6340	6035	6325	6050	6310	6.5065	6.5295
23	13	6000	6345	6015	6330	6030	6315	6045	6.5300	6.5060	7.5290
24	14	6.5007	6.5353	6.5020	6.5340	6.5035	6.5325	7048	7312	7.5060	7.5300
25	15	7000	7348	7012	7335	7025	7322	7038	7.5310	7.5050	8300
26	16	7.5006	7.5354	7.5018	7.5342	7.5030	7.5330	8040	8320	8050	8310
27	17	7.5000	7.5348	7.5012	7.5335	7.5025	7.5325	7.5035	8315	8045	8.5305
28	18	8.5005	8.5355	8.5015	8.5345	8.5025	8.5335	8.5035	8.5325	8.5045	8.5315
29	19	9000	9350	9010	9340	9020	9330	9030	9320	9040	9310
30	20	9.5005	9.5355	9.5015	9.5345	9.5025	9.5335	9.5035	9.5235	9.5045	9.5315

Table II.—ASSURED SONAR

Screen No.	Number of DD's	Station Numbers									
		1	2	3	4	5	6	7	8	9	10
31	1	2.5000									
32	2	3050	3310								
33	3	3000	3300	3060							
34	4	3025	3335	3.5070	3.5290						
35	5	3.5000	3.5325	3.5035	4.5290	4.5070					
36	6	4015	4345	4050	4310	5080	5280				
37	7	4.5000	4.5330	4.5030	5300	5060	6280	6080			
38	8	5.5010	5.5350	5.5035	5.5325	6060	6300	7080	7280		
39	9	6.5000	6.5340	6.5020	6.5320	6.5040	7300	7060	7.5280	7.5080	
40	10	6.5010	6.5350	6.5030	6.5330	7050	7310	8065	8295	9080	9280
41	11	7.5000	7.5343	7.5017	7.5325	7.5035	8305	8055	8.5290	8.5070	10280
42	12	8008	8352	8025	8335	8.5040	8.5320	9055	9305	9.5070	9.5290
43	13	8.5000	8.5345	8.5015	8.5330	8.5030	8.5315	8.5045	9.5300	9.5060	10.5287
44	14	9.5007	9.5353	9.5020	9.5340	9.5035	9.5325	10050	10310	10.5065	10.5295
45	15	10.5000	10.5348	10.5012	10.5335	10.5025	10.5322	10.5038	11310	11050	12300
46	16	11006	11354	11018	11342	11.5030	11.5320	12040	12320	12.5050	12.5310
47	17	11.5000	11.5348	11.5012	11.5337	11.5023	12325	12035	12.5315	12.5045	13305
48	18	12005	12355	12015	12345	12.5025	12.5335	12.5035	12.5325	12.5045	12.5315
49	19	12.5000	12.5350	12.5010	12.5340	12.5020	13330	13030	13320	13040	13310
50	20	13005	13355	13015	13345	13025	13335	13035	13325	13045	13315

*When only this number of screening ships is available, it is impossible to provide the high degree of protection afforded by the screens for which the "circle well protected" is given. Nevertheless they do provide very useful protection.

(a) If the radius of the circle to be well protected is known, then by finding this radius in the extreme right hand column of the table, the number of screening vessels required is at once apparent in the corresponding position in the column headed "Number of DD's". If additional screening vessels are available, they may be employed as "pickets," "plane guards," etc.

Screen No.	Number of DD's	Station Numbers										Radius in yards of Max. Circle well protected
		11	12	13	14	15	16	17	18	19	20	
11	1											•
12	2											•
13	3											•
14	4											•
15	5											
16	6											1 ship
17	7											500
18	8											750
19	9											1,000
20	10											1,500
21	11	7075										2,000
22	12	7080	7280									2,500
23	13	7.5070	8.5280	8.5080								3,000
24	14	8070	8290	9080	9280							3,500
25	15	8060	8.5290	8.5070	9.5280	9.5080						4,000
26	16	8.5060	8.5300	9070	9290	9.5080	9.5280					4,250
27	17	8.5055	9295	9065	9.5285	9.5075	10.5280	10.5080				4,500
28	18	9055	9305	9.5065	9.5295	10075	10285	11080	11.280			5,000
29	19	9050	9.5300	9.5060	10290	10070	10.5280	10.5080	11.5275	11.5085		6,000
30	20	10055	10305	10.5065	10.5295	11073	11287	11.5080	11.5280	12.5085	12.5275	6,500

RANGE, 1,500 YARDS

Screen No.	Number of DD's	Station Numbers										Radius in yards of Max. Circle well protected
		11	12	13	14	15	16	17	18	19	20	
31	1											•
32	2											•
33	3											•
34	4											1 ship
35	5											500
36	6											1,000
37	7											1,500
38	8											2,500
39	9											3,000
40	10											3,500
41	11	10080										4,500
42	12	11080	11280									5,000
43	13	10.5073	11.5275	11.5085								6,000
44	14	11.5075	11.5285	12.5085	12.5275							6,500
45	15	12060	13290	13070	14280	14080						7,500
46	16	13060	13300	13.5070	13.5290	14.5080	14.5280					8,000
47	17	13055	13.5295	13.5065	14285	14075	14.5275	14.5085				8,500
48	18	13055	13305	13.5065	13.5295	14075	14285	15085	15275			9,000
49	19	13050	13.5300	13.5060	14290	14070	14.5280	14.5080	15270	15090		9,500
50	20	13.5055	13.5305	14065	14295	14.5075	14.5285	15085	15275	15.5095	15.5265	10,000

(b) When sufficient screening vessels are not available to fill the stations required, a loose screen must be accepted. It is suggested that the stations required by the above table for the circle to be protected be placed on a maneuvering board and patrol sectors be assigned to screening vessels, who should adjust course and speed so as to cover the locus determined by the above points while patrolling their stations. Particular emphasis must be given to the flank stations, and this may be accomplished by reducing the patrol area assigned flank ships in order that this vital spot is not uncovered for too long a time.

DECLASSIFIED

Screen No.	Number of DD's	Station Numbers									
		1	2	3	4	5	6	7	8	9	10
51	1	3000									
52	2	3050	3310								
53	3	3,5000	4305	4055							
54	4	3.5025	3.5335	4.5065	4.5295						
55	5	4.5000	4.5320	4.5040	5.5285	5.5075					
56	6	5.5015	5.5345	5.5050	5.5310	6.5080	6.5280				
57	7	6.5000	6.5335	6.5025	7310	7050	8285	8075			
58	8	7010	7350	7035	7325	7.5060	7.5300	9080	9280		
59	9	8000	8340	8020	8.5320	8.5040	9300	9060	10280	10080	
60	10	9010	9350	9030	9330	9.5050	9.5310	11065	11295	12080	12280
61	11	10000	10343	10017	10325	10035	11310	11050	12295	12065	13280
62	12	11008	11352	11025	11335	11.5040	11.5320	12055	12305	13070	13290
63	13	12000	12345	12015	12330	12030	12315	12045	12.5300	12.5060	13.5285
64	14	13006	13354	13020	13340	13035	13325	13050	13310	14.5065	13.5295
65	15	14000	14348	14012	14335	14025	14322	14038	14.5310	14.5050	15297
66	16	15006	15354	15018	15342	15030	15330	15043	15317	15.5055	15.5305
67	17	16000	16350	16010	16340	16020	16200	16032	16317	16043	16.5305
68	18	17005	17355	17015	17345	17025	17335	17035	17325	17045	17315
69	19	18000	18350	18010	18340	18020	18330	18030	18320	18040	18310
70	20	19004	19356	19012	19348	19020	19340	19030	19330	19040	19320

*When only this number of screening ships is available, it is impossible to provide the high degree of protection afforded by the screens for which the "circle well protected" is given. Nevertheless, they do provide very useful protection.

(a) If the radius of the circle to be well protected is known, then, by finding this radius in the extreme right-hand column of the table, the number of screening vessels required is at once apparent in the corresponding position in the column headed "Number of DD's." If additional screening vessels are available, they may be employed as "pickets," "plane guards," etc.

Table IV.—SCREENING DISTANCE TABLE

Screened distance between stations equally spaced on circular screen tabulated with number of screening stations vs. circle on which positioned.

Number of stations	Circle Number (in thousands of yards)															
	2.5	3	3.5	4	4.5	5	5.5	6	6.5	7	7.5	8	8.5	9	9.5	10
4	3500	4200	5000	5600	6400	7000	7800	8500	9200	9900	10600	11300	12000	12800	13500	14100
5	2900	3500	4100	4700	5200	5800	6500	7100	7600	8200	8800	9400	10000	10600	11200	11700
6	2500	3000	3500	4000	4500	5000	5500	6000	6500	7000	7500	8000	8500	9000	9500	10000
7	2100	2600	3000	3500	3900	4300	4800	5200	5600	6000	6500	6900	7300	7800	8200	8600
8	1900	2300	2700	3100	3400	3800	4200	4600	5000	5400	5800	6200	6600	6900	7300	7700
9	1800	2100	2400	2700	3100	3400	3800	4100	4500	4800	5200	5500	5800	6100	6500	6900
10	1600	1900	2200	2500	2800	3100	3400	3700	4000	4300	4600	4900	5300	5600	5900	6200
11	1400	1600	1900	2200	2500	2800	3000	3300	3600	3900	4100	4400	4600	4900	5200	5700
12	1300	1600	1800	2100	2300	2600	2800	3000	3400	3600	3900	4100	4300	4600	4900	5200
13	1200	1400	1600	1800	2100	2300	2600	2800	3000	3300	3500	3800	4000	4200	4400	4700
14	1100	1300	1500	1700	1900	2200	2400	2600	2800	3000	3200	3500	3700	3900	4100	4300
15	1100	1300	1500	1700	1900	2100	2300	2500	2700	2900	3100	3300	3500	3700	3900	4100
16	1000	1200	1400	1600	1700	1900	2100	2300	2500	2700	2900	3100	3300	3500	3700	3900
17	1000	1100	1300	1500	1700	1800	2000	2200	2400	2600	2700	2900	3100	3300	3500	3700
18	900	1000	1200	1400	1600	1700	1900	2100	2200	2400	2600	2800	2900	3100	3300	3500
19	900	1000	1200	1300	1500	1700	1800	2000	2100	2300	2500	2700	2900	3000	3200	3300
20	800	1000	1100	1200	1400	1600	1700	1900	2000	2100	2300	2500	2600	2800	2900	3100
21	800	900	1100	1200	1400	1500	1700	1800	1900	2100	2300	2400	2600	2700	2800	3000
22	700	800	1000	1100	1300	1400	1600	1700	1800	2000	2100	2200	2400	2500	2600	2800
23	700	800	1000	1100	1300	1400	1600	1700	1800	2000	2100	2200	2400	2500	2600	2800
24	700	800	1000	1100	1200	1300	1400	1600	1700	1800	2000	2100	2300	2400	2500	2600

DECLASSIFIED

Screen No.	Number of DD's	Station Numbers										Radius in yards of Max. Circle well protected
		11	12	13	14	15	16	17	18	19	20	
51	1											•
52	2											•
53	3											1 ship
54	4											500
55	5											1,500
56	6											2,500
57	7											3,000
58	8											4,000
59	9											5,000
60	10											6,000
61	11	13080										7,000
62	12	15080	15280									8,000
63	13	13.5075	15275	15085								9,000
64	14	15075	15285	16.5085	16.5275							10,000
65	15	15063	16075	17.5275	17.5285	17.5085						11,000
66	16	16.5065	16.5295	17.5075	17.5285	19085	19275					12,000
67	17	16.5055	17.5295	17.5065	19285	19075	20275	20085				13,000
68	18	17.5055	17.5305	18.5065	18.5295	19.5075	19.5285	21085	21275			14,000
69	19	18050	18.5300	18.5060	19.5290	19.5070	20280	20080	21270	21090		15,000
70	20	19050	19310	19.5060	19.5300	20070	20290	20.5080	20.5280	21.5090	21.5270	16,000

(b) When sufficient screening vessels are not available to fill the stations required, a loose screen must be accepted. It is suggested that the stations required by the above table for the circle to be protected be placed on a maneuvering board and patrol sectors be assigned to screening vessels, who should adjust course and speed so as to cover the locus determined by the above points while patrolling their stations. Particular emphasis must be given to the flank stations, and this may be accomplished by reducing the patrol area assigned flank ships in order that this vital spot is not uncovered for too long a time.

Table V.—CLOSED CIRCULAR SCREENS

The following table gives the relative bearing of each station from the center of the disposition relative to the disposition course for equidistant closed circular screens for the number of screening ships indicated:

Number of ships	STATION NUMBER AND RELATIVE BEARING																							
	1	2	3	4	5	6	7	8	9	10	11	12	13	14	15	16	17	18	19	20	21	22	23	24
4	000	270	090	180																				
5	000	288	072	216	144																			
6	000	300	060	240	120	180																		
7	000	309	051	258	102	207	153																	
8	000	315	045	270	090	225	135	180																
9	000	320	040	280	080	240	120	200	160															
10	000	326	036	292	072	252	108	216	144	180														
11	000	328	032	296	065	264	097	232	130	200	163													
12	000	330	030	300	060	270	090	240	120	210	150	180												
13	000	332	028	314	056	276	084	250	110	222	138	194	165											
14	000	335	025	310	050	285	075	260	100	235	125	210	150	180										
15	000	336	024	312	048	288	072	264	096	240	120	216	144	192	168									
16	000	338	022	315	045	292	067	270	090	247	112	225	135	202	157	180								
17	000	339	021	318	042	297	063	276	084	255	105	234	126	213	147	192	168							
18	000	340	020	320	040	300	060	280	080	260	100	240	120	220	140	200	160	180						
19	000	341	019	322	038	303	057	284	076	265	095	246	114	227	133	208	152	189	171					
20	000	342	018	324	036	306	054	288	072	270	090	252	108	234	126	216	144	198	162	180				
21	000	343	017	326	034	309	051	292	068	275	085	258	102	241	119	224	136	207	153	190	170			
22	000	344	016	328	032	312	048	296	064	280	080	264	096	247	112	230	129	213	146	197	163	180		
23	000	344	016	329	031	314	046	299	061	284	076	268	092	252	108	236	124	220	140	204	156	188	172	
24	000	345	015	330	030	315	045	300	060	285	075	270	090	255	105	240	120	225	135	210	150	195	165	180

3250. Basis of Antisubmarine Screen.

(a) Antisubmarine Screens are based on consideration of the following:

(1) The screen in the direction of advance should be kept closed to the most effective screening distance between screening ships.

(2) The most effective screening distance is one and one-half times the assured sonar echo-range determined by the bathythermograph.

(b) The open circular and closed circular screens used as antisubmarine screens have the advantage of providing:

(1) More adequate antiaircraft protection in surprise air attacks.

(2) A more rapid transition into closed circular screens at the proper spacing and interval to provide the maximum antiaircraft protection to the screened ships.

(3) In case of frequent course changes for (1) Closed Circular Screen, no reorientation; (2) Open Circular Screen, the minimum of orientation, to cover the direction of advance of the disposition.

(c) The partial (bent line) antisubmarine screen has the advantage of providing the protection desired with the minimum number of screening ships.

3251. Screening Station Assignments—Tables for

(a) To promote uniformity and to reduce signaling, six tables of screening station assignments have been included as pages 3–10 to 3–13, inclusive, and 3–28 to 3–33, inclusive, for use in stationing screens. It will be noted that there are two basic forms of single screens:

(1) The partial (bent line) screen, for which tables I, II, and III have been prepared.

(2) The circular screen (both closed and open), for which special tables IV, V, and VI have been prepared.

(b) Tables I, II, and III are based on the following assumptions:

(1) Type of disposition. The body screened is either a single ship or is disposed within a circle. The largest circle well protected is given for each screen by the right-hand column of the tables.

(2) Sonar Conditions:

a. Table I—Assured sonar echo-range of 1,000 yards.

b. Table II—Assured sonar echo-range of 1,500 yards.

c. Table III—Assured sonar echo-range of 2,000 yards.

(3) Locus of outer limits of effective enemy firing position for 15 knot fleet speed versus assumed enemy torpedo run of 6,600 yards at 43 knots. There is little difference between torpedo danger zones and submarine limiting approach lines based on the above assumption and with the assumption of a 15-knot fleet speed versus assumed enemy torpedo run of 6,000 yards at 36 knots. The station assignments indicated in tables I, II, and III are equally applicable for both assumptions as differences involved are relatively small. This limiting locus of firing points is measured from the disposition center, or, in case the main body is a column or other formation where the screened ships are not closely and symmetrically spaced around the guide, the center of the smallest circle containing the screened formation. In the latter case the tables should be adjusted or modified to correspond.

(c) Spacing and intervals are based on the following:

(1) The screen should if practicable be on the locus of the outer limit of enemy favorable firing points. When insufficient ships are available to provide a tight screen on this locus, a looser screen is accepted, dependence being placed on the screening ships patrolling their stations. The important flank positions should always be filled.

(2) The distance between screening vessels should not unnecessarily exceed one and one-half times the assured echo-range determined by bathythermograph.

(3) The assured echo range and the size of the circle of the protected ships determine the screen to be used. When more screening vessels are available than are required for the screen, they should not be used to form a larger screen which would protect an unnecessarily large circle, but the additional units should be assigned to picket stations, aircraft guards, or, if desired, a change to an open or closed circular screen could be made.

(d) (1) Table IV is an aid to assist in the choosing of the correct station for screening vessels based on the screening distance desired, screening circle, and the number of ships available for screening duties. From this table stations for an antisubmarine or antiaircraft circular screen may be determined.

(2) Table V provides a ready means of determining the angular spacing and the relative bearing of each station from the center of the disposition, relative to the disposition course

or the selected screening circle for the number of ships available for screening duties (however, station assignments must be made).

 (3) The use of tables IV and V plus the original assignments of screening ships on the screen will determine with a minimum of signaling the station of any screening ship in a circular screen.

 (e) Table VI. (See paragraph 3263 (a) and page 3–28 for table and example.)

  (1) Table VI is a convenient method of reorienting open circular screens once the proper screen has been selected and station assignments have been made.

  (2) The officer in tactical command or screen commander will indicate by signal if table VI is to be used.

3252. Method of Selecting Antisubmarine and Antiaircraft Circular (open and closed) Screens.

 (a) Antisubmarine Screens.

  (1) Determine assured sonar echo-range.

  (2) Determine the screening distance (one and one-half times assured sonar echo-range).

  (3) From the number of heavy ships in the disposition and their positions relative to the disposition center, determine the approximate circle on which it is desired to place the screen. The interval between the screen and the circle of screened ships should never be less than 4,000 yards, a distance from 4,500 to 5,000 yards being a normal optimum, particularly for screened formations which are within a circle of over 1,500 yards radius.

  (4) In table IV under circle selected as in (3) above, go down that column until approximate screening distance (as determined in (2) above) is found, then look to the left along that horizontal line and find the number of equally spaced stations on the circle selected which it will be necessary to fill if closed circular screen is provided.

  (5) If sufficient screening ships are available to fill these stations, then this screen may be operated as a closed circular screen and be designated by signal as described in subparagraph 3253 below.

(6) If, however, insufficient screening ships are available to fill these stations but sufficient vessels are available to fill the stations in the forward semicircle or preferably a 240° arc of the circle, then this screen may be designated by signal as described in subparagraph 3253 below, and the screen may be operated as an open circular screen.

(7) If, however, insufficient screening ships are available to adequately form a screen as described on (6) above, then a partial screen must be used. The radius of the circle should not be diminished so much that the interval between the screen and the circle of screened ships is under 4,000 yards. Furthermore, the screen should always extend to 90° on either side of the formation's course, and these flank positions should always be filled. When this results in a spacing between screening ships more than one and one-half times sonar echo-range, they will depend upon station patrolling to increase the tightness.

(8)   (a) The above procedures are for the provision of optimum antisubmarine protection. However, it may be necessary to modify them in cases where they conflict with the requirements of antiaircraft protection.

    (b) See FTP 223, section 1200, for echo search plans and further details on screening.

    (c) Should one or more "tail backs" be required, it is solely necessary to assign the destroyers to those stations and then form a bent-line screen out of the remainder.

(b) Method of Selecting Antiaircraft Screen.

(1) The best position of screening ships to provide maximum antiaircraft protection, is in a full circular screen, equally spaced. After determining the circle on which the screen is to be disposed, the position of individual ships from the disposition center may be ascertained from table V. The screen may be designated by the method described in subparagraph 3253 (a) below.

3262. Method of designating circular screens.

(a) A circular screen is designated by an appropriate signal from the General Signal Book with a tack line followed by 4 or 5 numerals. The first 2 numerals after the tack line indicate the number of screening stations spaced equally on the circular screen. If there are less than 10 screening stations, the first numeral will be a zero. The third and fourth numerals, and if necessary, the fifth numeral indicate the radius of the circle in hundreds of yards. The designation of the screen does not necessarily mean that all the stations will be occupied. If the number of ships assigned to the screen are not sufficient to occupy all the stations, then the screen will operate as an open circular screen. (See subparagraph 3263.)

(b) Example of selection and designation of circular (closed and open) screen. Suppose it is desired to employ a circular form of screen, but only 9 ships are available. Assume that 1½ times the sonar range is 3,100 yards. Then by looking at table IV for a proper screen which will place the ships at a screening distance of 3,100 yards, it is found that a complete circular screen can be formed on Circle 4.5 with 9 ships. This is too close. It is desired to place the ships on Circle 6 or 7. Looking down column No. 6 a screening distance of 3,000 yards is found, which requires 12 stations for a complete circular screen. Therefore it is decided to form an open circular screen, and the signal TBC 4 tack 1260 is hoisted, which requires all screening vessels to place a 12-station screen from table IV and table V on the mooring board.

DECLASSIFIED

EXAMPLE

AXIS ROTATION BY UNIFORM ANGULAR RATE METHOD

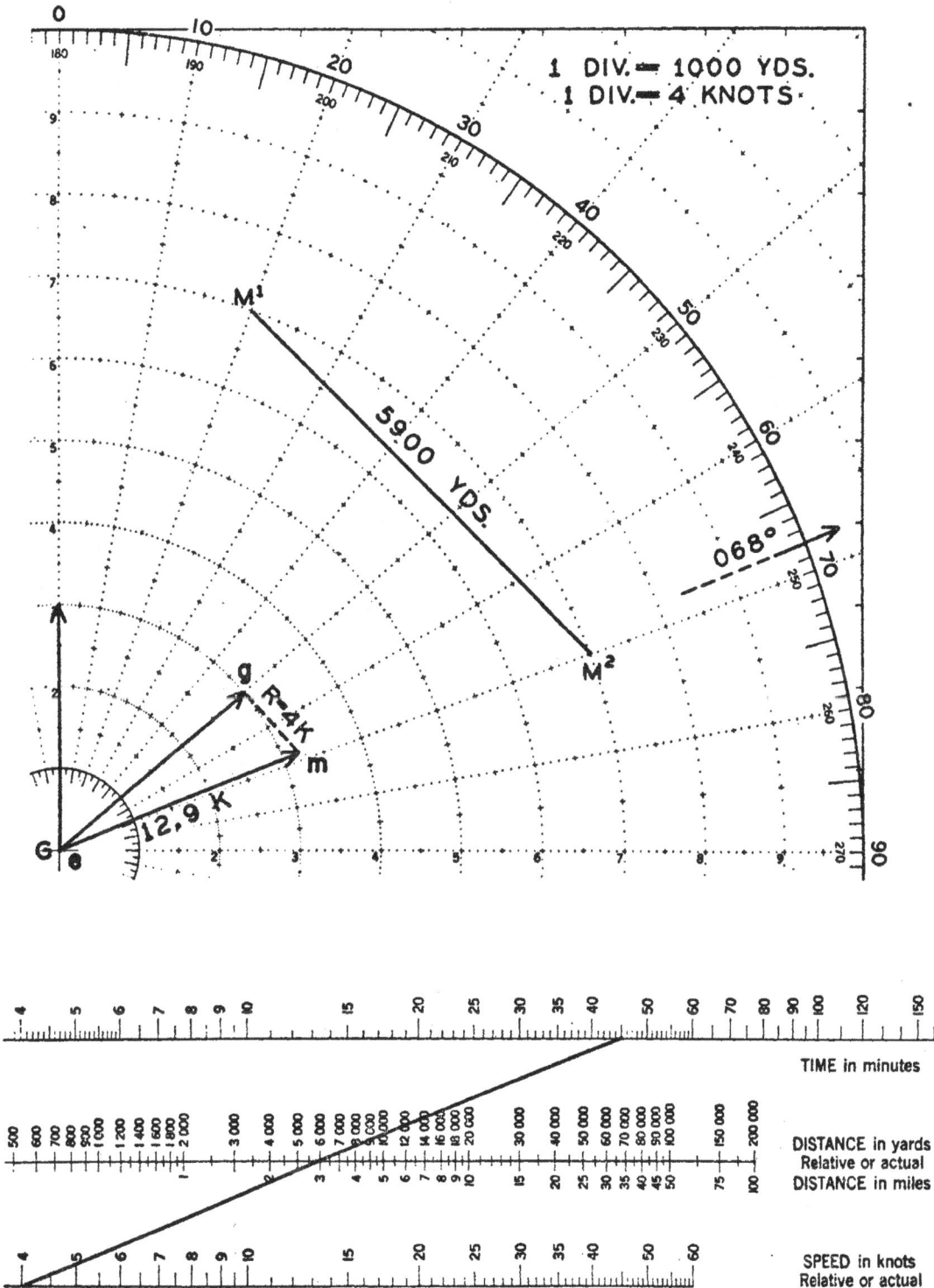

Figure 2.

DECLASSIFIED

3255. Axis Rotation by Uniform Angular Rate Method.

Change of front by uniform angular rate method—

> Signal "Change front of disposition on fleet center to right
> (left) to direction indicated (SIMULTANEOUS Method),
> commencing at _____, completing at _____."

This method is intended primarily for use at night or in greatly reduced
visibility. It is also advantageous if the effectiveness of the sonar screen is
to be maintained during the rotation. The time in which to accomplish the
maneuver must be selected so that no unit is required to slow below about 9
knots nor increase above flank speed (except when maximum power is available). If effective sonar screening is essential, the speed of sonar screen units
with spherical domes should not exceed 15 knots, with streamlined domes,
22 knots. Fleet speed should be not less than 12 knots, preferably greater.
In checking for speeds required, note that the unit for which the relative
motion is most nearly in the direction of the new course will require the
highest speed, that for which the relative motion is most nearly the reverse
of the new course the lowest speed. A sample problem and solution are
illustrated in the diagram.

Example

Maneuvering board solution appears on facing page.

Signal: Change front of disposition on fleet center to right to 050° (simultaneous method) commencing at 2215, completing at 2300.

Given: Present fleet course and axis 000°, speed 12 knots. New fleet course
and axis 050°. Speed of guide during maneuver 12 knots.
Ship station 7020.

Find: Course and speed of station unit to new position.

Solution: Ship at M1. New Station M2. Relative distance 5,900 yards.
Using logarithmic scales with "TIME TO COMPLETE" (45
Minutes), relative distance (5,900 yards), find relative speed (04
knots) for the maneuver. From *g* draw relative movement line
and lay off relative speed (*gm* 4) for the maneuver. Length of *em*
(12.9 knots) is required speed. Direction of *em* (068°) is required
course.

3260. Maneuvers with Circular Screens.

3261. For reorientation of closed circular screens see subparagraph 3245.

3262. Rotation of Closed and Open Circular Screens.—If the disposition or
screen commander at any time desires to rotate the screen as a whole, relative to the course, he may execute this maneuver by an appropriate general
signal ordering the screen to rotate in the direction and amount indicated in
the signal. Only upon execution of such a signal will the screen rotate in
this uniform manner. The officer ordering the maneuver should specify the

screening ships upon completion of this maneuver shall be exactly in screening stations as determined by the screen in use with stations determined relative to the course. The maneuver in effect rotates the screening ships into new stations, but the stations and station numbers remain fixed relative to the course. If the signal for rotation is accompanied by a time signal specifying the time of commencement and completion of the maneuver, the maneuver becomes rotation by uniform angular rate method, (See subparagraph 3254.) In the case of rotation of an open circular screen and upon completion of such rotation, it may be necessary to reorient to cover the advance of the disposition. This may be accomplished by the normal method of reorientation. (See subparagraph 3263.)

CONFIDENTIAL

Table VI.—POSITIONS IN CIRCULAR SCREEN BEFORE AND AFTER COURSE CHANGE

A—Total number of ships in the Screen.
B—Position in the Screen after course change.

Course change	A (total ships)	Pos. before 1 — B	Pos. before 2 — B	Pos. before 3 — B	Pos. before 4 — B
40 to 60 degrees to right	8	2	6	1	6
	9	2	6	1	6
	10	2	6	1	6
	11	2	6	1	6
	12	4	6	2	8
	13	4	6	2	8
	14	4	6	2	8
	15	4	6	2	8
	16	4	6	2	8
	17	4	6	2	8
61 to 80 degrees to right	8	4	8	2	8
	9	4	8	2	8
	10	4	8	2	8
	11	4	8	2	8
	12	6	8	4	10
	13	6	8	4	10
	14	6	8	4	10
	15	6	8	4	10
	16	6	8	4	10
	17	6	8	4	10
81 to 100 degrees to right	8	4	8	2	8
	9	4	8	2	8
	10	4	8	2	8
	11	6	8	4	10
	12	8	10	6	12
	13	8	10	6	12
	14	8	10	6	12
	15	8	10	6	12
	16	8	10	6	12
	17	8	10	6	12
101 to 120 degrees to right	8	6	10	4	7
	9	6	10	4	9
	10	6	10	4	10
	11	6	10	4	10
	12	10	12	8	11
	13	10	12	8	13
	14	10	12	8	14
	15	10	12	8	14
	16	10	12	8	14
	17	10	12	8	14
121 to 140 degrees to right	8	8	12	6	5
	9	8	12	6	7
	10	8	12	6	9
	11	8	12	6	11
	12	10	12	8	11
	13	12	13	10	13
	14	10	12	8	14
	15	14	15	12	14
	16	12	12	8	16
	17	12	12	8	16
141 to 160 degrees to right	8	6	7	4	7
	9	8	9	6	7
	10	8	9	6	9
	11	10	11	8	9
	12	10	12	8	11
	13	12	13	10	11
	14	10	12	8	14
	15	14	15	12	13
	16	14	16	12	15
	17	14	16	12	17
161 to 180 degrees to right	8	8	7	6	5
	9	9	7	8	5
	10	10	9	8	7
	11	10	9	8	9
	12	12	9	10	9
	13	13	9	12	9
	14	14	11	12	11
	15	15	11	14	11
	16	16	11	14	13
	17	16	11	14	15

Table VI.—POSITIONS IN CIRCULAR SCREEN BEFORE AND AFTER COURSE CHANGE—Continued

A—Total No. of ships in the Screen.
B—Position in the Screen after course change.

Position in the Screen after course change.

Position before course change

Course change	A B	5					6					7					8				
		A	B	A	B	A	B	A	B	A	B	A	B	A	B	A	B	A	B	A	B
40 to 60 degrees to right	8	1	15	1	16	1	10	5	15	10	16	3	8	3	15	3	16	3	11	12	15	14	16	14
	9	1	14	1	17	1	9	5	14	10	17	2	9	3	14	3	17	1	10	12	14	12	17	12
	10	3	14	1	--	--	10	5	14	12	--	--	10	5	14	4	--	--	9	11	14	11	--	--
	11	3	15	1	--	--	11	5	15	12	--	--	11	5	15	4	--	--	7	9	15	13	--	--
61 to 80 degrees to right	8	1	15	2	16	2	8	7	15	12	16	14	8	3	15	2	16	2	8	3	15	14	16	16
	9	1	14	2	17	2	9	7	14	13	17	17	9	3	14	2	17	4	9	5	14	14	17	16
	10	1	14	2	--	--	10	8	14	14	--	--	10	3	14	2	--	--	7	7	14	13	--	--
	11	3	15	2	--	--	11	8	15	15	--	--	11	5	15	2	--	--	10	9	15	15	--	--
81 to 100 degrees to right	8	2	15	4	16	4	8	10	15	15	16	16	8	5	15	2	16	2	8	9	15	15	16	16
	9	1	14	2	17	2	9	10	14	14	17	16	9	4	14	4	17	4	9	7	14	14	17	17
	10	1	14	4	--	--	10	9	14	13	--	--	10	4	14	4	--	--	10	5	14	13	--	--
	11	2	15	4	--	--	11	10	15	15	--	--	11	4	15	2	--	--	11	7	15	15	--	--
101 to 120 degrees to right	8	1	15	6	16	6	8	8	15	15	16	16	8	4	15	4	16	6	8	3	15	15	16	15
	9	1	14	4	17	6	9	7	14	13	17	16	9	4	14	4	17	2	9	5	14	14	17	17
	10	3	14	4	--	--	10	9	14	14	--	--	10	4	14	4	--	--	10	7	14	11	--	--
	11	4	15	6	--	--	11	11	15	15	--	--	11	2	15	4	--	--	11	9	15	13	--	--
121 to 140 degrees to right	8	2	15	6	16	6	8	5	15	13	16	13	8	2	15	4	16	2	8	3	15	13	16	16
	9	4	14	6	17	8	9	7	14	13	17	17	9	2	14	4	17	4	9	3	14	13	17	17
	10	4	14	6	--	--	10	5	14	13	--	--	10	2	14	4	--	--	10	5	14	11	--	--
	11	4	15	6	--	--	11	9	15	15	--	--	11	2	15	2	--	--	11	7	15	13	--	--
141 to 160 degrees to right	8	4	15	8	16	8	8	5	15	13	16	13	8	2	15	6	16	8	8	3	15	13	16	16
	9	4	14	6	17	10	9	5	14	13	17	15	9	2	14	6	17	8	9	1	14	13	17	15
	10	4	14	6	16	12	10	7	14	14	16	17	10	2	14	8	16	10	10	3	14	14	16	16
	11	6	15	10	17	17	11	7	15	15	17	13	11	4	15	8	17	10	11	5	15	15	17	17
161 to 180 degrees to right	8	6	12	12	--	--	8	3	12	7	16	11	8	2	12	6	16	10	8	5	12	7	16	9
	9	6	13	10	17	12	9	3	13	7	17	13	9	4	13	6	17	17	9	1	13	9	17	11
	10	6	14	10	16	17	10	3	14	9	16	16	10	4	14	8	16	16	10	3	14	7	16	12
	11	6	15	12	--	--	11	3	15	11	--	--	11	4	15	10	--	--	11	7	15	7	--	--

Table VI.—POSITIONS IN CIRCULAR SCREEN BEFORE AND AFTER COURSE CHANGE—Continued

A—Total No. of ships in the Screen.
B—Position in the Screen after course change.

Position before course change

Each position column (9 through 17) is divided into sub-columns **A** (total ships) and **B** (new position). Cell entries below are given as A:B pairs.

40 to 60 degrees to right

9	10	11	12	13	14	15	16	17
9:7, 10:7, 11:7, 12:5, 13:5, 14:5, 15:5, 16:3, 17:5	10:9, 11:11, 12:11, 13:13, 14:14, 15:14, 16:14, 17:14	11:9, 12:7, 13:7, 14:7, 15:7, 16:7, 17:7	12:9, 13:11, 14:13, 15:15, 16:16, 17:16	13:9, 14:9, 15:9, 16:9, 17:9	14:11, 15:13, 16:15, 17:17	15:11, 16:11, 17:11	16:13, 17:15	17:13

61 to 80 degrees to right

9	10	11	12	13	14	15	16	17
9:5, 10:5, 11:5, 12:3, 13:3, 14:3, 15:3, 16:3, 17:3	10:7, 11:9, 12:9, 13:11, 14:13, 15:15, 16:16, 17:16	11:7, 12:5, 13:5, 14:5, 15:5, 16:5, 17:17	12:7, 13:9, 14:11, 15:13, 16:15, 17:5	13:7, 14:7, 15:7, 16:7, 17:7	14:9, 15:11, 16:13, 17:15	15:9, 16:9, 17:9	16:11, 17:13	17:7

81 to 100 degrees to right

9	10	11	12	13	14	15	16	17
9:5, 10:5, 11:3, 12:1, 13:1, 14:1, 15:1, 16:1, 17:1	10:7, 11:7, 12:7, 13:9, 14:11, 15:13, 16:15, 17:9	11:5, 12:3, 13:3, 14:3, 15:3, 16:3, 17:3	12:5, 13:7, 14:9, 15:11, 16:13, 17:3	13:5, 14:5, 15:5, 16:5, 17:5	14:7, 15:9, 16:11, 17:13	15:7, 16:7, 17:7	16:9, 17:11	17:5

101 to 120 degrees to right

9	10	11	12	13	14	15	16	17
9:3, 10:3, 11:3, 12:2, 13:2, 14:2, 15:2, 16:2, 17:2	10:5, 11:7, 12:5, 13:7, 14:9, 15:11, 16:13, 17:15	11:5, 12:1, 13:1, 14:1, 15:1, 16:1, 17:1	12:3, 13:5, 14:7, 15:9, 16:11, 17:2	13:3, 14:3, 15:3, 16:3, 17:3	14:5, 15:7, 16:9, 17:11	15:5, 16:5, 17:5	16:7, 17:9	17:3

121 to 140 degrees to right

9	10	11	12	13	14	15	16	17
9:1, 10:1, 11:1, 12:2, 13:2, 14:2, 15:2, 16:4	10:3, 11:5, 12:5, 13:7, 14:9, 15:11, 16:11, 17:13	11:3, 12:1, 13:1, 14:1, 15:1, 16:2, 17:2	12:3, 13:5, 14:7, 15:9, 16:9, 17:11	13:3, 14:3, 15:3, 16:1, 17:1	14:5, 15:7, 16:7, 17:9	15:5, 16:3, 17:3	16:5, 17:7	17:2

141 to 160 degrees to right

9	10	11	12	13	14	15	16	17
9:1, 10:1, 11:2, 12:2, 13:4, 14:4, 15:4, 16:6	10:3, 11:3, 12:5, 13:5, 14:9, 15:7, 16:9, 17:11	11:1, 12:1, 13:2, 14:1, 15:4, 16:4, 17:4	12:3, 13:3, 14:7, 15:5, 16:7, 17:9	13:3, 14:3, 15:3, 16:1, 17:2	14:5, 15:3, 16:5, 17:7	15:5, 16:3, 17:3	16:3, 17:5	17:8

161 to 180 degrees to right

9	10	11	12	13	14	15	16	17
9:2, 10:2, 11:2, 12:4, 13:6, 14:6, 15:8, 16:8	10:1, 11:3, 12:3, 13:3, 14:11, 15:9, 16:7, 17:9	11:1, 12:2, 13:4, 14:4, 15:1, 16:1, 17:1	12:1, 13:1, 14:3, 15:3, 16:5, 17:3	13:2, 14:2, 15:4, 16:4, 17:4	14:1, 15:1, 16:3, 17:5	15:2, 16:2, 17:2	16:1, 17:3	17:1

ORIGINAL

79

Table VI.—POSITIONS IN CIRCULAR SCREEN BEFORE AND AFTER COURSE CHANGE—Continued

A—Total No. of ships in the Screen.
B—Position in the Screen after course change.

Position before course change

Course change		1							2							3							4					
		A	B	A	B	A	B		A	B	A	B	A	B		A	B	A	B	A	B		A	B	A	B	A	B
40 to 60 degrees to left		8	3	12	5	16	7		8	1	12	3	16	5		8	1	12	5	16	7		8	1	12	3	16	5
		9	3	13	5	17	7		9	3	13	5	17	7		9	3	13	5	17	9		9	1	13	3	17	5
		10	5	14	7				10	3	14	5				10	3	14	7				10	3	14	5		
		11	5	15	7				11	3	15	5				11	5	15	7				11	3	15	7		
61 to 80 degrees to left		8	3	12	5	16	7		8	1	12	3	16	5		8	3	12	5	16	7		8	1	12	3	16	5
		9	3	13	5	17	7		9	3	13	5	17	7		9	3	13	5	17	9		9	1	13	3	17	5
		10	5	14	7				10	3	14	5				10	3	14	7				10	3	14	5		
		11	5	15	7				11	3	15	5				11	5	15	7				11	3	15	7		
81 to 100 degrees to left		8	5	12	7	16	9		8	3	12	5	16	7		8	5	12	7	16	9		8	1	12	3	16	5
		9	5	13	7	17	9		9	3	13	5	17	7		9	5	13	7	17	9		9	3	13	5	17	7
		10	5	14	7				10	3	14	5				10	5	14	7				10	3	14	5		
		11	7	15	7				11	5	15	5				11	7	15	7				11	3	15	7		
101 to 120 degrees to left		8	5	12	7	16	9		8	3	12	5	16	7		8	5	12	7	16	9		8	3	12	5	16	7
		9	5	13	9	17	11		9	5	13	7	17	9		9	7	13	9	17	11		9	3	13	5	17	7
		10	5	14	9				10	5	14	7				10	5	14	9				10	3	14	5		
		11	7	15	11				11	7	15	9				11	7	15	11				11	3	15	7		
121 to 140 degrees to left		8	5	12	9	16	11		8	5	12	7	16	9		8	7	12	9	16	11		8	3	12	7	16	9
		9	7	13	11	17	13		9	5	13	9	17	13		9	7	13	11	17	13		9	5	13	7	17	11
		10	7	14	11				10	7	14	9				10	7	14	11				10	5	14	9		
		11	9	15	13				11	9	15	11				11	9	15	13				11	7	15	9		
141 to 160 degrees to left		8	7	12	11	16	15		8	7	12	9	16	13		8	9	12	11	16	16		8	5	12	9	16	13
		9	7	13	13	17	17		9	7	13	11	17	17		9	9	13	13	17	17		9	5	13	9	17	13
		10	9	14	13				10	9	14	11				10	9	14	13				10	7	14	11		
		11	11	15	15				11	11	15	13				11	10	15	15				11	7	15	11		
161 to 180 degrees to left		8	8	12	12	16	16		8	8	12	11	16	16		8	10	12	12	16	16		8	8	12	12	16	16
		9	8	13	14	17	17		9	9	13	13	17	17		9	10	13	14	17	17		9	9	13	13	17	17
		10	10	14	14				10	9	14	13				10	10	14	14				10	9	14	13		
		11	11	15	15				11	10	15	13				11	11	15	15				11	11	15	11		

USF 10B

Table VI.—POSITIONS IN CIRCULAR SCREEN BEFORE AND AFTER COURSE CHANGE—Continued

A—Total No. of ships in the screen.
B—Position in the screen after course change.

Course change	A	Position before course change			
		5 (B)	6 (B)	7 (B)	8 (B)
40 to 60 degrees to left	8	7	4	8	6
	9	7	4	9	6
	10	9	2	10	4
	11	9	2	11	4
	12	9	2	11	4
	13	9	2	11	4
	14	9	2	11	4
	15	9	2	11	4
	16	11	1	13	2
	17	11	1	13	2
61 to 80 degrees to left	8	7	4	8	6
	9	7	4	8	6
	10	9	2	10	4
	11	9	2	11	4
	12	11	1	12	2
	13	11	1	13	2
	14	11	1	13	2
	15	11	1	13	2
	16	11	1	13	2
	17	11	1	13	2
81 to 100 degrees to left	8	8	2	6	4
	9	9	2	8	4
	10	9	2	8	4
	11	11	1	10	2
	12	11	1	12	2
	13	11	1	13	2
	14	11	1	13	2
	15	13	1	13	2
	16	13	3	15	1
	17	13	3	15	1
101 to 120 degrees to left	8	8	2	6	4
	9	9	2	8	4
	10	10	1	8	2
	11	11	1	10	2
	12	11	1	12	2
	13	13	3	12	1
	14	13	3	14	1
	15	15	5	14	3
	16	15	3	16	3
	17	15	3	17	3
121 to 140 degrees to left	8	6	1	4	2
	9	8	1	6	2
	10	10	1	8	2
	11	10	3	8	1
	12	12	3	10	1
	13	12	5	10	3
	14	14	5	12	3
	15	14	7	12	5
	16	12	7	14	5
	17	14	9	--	7
141 to 160 degrees to left	8	6	1	4	2
	9	8	1	6	2
	10	8	3	6	1
	11	8	5	6	3
	12	10	5	8	3
	13	12	5	10	3
	14	12	7	10	5
	15	14	7	12	5
	16	10	9	12	7
	17	12	9	14	7
161 to 180 degrees to left	8	4	5	2	1
	9	6	5	4	1
	10	6	7	4	3
	11	8	7	6	3
	12	8	7	6	5
	13	10	7	8	5
	14	10	9	8	7
	15	12	9	10	7
	16	12	11	10	9
	17	14	11	12	9

Table VI.—POSITIONS IN CIRCULAR SCREEN BEFORE AND AFTER COURSE CHANGE—Continued

A—Total No. of ships in the Screen.
B—Position in the Screen after course change.

Course change			Position before course change																	
			9		**10**		**11**		**12**		**13**		**14**		**15**		**16**		**17**	
	A	B	A	B	A	B	A	B	A	B	A	B	A	B	A	B	A	B	A	B
40 to 60 degrees to left	9	8	13	12	—	—	10	6	16	6	10	8	14	8	12	10	16	10	17	12
	10	8	13	13	—	—	11	6	16	8	11	8	15	8	13	10	16	10	17	12
	11	10	15	13	17	—	13	6	17	10	13	8	16	10	14	12	16	14	17	14
	12	12	16	15	17	15	13	8	17	14	13	10	17	10	15	14	17	14	—	—
61 to 80 degrees to left	9	8	12	12	14	4	11	6	13	6	13	8	14	8	15	10	16	8	17	10
	10	10	14	14	14	4	12	6	14	8	14	8	15	8	15	12	16	10	17	12
	11	13	15	15	15	6	13	8	15	10	14	10	16	10	16	12	17	12	—	—
	12	15	16	16	15	6	14	10	15	12	15	12	16	12	17	14	—	—	—	—
81 to 100 degrees to left	9	10	12	15	14	4	11	8	13	4	13	6	14	6	15	6	16	8	17	10
	10	13	14	14	15	4	12	8	14	6	14	6	15	8	16	8	17	10	—	—
	11	13	15	15	16	4	13	10	14	6	15	8	16	8	17	12	—	—	—	—
	12	10	16	16	17	4	14	12	15	6	16	8	17	10	—	—	—	—	—	—
101 to 120 degrees to left	9	6	13	16	16	1	11	4	12	2	13	4	14	4	15	6	16	6	17	12
	10	8	14	15	16	1	12	4	13	4	14	6	15	8	16	6	17	8	—	—
	11	8	15	12	16	1	13	4	14	6	15	8	16	8	17	10	—	—	—	—
	12	10	16	14	17	1	14	4	15	2	16	10	17	10	—	—	—	—	—	—
121 to 140 degrees to left	9	4	13	10	14	3	11	2	12	2	13	4	14	2	15	4	16	4	17	4
	10	6	14	10	15	3	12	2	13	2	14	6	15	6	16	6	17	6	—	—
	11	8	15	10	16	3	13	6	14	4	15	8	16	6	17	6	—	—	—	—
	12	10	16	12	17	5	14	8	15	6	16	10	17	10	—	—	—	—	—	—
141 to 160 degrees to left	9	2	13	8	14	3	11	2	12	2	13	4	14	2	15	4	16	2	17	6
	10	4	14	8	15	3	12	1	13	4	14	6	15	4	16	4	17	6	—	—
	11	6	15	10	16	5	13	1	14	6	15	8	16	6	17	6	—	—	—	—
	12	6	16	10	17	5	14	1	15	6	16	10	17	10	—	—	—	—	—	—
161 to 180 degrees to left	9	2	13	6	14	5	11	1	12	2	13	4	14	1	15	2	16	1	17	2
	10	4	14	8	15	7	11	1	13	4	15	1	16	3	17	2	—	—	—	—
	11	4	15	8	16	7	12	3	14	4	15	1	16	2	—	—	—	—	—	—
	12	8	16	10	17	7	13	3	14	4	16	3	17	4	—	—	—	—	—	—

3262. Reorientation of Open Circular Screens.

(a) Reorientation of open circular screens, using table VI.

(1) On the maneuvering board plot the complete circular screen with all stations numbered relative to the present disposition course.

(2) Indicate the stations occupied on the present course, and the ships occupying those stations.

(3) If a new course is ordered, draw in the final course line. Number stations relative to this course.

(4) Enter table VI. In the left-hand vertical column is the amount of angular change that the new course is to the right or left of the old course. (Note.—Changes to the left are on separate pages from changes to the right.) At the top in the horizontal column is the ship's present station with reference to the old disposition course. Knowing the amount of change of course, and your present station, enter the table, and opposite the total number of ships in the screen, which is in column A, is your new station, which is in column B.

Example

Number of ships in screen: 14.
Your present station number: 9.
Signaled course change is 70° to right of present course.
Your new station is 3.

If table VI is not used the reorientation of open circular screens with each ship traversing a minimum of distance can best be accomplished by either one of the two following methods:

(1) The "Close the Gap" method, described below, for screens employing nine or more screening vessels. If there are less than nine screening vessels, it is recommended that the "End Around" or a bent line screen be used.

(2) The "End Around" method, described in subparagraph (c) below, employing eight or more screening vessels.

(b) Reorientation of Open Circular Screens by "Close the Gap" method.

(1) Set up maneuvering board as in subparagraphs (a) (1), (2), and (3) of subparagraph 3263 above.

(2) Indicate the stations that are to be filled after reorientation. Insofar as practicable the screen should be symmetrically disposed in the 120° arcs on both sides of the new course.

(3) In order that there will be no doubt as to which ship takes station one, when a change in course is ordered, the following rules are prescribed:

a. Should the new course line pass through an occupied station, that station immediately becomes station one on the course or to the right of the course, if there is an even number of ships in the screen.

b. Should the new course line pass between two occupied stations, the van ship on the unexposed flank with reference to the new course takes station one on the course or to the right of the course, if there is an even number of ships in the screen.

c. Should the new course line pass through a vacant screening station, which is adjacent to an occupied station, then the van ship on the unexposed flank with reference to the new course shall move into that station or to the right of it, if there is an even number of ships in the screen.

d. Should the new course line pass between two vacant screening stations, then the nearest ship takes station one on the course, or to the right of it if there is an even number of ships in the screen. However, if the course change is 180° (not recommended) the van ship on the right flank with reference to the new course will take station one on the course or to the right of the course, if there is an even number of ships in the screen.

"CLOSE THE GAP" METHOD

CASE I: COURSE CHANGE 30° OR LESS
12 SCREENING STATIONS – 9 SCREENING SHIPS
OLD COURSE 000° (T) – NEW COURSE 030° (T)

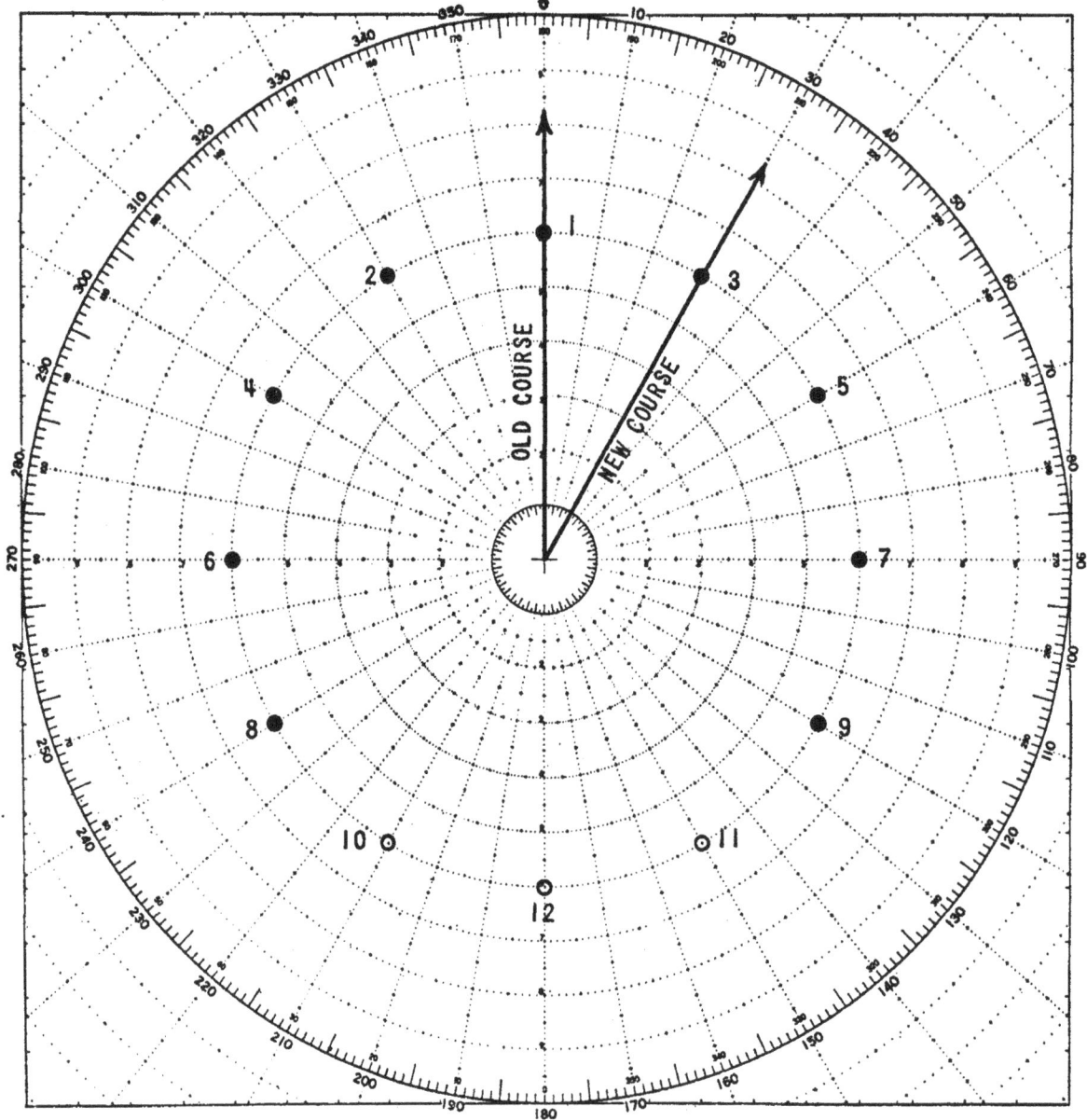

● = OCCUPIED STATIONS AT COMMENCEMENT OF EXERCISE
○ = UNOCCUPIED STATIONS AT COMMENCEMENT OF EXERCISE
→ = DIRECTION OF MOVEMENT

Figure 3.

REORIENTATION BY "CLOSE THE GAP METHOD"

IN OPEN CIRCULAR SCREENS
CASE II: COURSE CHANGE 90°
12 SCREENING STATIONS – 9 SCREENING SHIPS
OLD COURSE 0.00° (T) – NEW COURSE 090° (T)

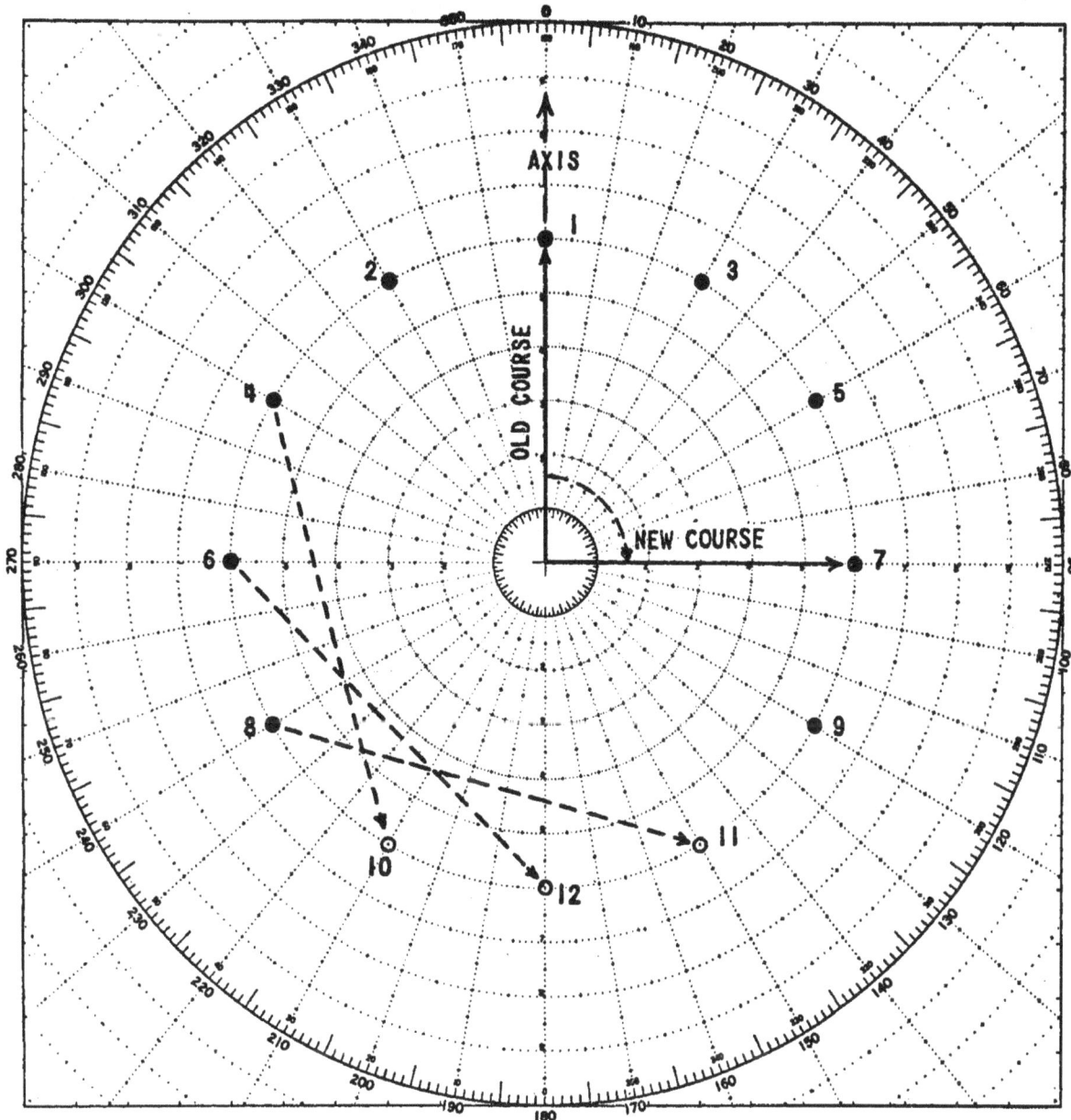

● = OCCUPIED STATIONS AT COMMENCEMENT OF MANEUVER
○ = UNOCCUPIED STATIONS AT COMMENCEMENT OF MANEUVER
--● = DIRECTION OF MOVEMENT

Figure 4.

"CLOSE THE GAP" METHOD

CASE III: COURSE CHANGE 135°
12 SCREENING STATIONS - 9 SCREENING SHIPS
OLD COURSE 000° (T) - NEW COURSE 135° (T)

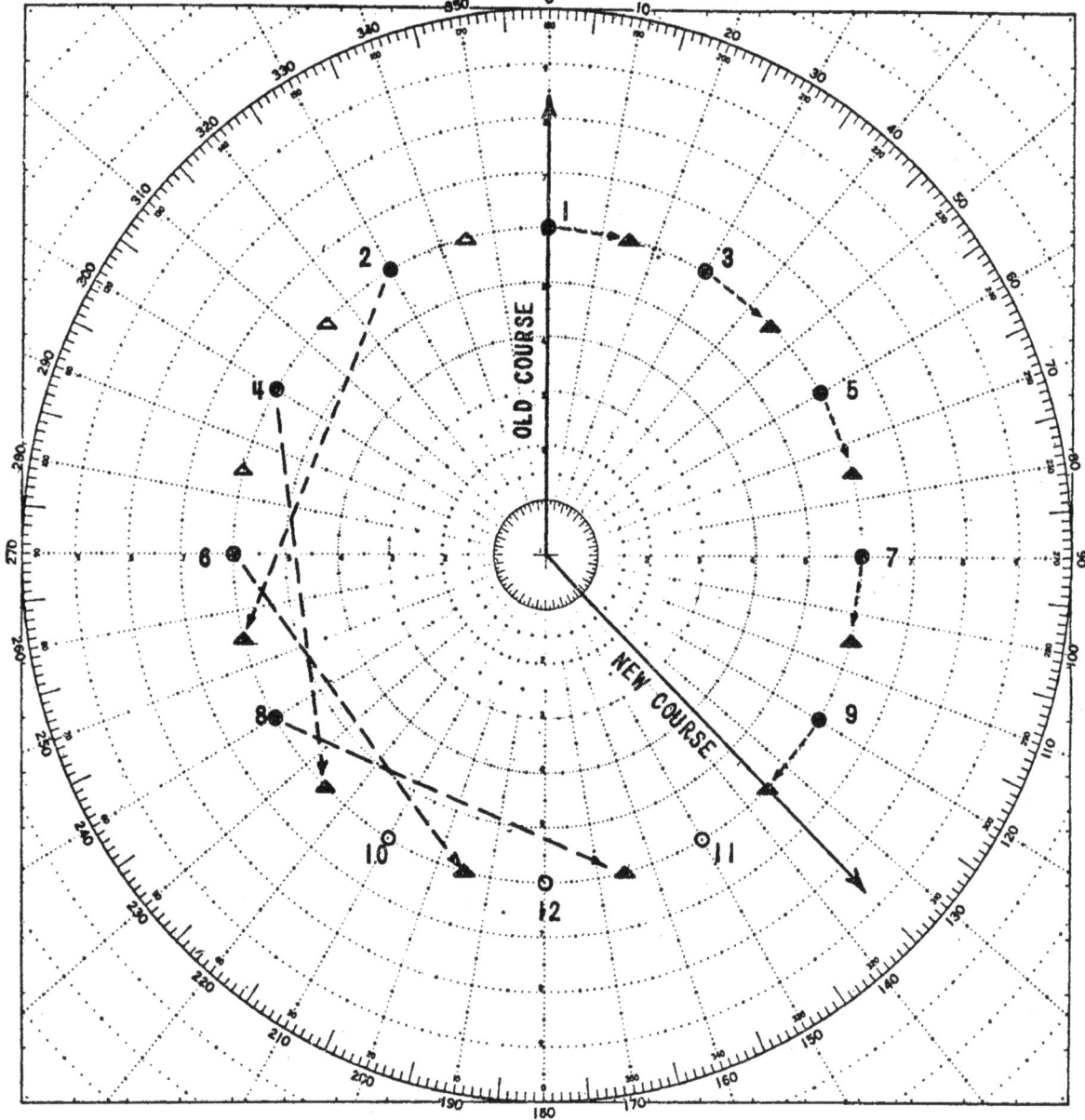

● = OCCUPIED STATIONS AT COMMENCEMENT OF EXERCISE

O = UNOCCUPIED STATIONS AT COMMENCEMENT OF EXERCISE

▲ = OCCUPIED STATIONS AT COMPLETION OF MANEUVER

△ = UNOCCUPIED STATIONS AT COMPLETION OF MANEUVER

→ = DIRECTION OF MOVEMENT

Figure 5.

(4) The ship to occupy station one having been established by subparagraph (3) above, the remaining ships to the right (left) of the new course line rotate in relative order to occupy vacant stations in the arcs extending 120° from the new course line.

(5) The ships not required to fill the 120° arcs each side of new course line may occupy those stations which most nearly equalize the spacing in the after 120° arc.

(6) On occasions it may be advisable for the screen commander to designate which screening ship is to occupy station one.

Case I—Course change of 30° or less with nine screening ships. (See diagram on page 3-38.)

(1) This course change does not expose the disposition flank, therefore all ships maintain present station. (The flank *is* exposed when the 000° to 090° or 270° to 360° quadrant with reference to the new course has any vacant stations.)

Case II—Course change of 90° with nine screening ships. (See diagram on page 3-39.)

(1) This course change exposes the flank of the disposition, but the new course does not pass through stations formerly unoccupied.

(2) In this situation enough ships in the rear of the formation with reference to the new course move in the opposite direction to the course change to cover the exposed flank; all other ships maintain present station.

Case III—Course change of 135° with nine screening ships. (See diagram on page 3-40.)

(1) This course change exposes the disposition flank, and the new course is into the former gap.

(2) In this situation enough ships on the side of the exposed flank with reference to the new course move in the opposite direction to the course change to cover the exposed flank; the ship on the least exposed flank with reference to the new course and in the van will take station one on the screen axis. Remaining ships on this flank rotate as necessary to fill vacant stations in the direction of the course change.

DECLASSIFIED

REORIENTATION BY "END AROUND" METHOD
IN OPEN CIRCULAR SCREENS

12 SCREENING STATIONS – 9 SCREENING SHIPS
OLD COURSE 000° (T) – NEW COURSE 090° (T)

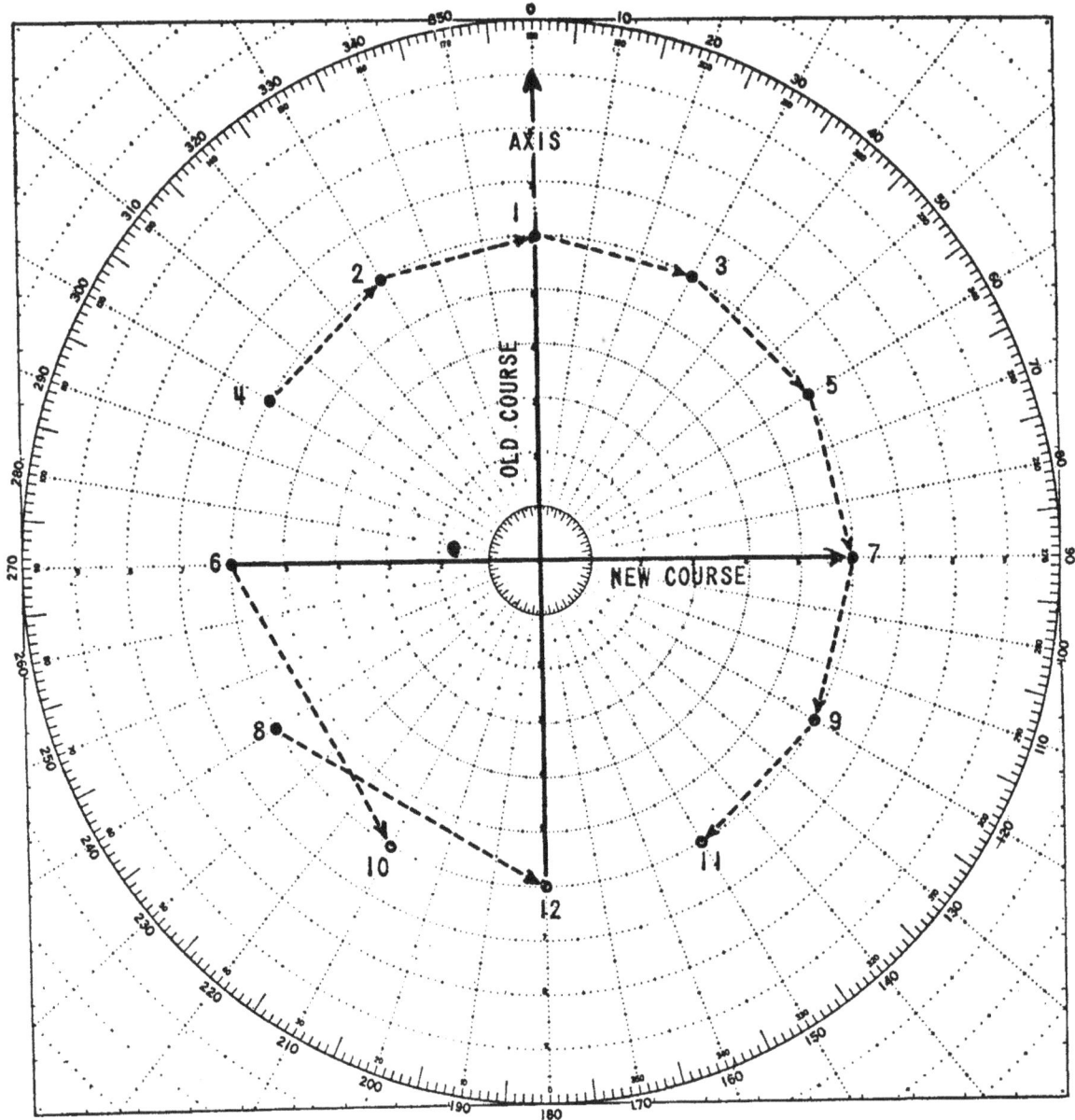

● = OCCUPIED STATIONS AT COMMENCEMENT OF MANEUVER
○ = UNOCCUPIED STATIONS AT COMMENCEMENT OF MANEUVER
----▶ = DIRECTION OF MOVEMENT

Figure 6.

(c) Reorientation of Open Circular Screen by the "End Around" Method.

    (1) Set up mooring board as in subparagraph 3263 (a) (1), (2), and (3) above, but draw in reverse of old and new course lines.

    (2) Indicate the stations that are to be filled. Insofar as practicable the screen should be equally disposed in the sectors 120° on each side of the new course.

    (3) a. Any ship on the reverse of the new course line, and all ships included between the reverse of the new course line and the reverse of the old course line, rotate in a direction opposite to the direction of the course change. All other ships rotate in the same direction as the course change. All ships will rotate in the direction indicated above until they are symmetrically disposed about the new course line, with all adjacent stations occupied.

    b. If the course change is such that there is no ship on the reverse of the new course line, nor between the reverse of the new course line and the reverse of the old course line, the course change is accomplished by a simple rotation of all ships in the direction of the course change.

    c. The van ship on the unexposed flank will always take station one on the course or to the right of the course, if there is an even number of ships in the screen.

Figure 6—Course change of 90°—12 stations with 9 screening ships. (See page 3–42.)

Figure 7—Course change of 150°—12 stations with 8 screening ships. (See page 3–44.)

3264. Special Notes on Screens.

(a) If one or more CL (AA) are present in the screen, it may be desirable that they maneuver with the screen, and that they be on the screen axis or reverse thereof.

(b) On a change of disposition course, the screening ships may be kept in the same relative position with respect to the new course by directing a rotation of the screen when a closed circular screen is used.

(c) The screen commander may hoist at the yardarm at the dip the appropriate numeral flag to indicate the station his flagship is to occupy. Other screening ships may similarly use numeral flags to clarify the situation in case of doubt.

"END AROUND" METHOD
12 SCREENING STATIONS – 8 SCREENING SHIPS
OLD COURSE 000° (T) – NEW COURSE 150° (T)

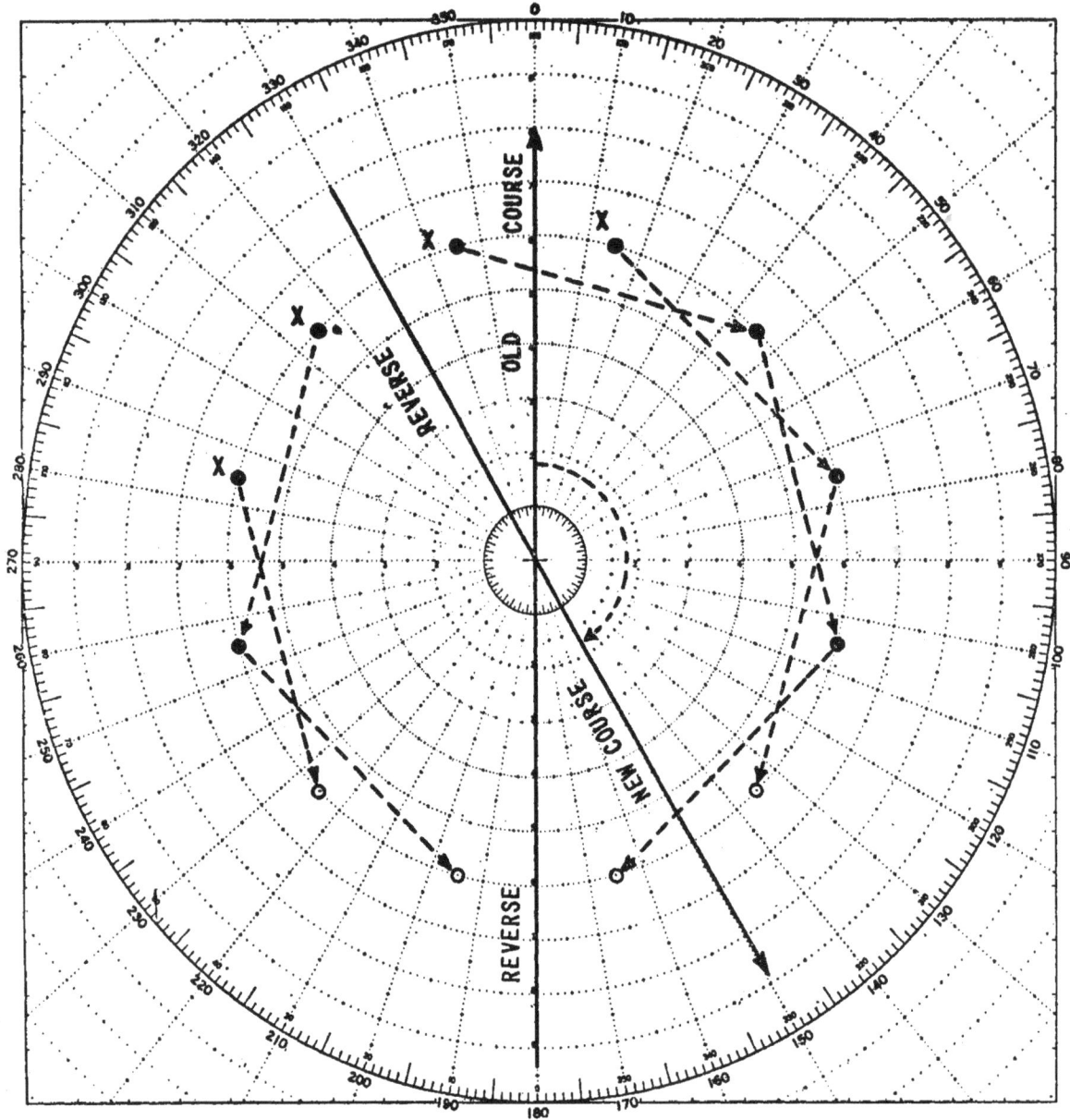

X = UNOCCUPIED STATIONS AT COMPLETION OF MANEUVER

● = OCCUPIED STATIONS AT COMMENCEMENT OF MANEUVER

O = UNOCCUPIED STATIONS AT COMMENCEMENT OF MANEUVER

--► = DIRECTION OF MOVEMENT

Figure 7.

(d) During the late afternoon the screen commander should inform all ships present of the names of ships in the screen and what station they occupy. If this is not practicable, he should designate who is in station one.

3265. Special Instructions For The Screen.

(a) Unless specific instructions have been issued by the officer in tactical command, the screen commander shall prescribe the antisubmarine screen, including instructions as to patrolling and zigzagging. (See FTP 223, section 1200; articles 4210 and 4336.)

(b) Unless otherwise directed, screening ships will not patrol stations when formation speed is 15 knots or higher.

(c) When screening ships patrol stations they will normally do so within 500 yards and 5° of bearing of assigned station, using speed as necessary to maintain station. Two knots above formation speed is generally adequate.

(d) Unless specific instructions have been issued by the officer in tactical command, the screen commander shall conduct sonar search in conformance with standard procedure outlined in FTP 223. (See section 1200.)

(e) Unless otherwise directed screening ships will echo-range continuously during night and day, conforming to standard sonar search procedure outlined in section 1200, FTP 223.

(f) Unless otherwise directed when a carrier or a battleship leaves the disposition, the two screening ships nearest the point where it passes through the screen will screen it without further orders. In case of a major ship, not a carrier or battleship, only one screening ship will accompany it.

(g) In large screens where it is not always possible for screening ships to observe others leaving, the screen commander should keep the screen advised.

(h) Should it be necessary to equalize fuel consumption, the screen commander should occasionally reassign the positions of ships which use the most fuel.

3270. Pickets.

3271. The use of antisubmarine, antiaircraft and anti-motor-torpedo boat pickets should be thoroughly considered. These pickets are effectual in attaining early radar contact with bogies, in visual sightings of bogies and in their destruction, in early radar contact with surface ships including surfaced submarines, in the interception and destruction of surfaced submarines, in the interception, investigation, and destruction of surface ships, in the inter-

and destruction or ~~~~or torpedo boats, in the rescue of survivors from crashed planes, both ~~~~ and enemy, in the salvage of important enemy information items, before the wreckage sinks, and in timely warning of pending dangers including navigational. They may also be useful as orbiting points for the combat air patrol and an orientation point for the antisubmarine patrol, as well as rendezvous points for air attack groups. When employed as "rendezvous points" for aircraft orbiting or rendezvousing (especially at night) they must cease patrolling and maintain prescribed station. They should take vigorous offensive action against attacking enemy forces when the situation so indicates, and should be ready to take over fighter direction of combat air patrols as necessary. They should generally be stationed at such distances as to be always on the search radar screens, and should normally never be beyond the radius of the very high frequency voice communication system.

3280. Stations and Station Keeping.

3281. Stations of ships and units in cruising dispositions are assigned to promote security through mutual support. Station keeping should be sufficiently accurate to fulfill this purpose.

3282. Commanders may interchange stations of similar ships to equalize fuel consumptions, etc., provided this is accomplished without jeopardizing other units or interfering with other operations.

3283. To minimize wear on director rotating mechanisms, fire-control radars and gun director range finders normally should not be used for station keeping.

3284. At all times make best use of all types of detection radars consistent with condition of radar silence in effect.

3285. All ships should know the maneuvering characteristics of other ships in the disposition. (Particular attention is directed to *Saratoga*.)

3290. Minesweeping Screens. (See part V.)

3300. Special Maneuver Instructions.

3310. Special instructions covering certain maneuvers by task forces, task groups, and simple screened units are set forth in this section. Fleet or tactical commanders may supplement but may not modify these special instructions.

3311. Fleet or tactical commanders shall specify when the maneuver instructions of this section 3300 or specified paragraphs or subparagraphs thereof are effective within their commands.

MANEUVER WITH SCREEN

A = SIGNAL UNDERSTOOD

B = SIGNAL EXECUTED

C = MANEUVER COMPLETED

APPROPRIATE
CORPEN   } WILLIAM
SIGNAL

⌐ DISPOSITION GUIDE

▷ UNIT GUIDE

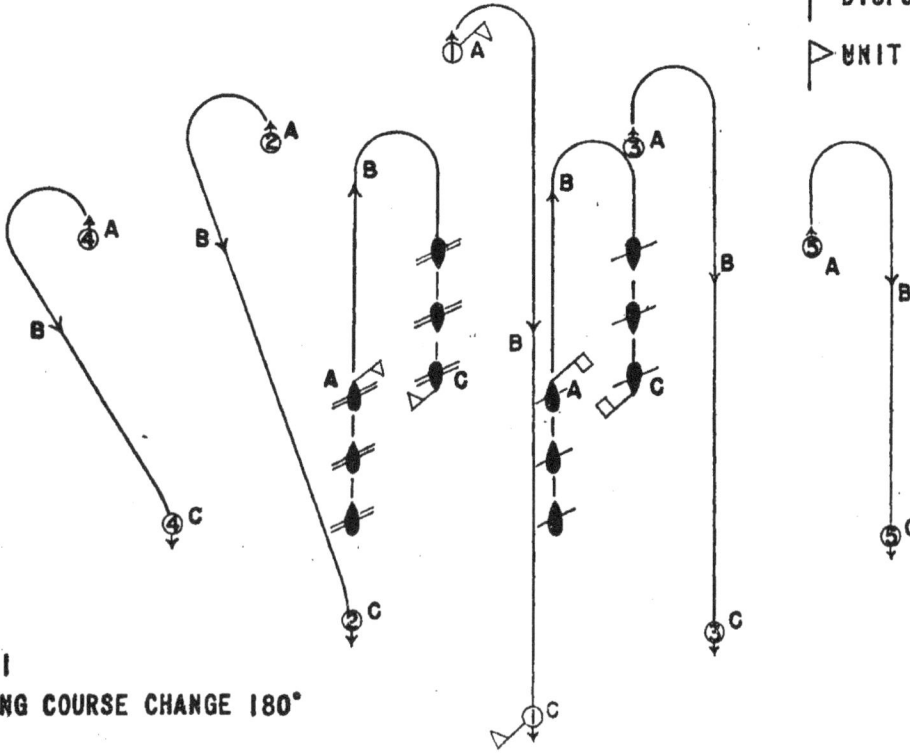

CASE I
SHOWING COURSE CHANGE 180°

Figure 8.

CASE I
SHOWING COURSE CHANGE 120°

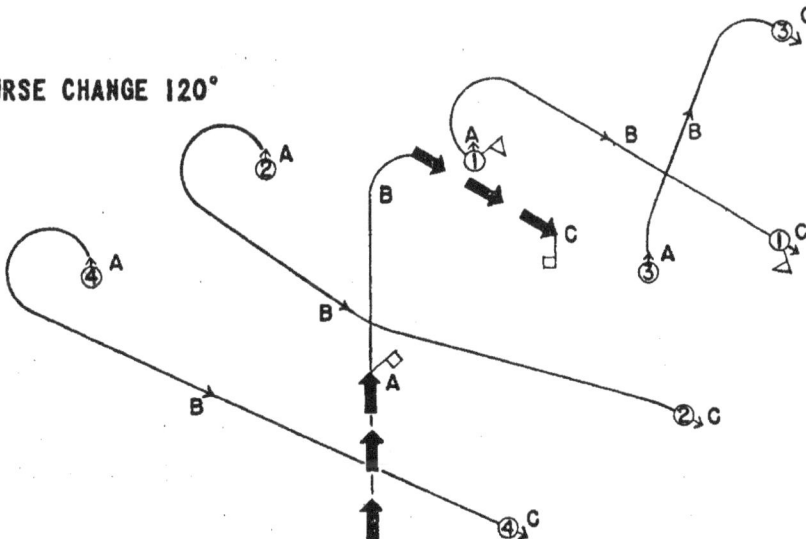

Figure 9.

... it is usually impracticable to handle large dispositions by the abbreviated procedures given below. However, when carriers and their attached screening units conduct flight operations within such a large disposition these special maneuver instructions may be placed in effect within the carrier unit by its commander.

3313. The instructions for cruising dispositions, section 3200; screens, paragraph 3240, and zigzag, section 3400, are not modified by any of the provisions of this section 3300.

3314. The General Tactical Instructions apply in all cases for which no special instructions are given herein, and for all maneuvers when section 3300 has not been made effective.

3320. Maneuvering With Closed or Open Circular Screen.

3321. Should it be desired to rotate the axis of a cruising disposition with a circular screen the uniform angular rate method (see diagram on page 3–24) should be prescribed for all ships, both in high and low visibility.

3322. Should it be desired to change the course or heading of a disposition with a closed circular screen, the screen should not be reoriented.

3323. Should it be desired to change the course or heading of a disposition with an open circular screen, the screen should be reoriented by "Close the Gap" method unless otherwise directed.

3324. When carrier dispositions are operating in light or variable winds the formation axis of the carrier(s) must be changed frequently in order to conduct flight operations most efficiently. Frequent rotation of the disposition axis requires high speed steaming by the support ships and the screen to reorient. In order to avoid this unnecessary steaming, the disposition axis may be left unchanged and the formation axis of the carrier(s) changed independently inside the support ships. In order to identify quickly the true bearing from the disposition center of a screening ship which reports contact, the disposition axis may be put on true North.

3330. Maneuvering with Bent-Line Screens.

3331. The special maneuvers described in this paragraph are intended to expedite changes of course by small dispositions without sacrificing good sonar protection. They are not generally suitable for dispositions in which the screened body contains large compound formations, particularly if the subdivisions of a compound formation are at reduced intervals.

DECLASSIFIED

MANEUVER WITH SCREEN

CASE II SHOWING COURSE CHANGE 60°

A = SIGNAL UNDERSTOOD
B = SIGNAL EXECUTED
C = MANEUVER COMPLETED

APPROPRIATE
CORPEN   } QUEEN
SIGNAL

⊢ DISPOSITION GUIDE

▷ UNIT GUIDE

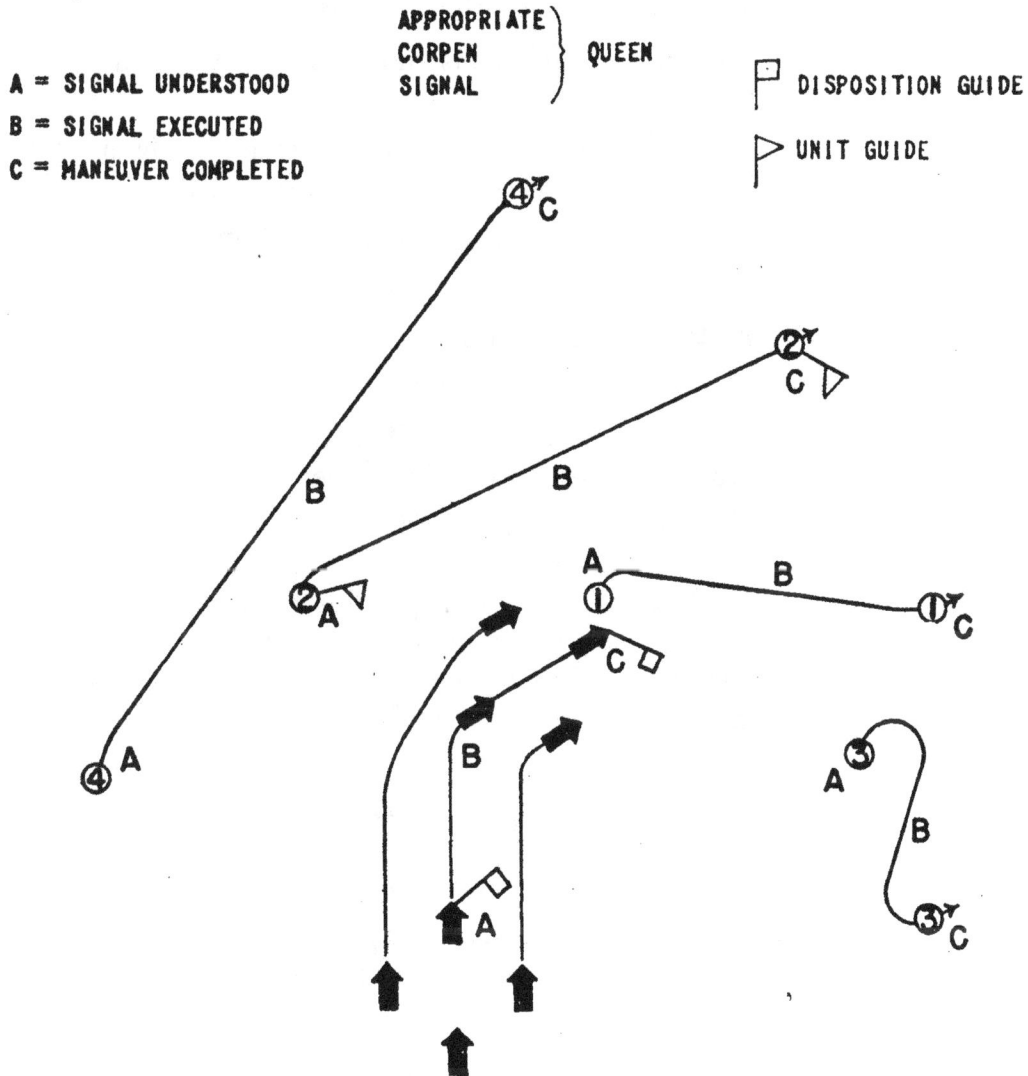

Figure 10.

DECLASSIFIED

3332. Case I. Change of course by 120° to 180°. (See figures on page 3-48.)

(a) This maneuver is primarily to be used for quick countermarch.

(b) Screening ships turn back individually through the disposition and proceed as directly as practicable to new stations, increasing speed as necessary and being careful to insure that best sonar coverage is maintained, especially on the flanks in the direction of turn. Ships on the axis turn in the signalled direction of the change; others turn outward. In the case of a carrier task group employing plane guard for flight operations adjustments must be made for the absence of the center (or lee center) screening vessel which takes up plane guard position. Start the turn:

(1) As soon as the signal is understood, if it is made by executive method.

(2) Ten minutes prior to time specified if signal is made in advance for execution at a future specified time.

(c) Screened station unit(s) commence evolutions:

(1) When the signal is executed, or

(2) At time specified if signalled in advance.

(d) Screened station unit procedures:

(1) If a screened station unit is in column, it will change by "follow the leader," unless otherwise signalled.

(2) If a screened station unit is in line of bearing of division (section) guides, each column will countermarch by "follow the leader." If but two columns are present and the interval is less than standard, each column shall change course outward. If more than two columns are present and the interval is less than standard, this maneuver should not be attempted.

(3) If the screened body consists of several single ship station units, they will change by simultaneous ship turns and then assume reversed symmetrical stations on the guide.

(4) If the screened body is disposed other than (1), (2), or (3) above, station unit commanders shall signal how the change is to be made.

3333. Case II. Change of course (and axis) of less than 120°. (See diagram on facing page.)

(a) This is the normal method of changing course (and axis). It is the preferred method for changes signalled in advance for execution at a future time.

DECLASSIFIED

(b) Screening ships maneuver to reorient the screens:

(1) As soon as the signal is understood if it is made by the executive method.

(2) Ten minutes prior to specified time if signal is made in advance for execution at a future specified time.

(3) In the case of a carrier task group employing plane guard for flight operations adjustment is made for the absence of the lee flank screening vessel which takes up plane guard position.

(c) Screened station unit(s) commence evolutions:

(1) When the signal is executed, or

(2) At the specified time if made in advance.

(d) Screened station unit procedures:

(1) If a screened station unit is in column, it will change by "follow the leader."

(2) If a screened station unit is in line of bearing of division (section) guides, each column will change by "follow the leader," the base unit (on the side toward which the turn is to be made) coming directly to the new course, other columns being conducted to their stations on the new course by the column leaders.

(3) If the screened body consists of several single ship station units, the guide will come directly to the new course, others maneuver to regain stations on the new course.

(4) If the screened body is disposed other than in (1), (2) or (3) above, station unit commanders shall signal how the change is to be made.

3334. When the foregoing maneuvers are signalled by the executive method in good visibility, the signal should be executed at the proper time for the disposition guide to complete the maneuver in correct position with respect to the screen guide.

3335. Case III. Change of course by simultaneous ship turns accompanied by reorientation of the screen.

Signal: Appropriate Turn Signal } TACKLINE—ROTATE SCREEN

(a) Procedure for screening ships is the same as for Case I when the turn is 120° to 180°; Case II when the turn is less than 120°.

(b) Screened units change to the new course by simultaneous turns when the signal is executed or at specified time if made in advance.

(c) Destroyers may need to swing wide to avoid screened station units.

3336. The foregoing maneuvers with screens are similar to but not to be confused with those designated by PREP-CORPEN signals for mixed British-U. S. forces. See appendix to General Signal Book (CSP 1846).

3340. Maneuvers in Emergencies.

3341. Turns performed in obedience to EMERGENCY-TURN signals shall be made with standard rudder at the last signalled speed. This does not apply to individual avoiding measures, covered separately in paragraph 4511. (See also subparagraph 3452.)

3342. Change of course (CORPEN) signals made under the EMERGENCY PENNANT shall be carried out in accordance with the General Tactical Instructions, except:

(a) The special maneuvers with screen prescribed in paragraph 3332 and paragraph 3333 shall be carried out by the screened station units changing immediately to the new course, and by screening vessels readjusting their positions relative to the screened station unit by the method indicated in the signal, at increased speed. CAUTION.—Case I should be used as an emergency maneuver only when no other means will effect reversal in the time available.

3343. When the disposition is being maneuvered by emergency turns through an indicated number of degrees the commander should, at intervals, when practicable, indicate the true course by signal.

3344. Unless the special maneuver instructions of section 3300 are in effect, changes of course of more than 90° should be made in two or more increments except in an emergency.

3350. Communications for Emergency Maneuvers.

3351. The preferred means for ordering an emergency maneuver by the officer in tactical command, or of announcing such maneuver initiated by a subordinate commander or commanding officer, is very high frequency voice radio, accompanied by flag hoist and/or proper whistle signal as appropriate to existing visibility. Plain language is permissible.

3352. Ships must be prepared to use immediately the keyed medium frequency bridge radio. Officers in tactical command should avail themselves of this circuit when circumstances warrant (i. e., position well known to

CONFIDENTIAL (cont.), using enciphered or unenciphered general signals as available time dictates.

3353. (a) WIMS vol. I shall not ordinarily be used to control night emergency maneuvers when only U. S. naval vessels are in company. Only officers in tactical command are authorized to use WIMS vol. I, and then only in exceptional circumstances, such as casualty to very high frequency voice radio. However, in order that WIMS vol. I may be effective when employed, all ships must be familiar with them, and drills in their application should be conducted at such times as circumstances warrant. Caution must be exercised to avoid confusing WIMS vol. I maneuver signals and night vertical fighting lights.

(b) WIMS vol. I shall always be used when in company with merchant ships.

3360. Carrier Task Force (Group) Maneuvers.

3361. The instructions of paragraphs 3360 and 3370 following, apply when task forces (groups) are maneuvered to conduct carrier air operations.

3362. (a) The Point Option System of Navigation shall be used whenever aircraft are expected to operate outside of sight contact with their carrier. Point Option is a point moving on a specified course and speed such that, at any instant, it represents the predicted position of the carrier, with an allowable error of less than half the radius of visibility.

(b) The Point Option System of Navigation shall also be used for carrier task force and carrier task group operations. In a carrier task force Point Option represents, at any instant, the predicted position of the guide task group; in a carrier task group it represents the position at any instant, of the guide. (See USF 75 and 77.)

3363. Routine air patrols will be flown when necessary. The complete daily air operating schedule should be made known to all carriers and unit commanders in the disposition. A skeleton air operating schedule should be supplied all other ships.

3364. Carriers engaged in flight operations shall display a FOX flag or flags where they can best be seen. FOX at the dip indicates that preparations are being made for impending flight operations or that there has been a temporary delay. FOX two-blocked indicates that a carrier is starting the turn into the wind to commence flight operations or that she is resuming flight operations after a temporary delay. FOX hauled down indicates that the carrier has completed flight operations.

3365. Carriers operating aircraft and with FOX two-blocked, have the right-of-way over all other ships.

3366. Carriers turning into or out of the wind, except in obedience to an executive method signal, shall, when the rudder is put over, blow one short blast on the whistle when turning to the right, or two short blasts when turning to the left.

3367. In order to obtain freedom of action for the operating carriers, it may be wise to assign "operating stations" as well as "cruising stations" for each carrier.

3368. Carriers operating aircraft should make general information signals at all times when not conforming to the course and speed of the guide.

3369. The lighting of all ships of a disposition during night carrier operations shall be in conformance to the lighting doctrine contained in USF 77.

3370. Methods of Conducting Flight Operations.

3371. For the conduct of air operations including routine patrols, two basic methods, viz, method ABLE and method BAKER, and one modified method, viz, method CHARLIE, are prescribed. The commander shall indicate in advance which method he desires to use. Normally this is method ABLE unless otherwise directed.

3372. Method ABLE.

(a) This method consists of maneuvering the disposition as a whole into the wind. It is normally employed for all extensive flight operations, and (in order to minimize danger of collision) for flight operations, during night or the low visibility of early dawn, late dusk, and bad weather.

(b) In bringing the disposition into the wind for air operations the commander should indicate by the choice of his maneuvering signal whether or not he desires to reorient the screen. In this connection he should indicate his desire for reorientation by an appropriate CORPEN signal, and his desire that no orientation take place by the use of a TURN signal.

(c) All ships should realize that the course originally signalled may not be into the existing wind, and shall be alert to conform to the course and speed of the guide as indicated by general information signals. These signals, made by the guide, shall designate the course and speed of the disposition while flight operations are in progress.

(d) Upon completion of flight operations, as indicated by the hauling down of FOX on all operating carriers, the commander will maneuver the disposition, by an executive method signal, to the desired true indicated course.

(e) On turning into the wind to conduct air operations by method ABLE, carriers should adjust their initial operating position to minimize interference between adjacent air groups or adjacent carriers. Once in a satisfactory position they should strive to maintain the course and speed of the guide. On completion of flight operations they must regain their assigned positions promptly. However, for all air operations at night or in reduced visibility and for all operations in which the true wind velocity is light (5 knots or less), carriers, once in a satisfactory operating position, shall conform to the course and speed of the guide, suspending operations temporarily when wind conditions are considered dangerous (near squalls, etc.).

(f) GUIDE. Because of the sensitive relationship between the wind and the technical details of launching and landing carrier aircraft, it is advisable to have the guide in an aircraft carrier during air operations by method ABLE. When a disposition is maneuvered into the wind for air operations by method ABLE, the guide should normally be placed in a carrier before the turn into the wind is commenced. If this is not done, however, the guide should remain unchanged until changed by signal. If the flight operations of other carriers continue longer than those of the guide, *the guide shall not shift*, but the operating carriers should make general information course and speed signals. The guide may repeat these general information signals in which case they designate the course and speed of the disposition.

3373. Method BAKER.

(a) This method consists of independent operations generally within the screen by carriers engaged in limited operations, such as launching or landing of routine patrols.

(b) The commander shall indicate sufficiently in advance whether or not method BAKER is to be used so that carriers scheduled to operate may have adequate time to gain an initial position well downwind and with sufficient speed to commence operations on schedule without delay. On occasions the commander may indicate that all routine flight operations shall be by method BAKER, unless otherwise directed.

(c) Carriers operating under method BAKER should endeavor to select an initial position which will permit screen protection, result in minimum separation from the disposition, and interfere least with heavy ships in the disposition center. In proceeding to their flying stations and in returning to their normal cruising stations, they should avoid embarrassing other ships in the disposition.

(d) When commencing the maneuver to take station, carriers shall hoist the signal "4th REPEATER VICTOR PREP" or "4th REPEATER ZEBRA GEORGE PREP." When about ready to turn they shall hoist FOX at the dip, two-blocking FOX and giving the appropriate whistle signal as the turn into the wind is commenced. Destroyers shall be alert to accompany carriers passing outside the screen. Upon completion of operations the carrier will haul down FOX, and regain assigned station.

3374. Method CHARLIE.

(a) This is not a distinct method, but a procedure which combines methods ABLE and BAKER with the principal aim giving maximum protection to carriers operating under method BAKER. For clarity it is called method CHARLIE. In this method the carrier(s) scheduled to operate aircraft proceeds to an initial position near the downwind arc of the screen and turns into the wind as in method BAKER. At an appropriate time before the carrier passes out of the screen the commander should turn the entire remainder of the disposition by method ABLE to parallel the course of the operating carrier(s). On completion of the flight operations, as indicated by hauling down FOX on all operating carriers, the commander should return the disposition to the desired course as in method ABLE, and the operating carriers should then regain their normal cruising station.

(b) The time to turn the disposition to parallel the operating carrier(s) should be chosen by the commander so as to gain most by the maneuver and will, naturally, depend on a number of factors. For example, two carriers might be scheduled to launch or land an entire deck load of aircraft by method BAKER. The commander might turn the remainder of the disposition by ABLE method almost as soon as the operating carriers turned, maintaining the disposition speed at the normal cruising speed. The operating carriers, proceeding at an increased speed for air operations, would then gradually advance through the disposition and might terminate the air operations close to the windward arc of the screen. In another case the disposition might be turned just in time to save an operating carrier from going outside of the screen at the upwind end of her run through the disposition.

63

(c) The disposition guide in method CHARLIE is handled exactly as in method ABLE.

(d) The commander may, but is not required to, signal in advance his intention of operating by method CHARLIE. He may at any time shift from BAKER to CHARLIE by hoisting an appropriate maneuvering signal. He should take cognizance of the dangers inherent in maneuvering a disposition at a time when the operating carriers are close to the heavy ships in the center.

3375. Speed Consideration. When operating aircraft the commander, in method ABLE, and the individual carriers in method BAKER, should, because of the loss of speed in turns, provide adequate speeds in advance of starting the turn into the wind. This should be done so that a minimum of time and distance will be lost in attaining the necessary relative wind speed on the launching or landing course.

3380. Battleship and Cruiser Air Operations.

3381. When it is planned to launch or recover battleship or cruiser planes simultaneously, the disposition may be maneuvered by the commander to conform in general to the movements of ships concerned. However, when one or more battleships and cruisers have aircraft to launch or recover at different times, the ships concerned should operate independently during the necessary flight operations, but should remain within the screen, when practicable.

3400. Zigzag. (See War Instructions, chapter 7.)

3410. Ships and dispositions shall zigzag during good visibility, including bright moonlight, in areas where enemy submarines may be encountered, unless the accomplishment of the task assigned will be jeopardized by the reduced speed of advance, increased fuel consumption, or both. The officer in tactical command should signal the time to commence zigzagging and cease zigzagging. Zigzagging should normally cease after evening twilight and commence prior to morning twilight, unless the phase of the moon requires that zigzagging be continued.

3411. When the disposition, as a whole, is ordered to zigzag, the speed in effect will remain unchanged unless signalled otherwise.

3420. Zigzag plans are contained in the following publications:

Plan 1 and Plans 3 to 10 inclusive—General Tactical Instructions.
Plans 19 to 26 inclusive—USF 10.
Plans 1Z to 43Z inclusive—Zigzag Diagrams, for Single Ships and Convoys, 1940.

DECLASSIFIED plan 1 and plans 3 to 10 inclusive are reproduced in appendix II with plans 19 to 26.

3422. For considerations in selecting zigzag plans see War Instructions, Chapter 7.

3430. Zigzagging by formations or dispositions containing only U. S. naval vessels, or allied men-of-war regularly attached and equipped with U. S. naval tactical and signal publications, shall be in accordance with section 37, General Tactical Instructions, as excepted below, and the optional special rules given in paragraphs 3450 to 3458, regardless of the source of the zigzag plan.

3431. The exception to the general rules prescribed in section 37, General Tactical Instructions, is as follows:

(a) The commander may order a translation, rotation, or change of front of a disposition without first ordering "Cease Zigzagging." When such a signal is executed all units cease zigzagging and carry out the disposition signal. This temporary suspension of zigzagging will not change the pattern nor the zone time hour of the zigzag plan in use.

3432. Whenever during a zigzag the signal to cease zigzagging and remain on the course being steered is executed, that course becomes the base course unless the signal is given to "resume zigzagging" in which case the original base course remains the base course.

3440. Zigzagging by dispositions containing merchant vessels, or allied men-of-war not regularly attached or not equipped with U. S. naval tactical and signal publications, shall be in accordance with Wartime Instructions for Merchant Ships, Vol. I (WIMS). Plans 1Z to 43Z only shall be used, and WIMS only shall be used to prescribe them.

3441. Attention is particularly directed to the difference in orientation of plan to time between the U. S. Naval Rules and WIMS Rules.

3450. The following special rules are prescribed for forces zigzagging under U. S. Naval Rules only and may be suspended by commanders thereof at discretion.

3451. Zigzag is automatically stopped upon receipt of any EMERGENCY maneuvering signals. Continue on present course unless signal directs otherwise. Zigzag will not be resumed until so directed by signal.

When zigzagging and an EMERGENCY-TURN signal is made to turn right or left an indicated number of degrees, use the following rules to determine the reference course to use in computing the course to turn to:

(a) If steady on a zigzag leg, use the course of that leg as the reference course.

(b) If in the act of turning to a new zigzag leg, use the course of the leg to which turning.

(c) If maneuvering independently at the moment, use the course being steered by the rest of the disposition.

(d) In other special situations rely on good tactical judgment, coupled with close observation of other nearby ships.

3453. When a change in zone time becomes effective, ships shall automatically cease zigzagging and resume the base course 10 minutes before the change of time is to become effective. They shall resume zigzagging on signal, using the same plan oriented to the new zone time.

3454. When a change of course of more than 5 degrees is signalled without a preliminary "cease zigzag" signal, ships shall:

(a) Cease zigzagging and resume base course:

    (1) When the signal is understood, if it is made by the executive method.

    (2) Ten minutes prior to the specified time when the signal was made in advance to be executed at a specified future time.

(b) Resume zigzagging on signal.

3455. When a change of heading is signalled using turn signals and without a preliminary "cease zigzag" signal, ships shall:

(a) Steady on the zigzag leg then in effect, and use the course of that leg as the reference course for the turn signal.

(b) Resume zigzagging on signal.

3456. When a change of course of 5 degrees or less is signalled ships shall not cease zigzagging but should absorb the change in the next leg.

3457. When any change of axis or a change of front is signalled without a preliminary "cease zigzag" signal, ships shall:

(a) Cease zigzagging without signal as in subparagraph 3454 above.

(b) Resume zigzagging on signal.

3458. When a change of disposition is signalled without preliminary "cease zigzag" signal, ships shall:

(a) Cease zigzagging without signal as in subparagraph 3454 above.

(b) Resume zigzagging on signal.

3460. The following tabular form may be used as a ready reference in conjunction with the zigzag instructions contained in paragraphs 3450–3458 inclusive:

Signal	Cease zigzagging automatic	Return to base course	Steady on present leg (reference course for turns)	Resume zigzagging—	
				Without signal	On signal
Emergency maneuvers	X		X		X
Turns	X		X		X
Change in disposition	X	X			X
Change of course greater than 5°	X	X			X
Change of axis	X	X			X
Change of front	X	X			X
Change in zone time	X	X			X

3500. Flight Operations.

3510. Routine.

3511. Routine flight operations comprise such of the regular patrols (inner, intermediate, combat) and regular searches (forenoon and afternoon), as may be directed or authorized.

3512. The day's flight operations should be divided between the carriers present in order that the daily flight load will be as equally distributed as possible. When conditions permit, battleships or cruisers may be directed to maintain patrols and conduct searches.

3513. So far as is practicable, individual ships should observe and keep a record of planes launched and recovered in order to minimize the danger of firing on friendly aircraft and to increase the prospect of observing forced landings.

3514. Unless otherwise ordered, recoveries terminating routine flight operations should be completed prior to end of evening twilight.

3515. Subordinates may exercise discretion with respect to routine flight operations as follows:

(a) When doubtful of the ability of the officer in tactical command to transmit signals by permissible means, and conditions are undesirable for flight, launching may be delayed until the officer in tactical command can be communicated with and his decision obtained.

(b) When minor and temporary difficulties exist, or will exist at the time specified for launching, launching may be slightly advanced or slightly delayed to avoid them. For example, if relative wind conditions are unsuitable but a prior leg or a subsequent leg of the zigzag will provide suitable conditions, a battleship or cruiser would be justified in advancing or delaying catapulting to take advantage of the zigzag.

(c) When light conditions are unfavorable but improving, launching may be delayed until they become satisfactory, unless the delay might jeopardize the mission of the flight.

(d) When beyond direct contact with the originating senior, flights should be held up or cancelled when conditions have developed or are in prospect which were not known to the originating senior and which clearly would render the flight unnecessary or undesirable. This general directive is intended to cover conditions arising from the action of other own forces or enemy forces as well as from weather and other natural causes.

3516. Air patrols should conform to the standard instructions of USF 74 and USF 75. For patrols by battleship and cruiser aircraft, the normal procedure is to assign low-numbered aircraft from low-numbered ships to low-numbered sectors or stations. When both cruiser and battleship aircraft are in the same flight all cruiser aircraft will be considered as having higher numbers than all battleship aircraft.

3517. Task forces having night fighter units should, from sunset until 1 hour before sunrise, when within range of enemy attacks, maintain night fighter units in the condition deemed necessary not only for defense, but, also, for such intruder and heckler missions as may be ordered.

3520. Special Flight Operations.

3521. Attack missions will be as ordered by the responsible commander.

3522. When so ordered the designated battleship or cruiser shall maintain two seaplanes on 10 minutes notice for launching and prepared to rescue crews of crashed or force-landed planes. One of the seaplanes should contain only the pilot and should be stripped of all armament, radio gear, and other nonessential equipment which may be safely removed. The other seaplane should contain the pilot and radioman and all gear necessary for navigation and communication. It is possible to recover three men in these two planes under the above conditions. The rescue planes and their parent ship shall guard the combat air-patrol frequency. When practicable in areas where enemy interception may be expected, rescue planes will be escorted by fighters from the designated carrier. These rescue planes shall be launched only on specific order from the officer in tactical command and, upon launching, will rendezvous over their parent ship and will not depart on their mission without first having been joined by their escorting fighters. Responsibility for safe navigation is a function of these escorting fighters.

3523. Depth Charge Alert Plane. When so directed by the officer in tactical command the designated battleship or cruiser shall maintain one seaplane ready for launching on 5-minute notice armed with the maximum load of depth charges. The depth charge alert plane shall be launched without signal when visual contact with a submarine is reported and recovery conditions are satisfactory, otherwise only on specific order from the officer in tactical command. Ship-plane communications as in subparagraph 3522. As a general rule, seaplanes on the battleships and cruisers of a carrier task force are not equipped with depth charges.

3524. Gunnery observation flights, when authorized by the officer in tactical command, shall be controlled by the officer commanding the unit requiring air-spot. Fighter director and radar guardships will be informed by the controlling officer of these flights.

3525. Aerograph-calibration flights for antiaircraft range finder calibration will be scheduled and controlled by the officer in tactical command, who will disseminate advance notice and comparison information when flight is completed.

3526. Training flights, when authorized or directed by the responsible commander, shall be controlled by the officer authorized to conduct them. The fighter director and radar guardships will be informed by the controlling officer of these flights.

3527. Due provision for rendezvous air space within a force should be made and these rendezvous air spaces should be known to all ships of the force.

3530. Aircraft Emergencies.

3531. Control. The officer in tactical command will normally issue the directive to make emergency recoveries of airplanes.

3532. Subordinate commanders, including the commanding officer of the parent ship from which the plane(s) was launched, may proceed with emergency recovery only under the following combined circumstances:

(a) The consequences of the subordinate's action will not be prejudicial to the mission on which the task force is engaged, and

(b) It is not possible to apprise the officer in tactical command of the situation and obtain permission prior to the recovery evolution.

3533. Rules governing the recovery of planes forced to land in the water, or their personnel, are as follows:

(a) A seaplane making a forced landing, but which is thereafter able to taxi, shall be recovered by the parent ship if close at hand, but otherwise by the most conveniently located ship able to hoist it in. The vessel thus recovering taxiing plane should maneuver independently as necessary, other nearby vessels keeping clear.

(b) When a seaplane capsizes or cannot be recovered, or a carrier plane lands in the water, the nearest destroyer will recover the personnel and sink the plane by gunfire. Parent ship will be notified of action taken at earliest opportunity, a statement being included as to status of the plane's confidential publications and personnel.

(c) Personnel landing in the water by parachute shall be rescued by the nearest destroyer when circumstances permit. The parent ship of rescued personnel shall be notified at the earliest opportunity. Life rafts shall be dropped to personnel by any ship passing close by when the tactical situation will not permit stopping.

3534. Aircraft forced to land in the water shall be guided by the following:

(a) A carrier plane should endeavor to land about 1,000 yards ahead or on the lee bow of a destroyer.

(b) A seaplane unable to land near parent ship but able to land near a destroyer should land as in (a).

(c) A seaplane forced down out of touch with the disposition should maintain receiver watch on the flight frequency in use prior to being forced down.

(d) In special cases, planes on water may be directed to make "MO's" on flight frequency or safety frequency, depending on the direction-finding ability of surface ships concerned.

3535. When cruisers or battleships must make emergency recoveries of aircraft, and their freedom of maneuver is cramped by nearby vessels, they shall hoist the signal "I am recovering aircraft by (_ _ _) method, first recovery to starboard (port)." Vessels in positions which would cramp the recovery maneuvers get clear. Remember for the CHARLIE method that—

(a) If the recovery turn is to starboard, a battleship or cruiser first turns to the left of the wind, then turns through the wind to a final recovery course about 45° to the right of the wind.

(b) If the recovery turn is to port, the above procedure is reversed. For cruisers having only one crane, and that on the port side, the recovery turn will always be to port.

DECLASSIFIED Lost plane and homing procedure shall conform to USF 77.

3540. Routine Requirements for Aircraft.

3541. In the absence of special instructions from the task force (group) commander, the ordnance loading for aircraft based on board when cruising is as follows:

(a) All aircraft—Full gun ammunition allowance.

(b) VF—No bombs.

(c) VSB or VTB:

    (1) On search—As directed by officer ordering the search.

    (2) On patrol—One or more depth bombs per plane to the limit permitted by operating conditions, with instantaneous impact fuze and hydrostatic fuze set for 25 feet.

(d) VSO and VOS (battleships and cruisers):

    On search or patrol:

        Two 100-pound bombs per plane, equipped with instantaneous impact fuzes.

    On gunnery observation:

        No bombs.

3542. Pilots of planes carrying bombs shall avoid passing over friendly ships.

3543. Personnel responsible for the navigation of aircraft shall employ the Point OPTION method of making ship and plane interception, unless otherwise directed. (See subparagraph 3362.)

3544. Precautions to prevent planes from becoming lost are—

(a) Planes on routine patrols shall close parent ships when thick weather threatens; and also about once an hour, on the alert for flashing light messages.

(b) Search planes should endeavor to fly around squally areas. If of too wide extent to permit continuation of the search, the planes shall return and report by message drop or flashing light their inability to search the entire area assigned.

(c) Planes which have returned from distant missions shall, in the absence of other instructions, take up an inner patrol ahead of parent ship, within flashing light range, awaiting recall, first checking in by flying close alongside the bridge of the parent ship, port side.

3545. Aircraft Approach and Recognition. The following special provisions should be fully understood by all pilots:

(a) Recognition procedure shall be carried out as outlined in USF 70.

(b) There is a dual responsibility in aircraft recognition, on the part of the pilot to observe prescribed procedure and on the surface ships to recognize friendly aircraft.

(c) When the current recognition procedure permits two or more directions of approach, the pilot must take care to avoid approaching from the direction of bright sunlight or on the bearing of an enemy air base.

(d) The same is true of a direction providing good cloud cover when another direction providing clear sky or else a solid overcast is available. (NOTE.—The object of (c) and (d) is to avoid any method of approach which is suggestive of enemy character.)

(e) Planes unable to comply with the prescribed recognition procedure shall endeavor to approach at low speed between 1,000 and 2,000 feet, making easy S turns, in order to indicate lack of hostile intent and enable ships to examine them for identification.

(f) Aircraft IFF shall be energized at all times during flight except when approaching a known enemy base or force which can interrogate our IFF. The officer in tactical command shall prescribe the detailed usage dependent upon the existing tactical situation and the possibility of the enemy's interrogation.

3546. Action on Sighting Submarine or Mine.

(a) A pilot sighting a submarine shall attack it with all available armament, instantly, if the submarine is near a favorable position for firing torpedoes at the disposition, and then mark the spot by float lights and repeated dives. One exception is made to the foregoing. When there is a destroyer within 1,500 yards of the submarine, the pilot shall withhold bombing to avoid disrupting the destroyer sonar attack. (See FTP 223.)

(b) A pilot sighting a mine shall mark its position and fly a tight spiral low over the mine. Attempts to explode floating mines by machine-gun fire must be undertaken with caution to avoid blast effects or fragments.

(c) In both cases the contact should be reported by most rapid permissible method, as early as possible after sighting. Necessary amplifying reports should also be made.

3541. Aircraft Availability. Daily, upon completion of flight schedule, the plane availability report together with the order of spot (in case of carriers) will be made by the type commander to the officer in tactical command. Available aircraft will be interpreted to mean total flyable by types on board, including planes temporarily out of commission for checks and minor repairs. Carriers will report separately, by types, available aircraft on overhead. Cruisers and battleships will report only if planes available are less than full allowance.

3550. Man Overboard.

3551. All ships will follow the wartime man overboard procedure given in section 32, General Tactical Instructions, except that a destroyer or other small ship may lower a boat when the nature of current operations justifies.

3600. Routine Activities in Task Forces.

3610. Zone Time.

3611. The officer in tactical command may, at discretion, prescribe the zone time to be used for regulating the internal activities of the command. Ordinarily, refinements smaller than one-half hour should not be used.

3612. Time designation in the text of despatches and reports shall be supplemented by the use of appropriate designating letter.

3620. Ship's Routine. The following are mandatory or desirable, as noted.

3621. Morning general quarters as required by subparagraph 2171 (b) (2).

3622. Whistle and siren shall be tested at sea following the motions of the officer in tactical command, normally at 1600.

3630. Routine Reports Underway are required as follows:

3631. Navigational position reports will be made, when requested, at 0800, after the meridian-altitude sight, and at 1800 by heavy ships and destroyer flagships. These reports are rarely requested.

3632. Aircraft Availability. (See subparagraph 3547.)

3633. Fuel on hand as of 0800 shall be reported as follows:

(a) *Destroyers.* Daily at 0800 to the screen commander who will forward the composite report to the task force (group) commander. This report is necessary at this time to facilitate the fueling of those destroyers which require oil and to give them sufficient time to pump ballast prior to fueling.

(b) head ships ... at 0800 to the type commander who will forward the composite report to the task force (group) commander when requested. The following classifications will be used:

ABLE—Fuel oil plus Diesel, barrels burnable, on hand.

BAKER—ABLE expressed as a percentage of total burnable which can be carried out.

CHARLIE—Fuel oil plus Diesel, barrels, consumed during preceding 24 hours.

DOG—Aviation gasoline, gallons, on hand (destroyers omit).

EASY—DOG expressed as percentage of capacity (destroyers omit).

(c) Normally ABLE will be the only report made unless otherwise directed.

3640. All ships shall be ready for towing and to be towed, subject to the following:

3641. Gear which is rigged shall not interfere with the ship's offensive power.

3642. Essential and fragile gear, such as hawsers, shall not be exposed to splinter damage.

3650. Other special preparations by all ships include the following:

3651. For fueling at sea, see section 5200 and "Fueling at Sea Instructions" (Cominch P–2).

3652. For fueling on reaching port, the pumping of water ballast shall be completed just prior to indicated fueling time unless pumping of water ballast is forbidden in that port, in which case pumping of water ballast shall be completed prior to the time of arriving at the outer limit of the area in which the pumping of water ballast is prohibited. Commanding officers, however, must retain the final decision whether or not to pump water ballast overboard, being guided by the degree of necessity of suppressing evidence of ship's movements, possibility of attack, stability of ships, weather conditions, and other military considerations.

3660. Identification. Ships must be fully prepared to identify themselves and to verify the identity of other friendly ships. This requires complete readiness of all regular and emergency means of identification; instruction and training of appropriate personnel in their use; and the posting in convenient places of the recognition signals which are current. See USF 70 and War Instructions, chapter 5.

3670. Measures to minimize the visibility of ships at sea are outlined below for guidance:

DECLASSIFIED

lights. Inspect own ship frequently. Observe other ships for lights, informing them thereof.

3672. Flashing light signals, both day and night, may be used only in accordance with USF 70.

3673. Glints from reflecting surfaces must be prevented in sunlight or bright moonlight. Check glass windows, aircraft wind screens, searchlights, bright metal fittings.

3674. Bright-colored and white objects must not be visible. Check white cap covers and clothes; white canvas.

3675. Smoke. Normally, by day steam smokeless; by night (and in fog) with a light-brown haze. Minimize galley smoke; prevent it, by securing the galley, when the tactical situation so demands.

3676. Tubes may be blown once each watch as considered practicable during conditions of reduced visibility and also when in waters where enemy contact is improbable. Unless otherwise directed by the officer in tactical command, blowing tubes in waters where enemy contact is probable shall not be commenced in bright moonlight or at a time earlier than $1\frac{1}{2}$ hours after sunset nor later than $1\frac{1}{2}$ hours before sunrise; and these limits should be extended in high latitudes during long twilights. Tactical commanders may encourage and require the use of soot blowers to the fullest practicable extent.

3677. Disposal of waste. One hour after sunset is prescribed for disposal of waste and daily pumping of bilges. Do not throw overboard anything that floats.

3678. The timing of blowing of tubes and disposing of waste shall not be such as to nullify the effects of an evasive course change made shortly after dark.

3679. Loud noises, including striking of bells and the use of topside loud-speakers, shall normally be prohibited during darkness and low visibility. Whistle signals and running lights may be used to prevent collision. (See paragraph 3622.)

3680. Reports required after return to port are as follows:

3681. Readiness for return to sea. Senior officers of each type keep in touch with their ships and inform the task force (group) commander of—

    (a) Estimated dates of readiness for return to sea.
    (b) Causes (repairs or deficiencies) which may delay or will delay individual ships.

DECLASSIFIED

(c) Dates upon which ships actually become ready.

(d) Important items of work and of supplies required, and the need for tender or yard availability.

3682. Average engine speed and fuel consumed in barrels for each day; amounts of fuel on hand at departure and arrival; and amounts received at sea, shall be reported by each ship to the task force (group) commander and senior of own type.

3683. Action report, submitted when the employment at sea has so warranted.

3684. Ships or units which have been sent on detached missions submit excerpts from war diaries covering operations while detached, to higher echelons of command if directed.

3685. Ships newly joining a task force shall furnish the task force and task group commanders with a copy of their ship characteristics card and three copies of monthly roster of officers, using air mail if not in company. If newly arrived in an area, send copies likewise to the area commander.

3690. Miscellaneous.

3691. Logistics. Immediately upon return to port take on fuel, gasoline, ammunition, and stores to capacity. Effect necessary repairs, and such desirable repairs and authorized alterations as can be accomplished within the time known to be available. Inform the senior present of own type of conditions which might delay readiness; and inform him immediately upon attaining readiness.

3692. Engineering maintenance measures. When in an inactive area, vessels are urged to request permission from the task force (group) commander and senior officer present to disable boilers or parts of machinery for specified brief periods to accomplish desirable repairs or adjustments.

3693. Comply with instructions in the Bureau of Naval Personnel Manual regarding distribution of the muster roll prior to sailing into dangerous waters. For the purposes of this requirement traverse on the high seas is considered as dangerous waters.

PART IV

FIGHTING INSTRUCTIONS

4000. GENERAL.

4100. Battle Plans and Dispositions.

4110. Chances of success in action are enhanced if the engaging force is suitably disposed and fights according to a prearranged plan.

4111. It is impracticable to provide explicit instructions for every possible combination of task force characteristics and tactical situations. Representative plans and dispositions are included in such form that they may be prescribed by brief signals. Through judicious use, concerted action may be obtained when, under stress of circumstances, a newly formed task organization is directed to undertake a task without a long period of indoctrination, or forces not previously in company are assigned a joint task.

4112. Commanders are expected to prepare other needed plans and dispositions, both for general application and, when time permits, for specific tasks. To avoid confusion, such plans and dispositions shall be distinguished by prefixing the task organization number to any other designation employed.

4200. Surface Action.

4210. Major Action. Battle dispositions, battle plans, and fighting instructions for the conduct of a major action are contained in War Instructions and General Tactical Instructions. The following paragraphs supplement and together with the above publications are prescribed as the basic standard in the U. S. Fleet.

4211. Adequate control is provided by general signal for—

(a) Forming the disposition.

(b) Specifying the battle plan.

(c) Conducting the engagement.

4220. Approach and Contact Dispositions.

4221. The stations of task groups (units) in approach dispositions shall conform generally to the typical approach disposition shown in diagram 54, General Tactical Instructions, except that the areas for the light forces shall be as prescribed in subparagraphs 4257, 4258, and 4259 herein. The distribution of light forces shall be in accordance with the number of the disposition indicated from table, paragraph 1114, General Tactical Instructions.

4224. The stations of task groups (units) in contact dispositions shall conform to diagrams 55, 56, and 57, General Tactical Instructions. Contact dispositions shall be in accordance with paragraph 1143, General Tactical Instructions.

4230. Battle Dispositions.

4231. Normal battle dispositions will conform generally to typical battle disposition shown in figure 11. Assignment of light forces to stations in a battle disposition may be made by use of the table in paragraph 1316, General Tactical Instructions. Sectors of radar responsibility shall be assigned for a battle disposition as designated in Part VI.

4232. In connection with their disposition for and employment in battle light forces will be governed by the following:

(a) The decision of the officer in tactical command as to the nature of the initial operations of the light forces will be conveyed to the flank commanders by the designation of a suitable battle plan, or by definite instructions. Such plans or instructions fall in one of three categories; namely:

    (1) Light forces assume the tactical offensive and attack immediately the battle line engages, and

    (2) Light forces assume the tactical defensive, withholding the attack until—

        (a) Specifically ordered by the officer in tactical command.

        (b) Particularly favorable circumstances warrant immediate offensive action, or

    (3) Light forces operate at discretion of flank commanders.

(b) In assigning light forces to stations in the battle disposition, the question of the type of torpedo which may be encountered must be thoroughly considered. Torpedoes of very pronounced characteristics have been reported. It is advisable, therefore, to adjust the stations of the light forces, and especially of the defensive elements, in order to prevent effective enemy torpedo fire. In so doing, it is wise to consider the question of mutual support, and not move the light forces of the defensive element into such an area as to (1) deny them the protection of own battle line, (2) deny them the chance to interpose between the enemy and own battle line.

(c) Such instructions may of necessity be changed hastily due to a change in the tactical situation. Flank commanders must be alert for orders changing the light force objectives, or when the situation demands immediate action, to act upon their own initiative. When making the decision as to the nature of the light force operations thus devolves upon a flank commander, such decision must be based on the general plan and consideration of strategical, tactical, and weather factors known to the flank commander.

4233. The flank commander will be responsible for the assignment to the flank forces of its immediate objective; for the disposition of types, or if the vessels of a type are not to be stationed in one group, for the disposition of the units of such type; and for the coordination of the operations of the units comprising the flank force. When change to a battle disposition from other fleet disposition involves a transfer of task units from one task group to another, flank commanders must effect assignment of units joining them in such manner that the chain of command is apparent. Communications follow the communication plan.

4234. Except by chance or surprise, a destroyer attack on an enemy battle line cannot be fully effective unless enemy light forces capable of offering effective opposition to such a destroyer attack can be destroyed, damaged, or intensively engaged by own light forces other than the destroyers engaged in making the torpedo attack. Two methods of conducting an attack by light forces in the van are—

4240. The Preliminary Attack.

4241. The object of the preliminary cruiser attack is to destroy, damage, or disperse the enemy light forces in order to clear the way for a destroyer torpedo attack on the enemy battle line to be initiated later; the period of delay depending upon the situation. The preliminary attack—

    (a) Requires a marked superiority in light force strength.

    (b) Must be made by light forces other than destroyers assigned to the torpedo attack group.

    (c) Cruiser phase may be made before or after deployment, but the torpedo attack should not be initiated until the battle lines are engaged.

    (d) Is usually made by cruisers only, but if cruiser strength is inadequate, destroyers not assigned to the attack group may be used.

    (e) Must be driven home; enemy light forces must be destroyed or driven off.

In the preliminary attack the normal objective of light cruisers will be the enemy destroyers and that of the heavy cruisers, the enemy cruisers, both heavy and light. The operations of the attacking cruisers and the distribution of their gunfire should, however, be governed by consideration of the relative value of enemy types in defending against the torpedo attack which is to follow. If, due to scarcity of cruisers, destroyers are employed in the force conducting the preliminary attack, they may be expected to operate as cruisers and our own cruisers must be so disposed and handled as to permit accompanying destroyers to use their torpedoes against the enemy cruisers.

4250. The Simultaneous Attack.

4251. The object of the simultaneous attack is to destroy, damage, or disperse enemy light forces simultaneously with the conduct of a destroyer torpedo attack on the enemy battle line. The simultaneous attack—

(a) To be successful should be conducted by an attack force superior in strength to the enemy light force.

(b) May be made by inferior force to relieve own battle line from an unfavorable tactical situation, by forcing the enemy battle line to maneuver or to prevent the enemy light forces from taking the initiative.

(c) Should be made after the battle lines are engaged.

(d) Need not be driven home in the face of superior opposition if the unfavorable situation of our own battle line has been relieved.

In this attack the normal objective of light cruisers is the defending destroyers and that of the heavy cruisers the enemy cruisers, both heavy and light; but preference as gun targets must be given to the enemy ships which are in position most effectively to oppose the destroyer attack, regardless of type. Cooperating cruisers must keep clear of destroyer attack points. Cruisers will retire with the destroyers, covering their retirement.

4252. Conversely, our battle line must, so long as enemy destroyers are in position to attack, be defended against such possible attack. The most effective defense of the battle line will be provided by a unit when it is stationed on or near the locus of torpedo firing points of the attacking destroyers, and interposed between such destroyers and own battle line, and so disposed as to permit a full broadside fire. Such locus will normally be an arc 12,000 to 14,000 yards from the center of own battle line. It is not essential that the the defensive unit physically occupy the area enclosing favorable torpedo firing points at the expense of damage from long range enemy fire but only that the position to which defensive units retire control the torpedo firing area at effective range. When the battle line is not engaged, retirement should be sufficient to gain its support.

4253. In order to permit rapid transmission of instructions to the flank forces, the following plans are provided for use with the general signal meaning "Light Forces will operate according to battle plan indicated":

Plan 1—Tactical offensive.
Plan 2—Tactical defensive.
Plan 3—Divided—part tactical offensive, part tactical defensive.

Plan 4—Make normal deployment, nature of initial operations to be decided when tactical situation is more definitely known.

Plan 5—Tactical offensive—Designated units prepare to make a preliminary attack.

Note.—If deployment is ordered before the order to attack is given, the designated units will take stations in the general vicinity of their normal deployment stations, but such as to facilitate the initiation of the attack.

Plan 6—Tactical offensive—Light forces in the van prepare to make a simultaneous attack.

Note.—If deployment is ordered before the order to attack is given, the light forces in the van will take stations in the general vicinity of their normal deployment stations, but as near to the enemy light forces as possible without becoming engaged.

Plan 7—Divided—Light force units designated prepare to make simultaneous attack—Units of light forces not designated operate defensively, but if practicable during the attack of the offensive units, move into the outer area and prepare to attack enemy battle line with torpedoes.

4254. Fighting strength is necessary in the flank unit most distant from own battle line in order to prevent the flank from being turned and own light forces being driven out of position.

4255. The most advantageous station for own attacking destroyers is that from which they can reach suitable torpedo firing points with the least exposure to enemy gunfire. This requires that van light forces operating on the tactical offensive be oriented with respect to the enemy objective, and not in a fixed area relative to own battle line. The position to be attained by the attacking destroyers will depend on comparative strength and distribution of enemy van light forces. When own light forces in the van are superior to the opposed enemy light forces, in an action on nearly parallel courses, this station will normally be about 22,000 yards from the center of own battle line, on a bearing 70° to 75° from the fleet axis.

4256. Cruiser action against enemy light forces either preliminary to or simultaneously with the attacking destroyers, normally will be most effective when initiated from two stations, one on each side of the station of the attacking destroyers.

4257. In view of the foregoing, in battle dispositions or initially upon deployment (if deployment is ordered direct from other than a battle disposition), units of the flank forces will be stationed in order away from own battle line as follows:

defensive element:

(a) Stationed at a distance of about 12,000 yards from the center of own battle line (less distance in reduced visibility, or if battle line support is required, or if probable characteristics of enemy torpedo are less than our own, and at more distance if enemy torpedo characteristics are greater than our own) at an angle from the fleet axis such as to permit interposing between the enemy and own battle line on the limiting locus of enemy favorable destroyer torpedo firing points. Stations of other flank units are calculated from the distance of the outer limit of Area A in which this defensive element is stationed. Should the flank commander desire to increase or decrease the distance of this element from the battle line he may do so by signal designating distance of outer limit of Area A from the center of the battle line. Should lack of time or other circumstances prevent a flank commander from designating area limits by signal, all unit commanders shall interpret the station taken by the flank commander as indicating the approximate stations the several units should occupy.

(b) Capable of effective defensive action against an unsupported attack of enemy destroyers in the opposed light forces. In estimating the required strength of this element it may be assumed that a light cruiser (modern) can provide effective defense against 4–6 destroyers; a heavy cruiser or light cruiser (old) 3–4 destroyers; a modern destroyer, 2 enemy destroyers. Old destroyers can provide effective defense against old destroyers and in such case in ratio 1 to 2 enemy destroyers.

(c) This defensive element of the flank force is not necessarily restricted to defensive action. Its initial task is the defense of own battle line against a surprise or early initiated attack by destroyers in the enemy van light forces. When our light forces are operating on the tactical offensive, or if a favorable opportunity occurs, it may be employed in an attack.

4258. A destroyer attack element:

(a) Stationed in an area outside (more distant from own battle line) of the defensive element.

(b) Capable of effective offensive action against the enemy battle line. This element should comprise one to four squadrons of destroyers (normally all destroyers of the van light forces not assigned to the defensive element) and in addition such cruisers as may be available to support the destroyers in an attack. When cruisers are limited the cruisers of the defending element may be directed to

TYPICAL BATTLE DISPOSITION

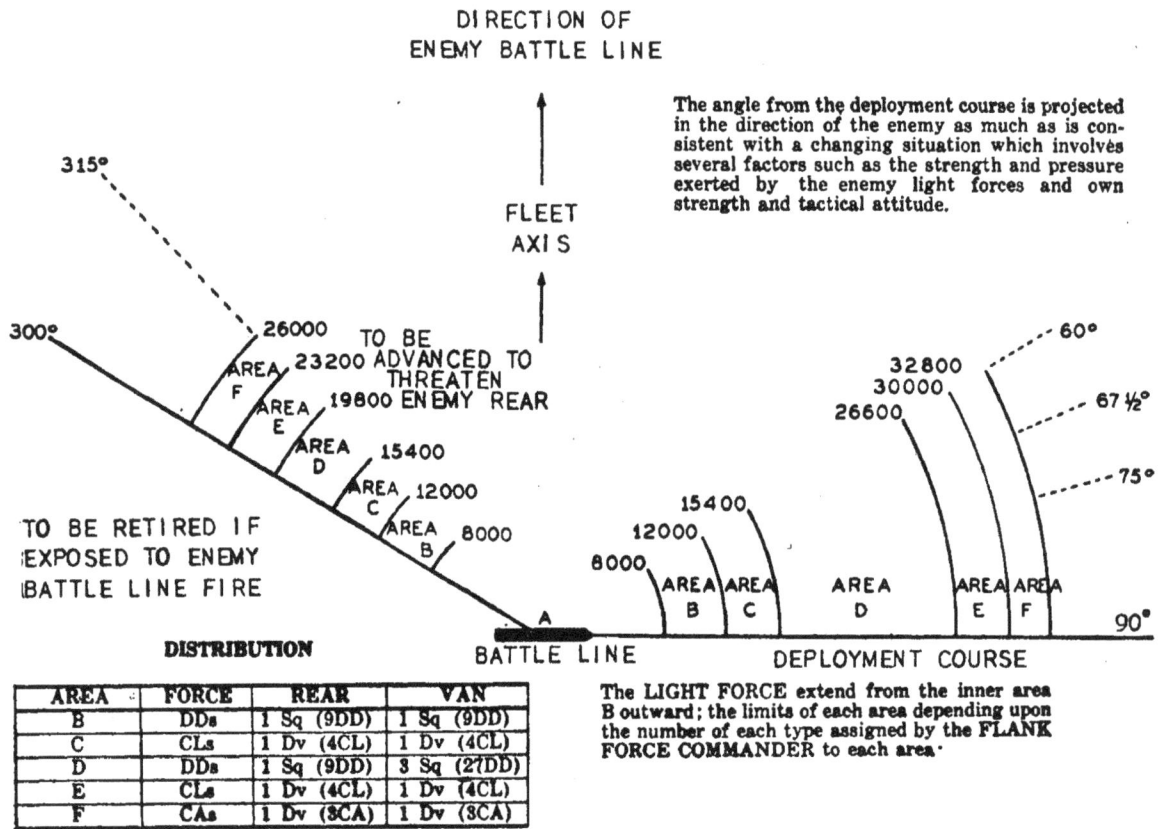

DIRECTION OF
ENEMY BATTLE LINE

The angle from the deployment course is projected in the direction of the enemy as much as is consistent with a changing situation which involves several factors such as the strength and pressure exerted by the enemy light forces and own strength and tactical attitude.

FLEET
AXIS

315°

300°

26000
23200   TO BE ADVANCED TO
AREA   THREATEN
F   AREA 19800 ENEMY REAR
E   AREA
D   15400
AREA 12000
C   AREA 8000
B

32800
30000
26600

60°

67 ½°

75°

15400
12000
8000

TO BE RETIRED IF
EXPOSED TO ENEMY
BATTLE LINE FIRE

AREA AREA
B   C

AREA
D

AREA AREA
E   F

90°

A
BATTLE LINE

DEPLOYMENT COURSE

DISTRIBUTION

AREA	FORCE	REAR	VAN
B	DDs	1 Sq (9DD)	1 Sq (9DD)
C	CLs	1 Dv (4CL)	1 Dv (4CL)
D	DDs	1 Sq (9DD)	3 Sq (27DD)
E	CLs	1 Dv (4CL)	1 Dv (4CL)
F	CAs	1 Dv (3CA)	1 Dv (3CA)

The LIGHT FORCE extend from the inner area B outward; the limits of each area depending upon the number of each type assigned by the FLANK FORCE COMMANDER to each area.

Figure 11.

operate in support of our attacking destroyers. Also cruisers of the strength element (paragraph 4259), may be used to support our attacking destroyers.

4259. A strength element:

(a) Stationed in an area outside (more distant from own battle line) of the destroyer attack element.

(b) Capable of preventing the turning of the light force flank and preventing the forcing of own light forces out of position. Preferably strong enough to drive the enemy light forces out of position. When own light forces are so superior to those of the enemy as to warrant the initiation of a destroyer attack, this strength element is used alone or in coordination with cruiser units of the destroyer attack element, or defensive element, to attack the enemy light forces preliminary to, or simultaneously with the initiation of own destroyer attack.

4259.1. An explanation of the typical battle disposition shown in facing figure 11 follows:

Areas for light forces in the van and rear are letters "B," "C," "D," "E," "F," etc., with "A" as the battle line station. The radius of the arc constituting the outer limit of B area will be 12,000 yards unless otherwise directed. This radius may be lessened in reduced visibility and should be increased to 14,000 yards, if more than one squadron of destroyers is assigned to area B after deployment. The radii of other areas should be determined by adding to the limiting radius of the area next toward the battle line, of an amount equal to the required maneuvering length plus 1,000 yards. The maneuvering length for a destroyer squadron is 3,400 yards, for other types, number of ships times distance.

For example:
Area B—1 Squadron DD —outer limit 12,000.
Area C—1 Division (4) CL—column 2,400 plus 1,000 = 15,400.
Area D—3 Squadrons DD —10,200 plus 1,000 = 26,600.
Area E—1 Division (4) CL—Maneuvering length 2,400 plus 1,000 = 30,000.
Area F—1 Division (3) CA—Maneuvering length 1,800 plus 1,000 = 32,800.
Signal "AREA. Take position in the disposition in ___ ___ designated."

TYPE "A" BATTLE DISPOSITIONS

A-1

ALL LIGHT FORCES IN THE VAN

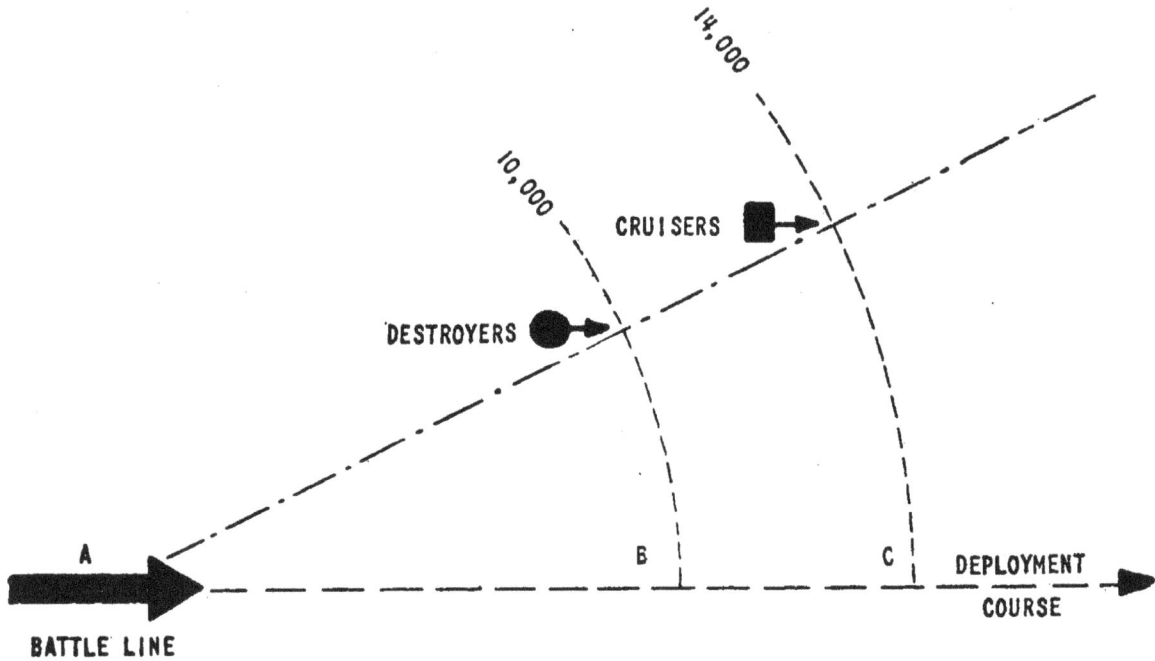

A-4

Same as A-1, except one destroyer is stationed 2,000
to 3,000 yards astern of rear ship of battle line.

Figure 12.

TYPE "A" BATTLE DISPOSITION

A-2

LIGHT FORCES EQUALLY DIVIDED

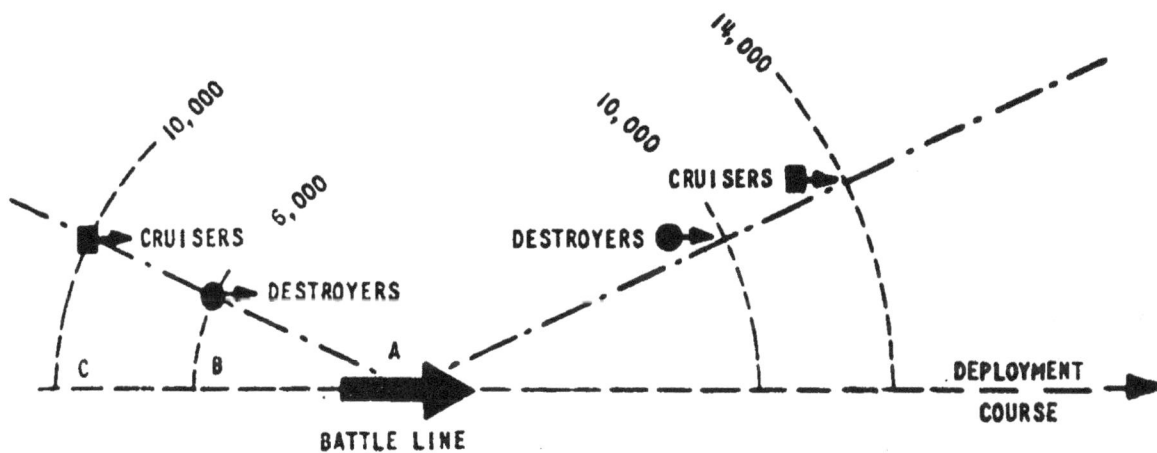

Figure 13.

TYPE "A" BATTLE DISPOSITIONS

A-3

**ALL LIGHT FORCES IN VAN IN B AREA, FORMED IN WEDGE
OR VEE AT DISCRETION OF LIGHT FORCE COMMANDER**

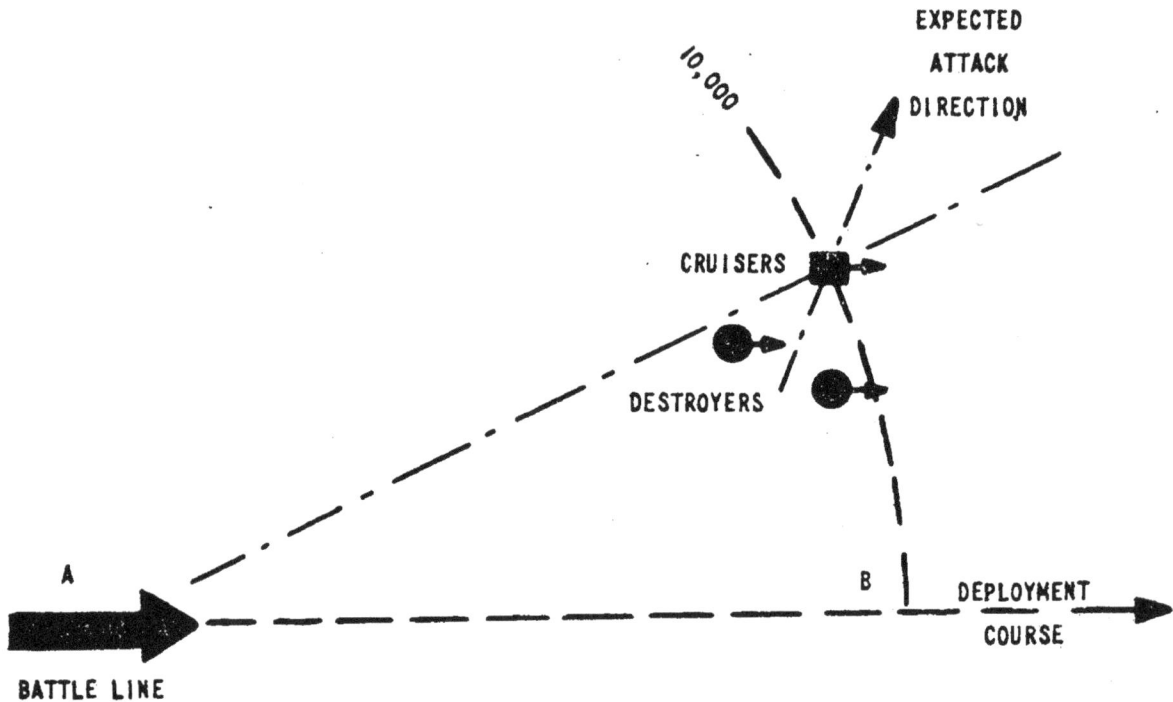

Wedge formation illustrated, vee similar. Note that
the reference direction of vee or wedge should point
in the direction in which it is expected to attack;
not in the direction of the deployment course..

A-5

Same as A-3, except one destroyer is stationed 2,000
to 3,000 yards astern of rear ship of battle line.

Figure 14.

TYPE B BATTLE DISPOSITION

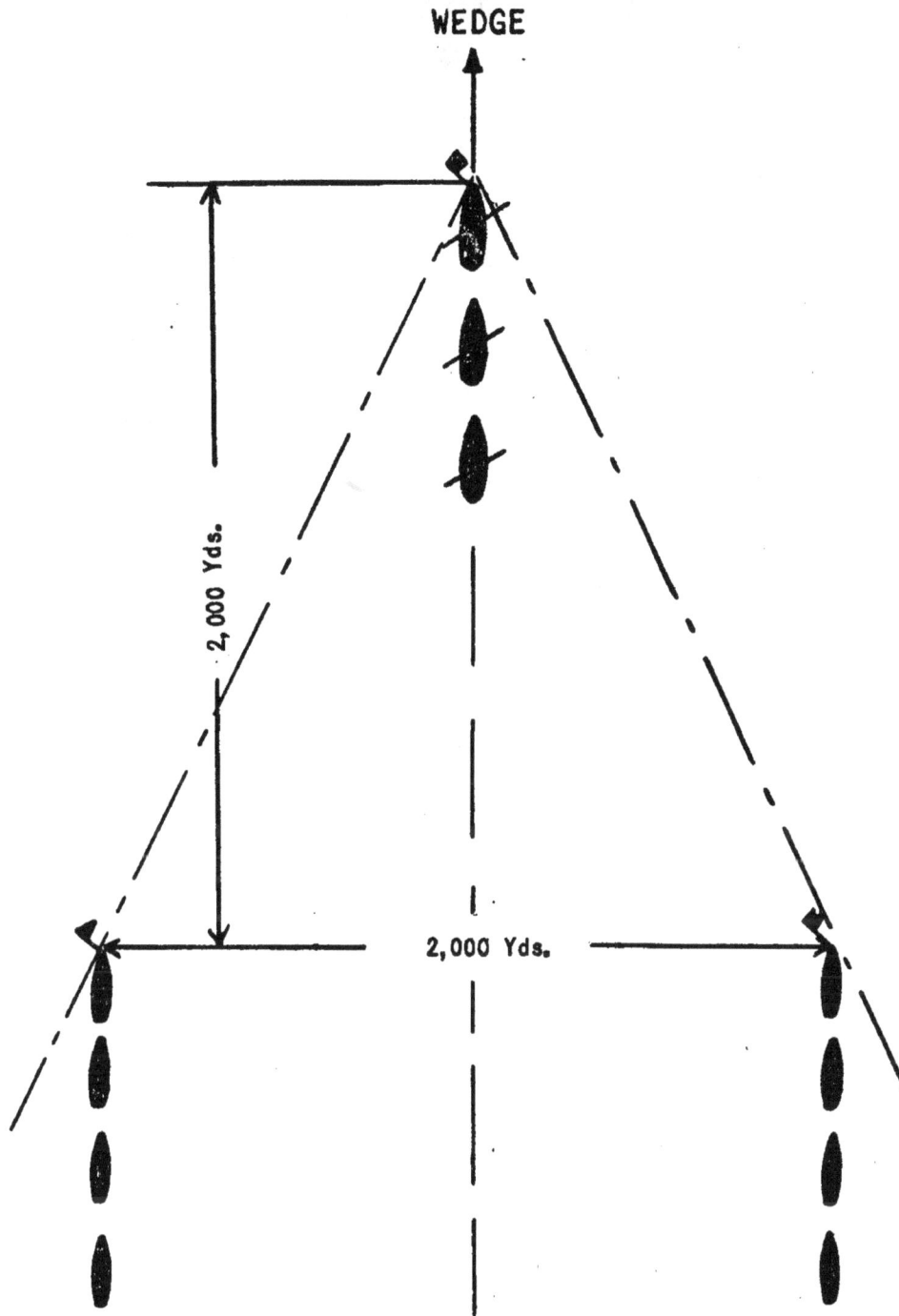

WEDGE

2,000 Yds.

2,000 Yds.

Illustrated for one division of cruisers and one squadron of eight destroyers, latter formed in two 4-ship attack units. Any other formation of attack units may be substituted. Distances may be varied to suit requirements.

Figure 15.

TYPE "C" BATTLE DISPOSITION

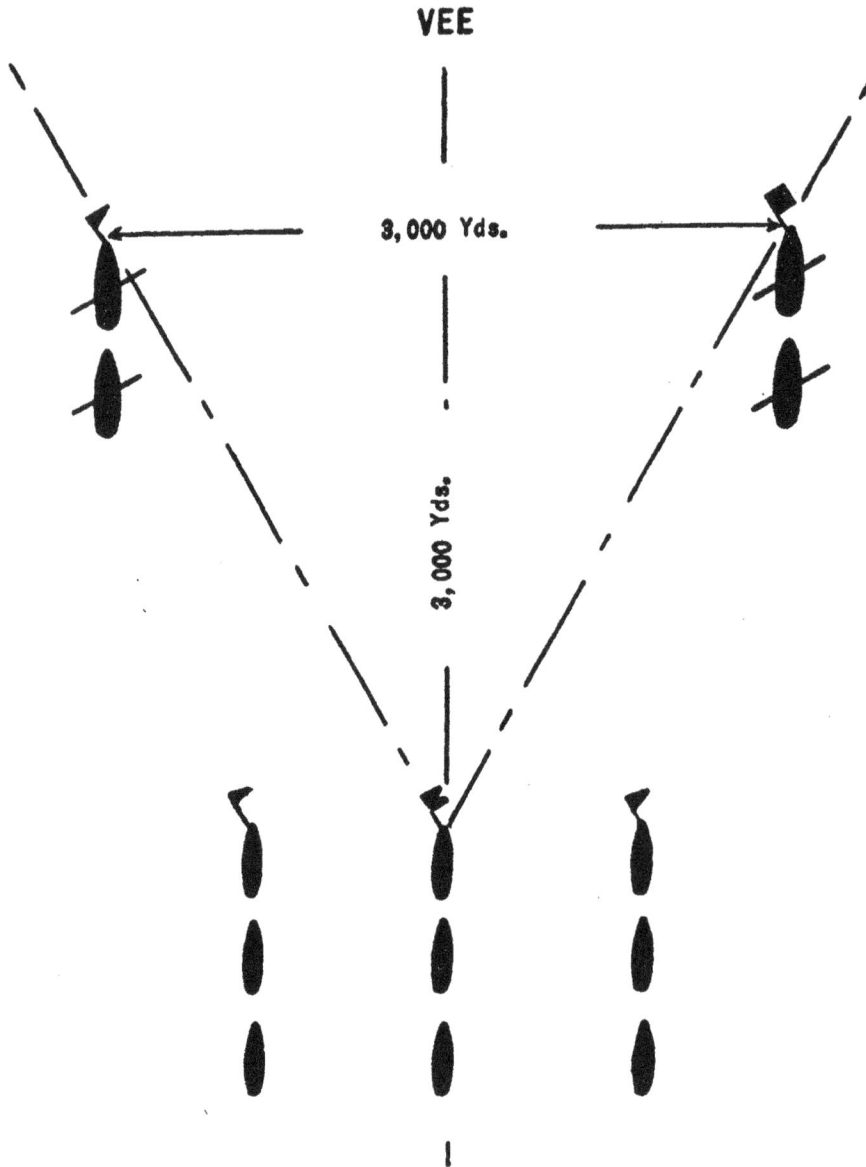

VEE

3,000 Yds.

3,000 Yds.

Illustrated for one division of cruisers and one squadron of nine destroyers, latter formed in three 3-ship attack units. Any other formation of attack units may be substituted. Distances may be varied to suit requirements.

Figure 16.

4261. Battle will be governed by a definite plan, normally previously prescribed, but such original plan is subject to modification or change, either prior to or during an engagement, as developments dictate. The battle plan may be prescribed by appropriate general signal, using the numerals and letters designating a typical battle plan from Chapter XIV, General Tactical Instructions; a plan contained herein; or other plan prepared by a responsible commander for a particular operation.

4270. Surface Action—Small Forces.

4271. Three typical dispositions, designated "A," "B," and "C" are provided for small forces in surface action, illustrated in figures 12 to 16 inclusive:

4272. Disposition "A" is adapted from a major disposition, with variants indicated for dispersing the light forces to suit different tactical situations.

    (a) (1) The "A" dispositions are suitable for either normal or emergency deployment of a disposition containing battleships and/or cruisers and destroyers.

          (2) When both battleships and cruisers are present the cruisers take station in van and/or rear as indicated by the light force distribution.

          (3) When cruisers are the only heavy ships present, they form the battle line. For night or low visibility attack, see paragraph 4276.

          (4) When cruisers and destroyers are assigned to the same area, they shall form as directed by the senior cruiser officer to suit existing circumstances. Vee or wedge formation, described later herein, should be used if applicable.

          (5) In all type "A" dispositions the angle to the deployment course at which light forces are stationed may be varied by the officer in tactical command or light force commanders as required by the tactical situation.

    (b) In assigning light forces in these type "A" dispositions, it must be remembered that these are typical dispositions and are not rigid. It is expected that commanders will exercise intelligent discretion in employing variations based on the existing situation. For example, should there be only cruisers and destroyers, the commander might station half of the destroyers in the van and half in the rear in a type A–2 disposition with the destroyers in closer to the battle line (cruisers). In the South Pacific, destroyers were often so assigned with those in the van at 5,000 yards and those in the rear at 3,000 yards. This was because of certain governing limitations in that area. Such modifications fall within the province of the professional judgment of the commander.

4273. For forces of the size contemplated, a complete battle plan for use in type "A" dispositions can usually be conveyed by the officer in tactical command signaling his general intention as to type of action, mean range, and whether light forces are to operate on the tactical offensive or defensive.

(a) For ease of signaling, such plans are designated by three characters, as follows:

Numeral—Type of Action	1 Normal	
	2 Reverse	
	3 Pursuit	
	4 Retiring	Significance same as for
	5 Delaying	typical plans of chapter
	6 Withdrawal	XIV, General Tactical Instructions

Letter—Range	E Extreme
	L Long
	M Medium
	C Close

Numeral—Light Force Operations	1 Both van and rear offensive.
	2 Both van and rear defensive.
	3 Van offensive, rear defensive.
	4 Van defensive, rear offensive.
	5 At discretion of light force commanders.

(b) As an example of the foregoing, the signal, "Action will be fought in accordance with BATTLE PLAN 2M4" would express the intention of the officer in tactical command to engage decisively on reverse courses, at medium range, with the van screening own heavy ships against enemy torpedo attack, and the rear attacking enemy van after it had been brought under fire by our own heavy ships.

4274. In addition, the following torpedo attack doctrine is effective in small forces, when no plan has been signaled or when circumstances justify a light force commander in departing from plan.

(a) The senior destroyer officer should consider assigning each squadron of his destroyers into multiple attack groups, normally three when there are six or more destroyers. These groups should attack from widely separated sectors for the purpose of insuring as practicable, that own torpedoes cover possible enemy evasive maneuvers.

(b) If a torpedo target is encountered before the heavy ships have commenced firing or before the torpedo attack units have been released, the destroyer commander or destroyer making contact, will inform the officer in tactical command. (See paragraph 4283.)

(c) If a torpedo target is encountered within torpedo range after the heavy ships have commenced firing, but before the torpedo attack units have been released, torpedo attack unit or destroyer making contact will fire torpedoes from station in the disposition without further orders, informing the officer in tactical command.

(d) If a torpedo target is encountered outside torpedo range after the heavy ships have commenced firing but before the torpedo attack units have been released, one torpedo attack unit close and launch torpedo attack, informing the officer in tactical command, who may release additional units to attack the same target.

(e) After torpedo attack has been delivered, torpedo attack units retire, employing own gunfire defensively, avoiding blanking fire of own heavy ships, and keeping officer in tactical command informed of general movements. Attack units, whose torpedoes are expended, proceed, as practicable, in order of preference, to—

    (1) Assigned rendezvous. It is customary to designate one or more rendezvous where destroyer divisions, and squadrons may reform before rejoining own main body. This reduces the danger of nonrecognition, and nonidentification.

    (2) Screening stations in van of battle line on locus of enemy torpedo firing, points, or

    (3) Fall in astern of battle line.

4275. Cruisers formed with torpedo attack units will support the attack of these units. In so doing they should avoid being caught between the opposing battle lines and should, once the torpedo attack is finished, regain their assigned stations promptly.

4276. Dispositions "B" and "C" are the wedge and vee formations, respectively, developed primarily for cruiser-destroyer attacks. Under special circumstances they may also be used for battleship-destroyer attacks. During night or low visibility, when contact has been made on enemy forces, and our force is constituted as above, it is often wise to take these dispositions, rather than the "A" disposition.

(a) Dispositions "B" and "C" automatically prescribe the accompanying battle plan if they are to be used against a heavily screened enemy formation.

(b) Dispositions "B" and "C" *do not automatically* prescribe the battle plan if they are to be used against nonscreened or lightly screened enemy forces—especially in night or low visibility attacks. In these cases, as well as in certain employments of the "A" dispositions, the most effective methods of making destroyer attacks have been obtained by the following:

(1) If the disposition is not discovered, to launch the torpedo attack without gunfire support either from the battleships (cruisers) or from the attacking destroyers themselves. If the attacking destroyers are discovered, or when their torpedoes strike the enemy target, to open fire with the guns of the supporting ships; and with own destroyer guns, if the situation so requires.

(2) If the disposition is discovered, to launch the torpedo attack under the supporting fire of the battleships (cruisers). In this case, the attacking destroyers should not open fire unless they themselves are discovered as it may be possible for them to deliver an undetected attack under the confusion caused by fire of own supporting ships.

4277. In certain situations, during night or low visibility where the location of an enemy is known within moderate limits, our force may be early disposed into an approach disposition with the destroyers advanced on each flank of the cruisers along the direction of advance (estimated enemy bearing line). This is equivalent to a scouting line with the support element (cruisers) astern of that line in such location as to be able to give adequate and timely support, if necessary. Then, when contact is made, the destroyers should be directed to attack without delay, without going through the deployment phase. The method of making these attacks would be that indicated in 4276 (b) above. In all of these attacks the heavy ships should be alert to avoid enemy torpedo water and to deny the enemy a suitable torpedo target. This may be accomplished in part by making radical changes of course at frequent intervals.

4278. If our force contains—

(a) Carriers; they shall form with their assigned screens on the disengaged side of the battle line, and by day maintain own and battle line combat patrols; by night, seek to avoid detection by evasive measures, or retire as directed, using night fighters if the situation so requires. Communication between carrier groups and battle line will be maintained by using linking destroyers for communications if necessary.

(b) Train; it shall form with assigned screens on disengaged side of battle line and proceed as directed.

4280. Attack Doctrine for Subordinate Commanders.

4281. Deliberate attacks on defined objectives are normally fully covered by written or signaled plans.

4282. Other attacks comprise attacks of opportunity, undertaken to exploit unforeseen favorable situations, or counterattacks initiated as defensive measures.

4283. Attacks of opportunity are necessarily limited by the peculiarities of each situation, by judgment of subordinate commanders and by the training they have given their personnel. These attacks are also strongly influenced by the ability of the officer in tactical command to exercise effective control under emergency conditions. Offensive action should be initiated by a subordinate when—

(a) The opportunity is clearly favorable.

(b) Exploiting the opportunity will not prejudice the mission of the task force.

(c) The opportunity probably is not apparent to the officer in tactical command.

(d) Lack of time or communication restrictions prohibit informing the officer in tactical command and awaiting his instructions.

4284. In fast developing situations, the officer in tactical command probably will be limited to indicating what he wishes accomplished. This requires that principal subordinates keep him and each other informed, particularly when cooperative action is involved. To this end, the command communication circuits, including very high frequency voice, must be kept clear of all nonvital traffic.

4300. Offensive Air Action.

4310. Doctrine and tactical orders for offensive air action by carrier air groups is contained in air type publications. No special plans are provided herein, since such actions usually develop suddenly from reports of air search, and the officer in tactical command is limited by time and conditions to ordering the attack and specifying the objective.

4311. In the case of a deliberate attack on a fixed objective, a detailed specific plan should be prepared in advance.

No special dispositions or plans are provided herein for surface forces, from which offensive air attacks are launched. If the air attack is launched when our surface forces are not deployed, the cruising dispositions are appropriate. If the air attack is launched after our surface forces are deployed, it is expected that the air component will operate separately on the disengaged side, and will itself be in a suitable protective disposition.

4330. Carrier task groups should remain tactically concentrated. The closeness of this concentration should, of course, be determined by the need for maneuvering searoom when conducting flight operations, whether offensive or routine, and for defense while under air attack. While no definite limiting interval is prescribed between task groups, the task group commanders should bear in mind the necessity for mutual support and for rapid and positive intergroup communications, both visual and very high frequency voice, and should remain sufficiently close to one another to achieve the above without breaking radio silence. This does not include VHF and UHF. Should it be impracticable to comply with the above, linking ships should be used.

4400. Repelling Enemy Attacks. (See War Instructions, chapters 7 and 10.)

4410. Enemy Surface Attack.

4411. Development of surface contacts in good visibility requires no special instructions since deliberate control by the officer in tactical command is the best counter measure. The following pertains to surprise surface contacts in low visibility.

4412. Contact reports should be made in accordance with the communication plan. Commanding officers must decide whether the contact warrants breaking any established condition of silence. As guides:

(a) Any visual or radar contact on an unidentified surface object inside 12,000 yards range from the ship making contact shall be considered an emergency contact.

(b) Reports of radar contacts on rain squalls, clouds, etc., are undesirable, but less so than delay in reporting a valid contact.

(c) A destroyer making first contact or destroyer nearest a cruiser making first contact, shall be prepared to investigate, if so directed. While investigating, the destroyer is exempted from carrying out maneuvers of the disposition as a whole, unless specifically directed to the contrary.

4413. Challenging an enemy is certain to provoke gun and/or torpedo fire. Do not challenge until completely ready to open fire.

...circumstances control procedures after contact has been reported:

(a) If in condition 1, suitably disposed, and seeking action, orders to attack may be instantly expected.

(b) If not in condition 1, not suitably disposed, guarding carriers or train, or seeking to evade action while reaching another objective, an emergency turn away may be expected.

(c) Ships maneuver independently to avoid if torpedoes or wakes are actually sighted. (See subparagraph 4511.)

(d) Illuminate only on order of the officer in tactical command.

(e) Open fire on order of the officer in tactical command or when illuminated or fired upon. (Also see subparagraph 4283.)

4420. Emergency Deployment, Night or Low Visibility.

4421. The most rapid, and, at the same time, the safest method of deploying, in an emergency, a sizeable carrier, transport, oiler, etc., force from a cruising disposition to a battle disposition is to maintain all heavy units on parallel courses until the heavy combatant ships and the screened ships have cleared one another by speed changes. Then the deployment course and battle disposition may be taken. Such a method is somewhat slower than might obtain if all ships dashed immediately to their battle stations, but it has the great advantage of safety, which is a very important item. In its present state of development and use, radar is not a sufficiently efficient device on which to base an emergency low visibility, high-speed deployment. The screened ships should take station in an area in a reverse direction to the enemy bearing line and at the limit of high-frequency voice.

4422. A cruising disposition which is best suited for antiaircraft defense may be entirely unsuitable for emergency deployment against enemy surface attack. The commander should, therefore, make his decision as to what type of disposition he plans to employ based on the probability of surface attack and/or air attack, or vice versa, and should ensure that his plans for emergency deployment are well understood in advance. It is advisable to have preliminary conferences on this matter prior to departure from port, in order that the doctrines for the deployment may be well understood but, failing in this, the commander should notify his subordinate commanders by signal of his deployment plans. (See cruising disposition 3R.) It is also advisable to exercise deployment at every opportunity.

4423. To obtain time to deploy from a cruising disposition, in the case of an emergency contact with a strong enemy surface force, an emergency turn away from the contact will probably be necessary. (See paragraph 4414 (b).) Such an emergency turn away should not only reduce the torpedo menace, but should also give the screened ships, such as transports or aircraft carriers which should not be subjected to gunfire, a chance to clear the disposition while the heavy combatant ships are concentrating for action.

4424. Should the emergency contact be so close as to make the turn away somewhat hazardous, it may be advisable to launch an attack employing light forces with the objective of delaying the enemy and of forcing him to indicate his intentions. Should this be successful, the deployment of own forces should be greatly facilitated.

4425. Should the danger from strong enemy surface forces greatly exceed the danger from air or submarine surface attack, an approach disposition may be more appropriate than a cruising disposition. In this case, the carriers would form with their assigned screens on the side away from the expected direction of enemy approach, at the limit of very high frequency voice radio range in order to maintain communications.

4426. The most difficult part of deployment from a cruising disposition is the "break away." If this is not carefully handled, serious collisions or great confusion may result with the ensuing loss of valuable time or valuable fighting units.

 (1) The following methods have proved successful. They are not to be considered the only methods but are to be considered rather as examples of approved tactics of deployment.

  (a) Should there be a "turn away" first. In this case, after the turn away has been completed, the deployments might then be effected as follows:

   (1) *Fast screened ships* (CV or CVL)—When forming a battle disposition similar to A–1 or A–2. To increase the speed of the screened ships to the maximum maneuvering speed available in order to clear the heavy combatant ships, which in this case, should be on a steady course and not zigzagging. The screening ships assigned to the screened ships should join them as they clear the disposition. The remaining screening ships should concentrate on the heavy combatant ships as designated which, as soon as the screened ships are clear, should deploy on the designated deployment course in the designated battle disposition.

   Once clear of the heavy ships, the screened ships should take station in a reverse direction from the enemy bearing line and at the limit of the very high-frequency voice range.

(2) *Slow screened ships* (transports, tankers):

(a) When forming a battle disposition similar to A-1. To increase the speed of the combatant ships to the maximum maneuvering speed available in order to clear the screened ships, which should continue course and speed. As soon as the heavy combatant ships have cleared, they should take the deployment course and speed and the light forces should take station in the van as called for in the plan.

Meanwhile, the screened ships, once they have been cleared by the heavy combatant ships, should maneuver to keep well clear of the battle disposition by taking station in a reverse direction from the enemy bearing line and at the limit of the very high-frequency voice range. The screening ships assigned to the screened ships should join them as the heavy combatant ships clear.

(b) When forming a battle disposition similar to A-2. To increase the speed of the combatant ships which belong in the battle line and those which belong in the van to the maximum speed available in order to clear the screened ships, which should continue course and speed. These ships should then proceed as in (a) above. To decrease the speed of the combatant ships which belong in the rear of the battle line, or to turn them through as large a turn as necessary to get them quickly into battle stations.

This maneuver should clear the screened ships, which should then proceed as in (a) above.

(b) Should no turn away be required:

(1) Fast screened ships (CV or CVL):

(a) When forming a battle disposition similar to A-1. This may be effected by employing plan (a) (1) above, or by employing (a) (2) (a) as desired.

When forming a battle disposition similar to A-2. This may be effected by employing plan (a) (1) above, or by employing plan (a) (2) (b) as desired.

(2) Slow screened ships (transports, oilers):

(a) When forming a battle disposition similar to A-1. This may be effected by employing plan (a) (2) (a).

(b) When forming battle disposition similar to A-2. This may be effected by employing plan (a) (2) (b) above.

4450. Enemy Submarine Attack. (See War Instructions, chapter 7.)

4451. The necessity for quick and independent avoiding action by screened ships in case a submarine or torpedo is sighted dangerously near is emphasized. The officer in tactical command, may be expected to signal a turn to which ships shall conform as soon as safe to do so. Individual ships close to the point of contact are not to consider this turn signal as mandatory, and are free to maneuver as most expedient to avoid being hit, having due regard to the General Prudential Rule and the obvious necessity for small fast ships to keep clear of larger ones.

4452. Screening Ship Procedures. (See FTP 223.)

Contact reports shall be made as provided in paragraph 4412, plus:

(a) A screening ship making day submarine contact sight or sound, shall hoist a large black pennant, keeping it two-blocked while contact is held; dipped, when contact is lost, and shall take action as follows:

(1) Sonar contacts:

(a) Should sonar contact made be within dangerous torpedo range of the screened ships, the screening ship shall immediately initiate an urgent attack, at at the same time inform the officer in tactical command giving her screen station number along with the bearing and range, and shall then evaluate the contact as submarine, nonsubmarine or doubtful, and make deliberate attacks as the circumstances indicate.

(b) After having attacked, as above, the screening ship shall inform the officer in tactical command giving her screen station number, if necessary, along with the bearing, range and estimated *new evaluation* of the contact

DECLASSIFIED

(c) The officer in tactical command may then, at discretion, based on above evaluation, assign additional ships from the screen to assist the ship making the first contact, or may assign planes from the ASP (antisubmarine patrol) and may order one or more of these ships and planes to remain on the scene of the initial contact until it is felt that danger to the force no longer obtains, or contact cannot be regained.

(d) Should one or more assisting ships be so assigned and have joined in the submarine search or attack, AFIRM and BAKER will normally be used by these units in lieu of the black pennant. (See Art. 1514, FTP 223.)

(e) Should the contact be a sonar contact on a submarine which is not within dangerous torpedo range of the screened ships, the screening ship should develop the contact and should then make deliberate attacks as circumstances indicate. When the screening ship has satisfied herself as to the nature of the contact, she should inform the officer in tactical command as to the location and established evaluation of the contact as prescribed in paragraph (1) above.

(2) Sight Contacts:

(a) Should the contact made be a sight contact, the screening ship should use guns, torpedoes, depth charges, and ramming, as appropriate, to prevent an aimed torpedo shot being fired at the screened ships and to destroy or damage the submarine.

(b) A screening ship making sight contact on a torpedo or torpedo wake should, if in position to do so, drop or throw depth charges with shallow setting near the torpedo to countermine it, and should use guns in an effort to detonate the torpedo or at least to indicate its course to the screened ships. (See subparagraph 4727.)

(c) 1. A screening ship assigned to develop a submarine contact should prosecute the hunt and attack until ordered to regain station in disposition, or until the submarine is definitely sunk. In this case the screening ship or ships should, before the disposition is beyond very high frequency

DECLASSIFIED

4-39

range, request directions from the officer in tactical command as to the number of hours to continue the search should the contact be lost.

2. If the original contact is evaluated non-sub, the screening ship should rejoin, after the disposition is well clear of the contact, but before the disposition is beyond very high frequency voice range.

4453. Airplane Procedure. Contact reports shall be made as provided in communication plan. (In addition see subparagraph 3546.)

4460. Enemy Motor Torpedo Boat Attack.

4461. Enemy motor torpedo boat attacks may be expected when in enemy controlled waters, and especially when in the vicinity of enemy territory suitable for concealing motor torpedo boats from discovery by daylight air reconnaissance. These attacks may be encountered in any of the following forms or combinations thereof:

(a) Low visibility attacks, supported by and coordinated with surface attack, submarine attack, air attack, or combinations thereof.

(b) Low visibility unsupported attacks.

(c) High visibility attacks, supported by and coordinated with surface attack, submarine attack, air attack, or combinations thereof.

(d) High visibility, unsupported attacks, suicidal in their nature.

4462. Repelling enemy motor torpedo boat attacks in *high visibility* requires no special instructions since deliberate control by the officer in tactical command is the best countermeasure. This deliberate control envisages the use of air power, gunfire, and maneuver. Own air power should be used, when possible, to destroy the enemy motor torpedo boats before they come into gun range. If they, nevertheless, succeed in pushing home their attacks, sufficient gunfire should be brought to bear to repel or destroy them before they reach the torpedo launching position, and violent maneuvers at high speed should be resorted to. Under favorable conditions, smoke should prove effective.

4463. Repelling enemy motor torpedo boat attacks in night or *low visibility* requires—

(a) Search.

(1) The employment of antimotor-torpedo-boat pickets. (See paragraph 3271.)

(2) The employment of a low level (about 1,500 feet) air patrol consisting of planes equipped with search radar, very high frequency voice, illuminating flares and float lights. The planes should search in and out in a section

radiating from the center of the disposition extended beyond and between the pickets. The out search should not normally be extended beyond the point where the pickets can no longer range on the search planes; the in search should be terminated when the search planes contact the pickets and establish reorientation.

(b) Action.

 (1) Air Contact:

  (a) A search plane making contact should: (1) Illuminate the motor torpedo boat with flares, (2) mark the extremities of the motor torpedo boat formation with float lights, and (3) should then extend the search to detect, if possible, additional attacking motor torpedo boats. Search planes are often capable of directing other planes to the attacking motor torpedo boats.

  (b) Planes equipped for night offensive operations (night fighters) should attack the motor torpedo boats, prior to their coming within range of the pickets, or of the screening ships of the disposition if no pickets are in use.

  (c) Should no additional motor torpedo boats be located and should the search plane be equipped for offensive action, it should then, unless otherwise directed, attack the most dangerous motor torpedo boat.

  (d) When air search and night fighters are available, pickets will normally endeavor to maintain their picket screens intact in order to give freedom of action to own night fighters. However, should no air search or night fighters be available, pickets should proceed to repel the attack.

 (2) Surface Contact:

  (a) Should the initial contact be made by a picket, that picket should repel the attack, falling back, if necessary, on own screen for support. One or more destroyers from the screen may be ordered to reinforce the picket, as necessary.

  (b) Should the contact be made by a screening ship, not a picket, that ship will not normally leave the screen, but will, instead, while maintaining her station within reasonable limits, take offensive action as necessary. All screening ships which are favorably situated should bring maximum gunfire to bear from all weapons when within effective gun range. It is preferable to open fire if possible before the enemy has closed to within 6,000 yards, and to use HC (high capacity) rather than AP (armor piercing). The HC projectiles with time fuzes should cut fuze settings to the advance range in order to position bursts close to the water.

(3) Effective avoiding maneuvers should be taken for the purpose of bringing the motor torpedo boats astern of the disposition. Individual ships are authorized to employ additional maneuvers, as necessary, to avoid torpedoes. (See paragraph 4511.)

(4) Smoke may also be found effective. (See paragraph 4462.)

(c) Illumination. (See War Instructions, chapter 8, section III.)

(1) Surface ships should not illuminate either with starshell or searchlight for the purpose of detecting motor torpedo boats.

(2) Starshell illumination should be used for control of gunfire only after the attacking motor torpedo boats have been detected and when other methods of fire control are not effective.

4464. Contact reports should be made in accordance with communication plan.

4500. Enemy Air Attack—General. (See War Instructions, chapter 7.)

4510. Experience with carrier task groups in the Pacific has shown that when repelling air attacks, carrier task groups should be maintained tactically concentrated and so disposed as to ensure:

(a) Most effective fighter direction and coverage.

(b) Maximum antiaircraft fire from all weapons.

(c) Mutual support between heavy ships and of heavy ships by the screen.

(d) Effective avoiding maneuvers under broad control by the officer in tactical command, with ships at foci of attacks supplementing signaled maneuvers as required.

4511. The supplemented maneuvers referred to in (d) above are indicated in the following:

An individual ship, a division commander, or a unit commander will maneuver to avoid torpedo attack or bombing attack having due regard for the existing situation and the danger of collision.

(a) This doctrine does not constitute an unrestricted license to individual maneuver. On the contrary, it denotes a definite two-fold responsibility to other ships in company; namely, to contribute a full share to mutual defense, and not to endanger others through bad seamanship.

(b) Although each ship must (and does) have the option of individual avoiding action, lack of restraint exacts heavy penalties. Ships become scattered. Mutual support is lost. Risk of collision is added to the dangers of enemy weapons. Difficulties of reforming, after the attack ends, are multiplied.

(c) However, there are also disadvantages in centralized control. The officer in tactical command may not be aware of an attack developing rapidly at a distance from the flagship, or if aware of it, his conception of the threatened bearing may be less accurate than that of subordinates closer to the spot.

(d) The crux of the situation often is not whether to maneuver, but when. The deleterious effects of radical maneuver are minimized if the officer in tactical command signals the basic turns, all ships start each turn simultaneously in the same direction, and individuals adjust course as need be.

4520. The form of disposition in which air attack is met is of fundamental importance. In general, the best repel-air-attack dispositions give poor antisubmarine protection and are extremely vulnerable to surprise surface attack. The "S" and "V" dispositions with the same first numeral given in appendix I are so related as to permit rapid transposition from one to the other, day or night.

4521. When a force is formed in an antisubmarine disposition and surprise air attack occurs, it should remain in that disposition unless another disposition is ordered.

4522. When a force is in action against comparable enemy surface forces, and a surprise air attack occurs, it shall retain the battle disposition until ordered to change.

4530. Discovery may be avoided by intercepting and destroying enemy snoopers while they are still beyond sight contact from the force or by taking advantage of local areas of bad weather. When a snooper which has made contact is destroyed, an evasive course change is in order, provided the situation permits a detour.

CONFIDENTIAL

4540. If our force is not being continuously tracked, an enemy attack group which is picked up by radar at considerable distances may be avoided, on occasion, by a high speed run on the reverse of the collision course, or by capitalizing on local areas of bad weather.

4550. Forms of enemy air attack which have been encountered or may be expected in the future are:

    (a) Torpedo attack.

    (b) Dive bombing.

    (c) Horizontal bombing.

    (d) Low level bombing.

    (e) Strafing.

    (f) Suicide landings.

    (g) Glider bomb and controlled high angle bomb attacks.

    (h) Glide bombing and rocket attacks.

Each may be employed alone or two or more forms may be coordinated. Several types of planes are capable of executing each form of attack.

4560. Defense measures consist of—

    (a) Destruction of attackers by fighter planes.

    (b) Destruction of attackers by gunfire.

    (c) Forming ships in an antiaircraft disposition.

    (d) Avoiding maneuvers.

    (e) Smoke.

    (f) Evasion through meteorological assistance.

    (g) Balloon barrages.

4561. No line of demarcation is prescribed at which fighter plane action should cease and gunfire take over. Ships shall exercise restraint in opening fire on enemy planes which are being attacked by our fighters. Nevertheless, the law of self-preservation must be respected. Ships will open fire on enemy planes menacing them or the disposition. Our own fighters will pull out when our antiaircraft fire becomes too dangerous.

4562. It may be necessary, during lulls in the enemy attacks, for a carrier to land planes which are out of gas or ammunition, or with wounded personnel. Surface units must be alert to this possibility and withhold fire on own incoming planes.

4563. The use of an antiaircraft disposition which presents the greatest fire power against attacking planes is obvious. The manner of forming such dispositions and their characteristics are indicated in part III.

4564. Smoke is very effective against aircraft especially for slow moving convoys. It has been found in the Mediterranean that for best defense—

(a) Against torpedo and low level bombing attacks. Smoke should be so placed that the horizon on bearing favorable for attack is obscured. In this case the convoy itself need not be obscured from the attacking planes.

(b) Against dive bombers, glide bombers, horizontal bombers. Smoke should be so placed that the convoy is blanketed, but not the escorts.

(c) White smoke is very effective even with the wind direction and atmospheric conditions unsuitable.

(d) Smoke should not be laid prematurely as it may disclose the general location of the convoy to search planes. It should not be laid too late as it may leave the convoy vulnerable to initial attacks.

4565. Evasion through meteorological assistance. The use of thick weather for the avoidance of air attacks of whatever nature is highly recommended. It has been frequently used by all combatants and has repeatedly proved effective. Because of this the close study of "weather maps" by all commanders, while in combat areas, is necessary.

4566. Barrage balloons. These have proven effective for slow speed convoys.

4570. Special day and night features of attack and defense with particular reference to gunfire and avoiding maneuvers are covered in the next two sections, 4600 and 4700.

4580. Contact reports of enemy aircraft shall be in accordance with communication plan. With the enemy definitely aware of the position of the force the benefits of rapid communication on any circuit outweigh any further advantages of radio silence.

4600. Enemy Air Attack—Day.

4610. Torpedo Attack.

4611. Enemy torpedo planes may approach at any altitude. At medium and high altitudes radar detection and fighter interception by low or high combat patrols comprise best defense.

4612. At low altitude they may escape radar detection until close in, whereupon gunfire assumes proportionally greater responsibility. Fire should be opened as soon as planes reach effective range of each battery, and in maximum attainable volume. Japanese planes have attempted to close to as little as 800 yards before dropping torpedoes. They will usually be below 500 feet when passing over or through the screen. Screening ships should make their shots count at this time.

4613. Against day torpedo plane attacks during the approach phase, maneuvers should, in general, turn the formation away from the approaching group of planes, as this increases the time the attacking aircraft are under fire and also the required run of the torpedo. However, once the attack is launched, it is best to turn towards the attacks forward of the beam; away from those abaft the beam. Timing the turn is very important. Turning early may bring about an increase in the number of guns able to bear but also may permit the enemy to change the direction of his attack to another favorable approach; turning late defeats its own purpose.

4620. Dive Bombing Attack.

4621. Dive bombers will usually approach at high altitude, reducing to about 10,000 feet just before starting their dives. Up to the diving point, radar detection and fighter interception are, as in the case of torpedo planes, the best defense.

4622. Maximum volume of fire should be developed by all batteries as planes reach effective range. Alertness in shifting target from a plane which has dropped and is pulling out to others still diving is essential. Ships within 2,000 yards of the one attacked can lend effective support.

4623. Against dive bomber attacks, the turn should be chosen to produce maximum relative wind during the dive of the first plane. Continuing the turn through one or more full circles is effective against remainder.

4630. Horizontal Bomber Attack.

4631. Horizontal bombers usually approach at high altitude and bomb in a tight formation. This altitude is always a compromise between safety, which is seriously affected if the aircraft come in low and are thereby exposed to more devastating antiaircraft fire, and accuracy, which is seriously affected if the aircraft come in high, because of the relative smallness of the targets and their maneuverability. Detection and interception again form the best defense. This type of bombing, especially against naval ships, has markedly decreased in popularity as its effectiveness has diminished, and it will probably be only infrequently used in the future, so long as dive bombing, low level bombing and torpedo attacks are effective.

4632. It is probable that the fire of only the 5-inch or larger antiaircraft guns will be effective. Unless the attackers are being dealt with by our fighters, fire should be opened by all ships in full director control as soon as a solution is obtained and effective range is reached.

4633. Against high altitude horizontal bomber attacks, a radical turn in either direction, commenced as the attackers start their steady dropping run, is effective. Starting to turn as bombers reach the release point is usually too late.

4640. Low Level Bombing Attacks.

4641. These attacks usually come in at about masthead height and endeavor to make low level direct hits. They combine the dangers of torpedo attack with the dangers of the bomb and strafing, and are made, very frequently, at night during moonlight. As it is not possible to distinguish them from torpedo plane attacks, it is wise to treat them as such and turn away unless the direction of attack and limited time available render turning towards them advisable.

4650. Strafing Attacks.

4651. Strafing attacks may be expected from torpedo planes, low level bombers, and dive bombers during or after their primary attacks, and from fighters which accompany them as low cover. The only effective defense is a high volume of well-directed automatic weapons fire.

4660. Suicide Landings.

4661. Many damaged Japanese planes, both with and without bomb loads, have attempted suicide landings on their targets. Several have been successful, and severe damage has resulted. The only effective defense is destruction by gunfire.

4670. Coordinated Attacks.

4671. Against any simultaneous coordinated attack by torpedo planes and other types, the action taken should be that best suited to nullify the torpedo or low level bombing attack.

4680. Glider Bomb and Controlled High Angle Bomb Attacks.

4681. These types of attacks are delivered on ships by aircraft using:

(a) Low altitude release with controlled glide of the bomb, or

(b) High altitude release with a vertical approach of the bomb.

These attacks may be accompanied by diversionary attacks of different types.

4682. (a) To deliver a glide bomb attack the aircraft approaches the target vessel on a parallel or reciprocal course such as to pass 3 to 5 miles on the beam, at an altitude of about 1,800–9,000 feet, releasing the missile when between 70° and 110° on the bow. The glider proceeds on ahead of the aircraft on release and is then turned toward the target.

(b) To deliver a controlled high angle bomb attack a group of three to six planes make a normal high altitude (about 22,000 to 37,000 feet) bombing run, dropping the bomb by use of the high level bombsight. The bomb is then controlled to the target.

4683. Countermeasures against these types of attack consist in jamming of electronic control signals and employing the usual methods of fighter protection, maneuvering, and gunfire. Smoke offers excellent protection, particularly in harbors. Radical maneuvering should be done at highest available speed. Against low level attacks of the glide bomb engage glider with close-in weapons.

4690. Glide Bombing and Rocket Attacks. These attacks are made from medium altitudes at angles of dive less than the nearly vertical angles of the true dive bombing. The angle of dive may vary from about 60° where the defense tactics are similar to those effective against dive bombers to about 30° where the defense tactics are similar to those effective against torpedo planes.

4700. Enemy Air Attack—Night.

4710. Enemy Tactics.

4711. Night aircraft attacks may be made with either torpedoes or bombs. The Japanese have shown a preference for the former, although they have made several successful attacks using low level bombing.

4712. Night aircraft attacks cannot be made without definite knowledge of the position of the target. Every effort should be made, therefore, to destroy any snoopers in the late afternoon and after dark. Night aircraft attacks often employ illumination of the target in more or less degree, but, with improvement in aircraft radar, the need for such illumination may be further reduced in future operations and enemy technique may change owing to their wider use of radar equipped planes.

4713. Torpedo planes require the least illumination for successful attack and have often attacked without artificial illumination. A ship in silhouette appears sufficient. In attacking, the torpedo striking group generally deploys on each side of the target at altitudes between 500 and 1,500 feet. If illumination is employed, a snooper then flies past the target dropping flares. Groups of one or two torpedo planes, which are in a favorable position, attack. In moonlight and twilight, planes may approach very low over the marker. The average dropping altitude under these conditions appears to be about 50 feet. After dropping, planes speed up and get clear of the formation at maximum speed.

4714. Night bombing may be done by horizontal, glide, or low level bombing. The first is the conventional day attack from low altitudes; the second is a shallow dive attack; while the third is similar to the torpedo attack except the bomb is released very near the side of the ship from a low altitude. For the first two types of attack, good illumination is required for the bombing plane to see the target from medium altitudes. The low level bombing attack requires about the same illumination as a torpedo attack.

4715. The enemy often use dim float lights to mark target course and reference points. They also often use brighter lights for illumination and silhouette. These brighter lights are provided by high candlepower parachute flares, which provide intense illumination, and which are generally dropped from altitudes of 2,000 feet or less, and are reported to burn from 3 to 8 minutes.

4720. Defensive Tactics—Night.

4721. Defense against air attack at night differs from day mainly in that primary reliance at night is on antiaircraft fire power and maneuvers instead of on fighter planes unless night fighters are available. The defense must come from one or a combination of the following factors:

(a) Concealment prior to the attack.
(b) Disruption of attack by night fighters.
(c) Gunfire.
(d) Maneuvers.
(e) Concealment during attacks.
(f) Harassing of enemy airfields (interdiction bombing and intruder missions).
(g) Jamming enemy radar equipment.

4722. When night air attack is expected, every effort should be made to throw off the enemy. This may be done by making radically evasive course changes, by seeking cover of bad weather areas, and by launching night fighters to shoot down any troublesome snoopers.

4723. Night fighters have effectively broken up night air attacks. They should not be vectored within gunfire range of the formation as the resultant restriction on ships' gunfire may permit hostile planes to press their attacks home unopposed. The control of the fighter director for the night fighters should be as prescribed in part VI. In making a decision as to whether or not to use night fighters in their present state of development, the officer in tactical command should weigh therein the hazards of recovery of the planes, the necessity for remaining on a course into the wind for this purpose, and the fact that at present the primary means of defense against night torpedo plane or low level bombing attack making an approach on a disposition is by timely radical maneuvers and by gunfire of ships.

4724. All ships should open fire with radar controllable batteries as soon as good set-ups are obtained, unless otherwise directed. Ships should never open fire unless computers have full radar or partial radar solutions (modified altitude) or unless the target is in sight. The 5″ or larger antiaircraft battery firing flashless powder and using mixed fuzes is the primary defense against aircraft at night as well as at other times. When there are only snoopers or flare planes present and it is evident that the force is being tracked, the 5″ or larger antiaircraft guns should open fire at a range of from 10,000–12,000 yards.

4725. Fire with automatic weapons may be opened only when the target is in sight, except that the 40-mm. guns may be fired in radar control from their own or from the 5″ or larger antiaircraft directors when the target is within 4,400 yards and is attacking.

4726. Success against enemy twilight or night torpedo attacks has shown that, among other things, high speed and repeated emergency turns have played an important part. In obtaining this success, it has been shown that it is normally wise to turn either away or towards float markers and flares. As attacks are pressed home, it is advisable to turn away from the closest plane; then, soon afterwards, to turn away from the next closest plane, unless the direction of the attack and the limited time available make turning towards them advisable. These maneuvers should be made at frequent and irregular intervals. However, in maneuvering, it must be borne in mind that continuous use of rudder results in drastic speed reduction which is disadvantageous because it markedly reduces the advance along the base course, and because it increases the chance of being hit.

4727. Any ship observing torpedoes being dropped or torpedo tracks in the water must immediately broadcast this information, including relative position and course of torpedo and reporting ship's call. In view of the fact that enemy torpedoes may now be of the acoustic type, and in further view of the fact that the location of an approaching torpedo may not be known and generally is not known to the probable target, it is recommended that any ship sighting a torpedo open fire at it using the automatic weapons. This fire not only will indicate the track of the torpedo, but may also detonate it.

In order to neutralize and harass enemy airfields during darkness, consideration should be given to the use of intruder fighters and interdiction bombing. Such action should prevent use of these airfields by the enemy for night attack missions.

4731. Destroyers and cruisers be prepared to use smoke, either funnel, chemical, or both, as the officer in tactical command directs. Funnel smoke, when used, should be laid between the probable heavy ship target and the source of illumination. This will destroy the silhouetting value of the illumination without depriving the target ship of all possibility of sighting planes, which are attacking "up-light," and taking them under visually controlled automatic weapons fire.

4732. Gunnery open-fire instructions presented in this section do not apply when, for tactical reasons, additional risk of attack must be accepted to increase chances for evasion, as for example, when a surface force is attempting to reach a bombardment or mining position undetected. In these circumstances ships must be apprised in advance of the desires of the officer in tactical command, and adhere to them fully unless actually attacked.

4800. Damaged Ships.

4810. A damaged ship shall report to the officer in tactical command at first opportunity by coded message, or enciphered general signal giving extent of damage, remaining speed and offensive power.

4820. Procedures.

4821. Continue on station if able to do so. If necessary to leave station, do so, if possible, without crossing the line of fire or hampering the movements of undamaged ships. If own movements are not under control, and it is possible to do so, warn ships which may be embarrassed thereby.

4822. If capable of proceeding at reduced speed, trail the disposition or proceed toward assigned rendezvous or nearest friendly base as judgment indicates.

4823. If towing is required, complete preparations as rapidly as possible.

4830. Exploit any opportunity to destroy enemy cripples.

4840. Prosecute damage-control measures with utmost diligence and tenacity. Many ships, in this war, enemy as well as our own, which would otherwise have been lost, have been saved by the heroic and intelligent conduct of the ships' personnel.

DECLASSIFIED

PART V

SPECIAL OPERATIONS

5000. GENERAL.

5100. Sortie and Entry. (See War Instructions chapter 11.)

5110. Sortie and entry procedures depend upon the composition of the task organization, geographical considerations, and probability of enemy opposition of various forms. In most cases special instructions will be required. Typical sortie and entry plans are contained in the General Tactical Instructions. These may be used as a guide modified for the special conditions of the port.

5120. Channel formations for sortie and entry shall be provided by task force commanders. (See paragraph 125 of foreword.)

5200. Fueling at Sea.

5210. Fueling at sea plans will vary to suit the composition of the force and circumstance existent at the time.

5220. Responsible commanders shall invariably include in their fueling plans a directive for action to be taken in case enemy contact is made during fueling.

5230. The following instructions are mandatory for all fueling operations, and need not be repeated in fueling plans.

    5231. Ships receiving fuel shall—

        (a) Discharge water ballast, completing just prior to indicated fueling time.

        (b) Shift oil, consistent with damage control limitations, so that reception rate will be a maximum.

        (c) Inform ship supplying fuel of requirements when time and signal traffic permit. Destroyers indicate provisions, supplies, and special items needed.

        (d) Display AFIRM if towline is desired; AFIRM TACK NEGAT if towline is not desired.

        (e) Display BAKER while actually receiving fuel.

        (f) Fifteen minutes prior to casting off, display PREP.

        (g) Inform officer in tactical command and ship delivering fuel the amount of fuel received.

5232. Ships supplying fuel shall—

(a) Shift oil as necessary, consistent with damage control limitations, to insure expeditious discharge.

(b) Heat oil as necessary.

(c) Display BAKER during actual pumping.

(d) Make necessary deviations from signalled fueling course and speed to counteract wind and sea conditions. Notify officer in tactical command if changes are so radical they will carry the fueling unit beyond protection of the screen before fueling is completed.

(e) If equipment or personnel are to be transferred, the necessary equipment must be ready. Normally the ship supplying fuel will furnish this equipment.

(f) It is advisable, whenever practicable during fueling, to transfer empty powder containers, empty cases, etc., to the tankers. Live ammunition for 5″ or smaller guns has been transferred in this manner from tankers to combatant ships.

5233. Ships not fueling zigzag independently behind screen unless fueling plan or orders prescribe otherwise. In order to expedite fueling, screening ships scheduled to fuel first should be astern of their respective fueling ships, ready to go alongside, 10 minutes prior to the scheduled time. Screening ships in the sonar screen which are to follow others in fueling should be relieved on station by the latter before proceeding to fuel unless there are sufficient screening ships available to obviate this necessity in which case they should proceed to their fueling stations upon the hoisting of "PREP" by the ship fueling.

5234. All ships not assigned definite guard ship duties maintain continuous surface detection radar all around search for periscopes.

5240. The technical aspects of fueling at sea are covered in Fueling at Sea Instructions, U. S. Fleet, (Cominch P-2).

5300. Security in Port.

5310. The senior officer present afloat in port shall be responsible for and issue the necessary instructions for the security of units in company. If at an established base, the senior officer present afloat shall consult local command and insure that his orders complement but do not abrogate existing orders for the port.

5311. When a commander in chief is present, the next senior shall function as senior officer present afloat unless otherwise directed.

5400. Rescue Facilities for Downed Aviators. (Refer to War Instructions, chapter 5, section VI.)

5410. The rescue of aviators downed at sea is a matter of unquestioned importance. Rescue service in carrier task force operations normally is provided by destroyers, submarines, and seaplanes, usually in conjunction with carrier aircraft. Fast coordinated action of these participating agencies by a central authority is frequently the first essential of a successful rescue. The officer in tactical command should provide such a central agency within his command and should insure that operation plans adequately provide for all rescue services.

5411. When submarines are assigned lifeguard duties, rescue procedure should be in accordance with the effective communication plan and doctrine.

5412. When seaplanes are assigned lifeguard duties, an appropriate number of battleship and cruiser planes should be maintained in condition ELEVEN during the carrier strikes to provide the rescue facilities. The decision to use these shipbased aircraft should be based on a number of factors, among the most important being wind and sea conditions in the rescue area, the range and speed of the rescue seaplanes, and the enemy activity in the rescue area. Likewise, the latest Point Option data should be furnished the ship(s) from which the rescue aircraft are to be launched. (See paragraph 3522.)

5413. When destroyers are assigned lifeguard duties, it is usually the result of a crashed plane, or a forced landing, in the vicinity of the formation, but it may be because of a similar accident in a more distant area. In the former case, the nearest destroyer should take prompt action to effect rescue of personnel in accordance with current doctrine; in the latter case, the rescue destroyer should be assigned by the officer in tactical command. In assigning this destroyer, the officer in tactical command should, at the same time, notify all carriers of her special mission, in order that pilots may be briefed as to the location of friendly ships detached from the formation. Destroyers normally should not be sent on rescue missions which require that they stop within effective range of active shore defense positions.

5414. Continuous fighter cover, whenever practicable, should be provided for the downed pilot, and for the rescue mediums, whether submarine, seaplane or destroyer.

5500. Photography.

5510. The importance of obtaining good photographic coverage of present and future enemy physical objectives, plus actual proof of damage inflicted on the enemy cannot be stressed too greatly. The planning and success of future operations depends greatly on adequate photographic coverage.

DECLASSIFIED

Where appropriate, naval directives shall include a definite plan, with alternates for inclement weather, for the coordinated use of available photographic facilities, aerial as well as submarine. Periscope photography should be used when deemed necessary. Consideration must be given to the limitations of aircraft or submarines involved, the opposition (aircraft, gunfire, navigational hazard, local control of the air over the target, etc.) to be expected, and to the fact that photographs are of no value unless promptly delivered to ships and/or bases which require them.

5512. Commands charged with obtaining aerial photographic reconnaissance should refer frequently to the latest instructions thereon.

5513. Based on the limitations of the photographic aircraft available and the distances involved, these planes should ordinarily be employed as follows:

(a) Heavy photographic aircraft to obtain high altitude vertical photographic coverage.

(b) Carrier based photographic aircraft to obtain—

(1) "Dicing mission" (Trimetrogon) of all beach lines;

(2) Complete vertical trimetrogon coverage of entire area;

(3) Large scale low altitude obliques of principal areas.

(c) Where carriers make strikes beyond the range of heavy photo squadrons, complete vertical coverage of the area by carrier planes will have to be added to (b) above as subparagraph (4).

5514. Where enemy fighter interception and/or intense antiaircraft fire may be expected, heavy photographic squadrons should not be required to go below 20,000 feet. This will permit vertical coverage of the objective and some obliques on an "opportunity" basis, with a long focal length camera. As possibility of enemy interception and antiaircraft fire decreases, the altitude of photography may be reduced. On long range missions where enemy fighter interception is certain, the photographic planes should be escorted by long range bombers.

5515. When carriers are making a strike on an area not covered previously every effort must be made to obtain the complete photographic coverage as outlined in subparagraph 5513. Of particular importance is the coverage required by subparagraph 5513 (b) as a second opportunity may not be available prior to landing of troops in amphibious operations. If the weather is inclement the best possible coverage must be obtained by using the trimetrogon installations.

5516. Photographs satisfactory for photographic interpretation usually cannot be taken within 2 hours of sunrise or sunset. To obtain the best estimate of damage inflicted by aerial strikes or bombardment, photographs must be taken after the strike or bombardment has been completed and after the smoke has cleared away.

DECLASSIFIED

DECLASSIFIED

5517. All negatives must be forwarded in accordance with current directives as soon as they have served the immediate needs of the officer in tactical command.

5600. Minesweeping Screens.

5610. Moored Mines.

5611. Minesweeping of moored mines is considered necessary when the depth of water is less than 500 fathoms. This is accomplished through the employment of minesweepers operating normally in minesweeping formations called "minesweeping screens." There are two general types of these screens. These are the inverted Vee as shown in diagram 3–C, appendix I, and a straight line formation. The inverted Vee formation gives best protection to the minesweepers but requires almost twice as many ships to cover the same area as does the straight line formation. It is normally employed in one of three formations:

(a) In a single large inverted Vee which sweeps ahead of the disposition, where the center minesweeper has both sweeping wires streamed and all other minesweepers have but one sweeping wire streamed.

(b) In a multi Vee formation where small Vees of five minesweepers each sweep ahead of each column of the screened disposition.

(c) In a multi Vee formation where Vees of three minesweepers each sweep ahead of the disposition with the flanks of the Vees overlapping.

5612. For a high-speed force the only minesweepers available are the high-speed minesweepers (DMS). These with 300 fathoms of sweeping wire streamed on one side, only sweep a path of 160 yards width at about 12 knots, and a minimum of 75 yards at 23.5 knots. Therefore, the screening distance, allowing for 25-yard overlap, should vary from 135 yards in the former case to 50 yards in the latter case. However, as echo ranging is not effective at speeds above 22 knots, minesweepers which are also echo ranging, should not be operated at speeds in excess of that figure. In this connection it is important to note that mines can only be swept up at slow speed, and that all that can be effected at high speed is exploratory sweeping. This exploratory sweeping will indicate whether or not mines are in the area. Once mines have been discovered the sweepers should slow to about 10 knots in order to clear an area through the minefield. Minesweeping screens

DECLASSIFIED

should therefore be stationed a distance of at least 2 miles in advance of the leading heavy ship of the force screened in order to provide opportunity for the force screened, in event mines are discovered, to reverse course or otherwise retire until clearance of mines has been accomplished.

5613. The above minesweeping gear will be effective against moored influence types as well as against moored contact types.

5614. For a slow force the minesweeping may be done by the above high-speed minesweepers or by the standard minesweepers (AM) or by the motor minesweepers (YMS).

5620. Influence mines (ground).

5621. Influence type ground mines include mines actuated by magnetic, acoustic, and other types of influence mechanisms. These mines should be swept for when their presence is suspected and when the depth of water is less than 30 fathoms.

5622. The technique of sweeping such mines is set forth in FTP 204, wherein is tabulated the width of swept paths for various field strengths and various depths.

5623. Magnetic mines may be swept by actuating their mine firing mechanism through the use of a magnetic field set up in electric "tails" streamed astern of a thoroughly degaussed minesweeper.

5624. Owing to the size of the magnetic minesweeper gear and characteristics of magnetic sweeping, the speed of the minesweepers is limited as follows:

    (a) DMS to 16 knots.

    (b) AM to 12 knots.

    (c) YMS to 8 knots.

5625. Since acoustic mines are fired ahead of the minesweeper, the sweeping speed is limited to 12 knots to permit the firing of the mine before it is dangerously close to the minesweeper.

5630. Drifting mines.

5631. Drifting mines of various types may be encountered. These include chemical horn, galvanic (antenna or contact), influence, and inertia. In general these mines are difficult to sweep but may be sighted and destroyed by gunfire. The antenna type of drifting mine can be swept by minesweeping gear similar to that used for sweeping moored mines.

5640. Minesweeping Interval.

5641. The minesweeping interval will depend upon composition of the force screened and the character of the waters through which the disposition will pass. It should be noted that minesweeping gear for sweeping moored mines can be employed simultaneously with the gear for sweeping acoustic mines with very satisfactory results. In this connection it should be further noted that the minesweeping gear for sweeping magnetic mines can also be used at this same time but the results in this case may not be entirely satisfactory.

5642. In event the swept channel is to be marked, provision should be made to assign danlaying vessels (for laying Danbuoys) to positions on the flank of the sweeping formation.

5700. Area Smoke Screens.

5710. Should it be necessary to cover an area with smoke, the method described in subparagraph 5711, using the army type smoke float, has been found highly effective. It is particularly useful in those areas where the wind is off shore, and where larger vessels might not be able to operate successfully. It results in a smoke screen of fairly uniform density.

5711. Method. A sufficient number of small boats, each adequately supplied with smoke floats, should be directed to proceed to a position 1,000 yards to 1,500 yards to windward of the area to be screened. Each of these small boats should be assigned an arc approximately 1,000 yards in length. On the order to "make smoke" each boat should proceed along its assigned arc and should drop a "smoke float" about every 100 yards. On reaching the end of its arc each boat should reverse its course and should repeat the above performance but should, in this case, drop its float midway between the smoke floats previously dropped.

5720. All ships in the area should also be directed to smoke in order to insure that the smoke laid is of the the heaviest density practicable.

5800. Area Screening and Special Purpose Screens.

5810. The following screening plan is designed to screen an area. It has been used effectively for covering a sortie or an entrance, and for screening transports and other ships at anchor or lying to.

5811. The basis of the screen is a figure 8 patrol track for each screening ship. Each patrol track covers a certain definite portion of the screening arc. The screening arc should normally be located on the limiting locus of favorable torpedo firing points for the torpedoes carried by enemy submarines in that area. It may, in some cases, be an arc of a circle, or a complete circle, but not necessarily so, depending of course, on the shape of the disposition to be screened and on the geographical characteristics of the area. Patrol stations, therefore, may be designated by a given arc of a circle, by grid coordinates or by any other convenient means.

5812. Method of Patrol. Each screening ship should pass through the midpoint of its patrol going in the same direction at the same time as the others. For convenience these times are on the hour, and each 15 minutes thereafter. For a patrol speed of 15 knots this gives a patrol arc of approximately 7,000 yards. Should it be necessary to patrol at less speed, the length of the patrol arc should be changed but *not the time*.

5813. Screening ships should adjust their stations on the screen to maintain formation and to thus insure that the arcs of the screen are rotated in the same direction at the same time. Where heavy currents are encountered, this may require considerable readjustment for the various screening ships.

5814. The direction of rotation is always viewed from *inside* the screen, The screening ships should pass through the *midpoints* of their patrols on the hour and half hour rotating the screen to the right, i. e., clockwise; and on the quarter-hour and three-quarters-hour rotating the screen to the left, i. e., counterclockwise. This is so important that every effort should be made to meet it. However, the patrol should not be "cut short" to accomplish it. Instead, any adjustment necessary should be made by speed changes.

5815. Prior to forming the above sonar screen the entire area to be enclosed should be thoroughly sonar swept to insure that no enemy submarines are inside the screen at its moment of forming.

5816. Ships, being screened, should be careful not to approach the sonar screen nearer than 3,000–4,000 yards. Should they close the screen nearer than this they may be within the range of enemy submarines which may be lying just beyond sonar range of own screen.

5817. All available screening ships should, if practicable, not be used in the outer screen. It is wise in this case to maintain several ships as spares for replacing screening ships which have to leave the screening line for any reason.

5818. If many screening ships are available, it is wise to form more than one sonar screen at an interval of about one and one-half times the assured sonar range. If insufficient screening ships are available, it may be necessary to contact the screen, which will reduce the area being screened, and will increase the danger of effective submarine attack.

5819. All screening ships should echo range in accordance with standard doctrine. (See paragraph 1200, FTP 223.)

5819.1. During daylight all screening ships should carefully coordinate navigational fixes with radar fixes so that accurate station keeping can be maintained after dark.

5819.2. During darkness, if sufficient screening ships are available, radar pickets should normally be used against surface attacks.

5819.3. All ships of the screening type, not assigned other duties, should be directed to report to the screen commander for assignment upon entering the screened area.

DECLASSIFIED

5820. Special Purpose Screen—Rotating A/A and A/S Screen Around Slow Speed Units.

5821. Asymmetrical Rotating Screen. By eliminating the requirement of complete symmetry about the screened units and accepting the slight unbalance of protection which this elimination implies, it is possible to construct a rotating screen which has none of the defects of the hexagonal screen but on the contrary possesses the simplicity of (1) a constant speed for all ships in the screen, (2) all legs steamed are of equal length, (3) once on station ships have only normal station keeping difficulties and ships remain properly spaced, (4) compensation for variation in speed of screened unit is simple.

5822. The rotating screens are presented in two different sets employing speed ratios of 3:1, 4:1, and 5:1. One affords protection inside or upon a circle of radius 500 yards, the other inside or upon a circle of 1,000 yards. In each set the screen moves around the screened unit at a distance which averages about 2,500 yards from the center of the unit screened.

5823. Provided that the speed-ratio is preserved, then the following facts are true:

(a) Adjustment of the screen to compensate for variation in speed of the screened unit may be made by varying only the speed of the screening ships. It is not necessary to steam different courses or turn upon different ranges or bearings.

(b) The screening speed may be changed at any desired instant without repositioning the screening ships and without regard to the positions of the screening ships at that instant.

5824. If the speed-ratio is changed, then it is necessary to reposition the screening ships before beginning screening operations with the new speed-ratio.

5825. From examining the tables it will be noted that for 8 knots or greater in the case of the screened unit the speed required of the screen is excessive. Under these circumstances the formation of a standard screen becomes practicable in which the patrolling of station in the usual manner is in order.

5826. Sonar Search Plan with a Rotating Screen. The principle to be observed in the sonar search with a rotating screen is that the search should be concentrated outboard. On legs ahead of the screened unit where antisubmarine protection is most important the search outboard will be in an area clear of interference from wakes. On the legs astern of the screened unit the efficiency of the sonar search outboard is greatly reduced by wakes. However, for a submarine to reach a firing position from astern considerable submerged speed will be required; therefore, sonar operators should be alert for high doppler somewhat masked by prevalent wake echoes. The sonar search should be conducted relative to the heading of the screening ship and not relative to the base course of the screened unit.

5827. Specific Sonar Searches.

    (a) If the number of screening ships is five or less, then the search should be from broad on the outboard quarter to the ships heading then slew aft to broad on the inboard bow and search forward to the ships heading. Slew aft to broad on the outboard quarter and repeat.

    (b) If the number of screening ships is six or more then the search should be from broad on the outboard quarter forward through the ships heading to 20° on the inboard bow, slew aft to broad on the outboard quarter and repeat.

5828. Antisubmarine protection is not satisfactory with less than 4–5 screening ships.

5-22

DECLASSIFIED

ROTATING ... AROUND SLOW SPEED UNITS — SPEED RATIO 3:1
RADIUS OF PROTECTED CIRCLE 500 YARDS
LENGTH OF LEG 2400 YARDS ;
ROTATING A/A AND A/S SCREEN NUMBER ONE

COURSE TABLE

LEG	0-1	1-2	2-3	3-4	4-5	5-6	6-0
COURSE RELATIVE TO BASE COURSE	090	180	270	314	344	017	045

SPEED-TIME TABLE

SPEED (Knots) OF SCREENED UNITS	3	4	5	6	7	8
SPEED (Knots) OF SCREEN	9	12	15	18	21	24
TIME (Mins.) ON LEG	8	6	4½	4	3½	3

SPACING TABLE — INITIAL STATIONS

NUMBER OF SCREENING SHIPS	1	2	3	4	5	6	7	8	9
1	000								
	2400								
2	000	204							
	2400	2100							
3	000	139	257						
	2400	2500	2200						
4	000	109	204	279					
	2400	2500	2100	2300					
5	000	082	168	237	294				
	2400	2400	2300	2200	2200				
6	000	066	139	204	257	304			
	2400	2600	2500	2100	2200	2200			
7	000	056	124	180	229	270	311		
	2400	2900	2900	2400	2300	2400	2300		
8	000	050	109	157	204	244	279	318	
	2400	2700	2500	2300	2100	2200	2300	2200	
9	000	046	095	139	185	223	257	288	323
	2400	2600	2400	2500	2300	2200	2200	2200	2250

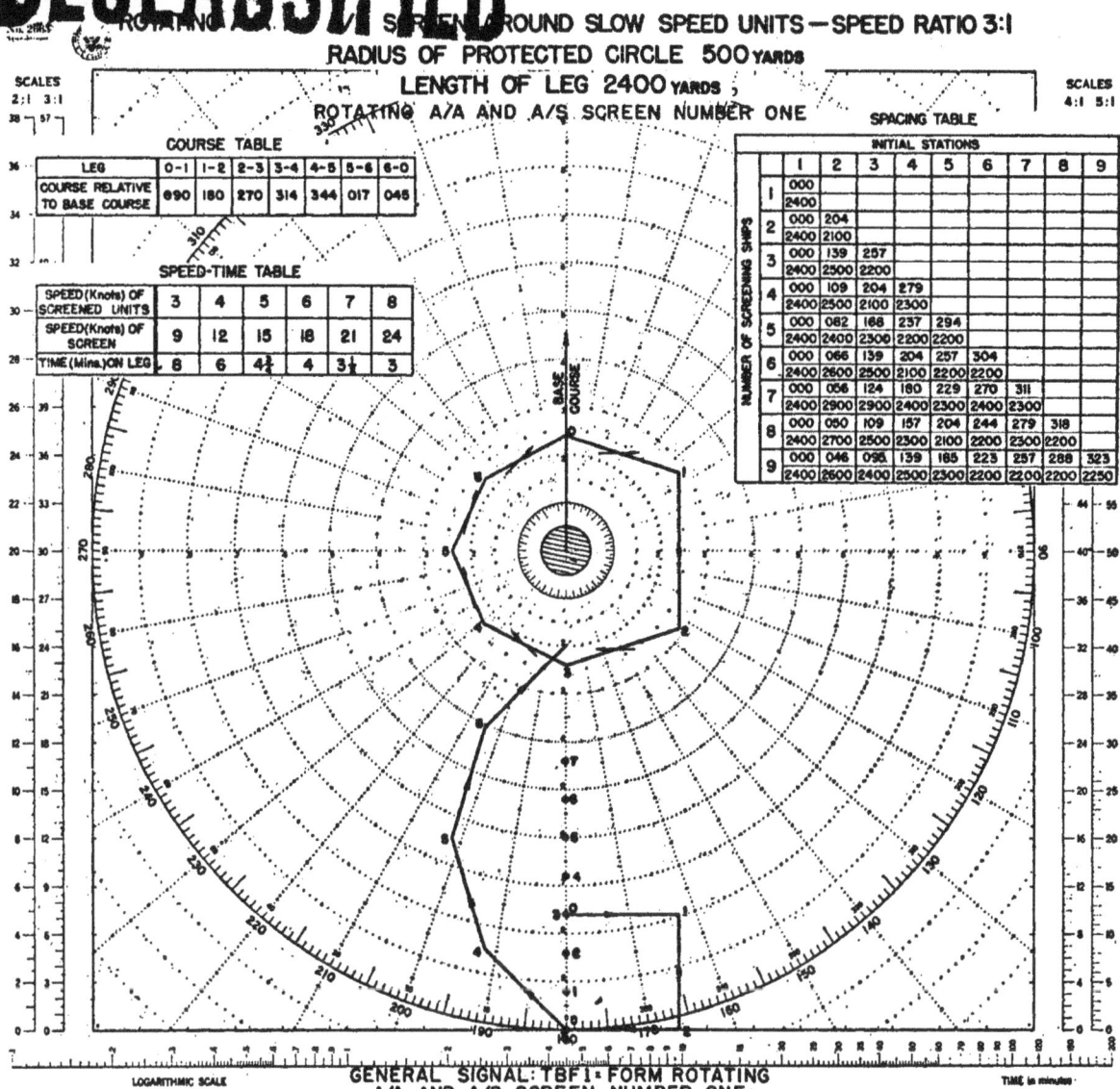

GENERAL SIGNAL: TBF1: FORM ROTATING
A/A AND A/S SCREEN NUMBER ONE

FIGURE 16 A

EXPLANATION OF DIAGRAM

The relative plot indicates a screen formed in an unsymmetrical seven-sided figure. Regardless of the number of ships available the standard seven-sided figure is used and ships are assigned station in accordance with the "Spacing Table." The navigational plot for the ship assigned to station one is shown below the relative plot. The navigational plot indicates the movement of station one for one complete 360° clockwise cycle. This plot indicates that the navigational distance traveled on each leg during the cycle is the same even though the relative distance varies. The navigational movement of the screened unit along the base course is shown by points plotted on the track and labeled 0 through 7.

SPACING TABLE—USE OF

Given the number of screening ships and a station assignment in the screen move vertically down the "Initial Stations" column until it intersects the horizontal row designating "Number of Screening Ships." At this intersection the top three figures indicate the relative bearing of the initial position of the station from the base course line and the bottom four figures the initial distance in yards from the center of the screened circle.

(REVERSE BLANK)

DECLASSIFIED

~~DECLASSIFIED~~

ROTATING A/A AND A/S SCREEN — ROUND SLOW SPEED UNITS — SPEED RATIO 4:1
RADIUS OF PROTECTED CIRCLE 500 YARDS
LENGTH OF LEG 2400 YARDS
ROTATING A/A AND A/S SCREEN NUMBER TWO

SCALES 2:1 3:1

SCALES 4:1 5:1

COURSE TABLE

LEG	0–1	1–2	2–3	3–4	4–5	5–6	6–0
COURSE RELATIVE TO BASE COURSE	097	180	263	302	343	017	058

SPEED-TIME TABLE

SPEED (Knots) OF SCREENED UNITS	3	4	5	6
SPEED (Knots) OF SCREEN	12	16	20	24
TIME (Mins.) ON LEG	6	4½	3½	3

SPACING TABLE

NUMBER OF SCREENING SHIPS	INITIAL STATIONS								
	1	2	3	4	5	6	7	8	9
1	000 2400								
2	000 2400	207 2300							
3	000 2400	136 2400	257 2600						
4	000 2400	107 2500	207 2300	279 2700					
5	000 2400	083 2400	168 2300	238 2600	294 2600				
6	000 2400	066 2600	138 2400	207 2300	257 2600	303 2600			
7	000 2400	058 2800	122 2800	180 2400	230 2700	270 2800	310 2700		
8	000 2400	051 2600	107 2500	158 2200	207 2300	246 2600	279 2700	316 2600	
9	000 2400	046 2500	094 2400	138 2400	186 2300	225 2500	257 2600	288 2600	320 2500

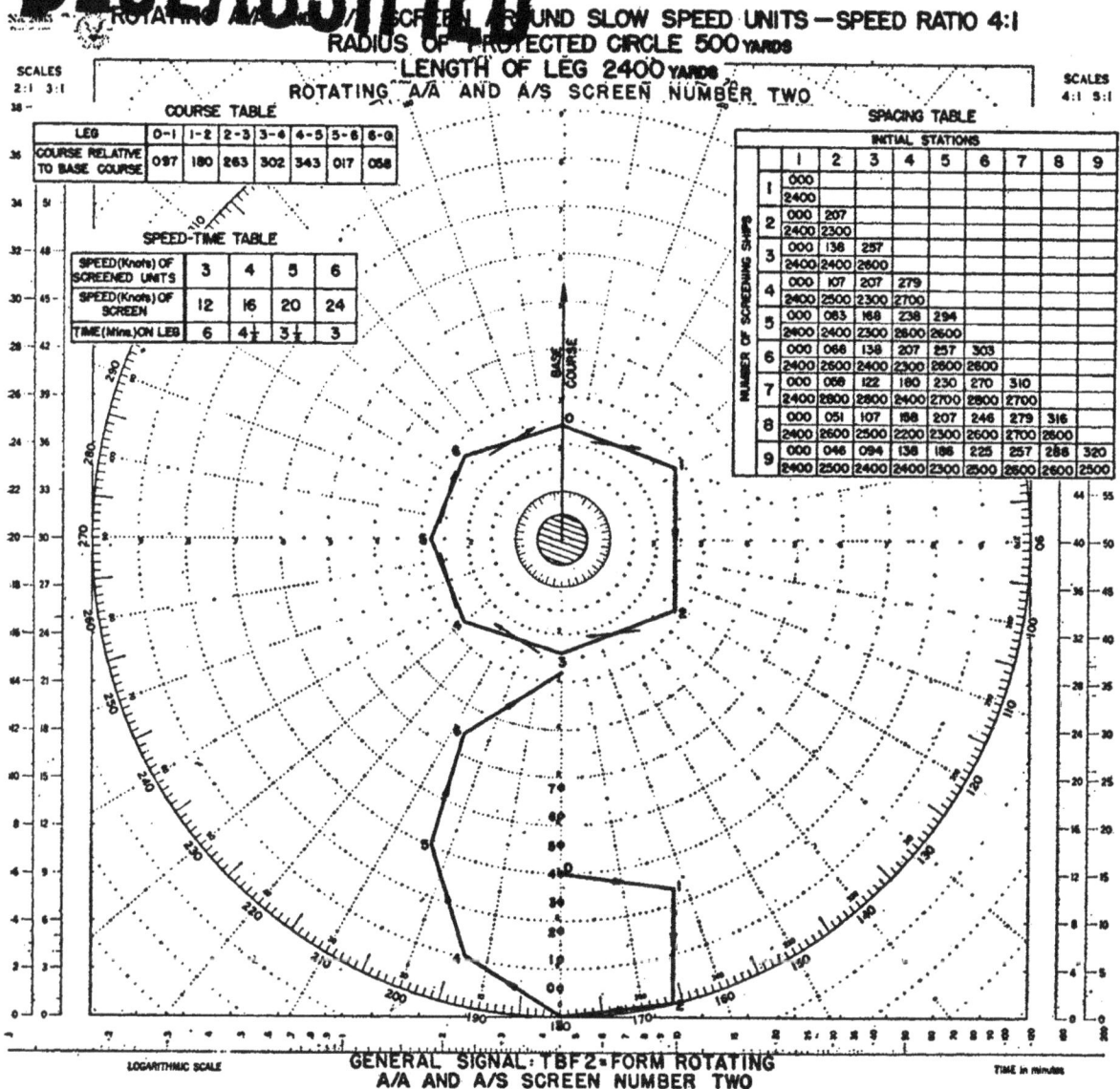

LOGARITHMIC SCALE

GENERAL SIGNAL: TBF2-FORM ROTATING A/A AND A/S SCREEN NUMBER TWO

TIME in minutes

FIGURE 16 B

EXPLANATION OF DIAGRAM

The relative plot indicates a screen formed in an unsymmetrical seven-sided figure. Regardless of the number of ships available the standard seven-sided figure is used and ships are assigned station in accordance with the "Spacing Table." The navigational plot for the ship assigned to station one is shown below the relative plot. The navigational plot indicates the movement of station one for one complete 360° clockwise cycle. This plot indicates that the navigational distance traveled on each leg during the cycle is the same even though the relative distance varies. The navigational movement of the screened unit along the base course is shown by points plotted on the track and labeled 0 through 7.

SPACING TABLE—USE OF

Given the number of screening ships and a station assignment in the screen move vertically down the "Initial Stations" column until it intersects the horizontal row designating "Number of Screening Ships." At this intersection the top three figures indicate the relative bearing of the initial position of the station from the base course line and the bottom four figures the initial distance in yards from the center of the screened circle.

(REVERSE BLANK)

CHANGE NO. 1

~~DECLASSIFIED~~

DECLASSIFIED

ROTATING A/A AND A/S SCREEN AROUND SLOW SPEED UNITS—SPEED RATIO 5:1
RADIUS OF PROTECTED CIRCLE 500 YARDS
LENGTH OF LEG 2400 YARDS

ROTATING A/A AND A/S SCREEN NUMBER THREE

COURSE TABLE

LEG	0-1	1-2	2-3	3-4	4-5	5-6	6-0
COURSE RELATIVE TO BASE COURSE	101	180	259	295	346	015	054

SPEED-TIME TABLE

SPEED (Knots) OF SCREENED UNITS	2	3	4	5
SPEED (Knots) OF SCREEN	10	15	20	25
TIME (Mins.) ON LEG	$7\frac{1}{2}$	$4\frac{1}{2}$	$3\frac{1}{2}$	3

SPACING TABLE

INITIAL STATIONS

NUMBER OF SCREENING SHIPS	1	2	3	4	5	6	7	8	9
1	000 / 2400								
2	000 / 2400	208 / 2400							
3	000 / 2400	138 / 2400	257 / 2700						
4	000 / 2400	107 / 2400	208 / 2400	290 / 2700					
5	000 / 2400	168 / 2400	237 / 2300	294 / 2600	/ 2700				
6	000 / 2400	067 / 2600	138 / 2400	208 / 2400	257 / 2700	304 / 2800			
7	000 / 2400	058 / 2600	122 / 2600	180 / 2400	230 / 2900	270 / 2900	310 / 2900		
8	000 / 2400	052 / 2600	107 / 2400	157 / 2200	208 / 2400	246 / 2700	280 / 2700	314 / 2700	
9	000 / 2400	048 / 2600	093 / 2380	138 / 2400	186 / 2300	226 / 2800	257 / 2700	288 / 2700	319 / 2600

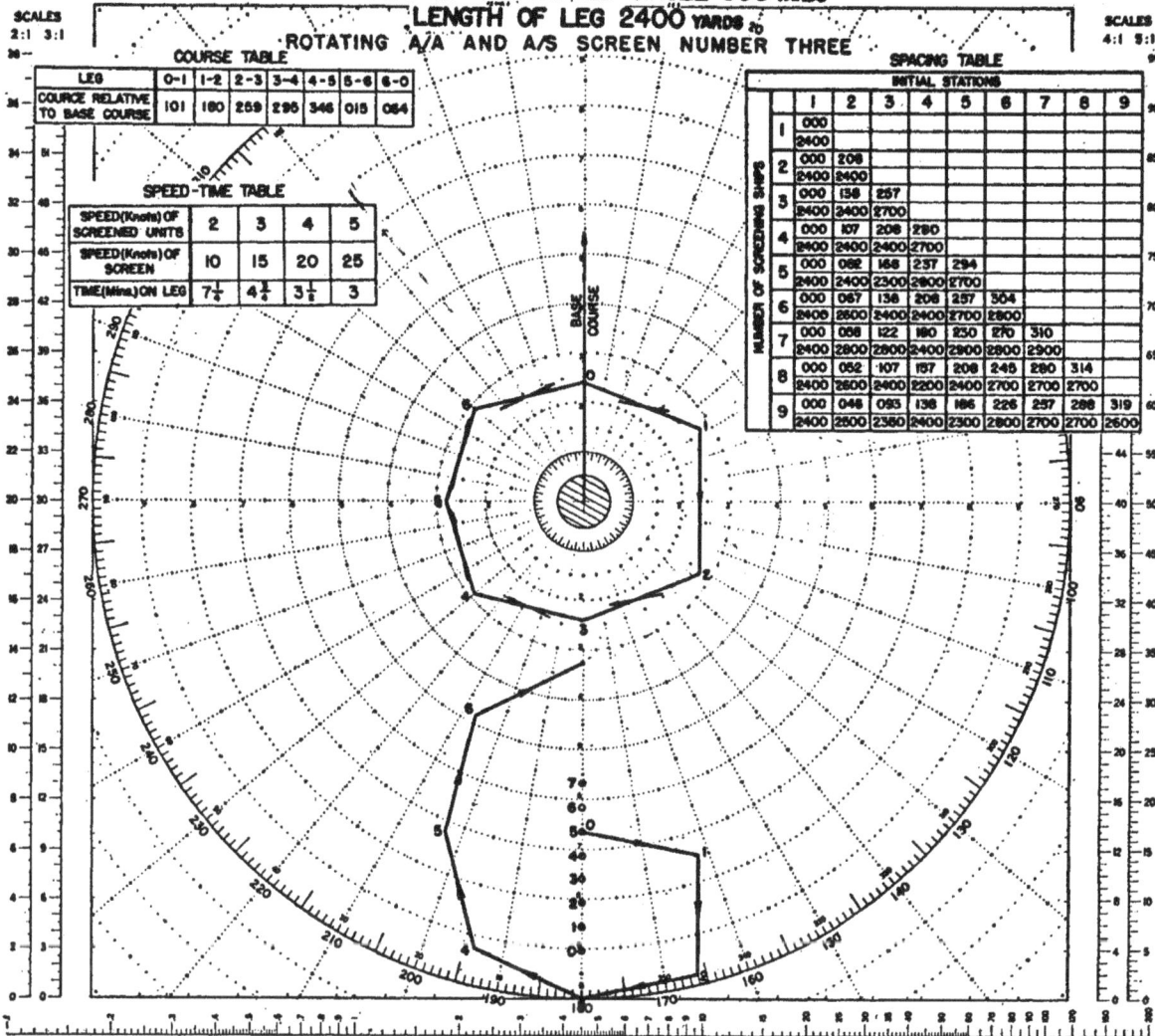

GENERAL SIGNAL : TBF3 · FORM ROTATING
A/A AND A/S SCREEN NUMBER THREE

FIGURE 16 C

EXPLANATION OF DIAGRAM

The relative plot indicates a screen formed in an unsymmetrical seven-sided figure. Regardless of the number of ships available the standard seven-sided figure is used and ships are assigned station in accordance with the "Spacing Table." The navigational plot for the ship assigned to station one is shown below the relative plot. The navigational plot indicates the movement of station one for one complete 360° clockwise cycle. This plot indicates that the navigational distance traveled on each leg during the cycle is the same even though the relative distance varies. The navigational movement of the screened unit along the base course is shown by points plotted on the track and labeled 0 through 7.

SPACING TABLE—USE OF

Given the number of screening ships and a station assignment in the screen move vertically down the "Initial Stations" column until it intersects the horizontal row designating "Number of Screening Ships." At this intersection the top three figures indicate the relative bearing of the initial position of the station from the base course line and the bottom four figures the initial distance in yards from the center of the screened circle.

ROTATING A/A AND A/S SCREEN AROUND SLOW SPEED UNITS – SPEED RATIO 3:1
RADIUS OF PROTECTED CIRCLE 1000 YARDS
LENGTH OF LEG 3000 YARDS
ROTATING A/A AND A/S SCREEN NUMBER FOUR

SCALES 2:1 3:1

SCALES 4:1 5:1

COURSE TABLE

LEG	0-1	1-2	2-3	3-4	4-5	5-6	6-0
COURSE RELATIVE TO BASE COURSE	090	180	270	315	343	017	046

SPEED-TIME TABLE

SPEED(Knots) OF SCREENED UNITS	3	4	5	6	7	8
SPEED(Knots) OF SCREEN	9	12	15	18	21	24
TIME(Mins) ON LEG	10	7½	6	5	4⅓	3¾

SPACING TABLE

NUMBER OF SCREENING SHIPS	1	2	3	4	5	6	7	8	9
1	000 / 3000								
2	000 / 3000	203 / 2650							
3	000 / 3000	139 / 3100	257 / 2800						
4	000 / 3000	108 / 3150	203 / 2850	279 / 2800					
5	000 / 3000	083 / 3000	167 / 2900	237 / 2750	294 / 2700				
6	000 / 3000	067 / 3250	139 / 3100	203 / 2650	257 / 2800	305 / 2750			
7	000 / 3000	057 / 3600	123 / 3600	180 / 3000	229 / 2850	270 / 3000	311 / 2850		
8	000 / 3350	051 / 3150	108 / 2850	157 / 2650	203 / 2700	244 / 2800	279 / 2700	318 / 2700	
9	000 / 3000	047 / 3200	094 / 3000	139 / 3100	184 / 2900	223 / 2750	257 / 2800	288 / 2700	323 / 2700

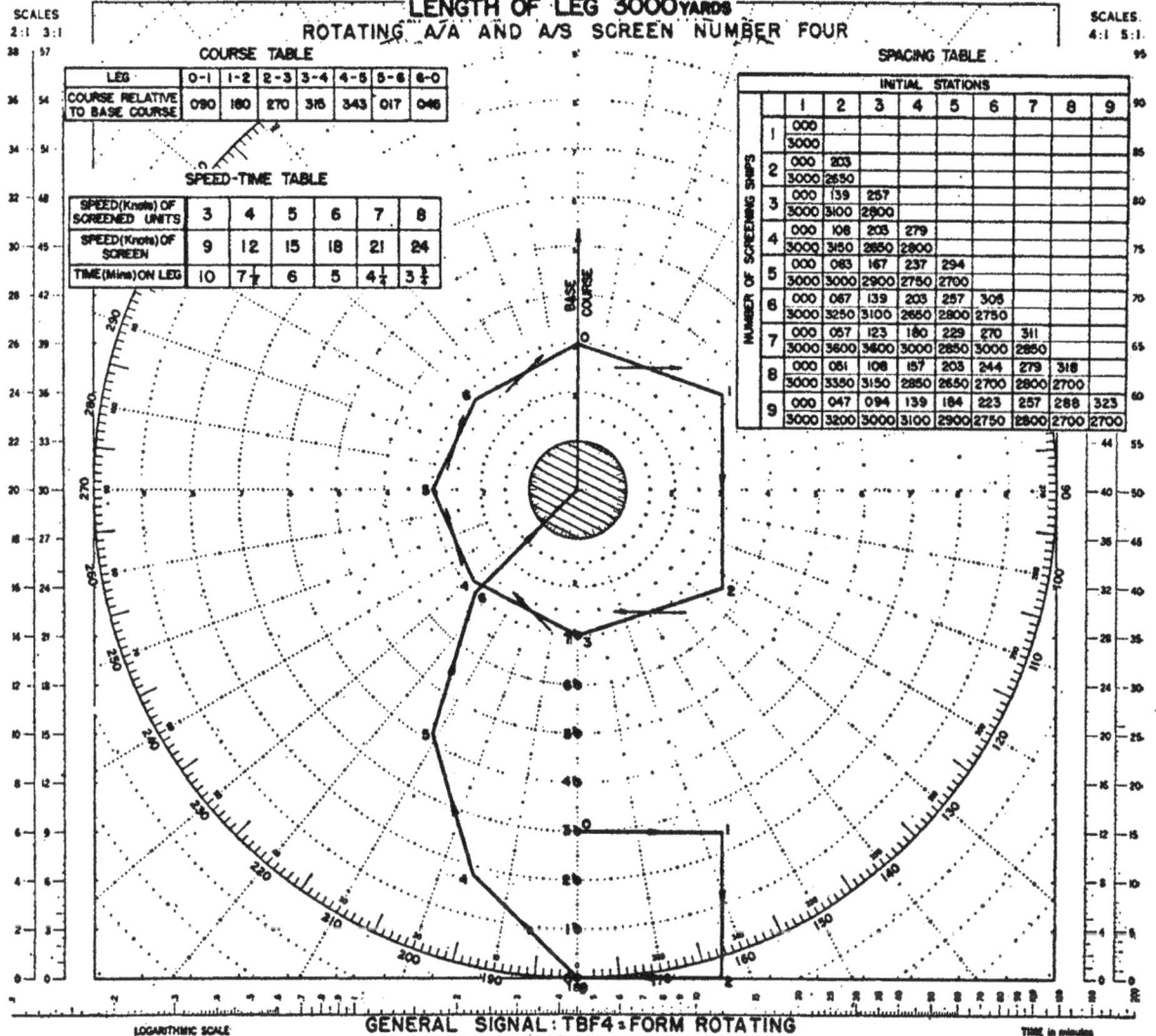

GENERAL SIGNAL: TBF4-FORM ROTATING
A/A AND A/S SCREEN NUMBER FOUR

FIGURE 16 D

EXPLANATION OF DIAGRAM

The relative plot indicates a screen formed in an unsymmetrical seven sided figure. Regardless of the number of ships available the standard seven sided figure is used and ships are assigned station in accordance with the "Spacing Sable." The navigational plot for the ship assigned to station one is shown below the relative plot. The navigational plot indicates the movement of station one for one complete 360° clockwise cycle. This plot indicates that the navigational distance traveled on each leg during the cycle is the same even though the relative distance varies. The navigational movement of the screened unit along the base course is shown by points plotted on the track and labeled 0 through 7.

SPACING TABLE—USE OF

Given the number of screening ships and a station assignment in the screen move vertically down the "Initial Stations" column until it intersects the horizontal row designating "Number of Screening Ships". At this intersection the top three figures indicate the relative bearing of the initial position of the station from the base course line and the bottom four figures the initial distance in yards from the center of the screened circle.

(REVERSE BLANK)

ROTATING A/A AND A/S SCREEN AROUND SLOW SPEED UNITS—SPEED RATIO 4:1
RADIUS OF PROTECTED CIRCLE 1000 YARDS
LENGTH OF LEG 3200 YARDS
ROTATING A/A AND A/S SCREEN NUMBER FIVE

COURSE TABLE

LEG	0-1	1-2	2-3	3-4	4-5	5-6	6-0
COURSE RELATIVE TO BASE COURSE	094	180	257	296	347	013	062

SPEED-TIME TABLE

SPEED(Knots) OF SCREENED UNITS	2	3	4	5	6
SPEED(Knots) OF SCREEN	8	12	16	20	24
TIME(Mins) ON LEG	12	8	6	4⅘	4

SPACING TABLE — INITIAL STATIONS

NUMBER OF SCREENING SHIPS	1	2	3	4	5	6	7	8	9
1	000 / 3000								
2	000 / 3000	208 / 3000							
3	000 / 3000	137 / 3150	257 / 3400						
4	000 / 3350	108 / 3350	208 / 3000	280 / 3400					
5	000 / 3000	083 / 3200	167 / 2900	238 / 3500	294 / 3400				
6	000 / 3000	068 / 3400	137 / 3150	208 / 3000	257 / 3400	303 / 3500			
7	000 / 3000	058 / 3700	122 / 3700	180 / 3000	231 / 3650	270 / 3500	309 / 3650		
8	000 / 3000	053 / 3450	108 / 3350	140 / 3100	208 / 3000	245 / 3400	280 / 3400	314 / 3600	
9	000 / 3000	046 / 3300	093 / 3200	137 / 3150	186 / 2950	227 / 3500	257 / 3400	290 / 3400	331 / 3050

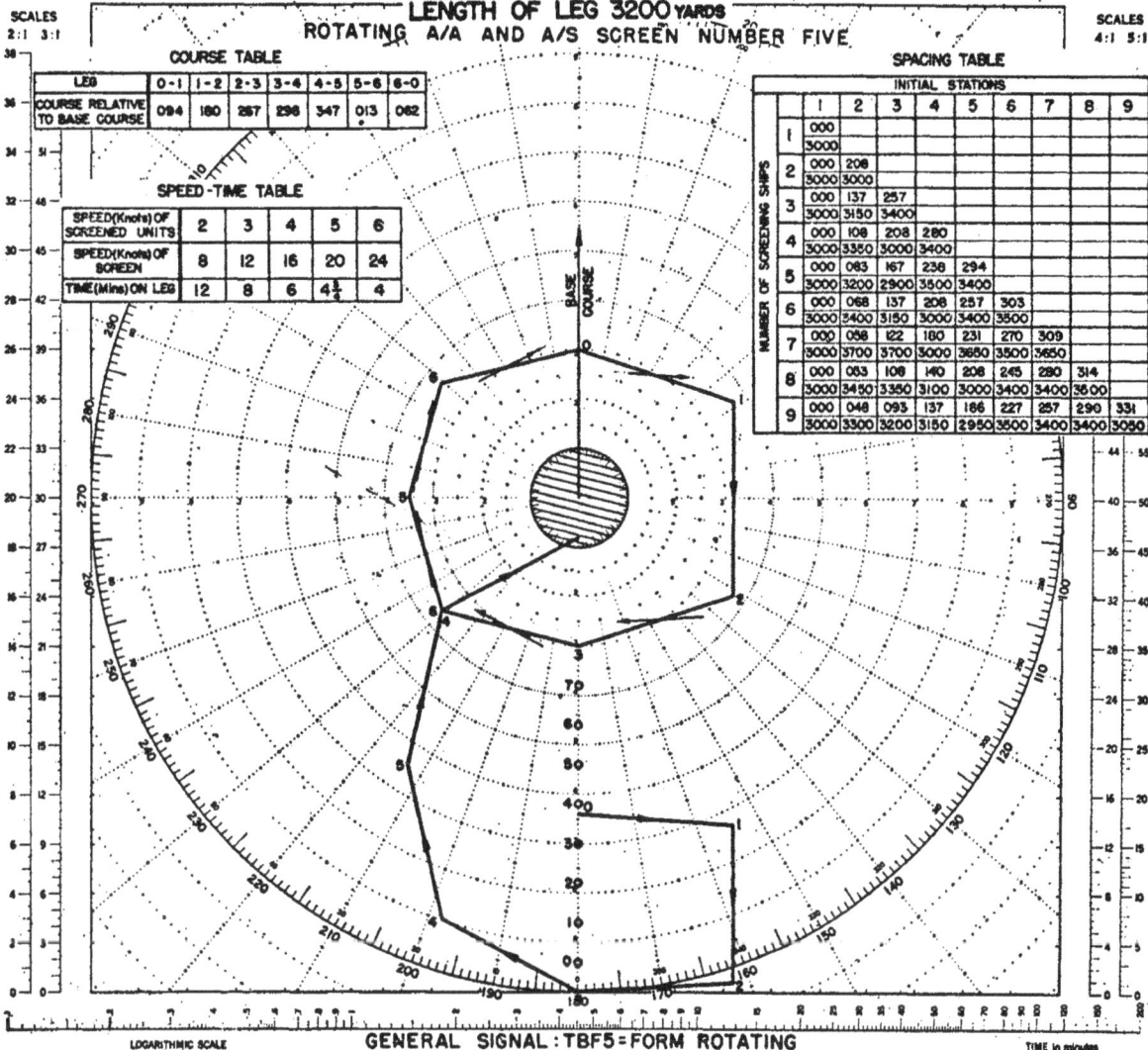

GENERAL SIGNAL : TBF5 = FORM ROTATING A/A AND A/S SCREEN NUMBER FIVE

FIGURE 16 E

EXPLANATION OF DIAGRAM

The relative plot indicates a screen formed in an unsymmetrical seven-sided figure. Regardless of the number of ships available the standard seven-sided figure is used and ships are assigned station in accordance with the "Spacing Table." The navigational plot for the ship assigned to station one is shown below the relative plot. The navigational plot indicates the movement of station one for one complete 360° clockwise cycle. This plot indicates that the navigational distance traveled on each leg during the cycle is the same even though the relative distance varies. The navigational movement of the screened unit along the base course is shown by points plotted on the track and labeled 0 through 7.

SPACING TABLE—USE OF

Given the number of screening ships and a station assignment in the screen move vertically down the "Initial Stations" column until it intersects the horizontal row designating "Number of Screening Ships." At this intersection the top three figures indicate the relative bearing of the initial position of the station from the base course line and the bottom four figures the initial distance in yards from the center of the screened circle.

(REVERSE BLANK)

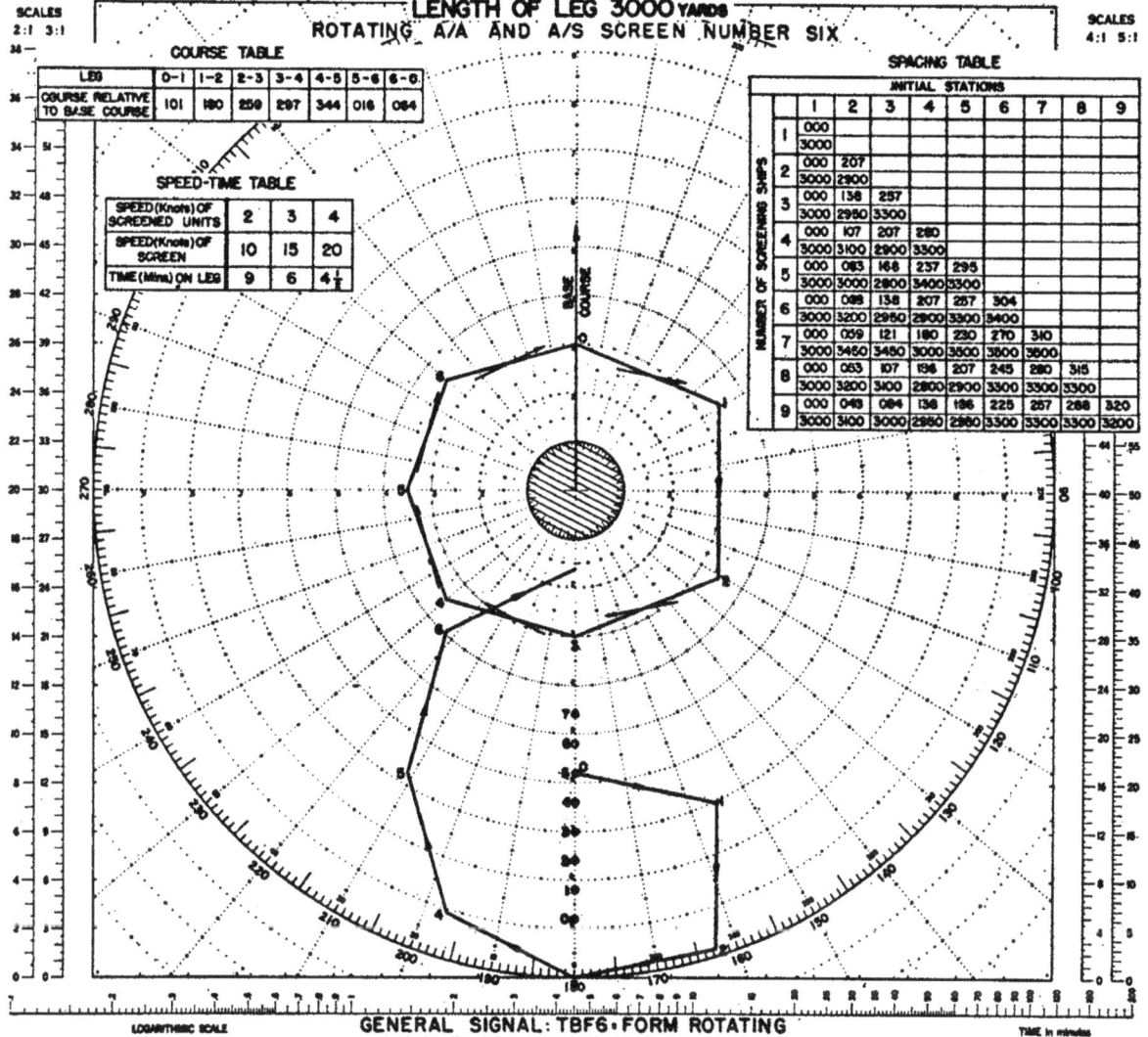

ROTATING A/A AND A/S SCREEN AROUND SLOW SPEED UNITS — SPEED RATIO 5:1
RADIUS OF PROTECTED CIRCLE 1000 YARDS
LENGTH OF LEG 3000 YARDS
ROTATING A/A AND A/S SCREEN NUMBER SIX

SCALES 2:1 3:1   SCALES 4:1 5:1

COURSE TABLE

LEG	0-1	1-2	2-3	3-4	4-5	5-6	6-0
COURSE RELATIVE TO BASE COURSE	101	180	259	297	344	016	064

SPEED-TIME TABLE

SPEED (Knots) OF SCREENED UNITS	2	3	4
SPEED (Knots) OF SCREEN	10	15	20
TIME (Mins) ON LEG	9	6	4½

SPACING TABLE

	INITIAL STATIONS								
NUMBER OF SCREENING SHIPS	1	2	3	4	5	6	7	8	9
1	000 3000								
2	000 3000	207 2900							
3	000 3000	138 2950	257 3300						
4	000 3000	107 3100	207 2900	280 3300					
5	000 3000	083 3000	168 2900	237 3400	295 3300				
6	000 3000	098 3200	138 2950	207 2900	257 3300	304 3400			
7	000 3000	059 3450	121 3450	180 3000	230 3300	270 3300	310 3600		
8	000 3000	053 3200	107 3100	196 2900	207 2900	245 3300	280 3300	315 3300	
9	000 3100	049 3000	084 2950	136 2950	196 3300	225 3300	257 3300	288 3300	320 3200

LOGARITHMIC SCALE   TIME in minutes

GENERAL SIGNAL: TBF6·FORM ROTATING
A/A AND A/S SCREEN NUMBER SIX
FIGURE 16 F

EXPLANATION OF DIAGRAM

The relative plot indicates a screen formed in an unsymmetrical seven-sided figure. Regardless of the number of ships available the standard seven-sided figure is used and ships are assigned station in accordance with the "Spacing Table." The navigational plot for the ship assigned to station one is shown below the relative plot. The navigational plot indicates the movement of station one for one complete 360° clockwise cycle. This plot indicates that the navigational distance traveled on each leg during the cycle is the same even though the relative distance varies. The navigational movement of the screened unit along the base course is shown by points plotted on the track and labeled 0 through 7.

SPACING TABLE—USE OF

Given the number of screening ships and a station assignment in the screen move vertically down the "Initial Stations" column until it intersects the horizontal row designating "Number of Screening Ships." At this intersection the top three figures indicate the relative bearing of the initial position of the station from the base course line and the bottom four figures the initial distance in yards from the center of the screened circle.

PART VI

SUPPORTING DOCTRINES AND INSTRUCTIONS

6000. GENERAL.

6010. The RAD Series of publications are promulgated for the purpose of making available the current best practices in the arts associated with the CIC doctrine. As indicated, it is not mandatory that these publications be followed; however, it must be pointed out that only by following these recommended practices can the necessary standardization be accomplished. When, due to the introduction of new equipment and/or new practices, a change to these publications appears necessary, fleet commanders should submit recommended changes without delay. The following are now available or under preparation.

RADONE A—	The Capabilities and Limitations of Shipborne Radar. (Under preparation.)
RADTWO A—	The Tactical Use of Radar in Aircraft. (Under preparation.)
RADTHREE—	Radar Operator's Manual.
RADFOUR—	Air Plotting Manual.
RADFIVE—	Surface Plotting Manual.
RADSIX—	CIC Manual. (Under preparation.)
RADSEVEN—	Radar Countermeasures Manual. (Under preparation.)
RADEIGHT—	Aircraft Control Manual. (Under preparation.)
RADNINE—	Tactical Use of Radar in Small Vessels. (Under preparation.)
RADTEN—	The Airborne Radar Operator's Manual. (Under preparation.)
RADELEVEN—	The Shipborne Radar Countermeasures Operator's Manual. (Under preparation.)
RADTWELVE—	The Airborne Radar Countermeasures Operator's Manual. (Under preparation.)

6011. The monthly magazine "CIC" is promulgated to the fleet in order to furnish the fleet information on CIC operations experienced by others.

6020. Definitions of terms used in CIC doctrine.

6021. Radar Area. The term "Radar Area" as used in the CIC and supporting doctrines is the maximum range of detection of aircraft by radar and for purposes of definition is defined as an area 100 miles in radius.

6022. In the CIC and supporting doctrines the term "TASK FORCE COMMANDER" is USED TO DENOTE THAT COMMANDER WITHIN THE RADAR AREA who is charged with the OVER-ALL COORDINA-

TION of the functioning of the CIC's in the various ships. This coordinating commander may be an officer in tactical command, a fleet commander, a task force, task group, or task unit commander. The term "task group (unit) commander" is used to denote the next lower echelon of command within the radar area.

6023. Special designations for ships are used in the CIC doctrine for purposes of identification of over-all coordinated functions. They may be assigned to individual ships, or more than one of the functions may be assigned a single ship. Normally the ship designated as special assistant to the task force (group) (unit) commander is his flagship; however, this is not mandatory and in certain tactical situations may not be advisable.

6030. In the CIC doctrine the special ship designations are defined as follows:

(a) *The Task Force (Group) (Unit) Combat Information Ship.*—The ship so designated shall be charged in addition to its intra-ship CIC functions, with the coordination of the inter-ship CIC functions of the various ships in the task force (group) (unit) so that the overall combat information available to command will be increased. This ship under the general direction of the task force commander will normally be given certain detailed duties to carry out for the task force commander.

(b) *Fighter Direction Ship.*—Any ship assigned the duties of "control of aircraft in an area." This assignment is normally assigned to aircraft carriers, when in the immediate vicinity; however, all ships with CIC's should have proper training and be capable of controlling aircraft.

(c) *Radar Guardship (Air and/or Surface).*—Any ship assigned the duties of surface and/or air surveillance of a given area. The ship should normally be equipped with a CIC and have a competent CIC team.

(d) *Radar Picket.*—Any ship stationed outside the antisubmarine or antiaircraft screen for the purpose of increasing the detection range of the formation especially for submarines, low flying planes and surface units.

(e) *Radar Intercept Ship.*—Any ship of the formation specifically charged with the duties of early detection of enemy radar transmissions.

(f) *Radar Jamming Ship.*—Any ship of the formation specifically charged with the duties of jamming and/or deceiving enemy radar in order to prevent the enemy from obtaining combat intelligence of own forces.

6100. General CIC Doctrine.

6110. Purpose. The fleet CIC doctrine is established to provide for—

(a) The coordination of all radars and other combat information within each ship and;

(b) The coordinated use of CIC's by ships operating together in various tactical organizations.

6120. Principle. Maximum combat efficiency of individual ships and task organizations can best be attained through full utilization of all available sources of combat information. By the evaluation of all available information by trained personnel, such data can be quickly disseminated to the flag and commanding officers, to other control stations concerned over interior communication circuits, and to other ships and aircraft via external communication facilities.

6130. The CIC doctrine is considered to be general in purpose and is supplemented by the following supporting doctrines: Task force (group) control, surface search, air search, fighter direction, recognition (IFF), and radar countermeasures which are contained in this chapter.

6140. The Combat Information Center.

6141. In order to carry out the intent of the CIC doctrine, a space designated as CIC shall be established in all combatant vessels (PF and larger) and in large amphibious vessels. In other craft adequate plotting facilities and communication circuits shall be established.

6142. The CIC team is charged with the function and responsibility of keeping the commanding officer and higher commands embarked informed of the location, identity, and movement of friendly and/or enemy aircraft and surface ships within the area. In addition, when the tactical situation indicates and the limitation of space and availability of trained personnel permit, any or all of the following functions will be required of CIC:

(1) Target indication.

(2) Control of aircraft in the area, both offensive and defensive.

(3) Control of small craft in the area.

(4) Navigation and piloting (amphibious landings, shore bombardments, etc.).

(5) Control of Radar Countermeasures.

(6) Assist in ASW operations.

6143. In order that combat information center teams may perform the above functions, it is essential that all shipborne radars be controlled initially by the combat information center. Combat information centers shall release fire-control radars for gunnery purposes prior to targets coming within tracking range of the battery served.

6150. Radar Security.

6151. Although radar transmissions are superfrequency radio signals, the greater power involved results in a receivable signal at ranges about two or three times farther than normal very high frequency radio communication transmissions on the same frequency. This type of transmission is quasi-optical in character, and normally reaches only to the optical horizon. Thus the condition of radar silence to be prescribed must be carefully considered in the light of the existing conditions. It is considered that a radar search should be conducted at all times when contact with the enemy is possible. An exception is when the necessity for remaining undetected is vital to the success of the mission and *outweighs the disadvantage of surprise enemy attack* which radar silence invites. In general, the intelligent use of radar will prevent being surprised. Although the use of radar may possibly disclose your presence, the information to be gained from it, plus the warning of impending attack, will usually far outweigh the negative value of radar silence.

6152. In certain tactical situations intermittent use of radar may be prescribed. This is a compromise measure, and should be used only in special circumstances. Its use will usually produce a *false security*. Normally the condition should be either complete radar silence in particular bands of frequencies or continuous search by assigned guard ships.

6160. Radar IFF and Radar Countermeasures Conditions of Silence.

6161. Correlation of Radar, IFF and RCM Silence. Any restrictions imposed upon the use of radar should be accompanied by a corresponding restriction upon the use of IFF or RCM transmitting equipment and be correlated with an appropriate condition of VHF radio silence. Officers who impose radar or other silence must always keep in mind the effect such action will have upon the over-all employment of radar, IFF and Radar Countermeasures as well as the inherent loss in combat information. (See paragraphs 6500 and 6600.)

6162. The following conditions of radar silence are prescribed. These conditions should be assigned for a given area (radar area) and made applicable to all ships or aircraft operating therein. These conditions apply equally to IFF and radar countermeasures transmitting equipment operating in the same frequency bands and should be correlated with applicable conditions of VHF radio silence.

Condition 1.—Maintain radar silence on all ship-borne radars.

Advantage.—No possibility of detection by enemy radar intercept receivers.

Disadvantage.—Force not prepared to repel enemy air or surface attacks, to detect presence of enemy outside of visual range, nor to recognize immediately contacts made. IFF system inoperative.

Condition 2.—Maintain radar silence on all ship-borne radar operating on frequency below 500 mcs.

Advantage.—Complete surface coverage, limited air coverage of low-flying aircraft. Limited air coverage by use of SM/SP radars. AA batteries ready.

Disadvantage.—Force not fully prepared to repel air attack with AA batteries because of limited air coverage and lack of target indication from air-search radar. Possibility of radar interception by enemy airborne intercept receivers under 150 miles, ship-borne 30 miles. IFF system inoperative.

Radars affected.—SA, SC, SK, SR, MK III IFF, TDY band.

Condition 2X.—Maintain radar silence on all ship-borne radars operating on a frequency below 500 mcs. except those on air radar guardships, pickets, IFF guardships, and task force (group) CIC ships.

Advantage.—Complete air and surface coverage with minimum interference.

Disadvantage.—Possible radar interception by enemy air-borne intercept receivers under 250 miles, ship-borne under 75 miles. Force not fully prepared, except on ships exempted, to repel air attacks with AA batteries because of lack of target indication from air search radars.

Condition 3.—Maintain radar silence on all ship-borne radars operating on a frequency below 2,000 mcs.

Advantage.—Complete surface coverage. Limited air coverage, including low flying with SM/SP radars and fire-control radars. Limited blind firing control of light AA battery.

Disadvantage.—No adequate early air warning coverage. Possible radar interception by enemy air-borne intercept receivers within 100 miles, ship-borne 25 miles. Force is not prepared to defend itself against enemy air attack. IFF system inoperative.

Radars affected.—SA, SC, SK, SR, MK3, MK4, MK12, Mark III IFF and TDY band.

Condition 3X.—Same as Condition 3 except air search radars on air radar guardships, pickets, IFF guardships, and task force (group) CIC ships not silenced.

Advantage.—Complete air and surface coverage with minimum interference.

Disadvantage.—Possible radar interception by enemy air-borne intercept receivers under 200 miles, ship-borne under 70 miles. Force not prepared to repel air attack with heavy AA battery because of lack of target indication on nonexempted ships and nonoperation of associated fire-control radars. Lack of target indication for light AA battery.

Condition 4.—Maintain radar silence on all ship-borne radars operating on a frequency below 5,200 mcs.

Advantage.—Practically no possibility of enemy interception through use of radar intercept receivers. Partial main and light AA battery radar control.

Disadvantage.—No warning of enemy air attack until visual contact is made. Limited warning of enemy surface attack outside visual contact range when force is equipped with SU, SO3 to 6 radars. No target indication for any battery and no radar control for heavy AA battery. IFF system inoperative.

Radars affected.—All except SO3 to 6, SS, ST, SU, Mark 8 Mod 3, 13, 29, 34.

Condition 5.—Maintain radar silence on all ship-borne radars designated for primary use in fire control.

Advantage.—Prevents enemy from interception of fire-control radar and thus prevents enemy from preparing to jam these radars when within effective range.

Disadvantage.—Fire-control radars not available for instantaneous use— No radar control of gunfire. Decrease in efficiency in overall air coverage.

Condition 5X.—Maintain radar silence on all ship-borne radars designated for primary use in control of main batteries.

Advantage.—Prevents enemy interception of radar used to control main battery to prevent presetting enemy jammers. Affords complete radar control for AA batteries.

Disadvantage.—Main battery fire-control radars not available for use. *Radars affected.*—Mark 3, Mark 8, Mark 13.

Condition 5Y.—Maintain radar silence on all ship-borne radars designated for primary use of the heavy AA battery.

Advantage.—Prevents enemy from interception of AA fire-control radars, thus preventing enemy from preparing to jam these radars when within effective range. Allows radar control of all except heavy AA battery.

Disadvantage.—Force not prepared to defend against air attack by use of radar in heavy AA battery.

Condition 6—Use radars as directed by current operation orders.

Condition 7.—For special assignment.

Condition 8.—For special assignment.

Condition 9.—For special assignment.

Condition 10.—Maintain radar silence on all air-borne radars.

Advantage.—Prevents possible detection of approach of airplanes on enemy by enemy use of radar intercept receivers.

Disadvantage.—Prevents use of IFF system either to identify self or recognize friend. Decreases plane search and attack efficiency by eliminating the use of radar.

Condition 11.—Maintain radar silence on air-borne radars operating below a frequency of 400 mcs.

Advantage.—None.

Disadvantage.—Prevents use of IFF system either to identify self or recognize a friend. Decreases plane search and attack efficiency by eliminating the use of radar in certain patrol type aircraft.

Radars affected.—ASE and IFF Mark III equipment.

Condition 12.—Maintain radar silence on all air-borne radars operating on a frequency below 2,000 mcs.

Advantage.—Prevents detection of approach of airplane to enemy by radar intercept receivers.

Disadvantage.—Prevents the use of the IFF system either to identify self or recognize a friend. Decreases plane search and attack efficiency by eliminating the use of radar in large numbers of carrier and shore-based planes.

Radars affected.—ASE, ASB, and IFF Mark III system.

Condition 13.—Maintain radar silence on air-borne radar operating on a frequency below 5200 mcs.

Advantage.—Prevents detection of approach of aircraft to enemy when equipped with radar intercept receivers.

Disadvantage.—Prevents the use of the IFF system either to identify self or recognize a friend. Decreases plane search and attack efficiency by eliminating the use of radar in a large number of carrier and shore-based planes.

Radars affected.—All except APS15, ASH (APS4), ASD (APS3), AIA (APS6).

6163. A condition of radar silence in a particular band of frequencies may be prescribed by signaling one condition of radar silence negative another condition of radar silence: *Example:* Condition 3 negative Condition 2 establishes radar silence between 500 and 2000 mcs.

6164. The following conditions of IFF silence are prescribed. These conditions should be assigned for a given area and made applicable to all ships or aircraft operating therein. Attention is called to the fact that the complete IFF system is silenced by the establishment of certain conditions of radar silence. (See subparagraph 6162.)

Condition 1.—All ship-borne transpondors and Interrogator-responsors deenergized.

Advantage.—None.

Disadvantage.—No electronic means of recognizing surface and/or air-borne targets with resultant confusion.

Condition 1A.—All ship-borne transpondors and Interrogator-responsors deenergized except I–R on radar guardships, radar pickets, fighter direction ships and task force (group) (unit) CIC ships.

Advantage.—No possibility of enemy triggering transpondors—allows recognition by force as a whole of air-borne targets. Prevents interference caused by over interrogation.

Disadvantage.—No electronic means of recognizing surface contacts with resultant confusion.

Condition 2.—All ship-borne transpondors deenergized.

Advantage.—No possibility of enemy triggering transpondors and thus determining identity of units and possible early detection.

Disadvantage.—No electronic means of recognizing surface contacts with resultant confusion.

Condition 2X.—All ship-borne transpondors deenergized except on radar guardships, IFF guardships, radar pickets, and ships joining formation.

Advantage.—Force recognition as a whole possible with minimum interference, possible to determine IFF code.

Disadvantage.—Possibility of detection and identification by enemy forces at slightly increased range if enemy radar equipment operates in IFF band.

Condition 3.—All interrogator-responsors deenergized.

Advantage.—No possibility of interrogating planes or ships in the vicinity and thus by the transmissions cause possible earlier detection and recognition by the enemy radar equipment operating in same band.

Disadvantage.—No electronic means of recognizing surface or aircraft with resultant confusion.

Condition 3X.—All ship-borne interrogator-responsors deenergized except on radar guardships, and pickets.

Advantage.—Recognition of air and surface contacts. Minimum use of IFF system thus preventing over interrogation and jamming of system.

Disadvantage.—Possibility of earlier enemy detection and identification if he has radar operating in IFF band.

Condition 4.—For future assignment.

Condition 5.—For future assignment.

Condition 6.—For future assignment.

Condition 7.—Use ship-borne IFF equipment as directed by current operation orders.

Condition 11.—All air-borne transpondors deenergized.

Advantage.—No possibility of earlier enemy detection by reradiation from planes caused by enemy radar operating in IFF band.

Disadvantage.—No electronic means available to recognize air contacts. IFF system inoperative.

Condition 11X.—All air-borne transpondors deenergized except two in each formation and in plane operating singly.

Advantage.—Electronic means of recognition of air-borne contacts plus possibility of reading IFF code.

Disadvantage.—Possibility of earlier enemy detection by reradiation from planes caused by enemy radar operating in IFF band.

Condition 12.—All air-borne transpondors A-band deenergized; G-band or "Rooster" in operation.

Advantage.—Electronic means of recognition (without code reading) by certain air search radars or special (G-band) interrogator-responsors, or in case of "Rooster operation" by preset interrogator-responsors.

Condition 13.—All air-borne interrogator-responsors deenergized.

Advantage.—No possibility of over-interrogation with attendant interference.

Disadvantage.—Plane cannot recognize, by use of IFF, friendly planes and/or ships.

Condition 13X.—All air-borne interrogator-responsors deenergized except those in flight leaders and patrol type aircraft.

Advantage.—Minimum interference caused by plane nondirectional interrogation. Allows flight leader and patrol planes to recognize, by use of IFF, friendly planes and/or ships.

Disadvantage.—Possibility of interference by use of nondirectional I-Rs.

6165. Opportunities for test and calibration of radars, IFF, and radar countermeasures equipment shall be exploited consistent with the prevailing condition of radar silence.

6170. Intership CIC Communications.

6171. For detailed information as to frequency and equipment for use in exercising the following intership control channels see USF 70.

6172. Intership CIC Control. Supervision and coordination of the flow of combat information between the CIC of the task force (group) (unit) CIC ship and CIC's of all ships in the force is a function of the task force commander assisted by the force CIC ship. The task force commander may delegate this authority to the task group or unit commanders assisted by the group or unit CIC ships. To facilitate this operation, voice radio circuits are assigned for comunication between ships. Further, the specific duties of the radar guardship, fighter direction ship, radar picket, radar, intercept ship or radar jamming ship are assigned to ships in the force depending on the extent of equipment installed and the state of training of personnel.

6173. Radar Control Orders. In order to abbreviate the flow of information and orders on the communication channels used in intership control and also to afford limited security the following radar control orders are established and defined:

(a) *Report.*—The ship addressed shall report the range and bearing of a designated air or surface contact at stated intervals (every minute for air contacts and every three minutes for surface contacts), and supply the necessary amplifying information which shall include course, speed, composition, altitude, or other information concerning the contact. Report may be used in conjunction with "size," "course," "speed," or "angels," etc., to obtain spot information.

(b) *Negat.*—The ship addressed shall cease reporting the designated air or surface target, but continue plotting all available information.

(c) *Estimate.*—The ship addressed shall provide a quick estimate of the angels and size of a designated air contact or size of the surface contact. This is a spot report concerned only with size and altitude of a designated contact. It pertains to controversial information upon which the task force (group) commander must base important tactical decisions.

(d) *Check Contact—(bearing)—(distance).*—The ship addressed shall check the designated contact for purposes of identification.

(e) *Recommend.*—Used by the reporting ship to indicate quickly to the appropriate CIC ship, the radar guardship, picket, intercept, jamming, or fighter direction ship best qualified to pick up a contact which is fading from the radars of the reporting ships. An example of such a transmission follows: "Hello William, this is Sugar. Raid one faded at one eight zero, fifty nine, Recommend Blue base, Over." This type transmission will be used, for example, by radar pickets or fighter direction ships deployed about a landing operation.

6174. To insure the orderly flow of combat information, four channels, usually voice radio, are designated for use within the Task Force. In certain tactical situations with large task forces, when the flow of information or inter group distances dictates, both inter and intra group channels should be set up. Any of the channels may be combined when required. The four channels are described below:

6175. The Radar Reporting Channel.

(a) The radar reporting channel is used to disseminate radar information, and to control the function of the radar guardships, radar pickets, radar intercept ships, radar jamming ships, and as required the fighter direction ships.

(b) The following are to be complied with on this channel in controlling the functions of the radar guardships, pickets, intercept and jamming ships and as necessary the fighter direction ships.

  (1) Control and coordinate air and surface radar searches by all ships in the task force (group) (unit) to insure maximum effective coverage, and to provide for reliefs in event of casualties.

  (2) Report to the task force (group) (unit) commander over this channel the initial air or surface contacts.

  (3) Report to the task force (group) (unit) commander the determination of friendly character of air or surface contact by ship first determining that fact.

  (4) (a) Reports of unidentified surface contact are made in plain language or encoded as required by existing instructions.

  (b) All reports of surface contacts shall be made in nautical miles.

  (5) The estimated size of the contact shall be given in the initial report. In case of surface contact the best estimate of the number shall be given. In case of air contact the arbitrary designations one, few (2 to 10), or many (10 or over), shall be used.

  (6) The task force (group) (unit) commander through the force (group) (unit) CIC ship shall indicate whether to report the nearest or the central ship in a group of surface contacts.

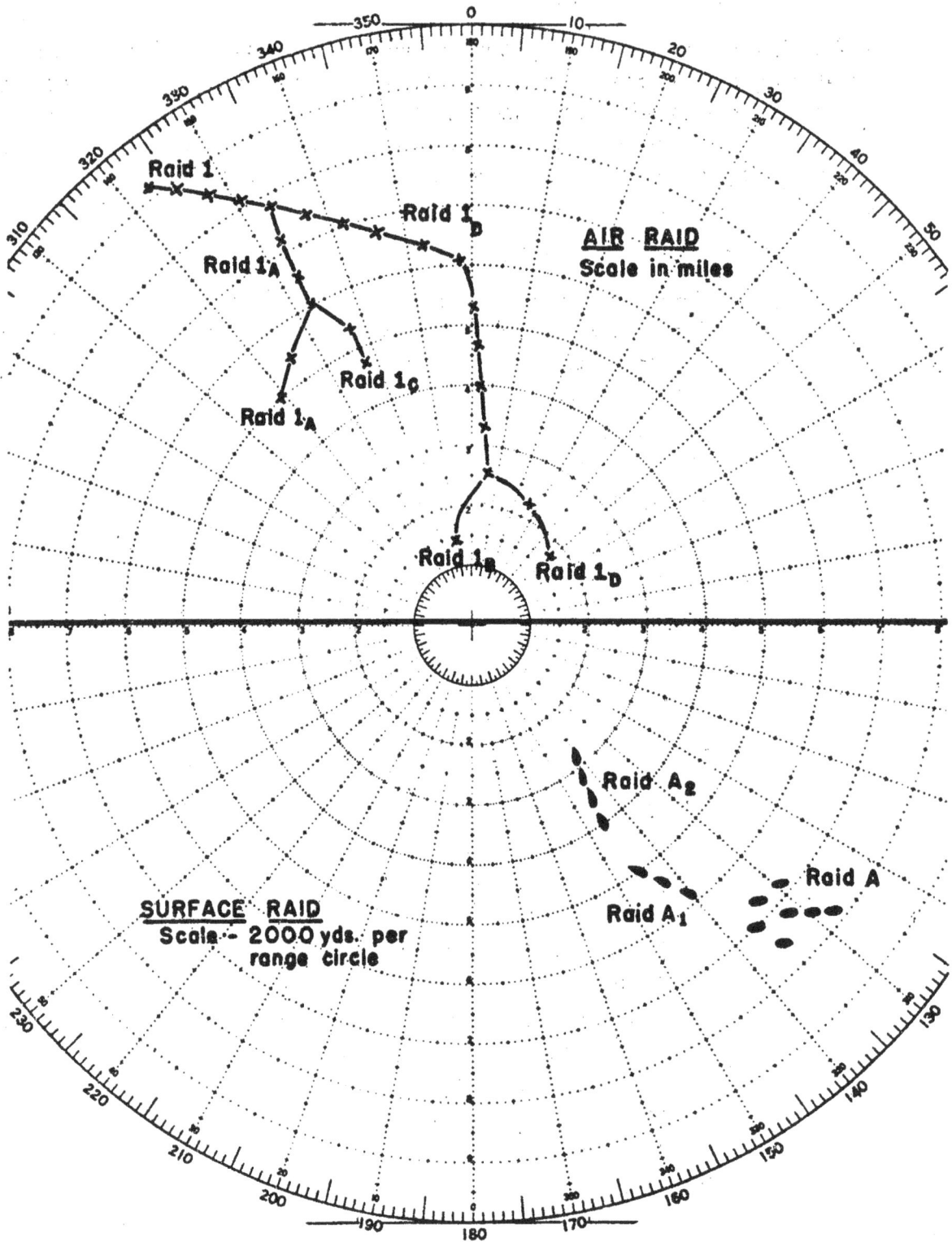

AIR RAID
Scale in miles

Raid 1

Raid 1$_B$

Raid 1$_A$

Raid 1$_C$

Raid 1$_A$

Raid 1$_B$

Raid 1$_D$

Raid A$_2$

Raid A

Raid A$_1$

SURFACE RAID
Scale - 2000 yds. per
range circle

Figure 17.

(7) Any ship in the force may be required to report an air or surface contact. The initial report shall include all available information; subsequent reports shall give the last plotted position of the contact; amplifying reports shall be made as new information becomes available.

(8) A radar guardship detecting a new air or surface contact while engaged in reporting another raid shall not, where possible, be required to report both at once. To promote over-all efficiency another guardship shall be directed to report the new contact by the coordinating ship.

6176. Radar Telling Net. Used for exchanging radar information of more than local interest between forces and/or land bases separated by distances too great to be covered by the radar reporting channel.

6177. The Warning Net. Used by the task force (group) (unit) commander for the dissemination of combat information as follows:

(a) For sounding alerts to the force of impending air or surface attacks.

(b) For designating raids, air or surface. When a raid splits, the components shall be designated as illustrated in the diagram in Figure 1. Numbers are assigned to air raids and letters to surface raids. Splits from an air raid shall be assigned letter subdesignations and splits from a surface raid shall be assigned number subdesignations.

(c) For keeping the task force informed of the progress of air or surface interceptions.

(d) For receiving emergency reports from any ship of the force of unidentified or enemy air or surface contacts close to the force when radar reporting channel is not available.

(e) For setting conditions of radar and IFF silence.

(f) For receiving emergency reports of radar jamming or deception by the enemy when radar reporting channel is not available.

(g) For warning the task force (group) (unit) of the intended launching or landing of night fighter aircraft.

6178. The Inter-Fighter Direction Channel. Used for the dissemination of information concerning fighter direction and to control the functions of the fighter direction ships.

(a) For purposes of security and to abbreviate terminology used in disseminating fighter direction information, the deck condition code is established. (See subparagraph 6179.)

(b) The force (group) (unit) CIC ships, as ordered by the task force (group) (unit) commander, will control the functions of fighter direction ships over the inter-fighter direction channel. Transmissions will be concerned with the following operations:

(1) Stationing and relieving of combat air patrols.

(2) The assignment of fighter direction ships to control the interception of designated raids.

(3) The allocation of combat air patrols to fighter direction ships for the interception of designated raids.

(4) Reinforcement of combat air patrols as required by the tactical situation.

(5) Reports concerning the flight deck conditions and status of air-borne aircraft from all carriers in the task group (unit), including returning air strikes.

(6) The expeditious transfer of control of interceptions between fighter direction ships when information fails for the controlling ship.

(7) The assignment of combat air patrols to the control of radar picket ships acting as fighter direction ships.

6179. Deck Condition Code. This code is intended to give brief positive information, with maximum security to CIC officers and the carrier flagship, concerning deck conditions and combat air patrols launched, landed, or to be launched or landed. Transmissions must be kept to a minimum.

Code Word	Meaning
a. Condition George	Deck fouled. Cannot launch or land CAP.
Condition George ———	Deck will be fouled for approximately ——— minutes.
Condition George Able ———	Deck fouled. Can you land ——— planes for me?
b. Condition Mike	Deck ready to land CAP.
c. Condition Love	Land CAP or landed CAP plus numbers.
d. Condition Fox	Ready to launch CAP.
Condition Fox ———	Division number(s) or CAP in readiness as indicated.
e. Condition How	Launch or Am launching 8 CAP.
Condition How plus or Minus ———.	Indicates exact number of planes to launch or that are being launched if number deviates from 8.

TASK FORCE CIC CONTROL DOCTRINE

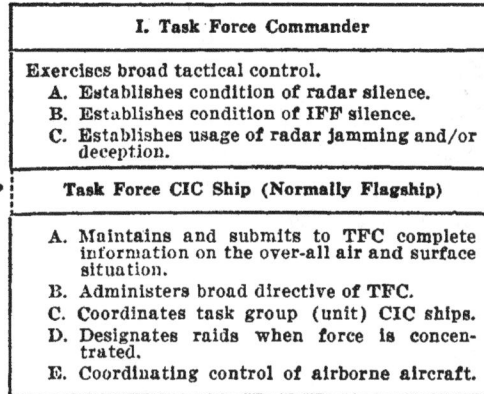

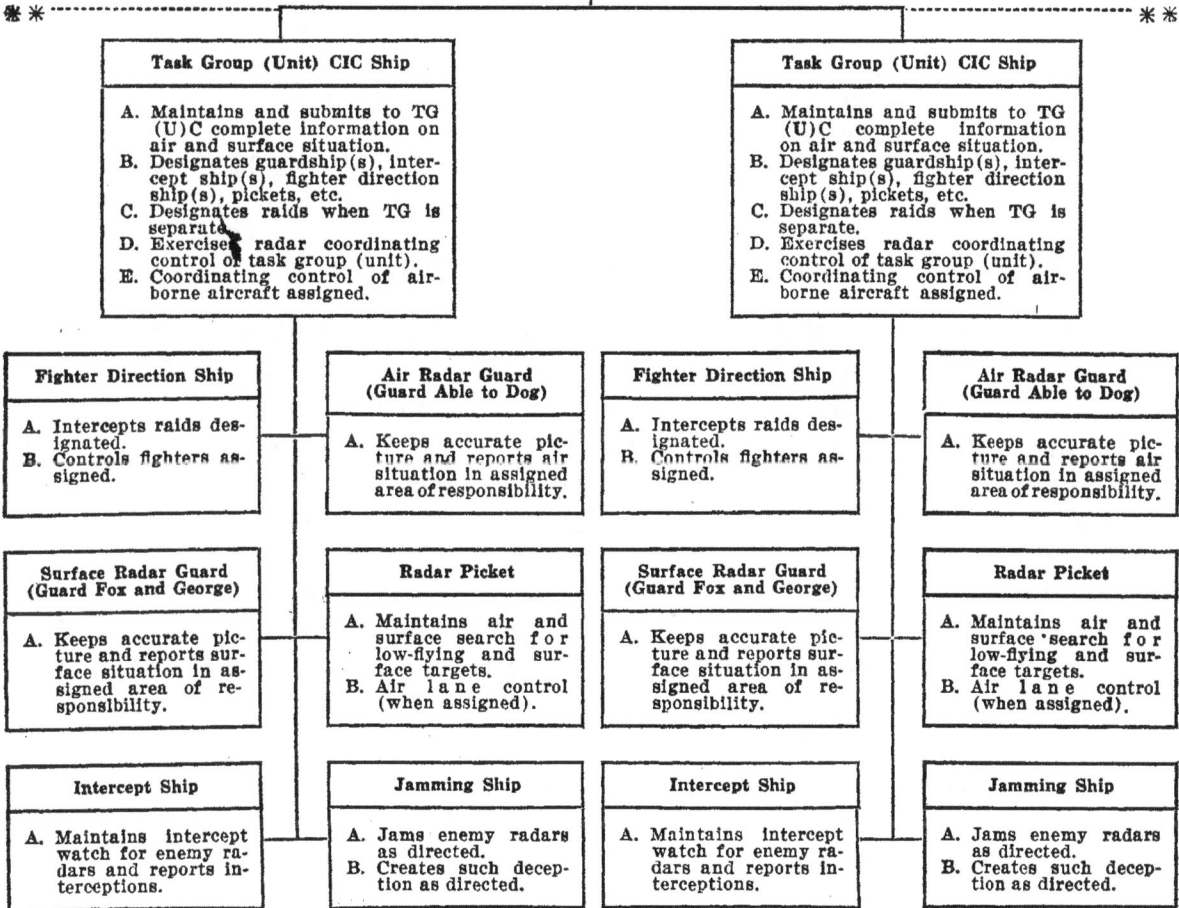

I. Task Force Commander

Exercises broad tactical control.
A. Establishes condition of radar silence.
B. Establishes condition of IFF silence.
C. Establishes usage of radar jamming and/or deception.

Task Force CIC Ship (Normally Flagship)

A. Maintains and submits to TFC complete information on the over-all air and surface situation.
B. Administers broad directive of TFC.
C. Coordinates task group (unit) CIC ships.
D. Designates raids when force is concentrated.
E. Coordinating control of airborne aircraft.

Task Group (Unit) CIC Ship

A. Maintains and submits to TG (U)C complete information on air and surface situation.
B. Designates guardship(s), intercept ship(s), fighter direction ship(s), pickets, etc.
C. Designates raids when TG is separate.
D. Exercises radar coordinating control of task group (unit).
E. Coordinating control of airborne aircraft assigned.

Task Group (Unit) CIC Ship

A. Maintains and submits to TG (U)C complete information on air and surface situation.
B. Designates guardship(s), intercept ship(s), fighter direction ship(s), pickets, etc.
C. Designates raids when TG is separate.
D. Exercises radar coordinating control of task group (unit).
E. Coordinating control of airborne aircraft assigned.

Fighter Direction Ship

A. Intercepts raids designated.
B. Controls fighters assigned.

Air Radar Guard (Guard Able to Dog)

A. Keeps accurate picture and reports air situation in assigned area of responsibility.

Fighter Direction Ship

A. Intercepts raids designated.
B. Controls fighters assigned.

Air Radar Guard (Guard Able to Dog)

A. Keeps accurate picture and reports air situation in assigned area of responsibility.

Surface Radar Guard (Guard Fox and George)

A. Keeps accurate picture and reports surface situation in assigned area of responsibility.

Radar Picket

A. Maintains air and surface search for low-flying and surface targets.
B. Air lane control (when assigned).

Surface Radar Guard (Guard Fox and George)

A. Keeps accurate picture and reports surface situation in assigned area of responsibility.

Radar Picket

A. Maintains air and surface search for low-flying and surface targets.
B. Air lane control (when assigned).

Intercept Ship

A. Maintains intercept watch for enemy radars and reports interceptions.

Jamming Ship

A. Jams enemy radars as directed.
B. Creates such deception as directed.

Intercept Ship

A. Maintains intercept watch for enemy radars and reports interceptions.

Jamming Ship

A. Jams enemy radars as directed.
B. Creates such deception as directed.

Indicates flexibility in that TFC may or may not be located in task force CIC Ship.
**Indicates flexibility in number of task groups (units) comprising task force.*

Figure 18.

f. Condition Jig ———	CAP is air-borne, division numbers as indicated by numerals.
Condition Jig ——— Xray ——— Zebra	CAP is air-borne, patrol(s) indicate preceding Xray is (are) high patrol(s). Patrol indicated preceding Zebra is low patrol.
g. Condition King	Launch all available CAP.

NOTE.—"Affirmative" or "Negative" may be used as an answer to any code transmission in which a question is asked or implied.

"Interrogatory" may be used to precede any "Condition" to frame the meaning as a question.

"Execute" may follow any of the above code transmissions from the CIC Ship to indicate an order that is to be carried out.

Code Word	*Meaning*
h. Condition Roger ——— (Call signs)	The indicated planes have been launched on long range search.
i. Condition Sugar ——— (Call signs)	The indicated planes have been launched on medium range air patrols.
j. Condition Tare ——— (Call signs)	The indicated planes have been launched on short-range air patrol.
k. Condition Unit ——— (Call Signs) ——— (Time)	Indicates divisions and time when a special combat air patrol will be on station over units operating on detached mission.

6200. Task Force (Group) (Unit) Control Doctrine. (See fig. 19.)

6210. The coordination of the operation of all ships' CIC's other than the major one of intradissemination of the tactical picture must be done by the task force commander (see subparagraph 6022) in certain broad aspects and in more detailed aspect by the task group (unit) commander. This coordinated control is required so that the multifunctions of CIC can be carried out within the group without the overloading of any one CIC.

6211. It is essential that the CIC's in individual ships be interrelated in their specific duties to such an extent that the task forces' radars and other information gathering sources are integrated into an effective whole. The "whole" is the group of ships operating within a given area. This will normally consist of a group of units operating under a task force commander in the same disposition. However, war experience has indicated that all units which are within radar range (about 100 miles) must coordinate their efforts to obtain maximum defensive and offensive efficiency in the functioning of CIC.

6220. **The Force Commander.** Upon the task force commander rests the responsibility for certain broad tactical decisions and assignments relating to the functioning of the combat information centers. It is important that all combatant groups within the radar area be guided by these decisions. The following are of major importance:

DECLASSIFIED

1. Conditions of radar silence.

2. Conditions of IFF silence.

3. The use of jamming and deception.

6230. Task Force CIC Ship. The task force CIC ship is the ship of the tactical organization, normally the flagship, designated by the task force commander to assist him in the efficient use of task force's information gathering sources. In general the TFCIC ship shall carry out the following:

(a) Maintain up to the minute information regarding the over-all air and surface situation, detection and location of enemy radars, and the use of radar countermeasures by the enemy.

(b) Disseminate task force doctrine and the directives of the task force commander pertaining to the use of radar, IFF, radar jamming and deception.

(c) Coordinate intertask group CIC activities including fighter direction and the control of air-borne aircraft.

(d) Designate raids when force is in tactical cooperation.

(e) Coordinate control of air-borne aircraft.

(f) Maintain complete information on the location and condition of all own radar intercept and jamming equipment and deception devices.

6240. Task Group (Unit) CIC Ship. The task group (unit) CIC ship is normally the flagship of the task group (unit) commander. This ship under the general direction of task group (unit) commander will be charged within its own group (unit) with—

(a) Assigning surface and/or air radar guardships, fighter direction ships, radar intercept ships, radar jamming ships and/or radar picket.

(b) Directing ships to challenge unidentified surface contacts, when doctrine does not cover this procedure.

(c) Designating surface and/or air contacts as raids when task group is separate.

(d) Enforcing conditions of silence as promulgated by the task force commander.

(e) Directing the use of radar jamming and deception equipment, where permitted by the task force commander.

6250. Relief for Task Force (Group) (Unit) CIC Ships. Because of the necessity of always having an effective coordination of all radars and information gathering sources, the task force (group) (unit) commander should designate relief

CIC ships together with the order in which these units shall assume task force (group) (unit) CIC duties. During cruising the function of task force CIC ship should be given to subordinates in order that they may be fully trained and ready to assume this important function when the tactical situation dictates. The task force CIC ship may also function as the task group CIC ship for the disposition of which it is a part. The task group (unit) CIC ship may also carry out the duties of the task force CIC ship when the task group (unit) is on a detached mission outside radar area of the task force commander.

6260. Assignment of Radar Guardships.

6261. Surface radar guardships will be assigned in accordance with the surface search doctrine. Air radar guardships will be assigned in accordance with the air search doctrine.

6262. When a commander is assigned an area of radar responsibility, he shall assign radar guardships for this area, enforce radar discipline for the condition of radar silence in effect, and provide for immediate relief in case of casualty. Such assignments and instructions must conform with the over-all instructions issued by the task force commander through the task force CIC ship if assigned.

6263. Normally fighter direction ships, task force (group) (unit) CIC ships and flagships will not be assigned as radar guardships, but will retain full use of their radars for their assigned primary responsibilities.

6264. Due to technical limitation it is inadvisable to assign radar guard duties to radar intercept and jamming ships because of the decrease in efficiency caused by the use of radar on the duties assigned.

6265. To facilitate the assignment of radar guardships the following designations are prescribed.

(a) Guard ABLE—Long range air search.

Object.—The detection, recognition, and maintenance of continuous track of all aircraft friendly and/or enemy, excluding aircraft within 30 miles when a guard BAKER is assigned.

(b) Guard BAKER—Short range air search.

Object.—The detection, recognition, and maintenance of continuous track of all aircraft friendly and/or enemy within 40 miles of the disposition, including antisnooper, antisubmarine patrol, etc., including their recognition by IFF and lookouts.

(c) Guard CHARLIE—Medium range air search.

Object.—The detection, recognition, and maintenance of a continuous track of all aircraft friendly and/or enemy within a 75–30 mile range from own disposition. This is an adjunct to guards ABLE and BAKER.

(d) Guard DOG—Low flying aircraft search.

Object.—The early detection and/or recognition of low flying aircraft approaching the disposition. In order to accomplish this it is essential that continuous plots of special low altitude patrol be continuously plotted in order to detect enemy aircraft immediately.

(e) Guard FOX—Long range surface search.

Object.—The early detection, recognition, and tracking of surface units friendly and/or enemy outside of disposition.

(f) Guard GEORGE—Short range surface search.

Object.—To exercise close surveillance of the area surrounding the disposition for early detection of submarines, PT boats, and other small craft.

(g) Guard ITEM—Recognition guard.

Object.—In a particular tactical situation when the normal radar guardship will not afford the proper recognition of friendly contacts an additional ship properly placed in the formation should be assigned these duties. For details see paragraph 6500.

6266. When sector assignments are necessary the following designations are prescribed:

(1) 90° sectors:
Sector GEORGE	350° to 100°
HOW	080° to 190°
ITEM	170° to 280°
JIG	260° to 010°

(2) 120° sectors:
Sector ABLE	350° to 130°
BAKER	110° to 250°
CHARLIE	230° to 010°

or

Sector DOG	290° to 070°
EASY	050° to 190°
FOX	170° to 310°

(3) 180° sectors:
| Sector KING | 260° to 100° |
| LOVE | 080° to 280° |

or

| Sector MIKE | 350° to 190° |
| NAN | 170° to 010° |

(4) 360° sector:
Sector OBOE

Unless otherwise ordered, these sectors are designated clockwise as true bearings.

6300. **Surface Search Doctrine.**

6310. **Purpose.** This doctrine is designed to provide task forces with standard instructions for obtaining maximum radar information about the existing surface situation. By placing particular responsibility in specified units better over-all protection will be accomplished.

6311. In order to obtain an effective surface search, the task force CIC ship shall coordinate the use of the surface search radars within the task force through the task group (unit) CIC ship if assigned. The duties of surface radar guardship shall be assigned to a sufficient number of ships to assure the accomplishment of the requirements of this doctrine.

6312. In the assignment of areas of responsibilities to the surface radar guardships, sectors and/or areas may be assigned. Whether a sector or a given area with reference to the fleet center is assigned will depend upon the existing tactical situation.

6313. When attack by submarines or motor torpedo boats is expected, it is advisable to establish special areas of responsibility to surface guardships to insure close-in surveillance within the task force. (Guard GEORGE.)

6320. **Surface Search Responsibility.**

6321. The task force CIC ship is responsible for the proper coordination of the surface search guardships.

6322. The task group (unit) CIC ship, when task groups are operating within the same areas but are not within the same formation shall coordinate the functions of the various surface radar guardships within the task group (unit) in consonance with the task force orders and doctrine in effect.

6330. **Surface Search Radar Control.**

6331. The task force CIC ship shall coordinate within the task force the use of all surface search radars.

6332. When two or more independent task groups are operating within the same radar area, this control will be exercised through the task group (unit) CIC ship.

6333. The surface radar guardships shall use all radar within the ship as required to carry out the functions charged.

6340. **Surface Search Communication Procedure.**

6341. **Communication Facilities.** The normal tactical radio facilities shall be used to coordinate surface search. Under conditions of a large number of contacts special reporting circuits shall be established.

6342. Reporting Procedure. Voice cards or flag signal procedure should not normally be used to transmit radar information unless security measures require. Abbreviated plain language should be used in reporting contact following the procedure set forth in this doctrine and USF 70.

6343. Call Signs. The call signs used on the radar reporting channel will be those assigned by the task force commander or higher authority. Call signs will be used only when one ship on the circuit is the addressee, or when more than one group are using the same frequency. Reporting ship will use call sign on initial contact. Thereafter, raid letter will identify information. Call sign shall always be used when range and bearing reported is from own ship.

6344. All reports will be made in true bearing and distance in nautical miles from fleet center; however, for initial contact, use of own ship as point of origin is permissible when necessary for speed.

6345. Authorized radar control orders are listed in subparagraph 6174.

6400. Air Search Doctrine.

6410. Purpose. This doctrine is designed to provide task forces with standard instructions for obtaining maximum radar information on the existing air situation.

6411. Classification of ships in the task group. For the purpose of allocating air search and fighter direction duties among ships in a task force, this doctrine establishes the following classes:

1. The fighter direction ship.
2. Air radar guardship.

6412. The Task Force (Group) (Unit) CIC Ship will be responsible to task force (group) (unit) commander for air search radar control, early air warning, and fighter direction.

6413. The fighter direction ships will be prepared at all times to assume the responsibility of intercepting unidentified aircraft using assigned aircraft.

6414. Air Radar Guardships will be responsible to the fighter direction ships for supplying appropriate data.

6420. Air Search Radar Control.

6421. The task force CIC ship or when task group (unit) is operating independently, the task group (unit) CIC ship represents command with regard to fighter direction, and air search radar control. In order to minimize radar interferences, normally no ships other than those listed in paragraphs 6411 and 6412 will use their air search radars except when required for identification purposes or target indication.

6422. Raid Designation. Raids will be designated by numerals by the task force CIC ship. In case a task group is within radar area but is operating independently of the task force as a whole, raid designations will be assigned through that task group CIC ship for raids under control of that group.

6423. Initial Reports. That ship which first detects unidentified aircraft will make the initial report. If other than the air radar guardship they will continue to report until an air radar guard ship starts reporting.

6430. Fighter Direction Doctrine.

6431. The purpose of fighter direction is to provide effective protection against air attack by the use of own defensive fighters.

6432. Attainment of this objective is dependent primarily upon three factors:

(a) The availability of fighters equal to or greater than enemy planes attacking and of adequate physical facilities for fighter direction.

(b) The advantageous positioning of the fighter aircraft and use of the fighter direction facilities.

(c) Thorough indoctrination and training of flying and nonflying personnel concerned with fighter direction.

6440. Fighter Direction Control.

6441. Fighter direction is a function of the task force commander who will normally delegate this function to the force or group CIC ship.

6442. In delegating this function, the task force commander must definitely delimit the forces and areas, including sea and land area, for the defense of which the task force (group) (unit) CIC ship is responsible.

6443. The fighter direction ship will—

(a) Carry out all orders from the task force (group) (unit) CIC ship relative to fighter direction and the use of air search radar as provided in air search radar doctrine.

(b) Be responsible for interception of raids allocated with fighters assigned.

(c) Inform the force (group) (unit) CIC ship of the status of fuel and ammunition in planes assigned in ample time to provide for their reservicing.

(d) Be responsible for the homing of aircraft assigned.

(e) Notify the task force (group) (unit) CIC ship of downed fighters.

(f) Enforce strict radio discipline.

(g) Maintain a high standard of efficiency by exercising fighter pilots and combat information center personnel attached in intercept problems.

6444. Tactical instructions and doctrine for combat air patrols are found in USF 74.

6445. The following basic principles will govern the tactical use of combat air patrols in making interceptions.

(a) Fighter coverage must be provided for the force or bases at all times when there is likelihood of air attack.

(b) No attack should be permitted to come in entirely unopposed.

(c) Fighters will be kept between raid and base. For fighter direction in low visibility see paragraph 6460.

(d) A number of fighters equal to or greater than the enemy must be vectored out to insure the thwarting of a determined attack.

(e) Interception of enemy aircraft will be effected at maximum distance from the base consistent with:

(1) Good communications.

(2) Optimum attack position.

(3) Due regard to the possibility of attack from other quadrants and the number of fighters remaining to thwart such later attacks as may develop.

(f) The number of separate flights of defending fighters used in the defense of an area must be kept small in order to simplify air command, fighter direction, and the radar picture. More fighters available generally means the more planes per flight, not more flights.

6446. The following conditions of readiness are established for defensive fighters:

(a) CONDITION ONE—About 75 percent of the defensive fighters air-borne, remainder at alert on deck. (When a large raid appears on the screen all fighters may be scrambled.)

(b) CONDITION TWO—Approximately 40 percent of the defensive fighters air-borne, remainder at stand-by on deck.

(c) CONDITION THREE—Approximately 10 percent of the defensive fighters air-borne, one-half of the remainder at stand-by on deck.

Note.—These conditions of readiness are independent of ship or other type plane readiness conditions.

6450. Fighter Direction Communications.

6451. Efficient communications quickly relay the orders of the fighter director out to the intercepting fighters. Good communications require that all messages be concise and in the correct fighter direction vocabulary. Strict radio discipline must be maintained to insure that the necessary orders will not be delayed or garbled by relatively unimportant or verbose messages. Unnecessary transmissions will be eliminated and, within flights, hand signals will be used for routine matters.

6452. All fighters and combat information center personnel must know the standard Allied Fighter Direction Vocabulary, CCBP 1102. All combat information center personnel must be thoroughly conversant with USF 70 and the communication plan issued by task force or task group commanders.

6453. Flight leaders must acknowledge all transmissions promptly. Orders from the fighter director must be acknowledged and repeated back; information messages will merely be receipted for.

6454. Upon sighting the enemy, the TALLYHO report must be transmitted in full at the earliest possible moment:

    (a) Sighting—"TALLYHO."

    (b) Own call sign—"This is (division call)—TWO–THREE."

    (c) Relative position of enemy in clock code—"TWO o'clock down 4 miles" (for information of other fighters in the flight).

    (d) Type and number—"18 Hawks, 9 Rats."

    (e) Altitude of enemy—"Angels 15."

    (f) Continuous reports by the flight leader shall be made reporting the progress of the attack and dispersion of the enemy group.

6460. Fighter Direction in Low Visibility (Night Fighter Direction).

6461. The interception of enemy aircraft at night and under conditions of low visibility requires an expert technique of control based upon precise information. The degree of precision is dictated by the limitations of the air-borne intercept radar. The duties of night fighter direction ship include all of those delineated in paragraph 6443. The degree of responsibility is in each case of higher and more detailed order in that the night fighter is completely dependent upon the night fighter direction ship. In addition to these duties the night fighter direction ship is charged with responsibility for—

    (a) Pre-launch communication checks.

    (b) Withdrawal of night fighters from own force AA range when enemy aircraft close to effective gun range.

    (c) Keeping the night fighters on assigned station, clear of any possible danger area or obstruction, and away from friendly strikes.

6462. A NIGHT FIGHTER **MUST NOT** BE LEFT ALONE OUT OF CONTROL!

6470. Visual Fighter Direction.

6471. A CIC watch officer qualified in fighter direction will be located in a position in the ship's superstructure, normally the lookout station, giving him as good all-around visibility as is possible, where he will carry out the following functions:

    (a) Coordinate lookout reports and pass them to CIC.

    (b) Keep a plot of raids as reported over the filter circuit from CIC.

    (c) Keep a plot of all fighter and antisubmarine patrols within visual range.

    (d) Be prepared to direct visual interceptions on planes when so directed by CIC.

6500. Radar Recognition and Identification Doctrine (IFF).

6510. For purposes of this doctrine the following general definitions which are applicable to all types of recognition and identification are quoted:

    (a) Recognition—is the process of determining the friendly or enemy character of another.

    (b) Identification—is that process of indicating your friendly character.

6511. "Identification of Friend or Foe"—is an electronic system installed in ships, aircraft, and shore facilities to recognize friendly contacts made by radar. It is all-important that the commander know the fundamental operating principles and limitations of the particular IFF system in current use. All IFF systems consist of the following units:

    (a) Interrogator-responsor—a unit which when actuated sends out a challenging signal of the proper characteristics and receives the reply from the transpondor challenged.

    (b) Transpondor—a unit which receives a challenge and automatically transmits a reply of a definte characteristic.

6512. The control of the IFF system is a function of the task force commander through the task force CIC ship, if assigned. He shall issue instructions regarding its use as appropriate to the existing tactical situation. The following is promulgated as a guide in the formulation of the required orders. In order that proper interservice coordination in the use of IFF may prevail the designated commander of an operation will issue general instructions. When none are issued this doctrine will be used.

6513. There are certain limitations inherent in any IFF system which must be recognized and taken into consideration when issuing orders for the use of IFF.

6514. SD 158 (4) is the Inter American-British instructions on the use of IFF.

6520. Air-borne Equipment.

6521. The use of air-borne transpondors and interrogator-responsors shall be governed by the conditions of IFF silence in effect. It is incumbent upon the task force (group) (unit) commander to take the necessary precautions that the air-borne IFF equipment is in proper operation and set on the proper code. The correct code settings are promulgated by the area and theater commanders. In the absence of instructions SD 158 (4) is used.

6522. The air-borne interrogator-responsor shall be used to a minimum consistent with absolute necessity.

6530. Ship-borne Equipment.

6531. The ship-borne transpondor shall normally only be energized as directed by the task force CIC ship.

6532. The ship-borne interrogator-responsor will be used only to obtain proper recognition and *will never be operated continuously* This equipment on all ships should be energized at all times when the condition of radar and IFF silence permit; however, the task force (group) (unit) CIC ship shall designate appropriate ship(s) to recognize contacts. None other than the ship(s) designated shall operate their interrogator-responsor except in emergencies.

6533. Normally the ship(s) nearest the contact or anticipated contact will be designated to turn on their transpondors.

6534. The IFF Mark III system operates in approximately the same frequency band as the air search radar equipment. It, therefore, may be considered as comparable in security to that of air search radar except that its power is less and, therefore, its transmission cannot be intercepted as far.

The task force commander, in declaring IFF silence, must weigh the advantages and disadvantages incurred by placing restrictions on electronic recognition.

6600. Radar Countermeasures Doctrine.

6610. Purpose. The fleet radar countermeasures doctrine is established to provide for—

(a) The coordination of radar countermeasures with radar and other combat information within the ship; and

(b) The joint use of radar countermeasures by ships operating together in various tactical organizations.

6611. The basic aims of radar countermeasures are—

(a) To obtain combat information of enemy forces from the enemy's employment of radar; and

(b) To prevent the enemy from obtaining through the use of his radar any accurate combat information of our own forces.

6612. For the purposes of this doctrine the term "radar countermeasures" (RCM) includes radar interception, radar jamming, and radar deception. It does not include communication countermeasures, nor does it include antijamming equipment or techniques. Communication countermeasures is treated in communication publications. Antijamming is considered to be a part of the equipment to which it is attached. It is NOT countermeasures.

6620. Radar Intercept Doctrine.

6621. All ships shall make maximum use of radar intercept equipment in order to obtain all possible information concerning enemy radar.

6622. When contact with the enemy is probable radar intercept ships shall be designated by the task force (group) commander or task force (group) CIC ship if assigned.

6623. The entire radar spectrum within the capabilities of the radar intercept equipment installed shall be kept under constant surveillance by designated intercept ships in order that new enemy frequencies may be discovered at the first opportunity.

6624. Emphasis should, however, be placed by specially assigned radar intercept ships on those bands known to be in use by the enemy.

6625. It is essential that RCM personnel be kept fully informed as to the status of all friendly radars, IFF, VHF, and UHF Radios, and navigational aids to prevent having these reported as enemy radars and to assist in the identification and analysis of spurious radar intercept receiver or signal harmonics. Task force commanders shall be kept informed of newly-established friendly radars at amphibious objectives in order that RCM personnel may be informed.

6626. The task force commander may direct ships equipped with radar direction finders to take simultaneous cross bearings on enemy radar signals reported in order to locate an enemy radar.

6627. Radar pickets should be chosen from ships having radar intercept equipment in order that the range of early warning for the force may be extended to the maximum possible.

6630. Radar Countermeasures Reporting Doctrine.

6631. Units experiencing enemy radar countermeasures, or who are engaged in radar countermeasures activities, must keep the task force (group) CIC ship fully informed of the situation having due regard for the existing communication load and the condition of communication silence.

6632. RCM reports shall be submitted in accordance with currently effective directives of the area commanders. In all cases, a copy of such reports shall be sent to the Chief of Naval Operations in order that research agencies may be kept abreast of the latest developments.

6633. Operational RCM reports shall be made to the task force commander, through the task force (group) CIC ship, and such other addresses as he may designate, as directed by current fleet orders. These reports should include the following:

(a) Interception of enemy radar signals.

(b) Location of enemy radars (if known).

(c) Enemy use of radar countermeasures.

(d) Own use of radar countermeasures.

6634. There is listed below the information which is pertinent and desired in various cases. No report shall be held up to obtain data not readily available. Amplifying reports shall be made to cover details not included in the original reports. *Indicates most important information.

(a) Enemy radar reports:

*(1) Frequency.

*(2) Pulse repetition rate.

*(3) Pulse width.

*(4) Location or bearing.

(5) Beam width.

(6) Rotation rate.

(7) Lobe-switching.

(8) Strength of signal (strong, moderate, weak).

(9) Type or use of radar (AS, SS, GCI, SLC, SFC, AAFC)

(b) Enemy radar jamming reports:

*(1) Frequency.

*(2) Effective band width of jamming.

*(3) Relative effectiveness.

*(4) Bearing limits.

(5) Type of jamming.

(6) Effectiveness of A/J techniques and equipments.

(c) Enemy window reports:

*(1) Bearing limits.

*(2) Range limits.

*(3) Radars affected and to what extent.

(4) Appearance of echoes.

(5) Effectiveness of defensive measures.

(d) Enemy radar deception reports:

*(1) Bearing.

*(2) Range.

*(3) Radars affected and to what extent.

(4) Appearance of echo.

6635. To provide proper intra ship coordination, all radar counter measures information shall be communicated promptly to CIC where it can be quickly evaluated and disseminated to the flag and commanding officers and control stations over internal communications circuits, and to other ships and aircraft as necessary via external communication facilities.

6636. Reports from aircraft shall be made to the base coordinating activity designated by the responsible air commander.

6637. The communications systems to be used in making operational RCM reports are set forth in fleet communication plans.

6638. Adequate internal communications among all countermeasures stations and between each countermeasures station and CIC must be provided.

6640. Basic Policies Governing Radar Jamming and Deception.

6641. Except as indicated in paragraph 6642 below, only the senior commander in an area of operations or commanders specially designated by the area commander may authorize the use of radar jamming and deception.

6642. The task force commander of major units when in actual contact with the enemy may authorize the use of radar jamming and deception of such a nature and of such a scope as will affect only the local tactical situation in their area.

6643. Prior to the employment of radar jamming and deception the commanders involved must weigh the local advantage against enemy reactions which may affect the operations in adjacent areas. Special care should be observed not to employ devices in one area that may prejudice the broader use of countermeasures in other areas, or give advance data concerning our devices that will be worth more to the enemy than a small local advantage gained.

6644. Any commander authorizing the use of radar jamming and/or deception shall ensure constant and intelligent supervision.

6650. Radar Jamming Doctrine.

6651. Radar jamming operations shall be conducted only as directed by The task force commander through the task force (group) CIC ship as appropriate.

6652. In general, radar jamming should be employed against specific enemy radars which are known or strongly suspected to be furnishing the enemy combat information of our own forces.

6653. Radar jamming when properly employed may be used to obliterate information on enemy radar scopes, to confuse enemy radar operators and possibly cause them to shut down their radar equipments, or to assist in deceptive operations employing electronic deception devices and window. Radar jamming is employed most advantageously in darkness, in conditions approaching zero visibility, in conjunction with the use of smoke, or in other circumstances where the enemy lacks visual observation.

6654. The advantages of radar jamming are—

(a) Enemy is fully or partially deprived of ability to determine composition, track, direct guns, or aim torpedos by radar; and,

(b) When used in connection with deceptive operations, the enemy may be caused to disperse his forces and lose local superiority where the real attack is launched.

6655. The limitations and disadvantages of radar jamming are—

(a) Enemy can frequently home on the jammer or locate it by a series of bearings. The direction of the jamming can generally be determined.

(b) If jamming of radars is attempted at extreme ranges, the jamming signal itself serves to alert the enemy before he detects the jamming ship or plane as a radar target.

(c) There is always some minimum range in electronic jamming operations within which the target echo stands above the jamming signal on a radar scope.

(d) Jamming effectiveness is difficult to predict since a well-prepared enemy may read through what seems to be adequate jamming.

(e) Effective jamming operations are difficult to carry out since the jammer must be exactly on the enemy frequency and remain so in spite of any shifts of frequency which may be made by the enemy radar.

(f) A jammer will only affect radars on the same frequency to which it is tuned as opposed to window which will affect all radars over a band of frequencies.

6656. The criterion of jamming effectiveness is the degree to which radar data is denied the enemy. Jamming should be continued even though the enemy does not turn off his radar. He may leave it in use in an attempt to read through the jamming or to give the impressions that the jamming is ineffective. With relation to jamming effectiveness the following factors should be considered:

(a) Screening is more effective when the jammer is between the radar and the target.

(b) Jamming is most effective when a number of ships jam simultaneously to minimize the possibility of the enemy homing on a single jamming bearing.

6657. Spot jamming is preferable to barrage jamming unless sufficient jammers are available to allow pre-tuning as closely as 1½ mcs., since the operator monitoring the jamming has actual control of the jamming and can follow any shift in enemy frequency. Barrage jamming requires much more equipment, but less trained personnel, and must be carefully monitored by continuously scanning the band covered to insure that the enemy radar is not looking through gaps in the jamming spectrum.

6658. Radar jammers will have little or no effect on radars operating farther away than about one and one-half times the distance to the optical horizon.

6659. Radar jamming should never be conducted indiscriminately simply because the enemy is using a radar. The more frequently jamming operations are conducted against the enemy, the more practice his operators receive in overcoming it, and a greater incentive is provided to his research and development agencies to provide tunable radars or radars on different frequencies than those previously employed. Shipboard fire control radars and shore based gun-laying radars should be jammed when encountered, especially if visual observation is denied the enemy. Air-borne radars should be jammed under conditions similar to the above. Never jam radars when outside their effective range (except in the case of jamming early warning radars in conjunction with window and deceptive operations) since this serves no useful purpose and merely alerts the enemy and extends the maximum range of his radar. Jamming is a function of CIC and all jamming operations will be coordinated and controlled by the task force (group) (unit) CIC ship.

6660. Window Doctrine.

6661. In some instances it is preferable to employ window rather than jamming when practicable for the following reasons:

    (a) Window affects all radars within a band of frequencies while radar jamming affects only those radars on the one frequency.

    (b) Window is easier to use effectively in certain situations by particular units.

6662. The effectiveness of window depends upon the following enemy radar characteristics:

    (a) Pulse width.

    (b) Beam width.

    (c) Polarization.

In general window is most effective against a radar having a long pulse width and a wide beam width in both horizontal and vertical plains.

6663. Window may be employed in the following instances:

    (a) Dropped by planes to destroy the accuracy of radar directed anti-aircraft fire and searchlights by confusing or obliterating the normal radar presentation.

    (b) Dropped by planes against enemy early-warning radar to simulate a large number of planes orbiting prior to an attack.

    (c) Dropped by planes in one area prior to making an attack in another area to disperse enemy intercepting forces.

    (d) Dropped by planes in conjunction with the use of radar jamming and other electronic devices in accordance with special deception plans.

    (e) Dropped by planes to cover a task force from enemy radars, either ship, shore-based or air-borne.

(f) Fired in 5''/38 shells and rockets to cover surface forces, especially in amphibious operations.

6664. The following factors must be considered in the operational employment of window:

(a) Window will affect our own radars that lie within its frequency band in that radar presentation will be impaired in the area where the window is sown.

(b) Window reaches its maximum effect about a minute after it is dropped from aircraft or ejected from shells or rockets. Allowance for this time lag should be made.

(c) Window persists from a few minutes to more than half an hour after being dropped or ejected depending upon the strength of the wind and the height at which the window container opens.

(d) Window is effective only in the area in which it is dropped or ejected. *Targets must be within* a window infested area to be protected. Window between ships to be covered and the enemy does *not* effect his obtaining combat information and therefore is useless.

(e) Window movement is controlled by the wind and may drift into an area not desired to be covered.

6670. Radar Deception Doctrine.

6671. Radar deceptive devices produce spurious echoes approximating those of ships and aircraft. They may be employed effectively to confuse search and fire-control radars and to divert enemy forces if used under circumstances in which their presence is not immediately betrayed.

6672. When employing radar deception due account must be taken of the possibility that our own forces will be deceived if not fully informed. Special care must be taken in the use of gulls (floating radar reflectors) since they may drift in an area for days.

6673. Radar deception can be used under the following circumstances:

(a) A single plane can simulate a large flight of aircraft to cause the enemy to divert his intercepting forces from the main attack.

(b) Aircraft can drop deceptive devices to simulate planes orbiting prior to attack. The planes then lose altitude and attack from a different direction coming in as far as possible under the enemy radar beams.

(c) Ground or surface forces can release various balloon-borne devices to simulate aircraft orbiting.

(d) Surface forces may release gulls at night when being trailed or when enemy attack planes or snoopers are in the vicinity in order to produce deceptive radar targets and divert the search forces of the enemy.

(e) Gulls may be launched to give the impression of a larger force than is actually present in the area.

(f) If weather and other conditions permit, carrier forces may launch at least one gull per ship present upon departure from the recovery area after the last strike on an objective.

6700. Gunnery Radar Doctrine.

6710. Several methods of radar gunnery control are available for using fire-control radars. The following methods are defined:

6711. Full Radar Control. A director is in full radar control when radar range, elevation and train data are used.

6712. Modified Radar Control. A director is in modified radar control when radar range and train data are used, elevation being obtained from stable element.

6713. Partial Radar Control. A director is in partial radar control when radar range is used; visual train data and visual or stable element elevation data is used.

6720. Proper radar target indication to the fire-control radars to insure their getting on the designated target is a function of CIC and is usually handled by a liaison officer in CIC who uses data available in that space.

6721. Fire-control radar with proper target indication from CIC should normally be used for directing illumination.

6730. When directors are under full or modified radar control, CIC is usually the best location to establish danger angles and bearing where use of guns will endanger other friendly units.

6740. With present fire-control radar equipment: (a) Radar range is usually more accurate than range finder range when distance between targets is outside the limits of radar discrimination. (b) Visual pointing and training is usually more accurate than by radar.

6750. The problem of shore bombardment differs from normal gunnery procedure in that the target to be taken under fire is usually not seen. Because of this it is necessary that the geographic position of the target and the ship be known at all times. The determination of the position of the ship is a function of CIC and the position of the target that of the shore fire-control party or spotting plane. When both are known the fire-control problem is solved in the usual manner. To assist in shore bombardments, various beacons and/or racons have been introduced into the fleet for test; however, their necessity is as yet unproven except where the topography of the shore makes landmarks difficult to determine.

6760. With the increased power and resolution of fire-control radars, spotting by radar has become more efficient and effective. Every opportunity to exploit this means of spotting should be taken. The exact range at which radar spotting is effective depends on the radars' performance and weather conditions.

6800. Air-Borne Radar Doctrine.

6810. Radar is installed in aircraft for the general purposes of (1) search for surface craft, (2) search for and interception of aircraft, (3) warning of approach of other aircraft, (4) control of weapons, (5) recognition and identification, and (6) navigation.

6820. The performance of a particular radar will be dependent on its design features, state of maintenance, and skill of operation.

6830. In the use of aircraft the capabilities and limitations of the radar in the plane must be known and its employment be directed to fully utilize the associated radar.

6840. Radar equipped aircraft should be employed in coordination with surface craft to (1) protect the formation, (2) exploit the offensive power of the combination, (3) extend the radar range of surface craft, and (4) search and attack operations.

6900. Illumination Doctrine. (See War Instructions, 1944, Chapter 8, Section III.)

PART VII

TRAINING

7000. GENERAL.

7100. Conduct of Exercises.

7110. Ships shall conduct training exercises at every opportunity in port and underway. They shall take full advantage of training offered by the numerous establishments maintained in various locations including outlying bases.

7120. Type and task force commanders shall coordinate training and insure that ships conduct intensive training in preparation for operations. Type commanders are responsible for standardizing methods.

7200. Requirements.

7210. The primary requisite of training is realism. To that end the element of surprise must be introduced frequently and the routine emergency and casualty drills for all departments must be held while ships are in various conditions of readiness for action.

7220. The word DRILL must be used in signaling or announcing all activities which might otherwise be confused with enemy action.

7300. Preparation of Standard Exercises.

7310. Type and task force commanders shall maintain standard exercises for training when utilizing service force facilities where available. They shall review these exercises as battle experience dictates and to accord with current training directives.

7320. For training as task forces at sea where service force facilities are not available, task force commanders shall utilize the exercises given in section 7400. Should changes be necessary, they shall forward recommended revisions to Cominch. (See paragraph 125.)

7400. Standard Task Force Exercises.

7410. Contents:

    I. Radar and Range Finder Comparison Tracking and Adjustment—Exercises 1–4.
    II. Battle Problems—Exercises 5–7.
    III. Bombing and Torpedo Exercises—Exercises 8–9.
    IV. Firing Practices, Aircraft—Exercises 10–11.

7420. General Instructions.

(1) Fleet and tactical commanders are enjoined to conduct frequent training exercises and when practicable daily surface and antiaircraft firing and frequent bombardment firing practices using reduced allowances, with the primary object of perfecting the ability to open fire instantly and accurately. Each exercise should include drill in shifting target from search to fire-control radars.

(2) Exercises should be balanced so that surface firing will not be neglected in favor of antiaircraft firing and that adequate bombardment firing is conducted.

(3) Preference should be given to sleeve firing over burst practices. Burst practices are the last expedient, their primary value being in testing performance of weapons and alertness of condition watch crews.

(4) Each condition watch should have frequent opportunity to open fire. During scheduled firing it is often practicable to have the stand-by section fire guns not manned by duty section.

(5) Plane towing targets for surface ship exercises shall remain within visual contact of surface ships in formation unless specifically ordered otherwise. Planes exercising under simulated attack conditions shall remain within radar range.

(6) Utilization of a vessel of the screen for an offset practice is authorized. Target ships will leave formation at discretion in order to be on station for commencing scheduled exercises at designated times. Should a cruiser be designated as a target, a destroyer will accompany it. In battle problems target should make changes of course and speed during simulated attacks.

(7) Ammunition allowances on firing practices are left to the discretion of commanding officers with the provision that ammunition expended on any run will be reduced as mush as possible so that additional runs and frequent practices may be fired without undue wear of guns. In order to obtain maximum training benefit under service conditions, commanding officers are authorized and encouraged to expend reasonable quantities of service ammunition in these exercises.

(8) Radar sleeves will be used whenever possible and antiaircraft as well as surface firing will be conducted in full radar control.

(9) Should it be desired to recover a sleeve, it will normally be dropped ahead of a destroyer for recovery.

(10) In these exercises commanders will consider the use of smoke by day and night and will conduct training in its use for screening against day and night air or surface attack.

(11) In carrier forces, ships should make maximum use of carrier launching maneuvers for tracking exercises during morning general quarters and at other times.

(12) During exercises ships and planes will employ IFF as directed by OTC insuring that IFF on ships is tested frequently.

(13) The signal ordering exercises may be followed by DESIG (class letter) to indicate the type of ship or aircraft (by indicating parent ship type) to conduct the exercise.

(14) Side designation may be accomplished by use of general signal, "Carry out exercise indicated, numeral preceding indicates side(s)."

(15) In all tracking runs ships shall drill in shifting from search to fire-control radars and shall devote at least half the time to tracking with optics blanked off, training in full radar control. Optical range finding, however, must be sufficient to ensure trained crews, and reliable range finder calibration data.

(16) In large formations the commander may find it convenient to hold certain firing exercises by types or groups and to set aside part of the day when type commanders may operate independently or separate from formation conducting both type and standard task force exercises.

(17) The exercises given hereafter are for use in normal task force operations using facilities of the force itself. Additional bombardment, surface, and antiaircraft practices including drone firings will be scheduled when opportunity permits using service force facilities.

7430. List of Exercises.

I. TRACKING AND CALIBRATION

Exercise 1(A)—Zero Calibration of Fire-Control Radars.

(1) Designated large ship(s) (target) steam on steady course for 10 minutes. Other ships take position abeam (in succession) so as to avoid radar echo interference, steam on course parallel to target(s), distance 1,500–1,700 yards and previously having determined proper setting of repetition rate knob, determine correct value of "zero" setting by "double range echo method."

(2) Ascertain that zero setting is applied correctly at all times. It is not sufficient to determine the "zero setting"; it must be applied and checked constantly because of changing electrical values during warming up periods of radar sets, and the possibility of mechanical slippage of clutch used to lock the "zero setting."

(3) Exercise 1(A) is preliminary to 1(B).

Exercise 1(B)—Radar-Optical Range Finder Comparison.

(1) Establish zero settings as in 1(A), if practicable; otherwise obtain and check preliminary setting by radar-optical range finder comparisons on nearby ships.

(2) Designated target ship(s) take station about 1,500–1,700 yards from guide on true bearing indicated. Remain on this station 5 minutes to permit radar zero setting. Open range to 5,000 yards and thereafter in 5,000 yard steps to 35,000 yards or prescribed distance, remaining at each range for 5 minutes and maintaining approximately the original bearing. Upon completion of exercise return to formation simulating attack on main body using only radar and sound for tracking. Ships of formation give way to target ship if necessary.

Exercise 2(A)—Surface Tracking Exercise.

(1) Designated ships form two groups—each group open to 30,000 yards to right and left of fleet guide between 40° and 70° on the bow, leaving the disposition in time to be in position at zero hour.

(2) Zero Hour—each group maneuver, simulating cruiser or battleship action, closing range so as to rejoin formation after having completed at least 1 hour of tracking exercise. In maneuvering, use a zigzag plan from USF 10 and constant speed. Immediately after the exercise is terminated, ships hoist signal indicating the zigzag plan and speed computed for opposing group. OTC in each group transmit zigzag plan and speeds used to opposite group commander.

Exercise 2(B)—Surface Tracking Exercise.

(1) Same as 2(A) except only one ship will be used as target on each side, zero hour will be 1 hour before sunrise.

(2) Upon rejoining formation targets fly signal giving speed and zigzag plan used. In large formations heavy ships not on axis repeat signal flown by target on their side.

(3) This simple exercise is designed to give all ships a daily tracking drill during morning general quarters when more complicated exercises cannot be conducted. It may usually be conducted as a matter of routine. It should be conducted, if possible, with two

targets in order to provide maximum training to ship and fire-control parties. Should this be impossible, it may be conducted with a single target, but, in this case, it may be expected that in large dispositions only those ships on the side of the target will achieve accurate results because of excessive range. Most ships on the other side will be limited to tracking about half of the time. Therefore, when a single target ship must be used, it should be stationed on alternate bows on alternate mornings.

(4) Each ship report to OCE plan number, basic course, and speed(s) followed by target's report of correct solution. If necessary, OCE can send out summary of results.

Exercise 2(C)—Surface Tracking Exercise—IFF.

(1) Same as 2(B) except target(s) energize shipboard IFF throughout exercise.

(2) Commencing at sunrise minus 1 hour each radar guard and BK marker ship in succession energize effective BK setting for 5 minutes, in order of visual call number (where call numbers are the same, precedence for that call number will be BB, Carriers, CA, CL, DD). Target(s) observe with BL and upon return to formation report BK discrepancies by visual.

Exercise 2(D)—IFF Observation and Check.

(1) This exercise permits check of performance of IFF and training of radar operators in recognizing signals. While it is being conducted all operators should be at radar to observe IFF indications on screen.

(2) Target may be (a) single ship to starboard—Target ONE/or (b) single ship to port, Target TWO/or (c) both targets ONE and TWO.

(3) Prior to zero hour designated target vessel(s) proceed to station(s) abeam of guide, Target ONE 8,000 and Target TWO 17,000 yards beyond assigned disposition screen. At zero hour turn on BK using setting No. 1. Five minutes later shift to setting No. 2 and thereafter at 5-minute intervals to other settings in succession.

(4) Beginning at plus 30 minutes each radar guard and BK marker ship in succession energizes effective BK setting for 5 minutes, order of ships in order of visual call number (if two or more call numbers are the same, precedence for that call number will be BB, Carriers, CA, CL, DD). Target(s) observe with BL and upon return to disposition report BK discrepancies by visual.

(5) Target(s) remain in position as long as practicable leaving in time to regain station in formation at plus 90 minutes without using excessive speed.

Exercise 2(E)—IFF Drill.

(1) (2) (3) Same as Exercise 2(D).

(4) Beginning at plus 30 minutes, OTC call various ships at random and direct each to turn on IFF. Ships called do not reply but merely turn on IFF with currently effective setting. Target ship(s) observe with BL and report "affirmative" or "negative." OTC orders vessel to turn off IFF and directs another vessel to turn on IFF, proceeding in a similar fashion until all ships have tested IFF or until exercise is ordered terminated. Ships receiving "negative" reports from target ship(s) effect repairs or adjustments immediately; OTC will have these ships retest later.

Exercise 3—AA Tracking and Aerograph Calibration of AA Range Finders.

(1) *Target.*—Carrier or cruiser plane equipped with aerograph.

(2) Plane makes high horizontal bombing runs over formation at specified altitude, being particularly careful that altitude is steady during each run. Ships record readings and times for comparison with aerograph readings forwarded after recovery. Time, 2 hours.

(3) Use fire-control radar as available in calibrating optical range finders.

Exercise 4(A)—AA Tracking and Range Finder Exercise.

(1) *Target.*—Two carrier planes unless otherwise designated.

(2) Planes make coordinated high-speed dive and glide bombing runs on heavy ships of the formation. Time, 2 hours.

Exercise 4(B)—AA Tracking.

(1) Plane(s) make high altitude bombing runs over force for 1 hour, using different speed and altitude for each run. Upon recovery, parent ship signal starting time of each run, course, speed, and altitude.
Note.—Utilize these exercises for training in full radar control tracking and for altitude calibration of AA radars.

Exercise 4(C)—Radar Test Flight.

(1) This exercise is designed to provide:

(a) Targets to determine maximum range of all search radars.

(b) Target at constant altitude each flight but varying altitude from day to day which will afford an opportunity to calibrate all sets for altitude determination.

(c) Training in coaching FD radar on target by air search radars.

(2) Procedure will be—

    (a) Flight of at least 2 airplanes will be launched in time to depart from directly over the formation at time and altitude designated by OTC.

    (b) Flight proceed to 120 miles relative and return. All ships track. Guard ships maintain search.

    (c) All ships coach FD radars on the target at maximum range on return flight.

    (d) Upon completion of flight all ships report by visual to type or group commander—

        (1) Range at which target lost on first leg.

        (2) Range at which target picked up on return leg.

        (3) Estimate of altitude.

        (4) Range in yards at which FD on target.

    (e) Upon completion of flight, carrier will report by visual to type or group commanders, who will inform their units—

        (1) True altitude of target.

        (2) Maximum distance of target from formation.

        (3) Any deviation of more than 200 feet from standard altitude.

Exercise 4(D)—Fire-Control Radar Elevation Adjustment.

    (1) The plane acting as target shall initially circle over formation at an altitude of from 2,000 to 5,000 feet. Fly a climbing course directly away from the formation to a range of 15,000 yards and altitude of not less than 8,000 feet. Ships adjust alignment of optical and radar line of sight in elevation. Plane fly directly toward formation at constant altitude to permit check at various position angles. Repeat as necessary.

Exercise 4(E)—Radar Tuning and Adjustment.

    (1) During this exercise any radar restrictions in existence are removed. Radar technicians on all ships will tune and adjust all radars for maximum performance commencing before zero hour while target is en route to station. In a large force, if interference among radars requires, OTC may specify restrictions on number of air search radars to be tuned simultaneously.

    (2) Target may be (a) single ship to starboard—Target ONE, or (b) single ship to port—Target TWO, or (c) both targets ONE and TWO.

(3) Designated target vessel(s) proceed to position 30,000 yards on beam of guide prior to commencement of exercise. At zero hour commence approach on formation converging slowly so as to regain station in formation in 1 hour. Remain at 22,000 yards from guide for about 10 minutes both going out and coming in.

Exercise 4(F)—Airborne Intercept Radar Calibration—VF(N).

(1) The purpose of this exercise is to test in daylight the performance of AI radar in night fighters.

(2) Two night fighters alternate as target and test plane (or any plane can be used as target); controlling fighter director plot exercise and vector testing plane into approximate radar interception position.

(3) Conduct at least one test at 20,000 feet altitude to check performance of radars under reduced atmospheric pressures.

II. BATTLE PROBLEMS

Exercise 5(A)—Surface Battle (Cruiser Attack).

(1) Destroyer commander assign two or more destroyers to attack group as directed by numeral following exercise designation; for example, "Exercise 5A2" specifies two destroyers for attack group. Destroyers leave formation in time to reach initial position, 25,000 to 30,000 yards between 40° and 70° on either bow of force, by zero hour. Reform screen with remaining destroyers.

(2) At zero hour attack group commence approach, using only radar and sonar for tracking. Follow standard zigzag plan and on completion of exercise report as in Exercise 2(A). Situation represents an early morning surprise contact. OTC maneuver formation as necessary to develop gunfire and avoid torpedoes. Cruisers and destroyers follow doctrine in protecting heavy ships.

(3) It is desirable to conduct this type of exercise with as many as three target groups making a combined approach from different bearings.

Exercise 5(B)—Surface Battle (Destroyer Attack).

(1) Same as 5(A) but initial position 20,000 yards. The attack group represents a division of enemy destroyers. Make a simulated torpedo attack against carrier, battleship, or main group, utilizing radar only to make approach. Own cruisers and destroyers simulate repelling the attack.

Exercise 5(C)—Surface Battle (Combined Attack).

(1) Exercise 5(A) and 5(B) combined to be conducted as an independent exercise. Exercise 5(B) shall begin when the attack group reaches about 16,000 yards.

(2) These exercises are designed—

    (a) To test doctrine for defense against surface attack and to train in use of this doctrine.

    (b) To provide training for destroyers in making torpedo attack.

    Note.—The foregoing exercises may be conducted by day or night.

Exercise 5(D)—Surface Battle (Combined Attack from Battle Deployment).

(1) Same as Exercise 5(C) but conducted by cruisers and destroyers against battle line of large formation when directed following battle deployment exercises.

Exercise 5(E)—Radar Reporting, Surface Contacts.

(1) OTC directs one ship to make a drill report.

(2) Designated ship makes sample "skunk" report, followed by suitable amplifying report; emphasis is on proper form and inclusion of all essential data; precede all such reports by the word "drill."

(3) When satisfied with reports, OTC designates another ship to make reports; continue in similar fashion until all ships have made sample reports or until exercise is ordered terminated.

(4) OTC may call upon any ship to (a) make amplifying report for any initial contact reported by another, or (b) hold, sweep, or watch the imaginary raid.

Exercise 5(F)—Same as 5(E) except that OTC may designate certain ships to work out sample raids and tracks before the exercise.

Exercise 6(A)—Group Aircraft Torpedo Attack—Carrier.

(1) The target may be any ship in the formation, but usually will be carrier, battleship, or train group.

(2) Carrier torpedo planes make repeated simulated attacks as a group during designated period of time, exercising at various evasive tactics and methods of approach. Planes take photographic records of attack and when possible drop waterfillable bombs to simulate torpedo release.

(3) Force, including intermediate air patrol, exercise at repelling attack. During group approach force maneuvers should in general be such as to bring attacking aircraft astern of the formation.

(4) This exercise should be frequently conducted at night or as a simulated night attack with maximum use of radar by ships and planes.

Exercise 6(B)—Group and Individual Aircraft Torpedo Attack.

(1) Same as Exercise 6(A) except that after completing first group attack, planes make individual attacks on single ships for 30 minutes.

Exercise 6(C)—Aircraft Torpedo Attack—Cruiser or Battleship.

(1) As far as practicable the same as Exercise 6(B) but conducted by cruiser or battleship planes.

Exercise 6(D)—Combined Aircraft Attack on Formation.

(1) Carrier striking group proceed when possible to at least 75 miles then simulate coordinated attack on Force from unannounced bearing. Designated ship exercise in fighter direction.

(2) Force, including combat patrol, exercise in repelling attack. No restriction on maneuvering. If fuel permits, maximum boiler power may be ordered. During the approach period, maneuvers should in general turn the formation away from the approaching group of planes.

(3) Time period during which this attack will be conducted will be designated in advance.

Exercise 6(E)—Combined and Individual Aircraft Attack on Formation.

(1) Same as Exercise 6(D) except that after group attack, planes make individual attacks on ships for 30 minutes.

Exercise 6(F)—Fighter Direction Problem One.

(1) At time specified a combat air patrol of at least four fighters shall be on station over designated fighter direction ship. Patrol leaders report fighter net frequency giving the number of planes with him, their angles, and how long they can operate at normal speeds.

(2) Call sign of the fighter direction ship shall be Rainbow Base and the fighters Rainbow One, Two, etc.

(3) The FDO shall divide the patrol into two groups, one to be sent out to act as an attack group and the other retained over the base for interception. The difficulty of these interceptions will depend upon the amount of control exercised by the FDO over the "attack group" and can be varied as desired.

(4) Upon completion of exercise FDO notify planes and vector them back to their base.

Exercise 6(G)—Fighter Direction Problem Two.

(1) Same as paragraph 1 of Exercise 6(D).

(2) Call sign of the fighter direction ship shall be Rainbow Base and the VF shall be Rainbow One, Two, etc. The collective call sign of the attack group shall be "Pirate." Individual call signs of the attack group shall be operational call signs assigned. The fighter direction ship shall guard the frequencies of both the attack group and the fighters.

(3) At an unspecified time (but within one-half hour of the zero time of the exercise) the attack group shall make a run on the fighter direction ship from a distance of at least 80 miles, at an altitude of at least 10,000 feet. Upon completion of their attack the group shall rendezvous, retire to approximately 50 miles and make a second attack simulating torpedo plane runs. In retiring the attack group should fly low enough so as not to be visible on radar screen.

(4) Fighter net and attack group frequencies as specified in despatch announcing the exercise.

Exercise 6(H)—Radar Reporting, Aircraft Contacts.

(1) Same as Exercise 5(E) except for imaginary "bogey" raids instead of "skunk" contacts.

Exercise 6(I)

(1) Same as Exercise 6(H) except that OTC may designate certain ships to work out sample raids and tracks before the exercise.

Exercise 6(J)—Close-in Tracking of Aircraft—Exercise of Radar Screening Teams.

(1) Single target plane, preferably a large bomber type, or a section of smaller planes if no large bomber available, take station about 20 miles abeam of disposition.

(2) At zero hour, commence making low altitude (200–1,000 feet) runs back and forth across disposition, withdrawing beyond visual range at times, circling disposition and orbiting to simulate past tactics of enemy torpedo bombers.

(3) Radar guardships track target continuously using all available radars; make reports as required by USF 10. At least one vessel by virtue of different range and bearing will usually be able to track bogey and must be alert to make report; OTC develop team work among guardships.

(4) Vessels exercise AA control parties at discretion.

DECLASSIFIED

(5) At about plus 30 minutes, or when ordered by OTC, target plane(s) climb to 5,000 feet and repeat runs.

(6) At about plus 60 minutes, or when ordered by OTC, target plane(s) climb to 10,000 feet and repeat runs.

(7) If more than one plane or group is available, they may be employed simultaneously at different altitudes.

Exercise 6(K)—Night Carrier Landings.

(1) This exercise shall be held preferably on a day when the base ship has the late air patrol duty. The night fighters shall be launched before the air patrol is taken aboard, and the flight deck left spotted forward after the late air patrol has been landed. The night fighters shall be landed after the ending of evening twilight.

Exercise 6(L)—Fighter Direction Problem Three (Night).

(1) This exercise is to be conducted during hours of darkness and will simulate an actual interception in every practicable respect. Varying conditions of visibility should be sought for successive problems, i. e., no moon, full moon, clouds, etc. Two night fighters will be used, alternating as interceptor and target. Night fighters shall be launched at least an hour before dawn, preferably on days when the base ship has the early air patrol duty. The night fighters can then be landed with the first air patrol.

(2) Procedure will be—

(a) Target will proceed to a point at least 40 miles from base and make a run on the ship or force. Interceptor will, under the control of the fighter director, follow vectors to a radar contact position on the target. The interception should be completed to the point of *visual identification*. Both planes will be plotted at all times and at the completion of exercise returned to base by the fighter director.

(3) The basic exercise outlined is capable of many variations and the fighter director and the pilots involved should exploit capabilities of material and skill of personnel to the fullest. Target should take reasonable evasive action both in course and altitude during the interception.

(4) When the exercise brings the interceptor within range of the force screen's antiaircraft fire, he shall be ordered to fire and break away as in actual practice.

(5) Other ships in formation should closely follow the exercise and be prepared to assume control if ordered. Advantage should be taken of the opportunity presented for checking radars for altitude determination.

DECLASSIFIED

(6) Upon order of the OTC, "window" may be dropped during the course of the exercise by the target.

Exercise 7(A)—Aircraft Squadron Combat.

(1) Fighter Squadron conduct VF vs. VF combat training in sector designated 20 miles outside screen.

(2) Camera guns will be used.

Exercise 7(B)—Aircraft Squadron Combat.

(1) Same as 7(A) except fighter planes attack multiplace planes for free gun and defensive formation training in sector designated. This exercise may be combined with dive and horizontal bombing exercises.

III. BOMBING AND TORPEDO EXERCISES

Exercise 8(A)—Dive, Glide, and Low Altitude Bombing.

(1) Bombing target will be towed by carrier or other designated ship.

(2) Designated aircraft groups conduct dive, glide, and low altitude bombing runs with miniature or water-filled bombs and strafing. OCE may designate use of live bombs (or rockets) at discretion.

(3) Screening ships simulate repelling attacks. Ships maneuver at discretion to bring batteries to bear, simulating insofar as possible actual protection of carrier.

Exercise 8(B)—Horizontal Bombing of Towed Target.

(1) Same as exercise 8(A), except horizontal bombing runs will be made instead of dive and glide bombing runs.

Exercise 8(C)—Torpedo Attack.

(1) Torpedo planes attack heavy ships in formation dropping water-fillable bombs at point of torpedo release. Use cameras.

(2) Ships maneuver to avoid attacks.

Exercise 8(D)—Coordinated Attack.

(1) Combinations of 8(A), 8(B), and 8(C) as prescribed.

Exercise 9(A)—Aircraft Slick Bombing.

(1) Aircraft as available conduct dive and/or horizontal bombing on slicks in sector designated 5 miles outside screen.

Exercise 9(B)—Antisubmarine.

(1) Conduct aircraft attack on surprise target which may be smoke float, slick, or shellfire.

(2) Use miniatures, water-fillable bombs, live bombs, or rockets as designated.

Exercise 10(A)—Section Free Machine Gunnery.

(1) VF tow sleeve for section of multiplace planes. Tow sleeve to pass over section on diagonal course with about 30 knots relative speed differential. Firing to be conducted in sector designated 10 miles outside screen.

(2) Sleeves will be dropped on carrier if practicable.

(*Note.—As far as possible conduct firing at high altitude.*)

Exercise 10(B)—Aircraft Fixed and Free Machine Gunnery.

(1) Same as 10(A), except aircraft as available conduct IBP fixed and free machine gunnery on towed sleeves in sectors designated 10 miles outside the screen.

Exercise 11—Aircraft Free Gunners—Ramp Firing.

(1) Aircraft sleeve will be towed across the ramp so that sleeve passes close aboard, but not over the deck. Planes on deck commence firing when sleeve comes within range and cease firing prior to limiting safety bearing on the quarter. Ships of the screen move forward as necessary to clear arc 120°–240° relative from carrier.

(2) Each gunner shall be attended by a safety observer in train.

V. FIRING PRACTICES—ANTIAIRCRAFT

Exercise 12(A)—AA Automatic Weapons "How."

(1) Designated ship(s) launch towing plane and stand-by plane equipped with sleeve on towline of not less than 900 feet. Plane will then make one "H" run from each side over heavy ships in succession from the van followed by similar runs over screening ships ahead of screen. (See FTP 191, Art. 1J7.) Force commander may direct plane to make additional runs. When practicable, and when necessary to provide firing opportunity, two or more screening ships may be directed to take station ahead of screen, other screening ships adjusting screen as necessary to provide effective antisubmarine protection for heavy ships.

(2) Towing plane will approach at such an angle as to insure a clear range; for leading heavy ships this normally should be from slightly abaft beam. Commander screen assist by moving flank screening ships forward.

Exercise 12(B)—AA Automatic Weapons "George."

(1) Same as Exercise 12(A) but "G" runs with towline of maximum length.

Exercise 12(C)—AA Automatic Weapons "Tare."

(1) Same as 12(A) or 12(B) except that plane flies past ships at ranges from 800 to 2,000 yards, altitude of sleeve 500 feet. Ships fire when they consider it safe to do so. Plane flies past all ships in column or around entire formation before turning for next run. Continue making runs during designated time period.

Exercise 12(D)—Large Caliber AA "Baker."

(1) When carrier planes equipped with towing reels are available, fire BAKER runs, using radar sleeve. When practicable provide multiple target runs.

Exercise 12(E)—All Calibers AA "George."

(1) Same as 12(D) except fire GEORGE runs with all calibers.

Exercise 12(F)—AA "Tare."

(1) Same as 12(E) except fire TARE runs with all calibers against multiple targets.

Exercise 13(A)—Burst Represents High Altitude Bomber.

(1) This exercise is to train and test alertness of condition watch crews.

(2) Burst target to be antiaircraft or starshell projectile, fired as surprise by designated ship during designated time interval, personnel not on watch keeping clear of battery.

(3) Position angle of burst to be about 40°—altitude 6,000 to 12,000 feet on any clear bearing.

(4) All ships which can safely do so, fire at burst with 3" and 5", condition watch crew, 1 round per gun. OCE note times of opening fire by each ship.

Exercise 13(B)—Burst Represents Torpedo Plane or Dive Bomber.

(1) Same as 13(A) except in small formations designated ship fire multiple burst targets to represent various types of close in air attacks. In large formations designated ship(s) fire burst targets during specified time interval.

(2) Any ship which can safely do so take burst target under fire with any or all batteries, condition watch crew, small number of rounds (one 5-inch, six 40-mm., ten 20-mm.). OCE note time of opening fire by each ship.

(3) 5" and 3" must not be fired unless burst will be at least 700 yards horizontally from any ship.

Exercise 13(C).

(1) Same as 13(B) except each ship which can safely do so fire multiple burst targets.

Exercise 13(D)—Surprise Flare (Simulated Dive Bomber).

(1) Plane flies at about 5,000 feet. At intervals drop flares about 1,000 yards from formation. Ships which can safely do so open fire on any target with one or two rounds from 5″ and 3″ guns when plane is clear. Limit ammunition to one round per gun per target.

Exercise 13(E)—Surprise Flare (Simulated Glide Torpedo or Bombing).

(1) Same as Exercise 13(D) except plane drops flares at 3,000 to 5,000 yards from formation.

Exercise 14—Automatic Weapons Against Balloons or Kites.

(1) Individual ships conduct automatic weapon practice against balloons or kites.

VI. FIRING PRACTICES—SURFACE

Exercise 15(A)—Surprise Simulated Submarine (Float Light Practice).

(1) By zero time, screen take stations between 315° and 045° relative to axis unless otherwise ordered; designated destroyer be in position between 1,500 and 2,000 yards on designated beam of rear heavy ship making maximum speed practicable and at least 5 knots greater than the guide.

(2) At zero time destroyer drop float light astern and announce SURPRISE on TBS. If float light fails to ignite, drop additional lights at 60-second intervals until satisfactory target is obtained, announcing SURPRISE TWO, etc., on TBS. Repeat this procedure for each heavy ship in succession from the rear, commencing when abeam.

(3) Not earlier than 90 seconds after SURPRISE, if float light has ignited, ship which has float light approximately abeam open fire with automatic weapons and 5″ if desired.

(4) When leading heavy ship ceases firing exercise is completed, screen and target vessel resume original stations in formation unless otherwise directed.

(5) This exercise may be conducted by day or night.

Exercise 15(B).

(1) Same as 15(A) except that airplane flies low over formation and releases float light outside screen.

Exercise 16(A)—Offset Battle Practice.

(1) Heavy ships as designated conduct offset firing at desired ranges.

(2) One of the two ships should remain in vicinity of force so that other ships may observe results. Rear ship in right-hand group and leading ship in left-hand group may be targets. Practice may be fired as a duel.

(3) Maneuver as practicable.

(4) Use radar to fullest extent possible.

(5) All offset firing should be to the right.

Exercise 16(B).

(1) Same as 16(A) except detach two destroyers for offset duel at ranges between 5,000 and 10,000 yards.

Exercise 16(C)—Offset Practice (Main and Secondary Batteries as Desired).

(1) By zero time screen take stations between 315° and 045° relative to axis. Heavy ships in column, or as ordered by OTC. At zero time, without signal, target destroyer start approach from ahead and pass counter-clockwise around formation at speeds between 15 and 30 knots on courses to maintain range from firing ship between 10,000 and 15,000 yards. Use slower speeds on run aft, and high speeds on run across rear and toward van. Heavy ships fire in succession unless otherwise directed. Maneuver as desired to bring batteries to bear without embarrassing other heavy ships.

(2) During each gunfire period at intervals of 3 minutes or greater target change speed at least once and maneuver.

(3) Target record time (zero time for each firing ship in time of first flash) and true bearing of firing ship and MPI of splash (for each salvo) as practicable. When convenient, target furnish each firing vessel target courses and speeds, and speeds during gunfire and fall of shot observations.

(4) Firing vessel indicate commence firing and cease firing by use of BAKER. As target comes within range each ship open fire if range is clear of screening vessels. Only one ship may fire at a time. Each side of the formation is considered divided into a number of sectors equal to the number of heavy ships present. Heavy ships should not fire outside their sectors until the preceding ship has obviously ceased fire. Ships may fire on both sides as target rounds formation.

(5) Use 70 mils offset for battleship main battery B L & P and all types 8'', 6'', and 5'' ammunition; use 2,000 yards offset for battleship main battery AP. Cease firing when range is 9,000 yards or less. Use target ammunition if available. Prior to zero time inform OTC info target vessel if AP will be fired.

Exercise 16(D)—Phase Calibration Practice.

(1) The purpose of this exercise is to check previous calibration firing for possible changes of I. V. caused by new index of powder or erosion of the guns. Normally only one phase will be fired, at expected battle range for each type ship, limiting ammunition fired to one full or two split salvos.

(2) The target will take station abeam of firing group. At time designated, target group and firing group maneuver to open to firing range at which time base course and speed will be resumed. Target group report when ready. Heavy ship firing order will be in order in column. Firing vessel take station with target bearing 2° forward of beam and maintain accurate station. Report when ready. Other ships in firing group maintain approximate stations on firing ship. Target group may also fire if desired.

(3) Firing and target ship record true bearings on each other and on splash as each salvo lands. Target take accurate rake data, reporting rakes after each salvo. Firing vessel and target take sextant angles limiting splashes to determine pattern size.

Exercise 17—Automatic Weapon Firing at Fast Target (Simulated MTB).

(1) Designated DD tow point of aim target at high speed past formation. Ships fire with automatic weapons when arcs are clear, shifting position in formation as necessary to get better firing arc.

Exercise 18(A)—Star-Shell Duel—Day.

(1) Two designated vessels leave force and conduct star-shell duel by daylight at safe distance from formation.

(2) Practice to be conducted as for night contact and star shells placed to give effective illumination as by doctrine.

(3) Reporting of contact, challenging, and ship's procedure of opening fire should be made part of above exercises.

Exercises 18(B) and (C).

(1) Same as 5(B) and (C) except fire star shells.

Exercise 18(D)—Star-Shell Duel—Night.

(1) Same as 18(A) but conducted at night.

VII. COUNTERMEASURES AND DECEPTION EXERCISES

Exercise 19(A)—Radar Intercept Tracking—Surface.

(1) The purpose of this exercise is to give ships practice in tracking a target (employing radar) without the use of their own radars. The target may be either a ship or aircraft.

(2) Target takes station about 40,000 yards from force (50 miles for aircraft target); at designated time make radar approach on the force, using various courses and speeds; record all movements for comparison.

(3) Ships track target using radar intercept receivers and directional antennas only; record data for comparison.

(4) Ships participating submit brief reports (three copies to the type commanders who will make further distribution as directed by the commander-in-chief of the fleet concerned.

Exercise 19(B)—Radar Intercept Tracking—Aircraft.

(1) Same as Exercise 19(A) except air group(s) make closing run on force, tracking the force radars with radar intercept receivers and directional antennas only.

Exercise 20(A)—Radar Jamming—Self-screening.

(1) The purpose of this exercise is to give ships practice in tracking a target which is screening itself by radar jamming. The jammer may be carried either in a ship or aircraft.

(2) Target (jammer) take station about 40,000 yards from force (50 miles for aircraft target); at designated time intercept and jam specified type of radars; close force on various courses and speeds; maintain a record of all movements for comparison.

(3) Ships attempt to track target with the specified type of radars; maintain record of all data obtained; note particularly range at which jamming becomes ineffective; record all adjustments made to minimize effects of jamming; obtain scope pictures and sketches where practicable.

(4) Submit brief report as for Exercise 19(A).

Exercise 20(B)—Radar Jamming—Off-Target.

(1) Same as Exercise 20(A) except that jamming ship or plane attempts to screen other targets (ships or planes) which are being tracked by the force radars.

Exercise 20(C)—Radar Jamming—Force-Screening, Surface.

(1) Jammer-equipped ships form screen for force in direction of attack group; intercept and jam attack group radars of specified type.

(2) Attack group take station about 40,000 yards from force; at designated time make closing run on the force; using information from the specified type of radars only attempt to determine the course, speed, and disposition of the force, and gain favorable attack position.

(3) Submit brief report as for Exercise 19(A).

Exercise 20(D)—Radar Jamming—Force-Screening, Air.

(1) Same as exercise 20(C) except that attack group consists of planes, making closing run on the force from about 50 miles using information from specified type of air-borne radar only.

Exercise 21(A)—Window—Air-borne.

(1) The purpose of this exercise is to give ships practice in tracking planes employing Window as a screen.

(2) Three or four planes of a squadron make closing run on the force, at designated time, dropping Window as necessary to jam specified type(s) of radars; remainder of squadron make attacks through the Window.

(3) Ships of the force attempt to track attacking planes through the Window using specified type(s) of radars only; obtain scope pictures and sketches where practicable.

(4) Submit brief report as for Exercise 19(A).

Exercise 21(B)—Window—Rocket or Shell, Offensive.

(1) Attack group equipped with rocket or shell Window take station about 40,000 yards from force; at designated time close the force, dispensing Window as necessary to screen self against specified type(s) of radars.

(2) Ships of the force attempt to track attacks ships through the Window Screen.

(3) Submit brief report as for Exercise 19(A).

Exercise 21(C)—Window—Rocket or Shell, Defensive.

(1) Ships equipped with rocket or shell Window form a screen for the force in the direction of the attack group; screen force by dispensing Window as necessary to jam specified type(s) of radars.

(2) Attack group form about 40,000 yards from the force; at designated time close the force, attempting to gain favorable attack position using information from specified type(s) of radars only.

(3) Submit brief report as for Exercise 19(A).

Exercise 22(A)—Radar Deception—Decoys, Offensive.

(1) The purpose of this exercise is to give ships practice in distinguishing between echoes from decoys and those from actual targets, and to gain experience in the tactical employment of radar false echo reflectors (other than Window).

(2) Attack group equipped with radar decoys take station about 40,000 yards from force; at designated time close force and employ decoys, towed, captive, or free, attempting to gain favorable attack position.

(3) Ships of force track attack group with specified type(s) of radars; attempt to distinguish between actual attacking and decoy ships.

(4) Submit brief report as for Exercise 19(A).

Exercise 22(B)—Radar Deception—Decoys, Defensive.

(1) Same as Exercise 22(A) except force employs radar decoys in an effort to evade attacking group; attack group use only specified type(s) of radars and attempt to intercept force and gain favorable attack position.

Exercise 22(C)—Radar Deception—Moonshine.

(1) Air group(s), with three or four planes equipped with Moonshine, take station about 75 miles from force; at designated time commence closing force; employ Moonshine-equipped planes from various directions; make actual attack with major force from a different direction.

(2) Ships of the force track air group(s) with specified type of radars; force fighter director attempt to intercept main attack group with combat air patrol, using information from the specified type of radars only.

(3) Submit brief report as for Exercise 19(A).

Exercise 22(D)—Radar Deception—Peter.

(1) Attack group, equipped with Peter, take station about 40,000 yards from force; at designated time close force employing Peter; use own radars to keep an accurate relative plot on designated ship(s) of the force for comparison.

(2) Ships of the force attempt to track attack group using specified type of radars only; record complete tracking data for comparison.

(3) Submit brief report as for Exercise 19(A).

VIII. FLAG HOIST EXERCISE

Exercise 23(A)—Internal Flag Hoist Drill.

(1) For use at sea or in port. Designated ships conduct exercise during specified times hoisting signal meaning "I am exercising at flag hoist drill" at fore truck in order to keep yardarms clear for drill.

(2) For first half of period, divide signal and quartermaster personnel into two groups. Assign call of a tactical unit commander to the more experienced group and own ship's call to other group. Conduct drill between port and starboard yardarms. Senior group make hoists using tactical calls, General Signals, International Code, Signal Vocabulary, WIMS, etc., which the other group will interpret making proper response by flag hoist. Intersperse with incorrect signals or those having no meaning.

(3) During second half of period signal officer or leading signalman sings out calls and signals to be hoisted and interpreted by each group simultaneously. Group first two blocking with correct interpretation scores one "beat."

Exercise 23(B)—Flag Hoist Drill.

(1) For use in port or at sea. SOP (or designate OCE) designate participating unit(s) (vessels) and indicate time of commencement. Make hoists containing appropriate calls and signals in various systems interspersed with incorrect signals or signals having no meaning. Participants make appropriate response by flag hoist. Fly hoist meaning "I am exercising at flag hoist drill" |during exercise.

(2) Responsible unit commanders and ships be alert to detect and call attention to improper hoists and relaying procedure.

Exercise 23(C)—Use of General Signal Book.

(1) For use only at sea during periods of reasonable tactical security. OTC (or designated OCE) after appropriate signal, transmits *via TBS* addressee(s) and text (meaning) suitable for encoding| as a Flag Hoist. Each ship two blocks flag hoist consisting of proper calls and signal as promptly as possible without regard to visual responsibility. Haul down with flag ship.

(2) OTC will preface each exercise transmission with the words "Drill Message." Announcement of "Cease Present Exercises" will terminate exercise.

Exercise 23(D)—Signal Drill in Methods of Minimum Visibility.

(1) For use in port or at sea. OTC designates two ships to conduct exercise 22(D) including a time signal for commencing and completing the exercise. During specified period the designated ships will hoist general information signal meaning "I am exercising for communication drill purposes only; no ship movement involved."

(2) Exchange despatches, signals, etc., by semaphore, searchlight (small iris or filter), blinker gun, aldis lamp or binocular mounted

blinker. Employ methods of lowest practicable visibility at the moment. Binoculars or glass should be required for reception.

(3) Sending of code despatches, repeated back, is best test of accuracy.

IX. RECOGNITION AND IDENTIFICATION EXERCISE

Exercise 24(A)—Aircraft Recognition Procedure.

(1) For use only at sea. OTC (or designated OCE) hoists general signal addressed to ships in company "Carry out exercise 23(A)," designating an individual ship. When the signal is understood the designated ship will challenge the OCE as though he were an approaching aircraft. The OCE will make the aircraft reply to challenge. As soon as proper reply to challenge is received ship makes hoist informing accompanying vessels of the friendly nature of the "aircraft." When all vessels have acknowledged "friendly" signal, the designated ship hauls down general information hoist and informs "aircraft" (OCE) by flashing light that her identity has been established as friendly within the formation. This terminates the exercise.

Exercise 24(B)—Emergency Identification by Night Fighting Lights.

(1) First Method (Individual). OCE hoists general information signal meaning "For communication drill purposes only; no ships' movements involved," and then flashes signal meaning "Use night fighting lights" to ships in succession. When this signal is received, ships called turn on night fighting lights correctly set up for the period, and, by flashing light directed towards the OCE, indicate the color sequence from top to bottom of the display. OCE receipts for response whereupon ship turns off display.

(2) Second Method (Simultaneous). This method will be used when the night fighting light displays of the ship(s) can be seen readily by the OCE who hoists signals meaning "For communication drill purposes only; no ship movement involved," and "Use night fighting lights" designating the ship or ships to be exercised. The designated ship(s) immediately turns on night fighting lights correctly set up for the period. No further signals are required. After OCE checks displays by glass, he executes the general information signal whereupon ship(s) turn off night fighting light display.

(3) This exercise is for use only at sea.

Exercise 24(C)—Recognition Procedure With Merchant Ships.

(1) For use at sea only. OCE hoists signal with meaning "Carry out exercise 23(C)" addressed to an individual ship. When understood OCE hoists the International Call Sign of any allied merchant vessel. The ship designated for exercise immediately challenges and carries out the correct merchant ship recognition procedures (with the OCE making proper responses for vessel whose International Call she is flying). Upon satisfactory completion of the exercise OCE haul down merchant vessel's call.

(2) Procedure may be repeated with other ships in formation in succession using different International Call Sign with each.

Exercise 24(D)—Major War Vessels Recognition Procedure.

(1) For use at sea only. OCE hoists general information signal "For communication drill purposes; no ship movement involved"; and designates an individual ship in formation to "carry out Exercise 23(D)." Designated ship will immediately challenge the OCE by the method of lowest practicable visibility using the current procedure in use between major war vessels. When exercise is satisfactorily completed OCE executes the general information signal, or else designates another vessel to carry out the same exercise.

X. MOTOR TORPEDO BOAT EXERCISES

Exercise 25(A)—Motor Torpedo Boat Attacks.

(1) The purpose of this exercise is—

(a) To train air and surface forces in detecting and repelling motor torpedo boat attacks.

(b) To train motor torpedo boats in search and attack operations against surface forces.

(c) To improve present antimotor torpedo boats doctrine.

(2) Procedure will be—

(a) A surface force will be operating in a limited area during certain specified hours. This force may be in any applicable disposition set forth in USF 10.

(b) MTB's will search for, locate, and simulate an attack on the surface force during the specified hours. The OTC of the surface force is the officer conducting the exercise.

(c) The surface force may employ an antiair patrol and antimotor torpedo boat pickets, if desired. The air patrol should be prepared to drop flares to illuminate and float lights to mark the position of the motor torpedo boats at night.

(d) Both the MTB's and the surface force will be prepared to use smoke screens tactically when scheduled.

(e) Surface forces may use star shell to illuminate the attacking MTB's after they have been detected.

(f) The surface force or air patrol will not listen in on the MTB's voice radio maneuvering circuit.

(g) Each ship of the surface force will indicate gunfire on MTB's by use of 36-inch searchlight kept continuously on each target taken under fire.

(h) Each MTB will fire one white Very star in the direction of the target to indicate simulated torpedo fire, and will close the range and turn its searchlight on the target fired at.

(i) Whenever any MTB approaches a surface ship undetected to within 2,000 yards and indicates having fired torpedoes at that ship, the ship will be considered out of action, will turn on its running lights, will leave the formation and trail it at about 5,000 yards astern.

(j) Any MTB receiving simulated gunfire as indicated in the table below shall turn on running lights, reverse course, and withdraw from the action at 1,000 r. p. m.

Gunfire from:	For
One (1) ship	30 seconds.
Two (2) ships	20 seconds.
Three (3) or more ships	15 seconds.

(k) Upon completion of the first attack, MTB's rendezvous 2,000 yards astern of the rear surface ship in the formation. Further attacks may be ordered by the OCE if time and weather conditions permit.

(3) Brief reports will be submitted if directed by the commander in chief of the fleet concerned.

XI. BOMBARDMENT EXERCISE

Exercise 26—Bombardment.

(1) Bombardment firing exercises against uninhabited coasts or by-passed enemy territory may be conducted by forces en route to and from operations.

(2) These exercises should follow the procedure set forth in current instructions and appropriate type doctrines.

(3) Where practicable they should include—

    (a) Direct fire at short and long ranges.

    (b) Indirect fire with offset point of aim.

    (c) Indirect fire with "Point Oboe" (selected point unsuitable for ranging) as point of aim.

    (d) Indirect fire on reverse slope.

(4) To obtain maximum benefit from the practice, charts should be prepared, target areas assigned, and firing scheduled as for actual operations. Most training will be in prearranged fire. It may be possible under some conditions, however, to send vessels with shore fire-control parties embarked close enough inshore to permit direct spotting and training in control of fire.

APPENDIX I TO USF 10B

CRUISING DISPOSITIONS

(See Section 3200)

Check-off list for instructions to accompany cruising dispositions.

  (a) Definition.

  (b) Purpose, or use.

  (c) Order of forces.

  (d) Position of guide.

  (e) Function of center.

  (f) Station of ships.

  (g) Establishment of searches and patrols.

  (h) Instructions for emergency deployment.

  (i) Tactical communications.

  (j) Miscellaneous instruction.

CRUISING DISPOSITION 3-C

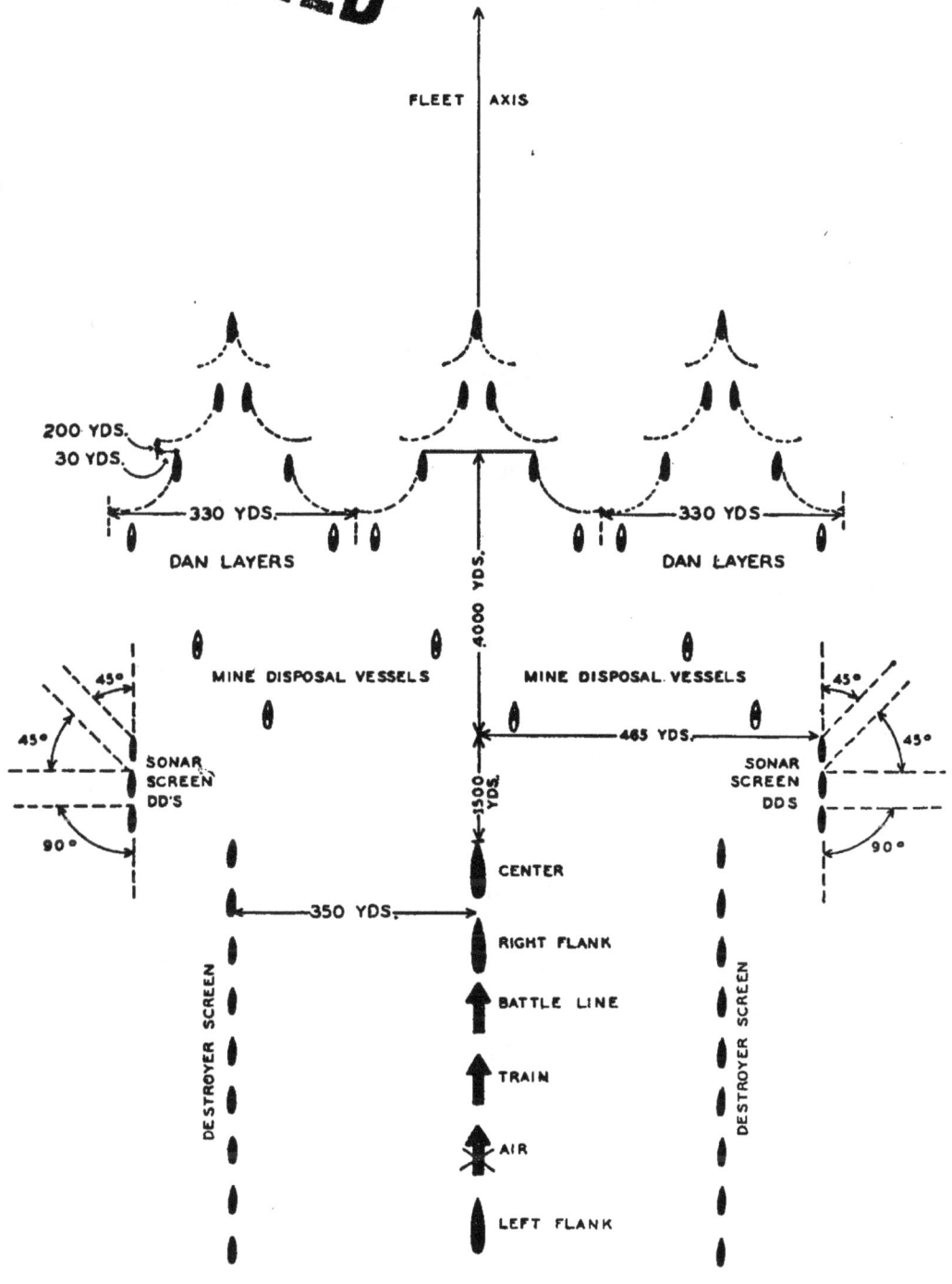

FLEET AXIS

200 YDS.
30 YDS.

330 YDS.

DAN LAYERS

4000 YDS.

330 YDS.

DAN LAYERS

45°

45°

SONAR
SCREEN
DD'S

90°

MINE DISPOSAL VESSELS

MINE DISPOSAL VESSELS

465 YDS.

45°

45°

SONAR
SCREEN
DDS

90°

1500 YDS.

CENTER

DESTROYER SCREEN

350 YDS.

RIGHT FLANK

BATTLE LINE

TRAIN

AIR

LEFT FLANK

DESTROYER SCREEN

1 DIV. HORIZONTAL = 100 YDS.
1 DIV. VERTICAL = 1,000 YDS.

NOTE

SCALE

Figure 19.

CRUISING DISPOSITION 3.D.

(a) Cruising Disposition 3—Cruise multiple column of task groups.

(b) This disposition is for use in traversing a swept channel in wake of mine sweepers.

(c) Natural order from van to rear is—
Center.
Right flank.
Battle line.
Train.
Air.
Left flank.

(d) The fleet guide is in the leading ship of the center column. All heavy ships follow as exactly as possible the course(s) made good by the guide.

(e) ———.

(f) Commander left flank destroyers assign destroyers to left flank sonar screen; commander right flank destroyers assign destroyers to right flank sonar screen.

(g) Air patrols will normally be launched before entering the swept channel and recovered after clearing it.

(h) ———.

(i) Communications as prescribed by USF 70 for normal tactical organization.

(j) (1) The axis spacing between task group guides is variable. In forming the disposition, take distance 1,000 yards between ships in the center column, leaving no gaps. Available destroyers spread to cover both flanks.

(2) All ships energize degaussing gear.

(3) Destroyers in wing columns stand continuous echo-ranging watch unless otherwise directed.

(4) Destroyers making sight or sonar submarine contact will proceed immediately to attack.

(5) Maneuvers by capital ships to evade air attack must limit lateral displacement from the column to approximately 200 yards.

DECLASSIFIED

CRUISING DISPOSITION 3-L

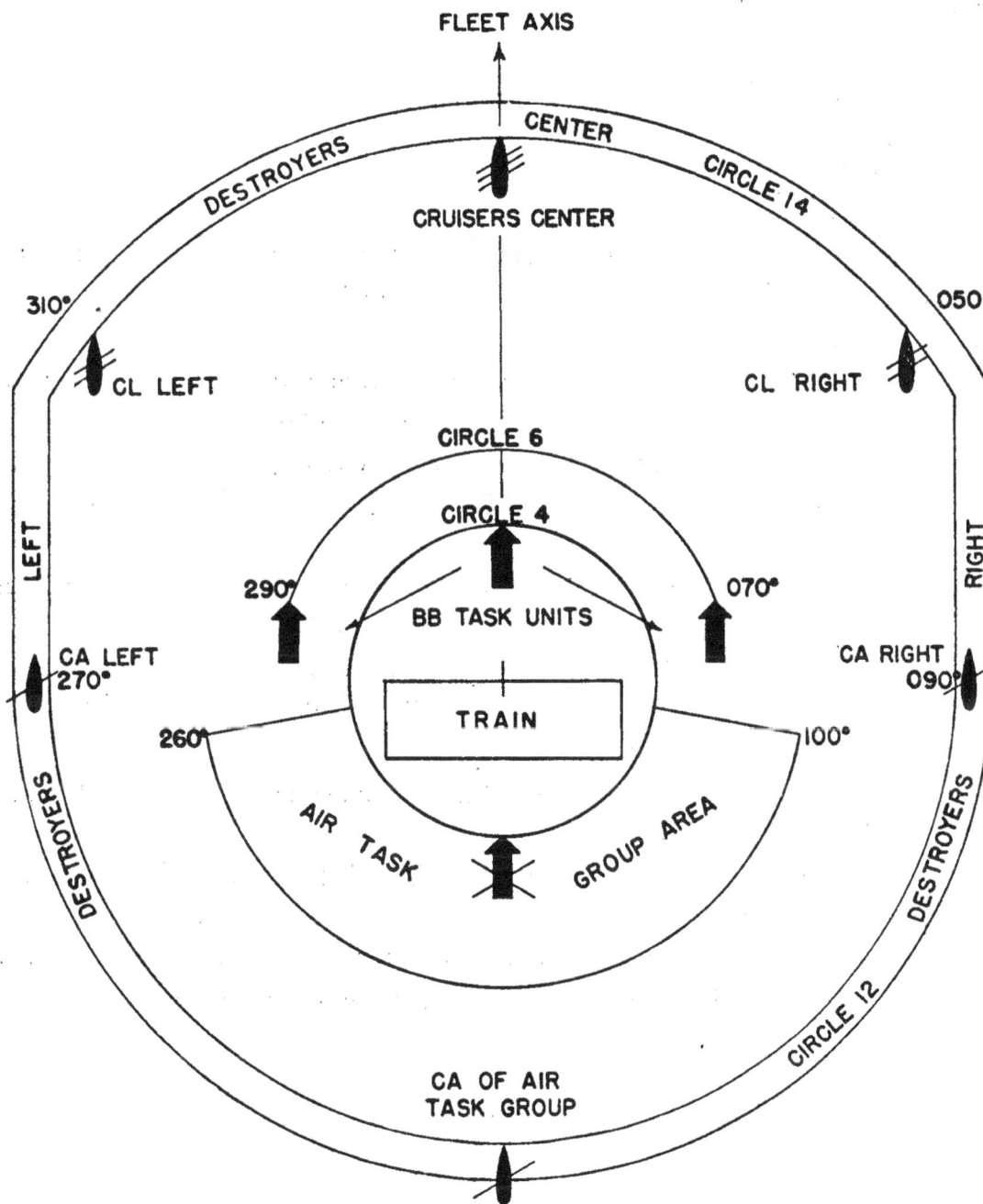

Figure 20.

CRUISING DISPOSITION

(a) Cruising Disposition 3-R is a night or low visibility disposition.

(b) It is suitable for the defense of carriers and train.

(c) (1) light forces are stationed in a single outer screen and as close antisubmarine screening vessels in proximity to the heavy ships. The outer screen is not circular; in shape it approximates the locus of firing points for torpedoes aimed at the fleet center. Cruisers will normally be stationed by divisions, destroyers singly or in pairs.

(2) Battleships are stationed by divisions or smaller units to provide a concentration of main battery fire on any bearing from which penetration of the screen is threatened and to permit individual station unit maneuvers to dodge torpedoes.

(3) Station assignments are indicated in the diagram, but may be varied by the officer in tactical command to suit existing conditions. If train and carriers are both present they occupy the areas indicated. If only one is present it occupies the fleet center.

(d) The fleet guide is normally in the train at the fleet center. If the train is not present, the guide is in the battleship station unit nearest fleet axis.

(e) Regardless of the station occupied by the guide, any rotation of the fleet axis will be performed about the fleet center.

(f) Unless otherwise prescribed, the train formation will be as compact as practicable, consistent with safety of maneuver. Columns should be limited to four ships in length, distance between ships 600 yards, interval between columns 1,000 yards.

(g) The officer in tactical command will direct the establishment of patrols.

(h) Deployment of the battle line will not be executed as a standard evolution from this formation. For emergency deployment, battleship station units change course by division columns to signaled deployment course and work gradually into column on van division, using course angles sufficiently small to avoid blanking main battery fire. Light forces form in signaled battle disposition by most expeditious routes. Train and air task groups change course to reverse of enemy bearing until well clear, then parallel battle line, or proceed as otherwise signaled. Screens assigned to train and air task groups accompany them.

(i) Communications as prescribed by USF 70 for normal tactical organization.

(j) All screening vessels stand continuous echo-ranging watch unless otherwise directed. Use supersonic gear in accordance with current doctrine.

CONFIDENTIAL DECLASSIFIED

CRUISING   DISPOSITION   3 - R

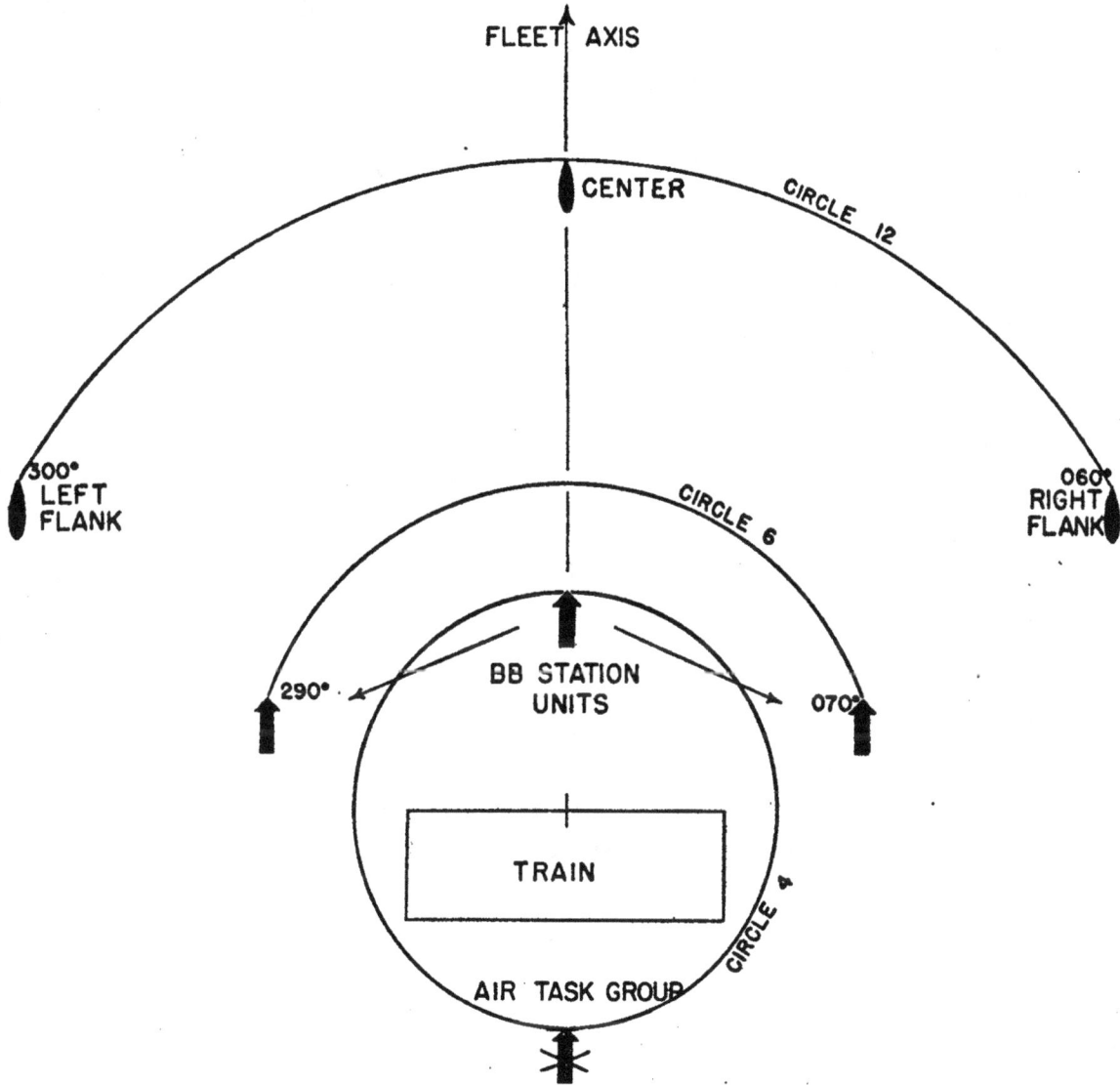

Figure 21.

DECLASSIFIED

CRUISING DISPOSITION 3-R

(a) Cruising Disposition 3-R is a low visibility or night READY cruising disposition.

(b) It is intended for use in proximity to enemy forces of comparable strength. Dependence for warning of surprise cruiser and destroyer raids or air attack is placed in radar ships and the usual all around screens of typical cruising dispositions are replaced by close screens on heavy units.

(c) Station assignments are as indicated in the diagram, but may be varied by the officer in tactical command to suit conditions. Station units are concentrated to facilitate handling during changes in course and/or axis and to make possible rapid deployment, even at night. Each task group screen take the screen formation prescribed by task group commander. If the train is not present, the air task group will occupy the fleet center.

(d) The fleet guide is normally in the train at the fleet center. If the train is not present, the guide is in the battleship station unit nearest fleet axis.

(e) Regardless of the station occupied by the guide, any rotation of the fleet axis will be performed about the fleet center.

(f) Unless otherwise directed, the train formation will be as compact as practicable, consistent with safety of maneuver. Columns should be limited to four ships in length, distance between ships 600 yards, interval between columns 1,000 yards.

(g) Searches and patrols will be established in accordance with instructions from the officer in tactical command.

(h) Emergency deployment may be ordered from this disposition during darkness. Battle line station units take deployment course by division column movement and work gradually into column on van division, using course angles small enough that own after turrets are not blanked. Battle line screens continue to screen until directed by commander battle line to join van inner area destroyers. The flank which will be in the van on deployment occupy the outer areas, center proceed to van inner areas. The flank which will be in the rear on deployment occupy the inner areas. Air take station 10 miles on disengaged side, forward of beam of battle line. Screens assigned to these task groups accompany them. The fleet guide and fleet center shift to the van battleship division on deployment.

(i) Communications as prescribed by USF 70 for normal tactical organization.

(j) All sonar equipped ships stand continuous echo-ranging watch unless otherwise directed. Use supersonic gear in accordance with current doctrine.

DECLASSIFIED

CRUISING DISPOSITION 3-V

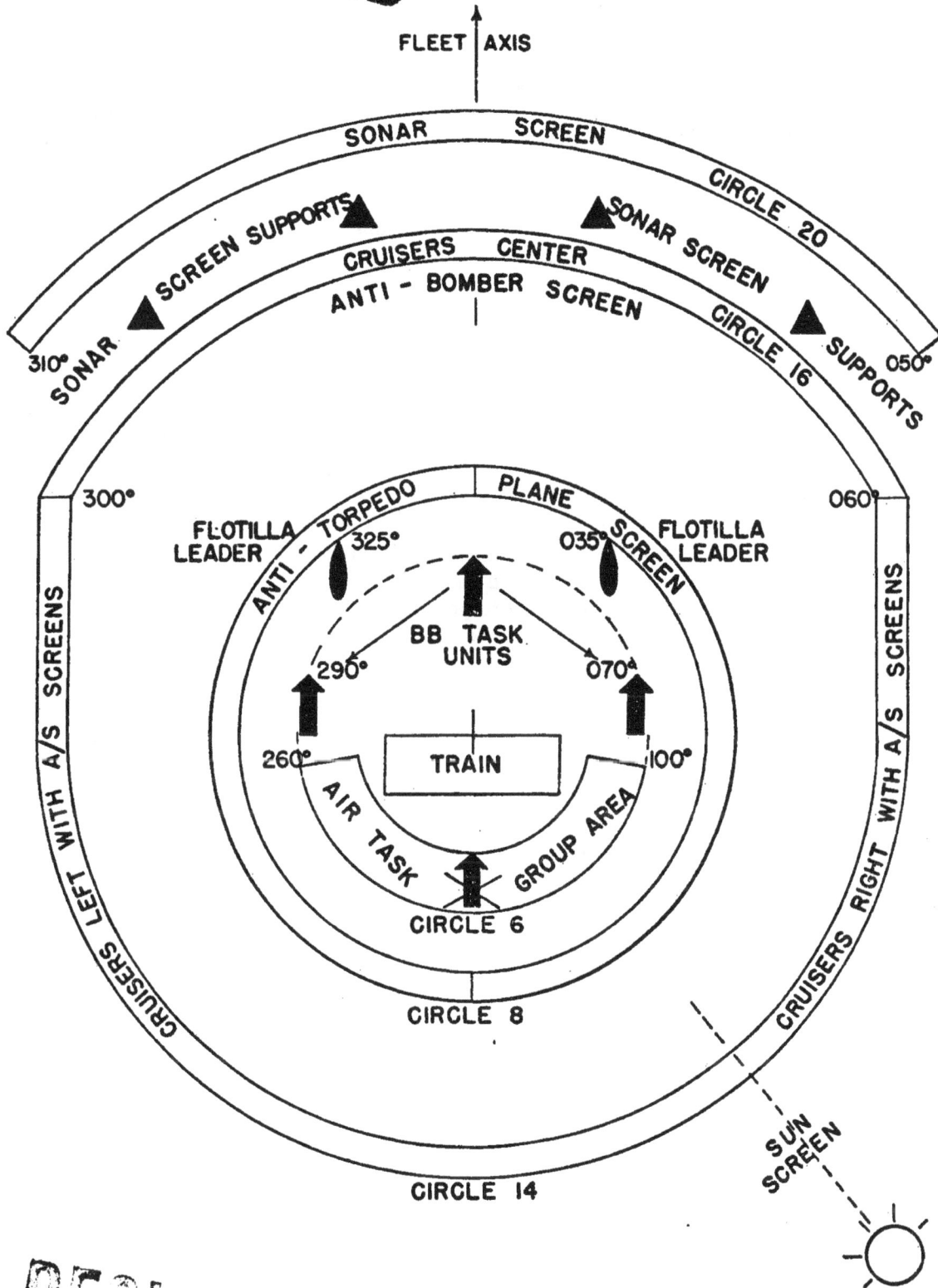

FLEET AXIS

SONAR SCREEN

CIRCLE 20

SCREEN SUPPORTS ▲

▲ SONAR SCREEN

CRUISERS CENTER

ANTI - BOMBER SCREEN

CIRCLE 16

310° SONAR

▲ SUPPORTS

050°

300°

060°

FLOTILLA LEADER

ANTI - TORPEDO PLANE SCREEN

325°

035°

FLOTILLA LEADER

CRUISERS LEFT WITH A/S SCREENS

290°

BB TASK UNITS

070°

CRUISERS RIGHT WITH A/S SCREENS

260°

TRAIN

100°

AIR TASK

GROUP AREA

CIRCLE 6

CIRCLE 8

CIRCLE 14

SUN SCREEN

Figure 22.

DECLASSIFIED

p. 1–8

CRUISING DISPOSITION 3-V

(a) Cruising Disposition 3-V is a day high visibility disposition.

(b) It is suitable for defense against both aircraft and submarine.

(c) (1) Station assignments are indicated in the diagram, but may be varied by the OTC to suit existing conditions. If train and carriers are both present, they occupy the stations indicated. If only one is present, it occupies the fleet center. Battleships are stationed by divisions or smaller units to permit independent station unit maneuvers to develop maximum fire and avoid torpedoes or bombs.

(2) Unless otherwise directed, the train formation will be as compact as practicable consistent with safety of maneuver. Columns should be limited to four ships in length, distance between ships 600 yards, interval between columns 1,000 yards.

(3) The antihorizontal bomber screen is composed of available cruisers and destroyers. It is located on circles 16 (van) and 14 (flanks and rear). Individual station units should be as powerful as practicable, observing the principle that circumferential distance between units shall not be more than 8,000 yards. Destroyers of each station unit do double duty as antisubmarine screens for cruisers.

(4) The outer antisubmarine screen (sonar screen) is stationed on circle 22 and the sonar screen supports on circle 19. Sonar screen and supports are units of the center, under immediate command of commander sonar Screen. The center of the sonar screen is on the fleet axis unless otherwise directed by the OTC.

(5) The antitorpedo plane screen is stationed on circle 8. It is composed of the flotilla leaders, air task group cruisers, and battle line inner antisubmarine screens. All ships in this screen are stationed singly to permit developing maximum volume of fire from short-range weapons against torpedo plane attack. Units of this screen will retain their basic task unit designations.

(6) Whenever a carrier passes outside the antitorpedo plane screen in launching or recovering aircraft, the nearest air task group cruiser will accompany the carrier. Remaining antitorpedo plane screens spread to close the gap.

(d) The fleet guide is normally in the train at the fleet center. If the train is not present, the guide is in the battleship station unit nearest fleet axis.

(e) Regardless of the station occupied by the guide, any rotation of the fleet axis will be performed about the fleet center.

(f) The task group commanders are responsible for stationing individual ships.

(g) Searches and patrols will be established on orders from the officer in tactical command.

(h) Deployment of the battle line will not be developed directly from this formation.

(i) Communications as prescribed by USF 70 for normal tactical organization.

(j) All sonar equipped ships stand continuous echo-ranging watch unless otherwise directed. Sonar screen utilize supersonics in accordance with current doctrine. Sun Screen—commander right and left flank each designate one section of destroyers as sun screen. On signal from the OTC to "station sun screen," the section from the flank nearest the bearing of the sun will take stations, one ship 10° right, the other 10° left of the bearing of the sun from the fleet center at maximum visual signal distance outside the outer screen. This unit will rotate around the fleet center as the azimuth of the sun changes. Once stationed, the sun screen will not be relieved by the other flank as a result of any change in bearing of the sun or rotation of the fleet axis. Unless otherwise directed, the sun screen will, without signal, rejoin the formation by one-half hour after local sunset.

CRUISING DISPOSITION 4-LS

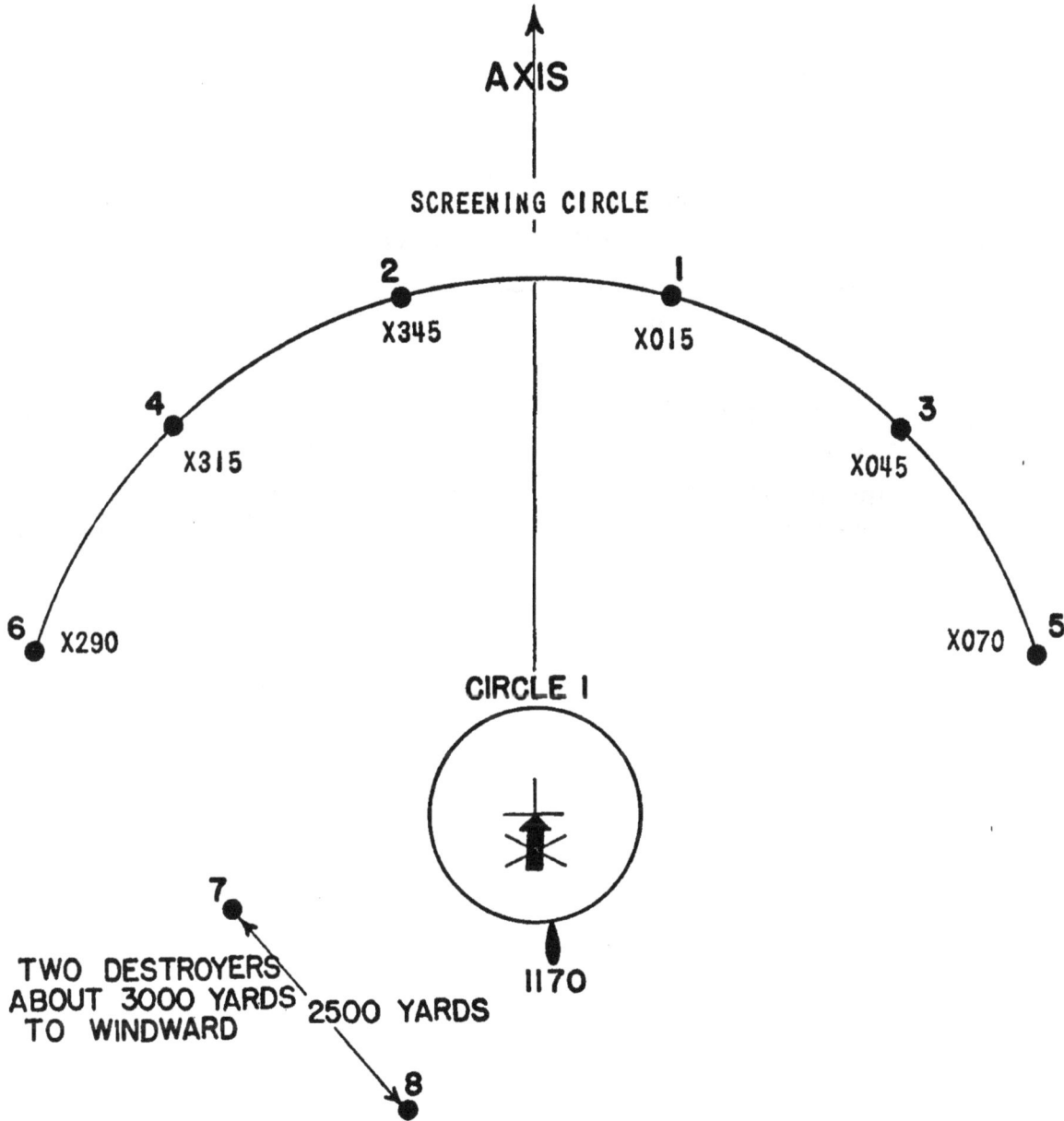

AXIS

SCREENING CIRCLE

2
X345

1
X015

4
X315

3
X045

6   X290

X070   5

CIRCLE I

1170

7

TWO DESTROYERS
ABOUT 3000 YARDS   2500 YARDS
TO WINDWARD

8

Figure 23.

(a) Cruising Disposition 4-LS is a combination low visibility and antisubmarine cruising disposition.

(b) It is suitable for use of a small carrier force cruising at night or in low visibility day conditions, or during any condition of light when heavy ship protection against submarine attack is a paramount factor.

(c) ———.

(d) The guide is normally in the carrier at the fleet center.

(e) Any rotation of the axis will be performed about the center.

(f) Station assignments are indicated on the diagram, but may be varied by the officer in tactical command to suit existing conditions. The screening ships will be stationed in accordance with the instructions contained in part III.

(g) Patrols and searches will be established in accordance with instructions from the officer in tactical command.

(h) ———.

(i) Communications as prescribed by USF 70 for an undivided task force, unless other specific instructions are issued by the officer in tactical command.

(j) All sonar equipped ships stand continuous echo-ranging watch unless otherwise directed. Sonar screen utilize supersonics in accordance with current doctrine.

CRUISING DISPOSITION 4-V

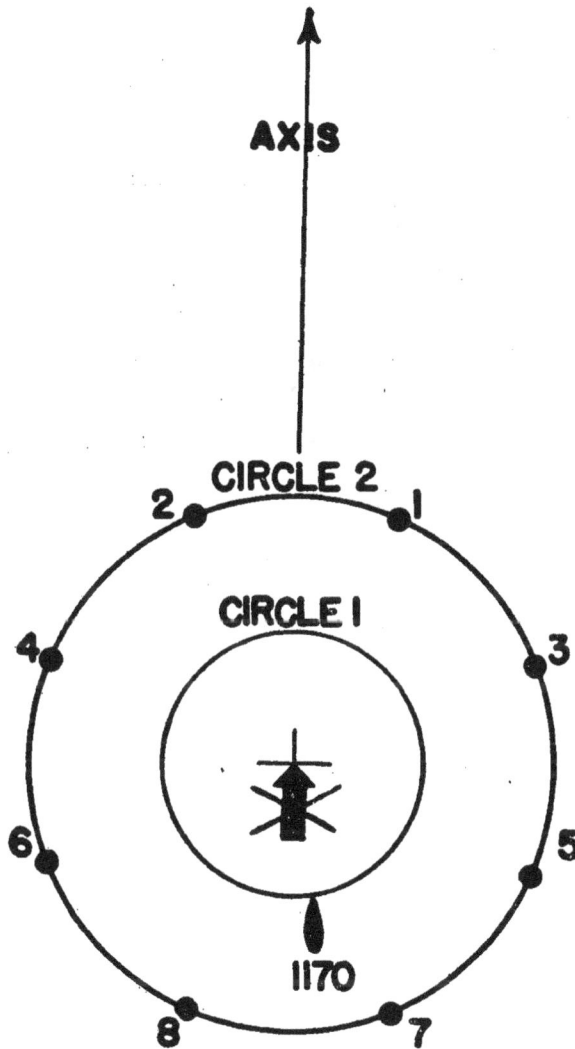

Figure 24.

CRUISING DISPOSITION 4-V

(a) Cruising Disposition 4-V is a high visibility disposition.

(b) It is devised primarily for defense of a small carrier force against probable or actual enemy air attack. Transformation between Cruising Disposition 4-LS and 4-V can be made rapidly and easily.

(c) ———.

(d) The guide is normally in the carrier in the fleet center.

(e) Any rotation of the axis will be performed about the center.

(f) Station assignments are indicated on the diagram, but may be **varied by the** officer in tactical command to suit existing conditions.

(g) Patrols and searches will be established in accordance with instructions from the officer in tactical command.

(h) ———.

(i) Communications as prescribed by USF 70 unless other specific instructions are issued by the officer in tactical command.

(j) All sonar equipped ships stand continuous echo-ranging watch unless otherwise directed. Sonar screen utilize supersonics in accordance with current doctrine.

CRUISING DISPOSITION 5-LS

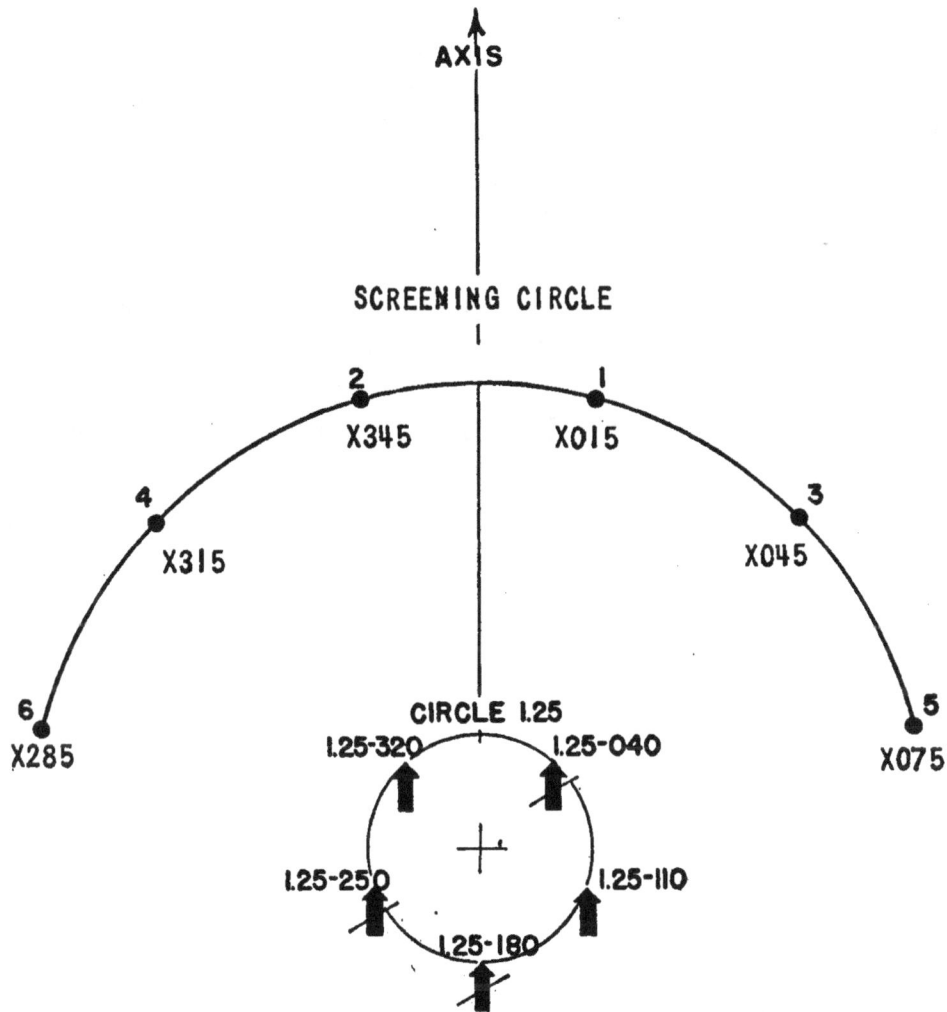

AXIS

SCREENING CIRCLE

2
X345

1
X015

4
X315

3
X045

6
X285

CIRCLE 1.25

1.25-320   1.25-040

1.25-250   1.25-110

1.25-180

5
X075

Figure 25.

CRUISING DISPOSITION 5-LS.

(a) Cruising Disposition 5-LS is a combination low visibility, and antisubmarine cruising disposition.

(b) It is suitable for use of a carrier force cruising at night or in low visibility day conditions, or during any condition of light when heavy ship protection against submarine attack is a paramount factor.

(c) ———.

(d) The guide is normally in the battleship farthest advanced along the axis.

(e) Any rotation of the axis will be performed about the center.

(f) Station assignments are indicated on the diagram, but may be varied by the officer in tactical command to suit existing conditions. The screening ships will be stationed in accordance with the instructions contained in part III.

(g) Patrols and searches will be established in accordance with instructions from the officer in tactical command.

(h) Deployment from this disposition is unlikely. However, if an enemy surface attack should develop, emergency deployment will be effected by the battleships turning to the deployment course, and by the carriers forming on the disengaged side.

(i) Communications as prescribed by USF 70, unless other specific instructions are issued by the officer in tactical command.

(j) All sonar equipped ships stand continuous echo-ranging watch unless otherwise directed. Sonar screen utilize supersonics in accordance with current doctrine.

DECLASSIFIED

SPECIAL CRUISING DISPOSITION 5F (FUELING)

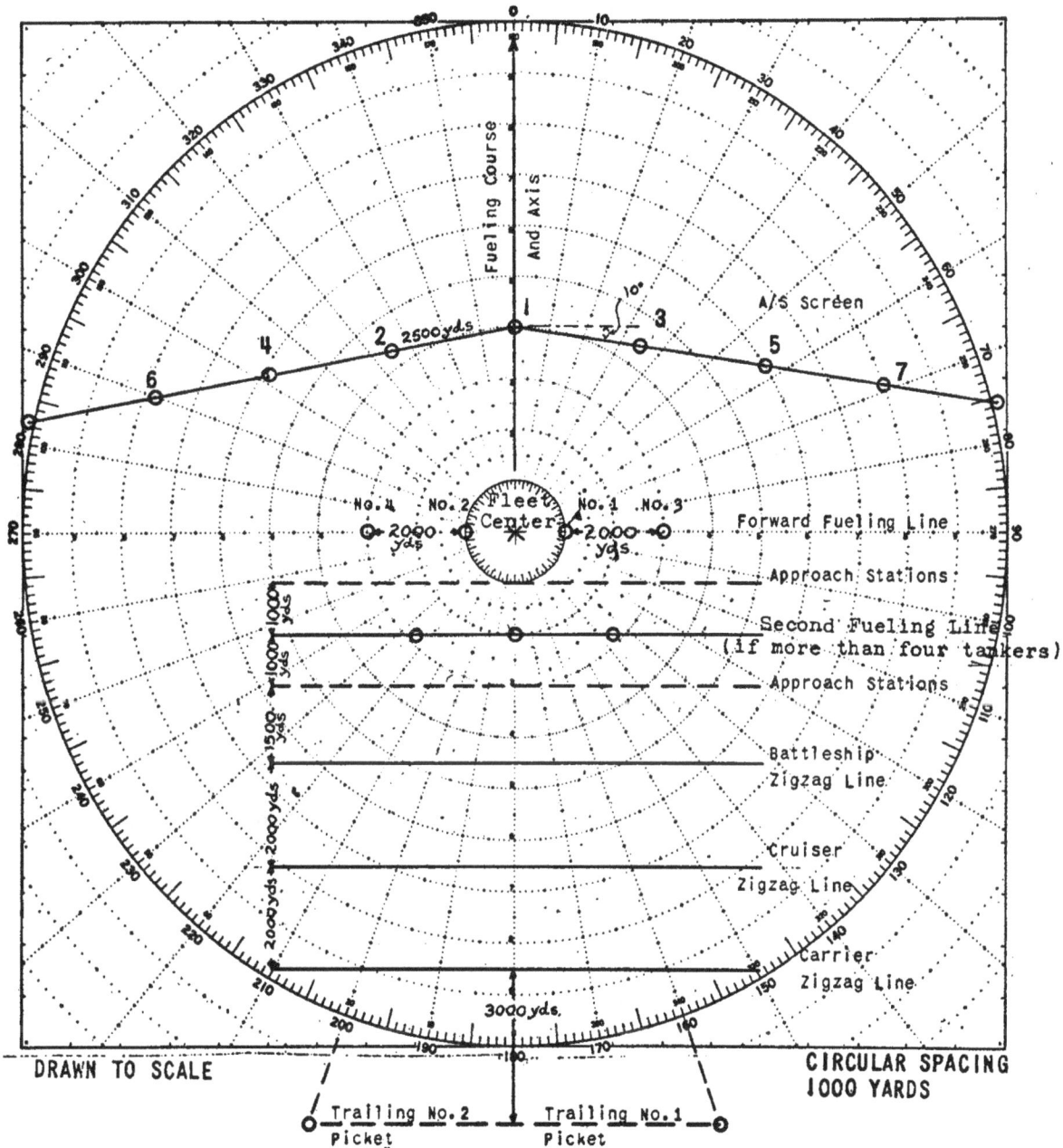

Fueling Course And Axis

A/S Screen

2 2500 yds 3 5 7

4 6

No. 4 No. 2 Fleet Center No. 1 No. 3 Forward Fueling Line
2000 yds 2000 yds

Approach Stations

1000 yds Second Fueling Line (if more than four tankers)

Approach Stations

1500 yds Battleship Zigzag Line

2000 yds Cruiser Zigzag Line

Carrier Zigzag Line

3000 yds.

DRAWN TO SCALE   CIRCULAR SPACING 1000 YARDS

Trailing No. 2 Picket   Trailing No. 1 Picket

Figure 26.

DECLASSIFIED

CRUISING DISPOSITIONS.

(a) Cruising disposition 5—First carrier force day fueling disposition.

(b) This disposition is for use of a carrier force for fueling with defense against submarines. It permits a rapid execution of fueling and antisubmarine defense for the force.

(c) Natural order from van to rear—

> Antisubmarine screen.
> Oilers as fueling vessels first line.
> Oilers as fueling vessels second line.
> Battleships.
> Cruisers.
> Carriers.
> Trailing pickets.

(d) The fleet guide is the right center fueling vessel in the forward fueling line.

(e) Regardless of the station occupied by the guide any change of fueling course and therefore change of the front of the formation will be performed about the fleet center.

(f) Unless otherwise prescribed the ships in the battleship, cruiser, and carrier lines will be formed in compact line, insofar as possible, consistent with safety of maneuvers.

(g) The officer in tactical command will direct the establishment of patrols.

(h) For emergency deployment heavy ship units on zigzag lines will maneuver clear of fueling units in succession from the rear.

(i) Communications as prescribed by USF 70 for normal tactical organization.

(j) All screening vessels stand continuous sonar search unless otherwise directed. Carry out search procedure in accordance with section 1200, FTP 223. The screen commander designates the forward antisubmarine screen vessels, the trailing pickets and any other screening lines or stations. Tanker escorts are usually stationed in the low number stations in the forward screen. Normal order for fueling screening vessels is from flanks of forward screen. Ships alternating from each flank. Upon completion of fueling screening vessels take forward screening stations outboard of tanker escorts and on same side of screen as previously stationed. As each screening ship rejoins on completion of fueling, screening ships on that flank shift one station outboard.

CRUISING DISPOSITION 5-R

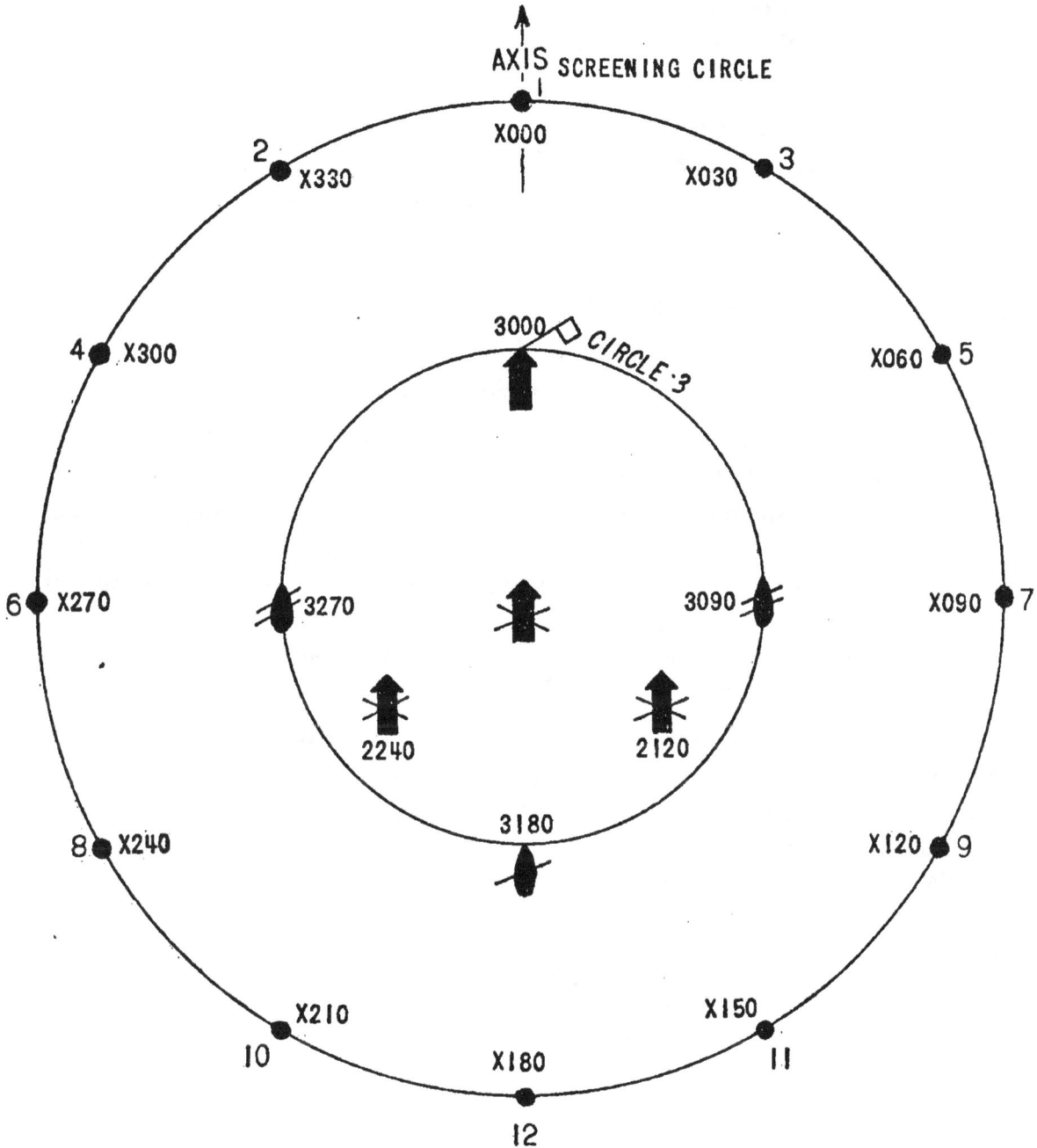

AXIS SCREENING CIRCLE

X000

2 X330   3 X030

3000 ◇ CIRCLE 3

4 X300   X060 5

3270   3090

6 X270   X090 7

2240   2120

8 X240   X120 9

3180

X210   X150

10   X180   11

12

3 Carriers – CV's and/or CVL's;
3 or more heavy ships – BB, CA, CL;
12 Destroyers.

Figure 27.

CRUISING DISPOSITION

(a) Cruising Disposition 5-R is a normal carrier force day or night high visibility disposition.

(b) It is suitable for use of a carrier force for defense against both aircraft and submarines. It permits a rapid shift to cruising disposition 5–V, the air defense disposition. Surface attack not probable.

(c) — — —.

(d) The fleet guide is normally in the ship at the center. With a carrier center of disposition, and independent carrier air operations contemplated, the guide will be shifted to the leading heavy ship along the fleet course. When the disposition is maneuvered into the wind for air operations, the guide will be as designated by OTC.

(e) Any rotation of the axis will be performed about the center.

(f) Station assignments are as indicated in the diagram.

    (1) The carriers normally taking stations equally spaced.

    (2) Heavy ships equally spaced on circle 3. They should be alternated with the carriers to provide an alternate heavy ship—carrier—heavy ship.

    (3) Station assignments are indicated on the diagram, but may be varied by the officer in tactical command to suit existing conditions. The screening ships will be stationed in accordance with the instructions contained in part III.

    (4) When an AO is present, it will take station in center of disposition. The CV taking station 2000.

(g) Searches, patrols, and offensive air operations as ordered by OTC.

(h) Deployment from this disposition is unlikely. However, if emergency deployment is ordered, heavy ships will deploy on the heavy ship in the van on deployment course. Carriers and AO retiring towards disengaged side. Screen divide as previously designated by screen commander.

(i) Communications as prescribed in USF 70, unless other instructions are issued.

(j) All sonar equipped ships stand continuous echo-ranging watch unless otherwise directed. Sonar screen utilize supersonics in accordance with current doctrine. Radar sectors as ordered.

CRUISING DISPOSITION 5V

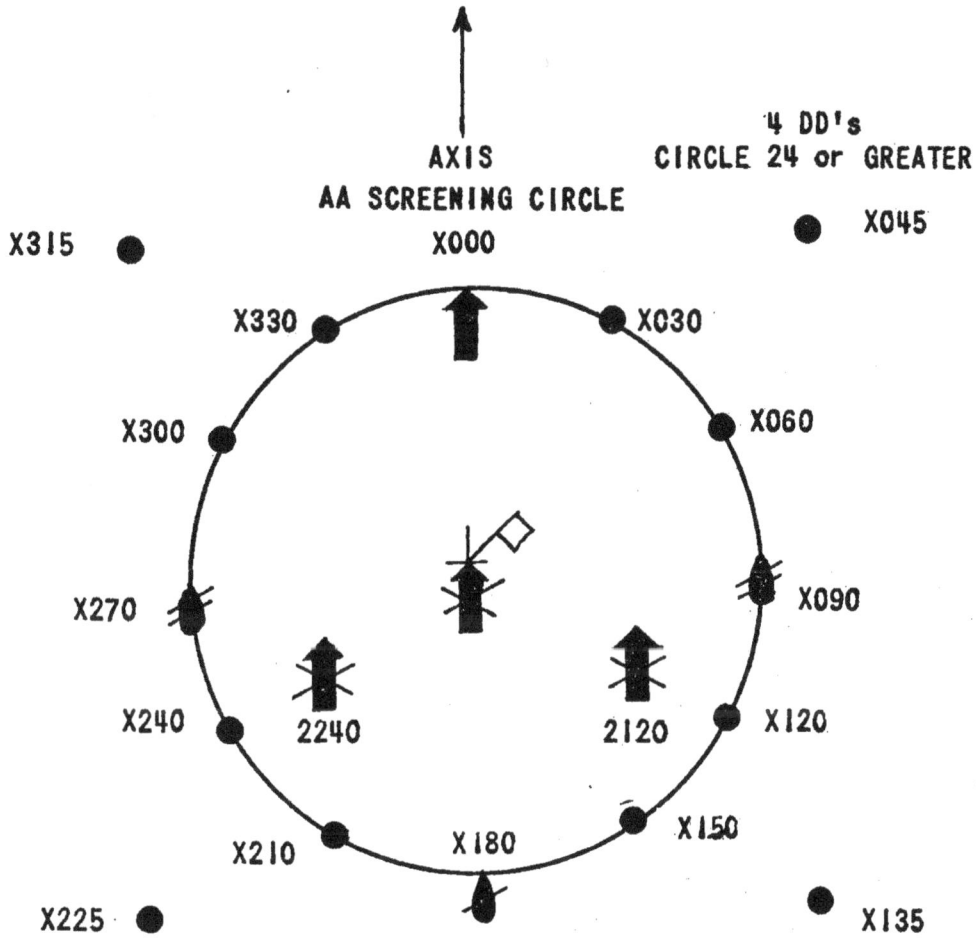

Figure 28.

3 Carriers – CV and/or CVL's;
3 or more heavy ships – BB, CA, CL;
12 Destroyers.

CRUISING DISPOSITION

(a) Cruising Disposition 5-V is an air defense disposition.

(b) Suitable for use by a carrier force for defense against actual air attack. This disposition normally to be formed from 6-R. Upon completion of attack, and additional attacks unlikely, disposition will be changed to 6-R.

(c) _____.

(d) The guide is the ship in center of disposition. The signal to assume this disposition automatically shifts guide to center ship of existing disposition. If no ship is in center the flagship of OTC becomes and remains the guide.

(e) _____.

(f) Station assignments are in general as indicated. Stations on AA screening circle should be assigned in accordance with part III. Pickets, if used, should be stationed beyond circle 20.

(g) Air operations as ordered by OTC.

(h) _____.

(i) _____.

(j) _____.

DECLASSIFIED

CRUISING DISPOSITION 5-W

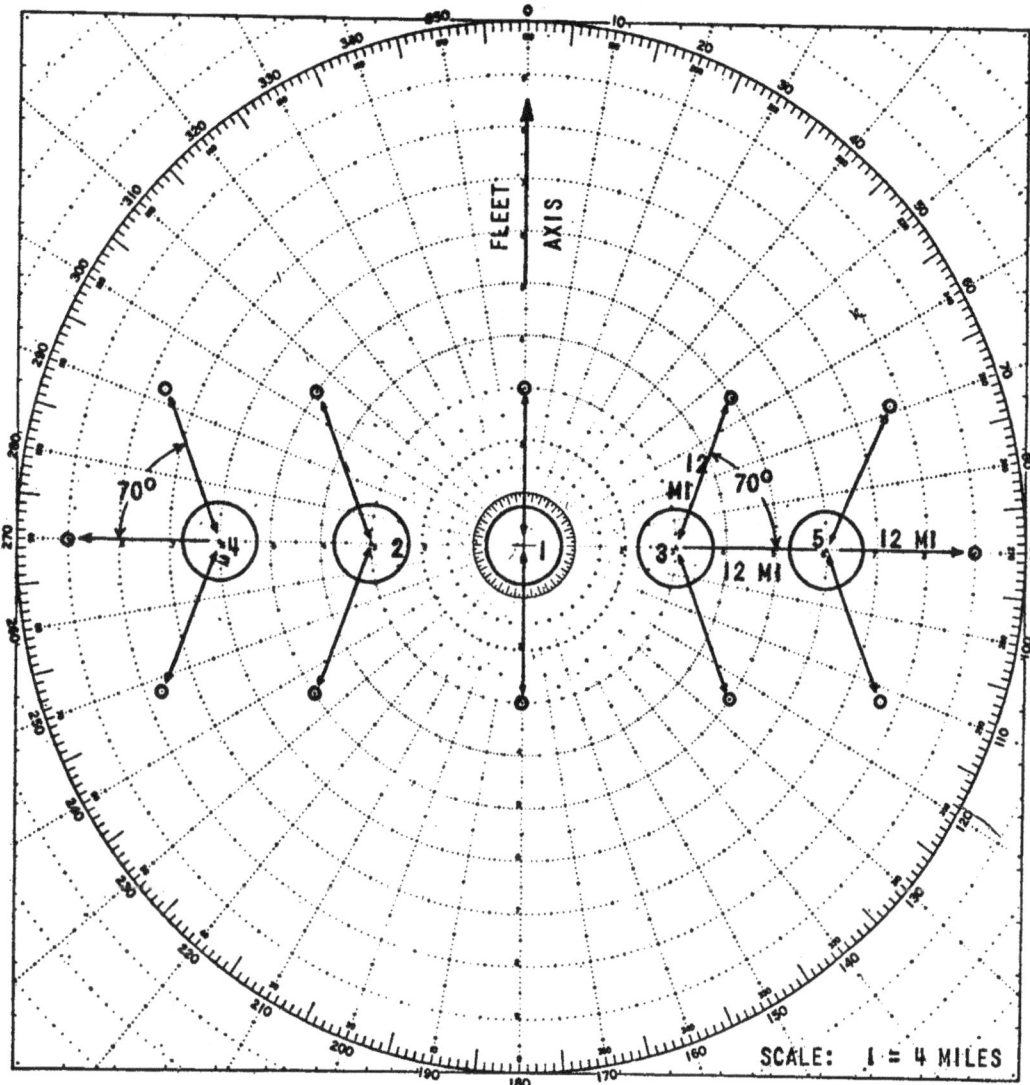

O = DD PICKET

DESTROYER PICKET STATION INSTRUCTIONS

1. When less than 5 TG's are present, TG's in stations #2 and/or #3 will place an additional picket at the position normally occupied by the next adjacent missing Task Group.

2. TG's assigned a total of 8 or less screening ships – Station no pickets.
   TG's assigned a total of 9 or 10 screening ships – Station 1 picket in picket station assigned that group that is nearest the fleet course.
   TG's assigned a total of 11 screening ships – Station 2 pickets, in picket stations assigned that group nearest fleet course.
   TG's assigned a total of 12 or more screening ships – Fill all Task Group picket stations.

Figure 29.

CRUISING DISPOSITION 5-W

(a) Cruising Disposition 5-W is a column or line of bearing of carrier task groups.

(b) It is primarily an attack formation, offering sufficient sea room for each task group to operate large numbers of aircraft. It is also suitable as a cruising disposition when it is desirable to maintain a narrow front to avoid detection by enemy patrol boats or to conduct the task force through narrow water.

(c) (1) Station units are two, three, four, or five carrier task groups stationed relative to the fleet center and axis as follows, using rectangular coordinates:

Station No.	Station
1	0
2	24 L
3	24 R
4	48 L
5	48 R

(2) Lateral spacing is 1,000 yards.

(3) Carrier task groups will be assigned stations by the OTC.

(d) The guide will be the carrier task group in station no. 1.

(e) Regardless of the station occupied by the guide, any rotation of the fleet axis will be performed about the fleet center. The formation axis of task groups need not coincide with fleet axis.

(f) Each carrier task group commander will dispose the ships of his task group at discretion, employing Cruising Dispositions in USF 10 or dispositions prescribed by himself. When oilers are present with a task group, the carrier task group commander will station them in the center of his disposition. The oilers' escorts will be stationed with the destroyers of the carrier task group.

(g) (1) Each carrier task group will maintain its own combat air patrol and antisubmarine patrol.

(2) Special air searches, scouting missions and air pickets will be established on orders of the OTC.

(h) In the event of surface radar contact in low visibility, or submarine contact or actual or threatened air attack, the carrier task group commander will maneuver his task group as required by the situation. He will keep the OTC and the other task group commanders in the disposition informed of his movements. The other carrier task group commanders will maneuver their task groups as necessary. Stations in the disposition, fleet course, and speed will be resumed as soon as practicable.

(i) (1) Carrier task group commanders are authorized to increase the distance from the fleet center to attain freedom of movement. It is important that task groups remain within TBS or visual communication range of the fleet flagship.

(2) All sonar equipped ships except screening ships shall stand continuous listening watch. Screening ships will utilize sonar equipment in accordance with current doctrine.

(3) Radar guard and identification guardships will be designated and radar sectors will be assigned by each carrier task group commander so as to give all around coverage for each task group.

(j) ———.

CRUISING DISPOSITION 5-X

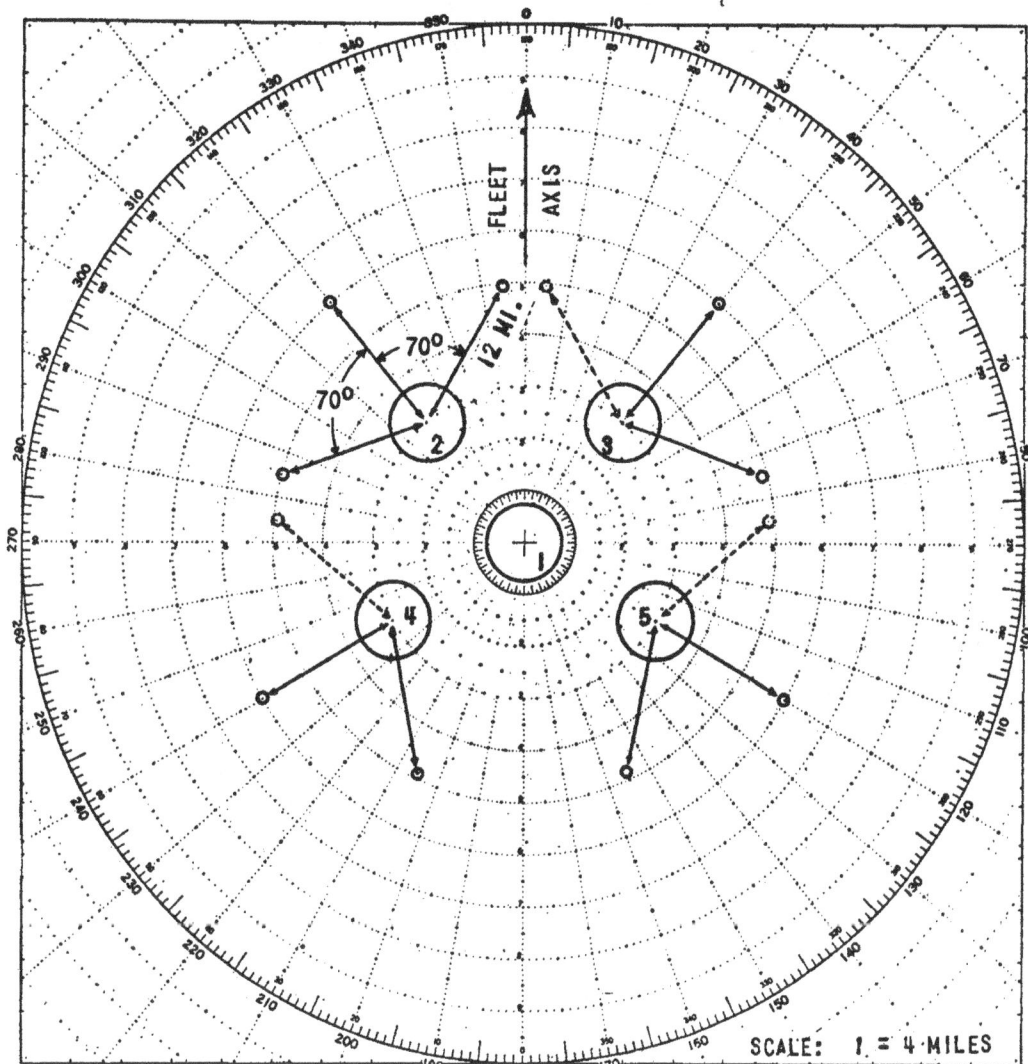

SCALE: 1 = 4 MILES

○ = DD PICKET

○ = DD PICKET NOT FURNISHED

CIRCULAR SPACING 1000 YDS.

DESTROYER PICKET STATION INSTRUCTIONS

1. When any TG picket station is nearer than 6 miles to the next adjoining picket station, the TG in the lowest station number will furnish the picket.

2. When less than 5 TG's are present, the TG in station #1 will place a picket at the position normally occupied by the missing TG or TG's.

3. TG's assigned a total of 8 or less screening ships - Station no pickets.
   TG's assigned a total of 9 or 10 screening ships - Station 1 picket in picket station assigned that group that is nearest the fleet course.
   TG's assigned a total of 11 screening ships - Station 2 pickets, in picket stations assigned that group nearest fleet course.
   TG's assigned a total of 12 or more screening ships - Fill all Task Group picket stations.

Figure 30.

CRUISING DISPOSITION

(a) Cruising Disposition 5 X is circular disposition.

(b) It is suitable for defense of large carrier task groups against submarines and aircraft.

(c) (1) Station units are three, four, or five carrier task groups stationed on bearings from the fleet center relative to the fleet axis as follows:

Station No.	Circle No.	Bearing of Center of Task Group from Fleet Center
1	0	000°
2	24	320°
3	24	040°
4	24	240°
5	24	120°

(2) Circle spacing is 1,000 yards.

(3) Carrier task groups will be assigned stations by the OTC.

(d) The guide will be the center of the carrier task group occupying station no. 1.

(e) Any rotation of the fleet axis will be performed about the fleet center. The formation axis of the task group need not coincide with the fleet axis.

(f) Each task group commander will dispose the ships of his task group at discretion, employing Cruising Dispositions in USF 10, or dispositions prescribed by himself. When oilers are present with a task group, the task group commander will station them in the center of his disposition. The oilers' escorts will be stationed with the destroyers of the carrier task group.

(g) (1) Carrier task groups in stations 4 and 5 (or the downwind groups if the fleet axis is not into the wind) move out prior to flight operations (Method ABLE) if necessary. Maintain visual and TBS communication with task force commander by linking vessel.

(2) Each carrier task group will maintain its own combat air patrol and antisubmarine patrol, unless task force antisubmarine patrol is specifically prescribed.

(3) Special air searches, scouting missions, and air pickets will be established on orders of the OTC.

(h) In the event of surface radar contact in low visibility, or submarine contact, or actual or threatened air attack, the task group commander will maneuver his task group as required by the situation. He will keep the OTC and the other task group commanders in the disposition informed of his movements. The other task group commanders will maneuver their groups as necessary. Stations in the disposition, fleet course and speed will be resumed as soon as practicable.

(i) (1) Task group commanders are authorized to increase the distance from the fleet center to attain freedom of movement, bearing in mind the necessity for maintaining visual communication with the fleet flagship.

(2) All sonar equipped ships except screening ships shall stand continuous listening watch. Screening ships will utilize sonar equipment in accordance with current doctrine.

(3) Radar guard and identification guard ships will be designated and radar sectors will be assigned by each task group commander so as to give all around coverage for each task group.

(j) ——————.

DECLASSIFIED

CRUISING DISPOSITION 5-XT

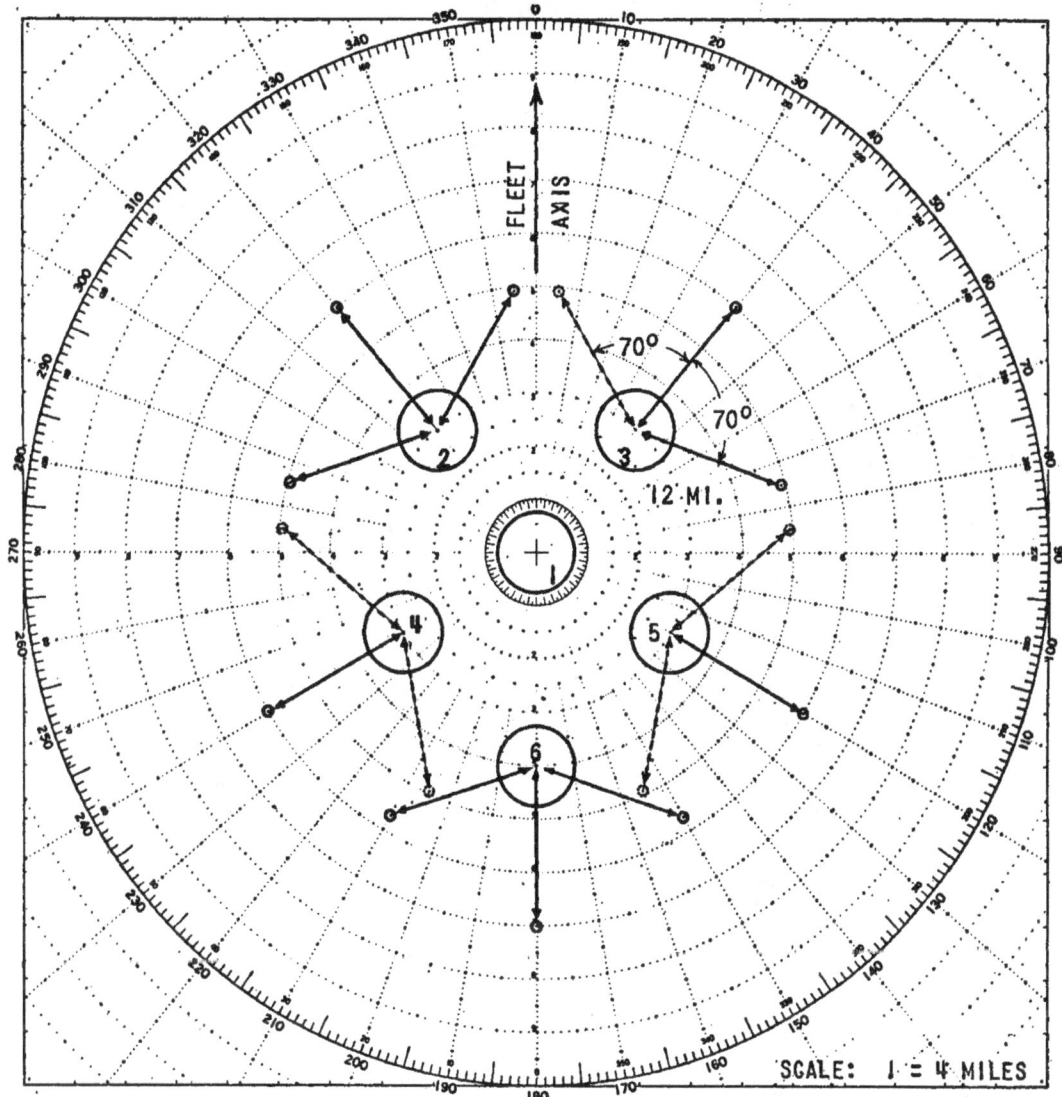

O = DD PICKET
◌ = DD PICKET NOT FURNISHED

SCALE: 1 = 4 MILES

CIRCULAR SPACING 1000 YDS.

DESTROYER PICKET STATION INSTRUCTIONS

1. When any TG picket station is nearer than 6 miles to the next adjoining picket station, the TG in the lowest station number will furnish the picket, except in the case of TG Station #6 which will fill all three picket stations assigned that group.

2. When less than 5 TG's are present, the TG in station #1 will place a picket at the position normally occupied by the missing TG or TG's.

3. TG's assigned a total of 8 or less screening ships — Station no pickets.
   TG's assigned a total of 9 or 10 screening ships — Station 1 picket in picket station assigned that group that is nearest the fleet course.
   TG's assigned a total of 11 screening ships — Station 2 pickets, in picket stations assigned that group nearest fleet course.
   TG's assigned a total of 12 or more screening ships — Fill all Task Group picket stations.

Figure 91.

DECLASSIFIED

Ap. 1-26

CRUISING DISPOSITION 5–XT. DECLASSIFIED

(a) Cruising Disposition 5–XT is a circular disposition.

(b) It is suitable for defense of large task groups against submarines with limited protection against aircraft. It is intended for use when possibility of enemy air attack is remote, and it is desirable to form a task group composed of heavy support ships with screen.

(c) (1) Station units are three, four, or five carrier task groups and one task group composed of support ships and screening ships from the carrier task groups as designated by the task force commander, stationed on bearings from the fleet center relative to the fleet axis as follows:

Station No.	Circle No.	Bearing of Center of Task Group from Fleet Center
Carrier Group 1	0	000°
Carrier Group 2	24	320°
Carrier Group 3	24	040°
Carrier Group 4	24	240°
Carrier Group 5	24	120°
Support Group 6	32	180° (area centered on station).

  (2) Circle spacing is 1,000 yards.

  (3) Task Groups will be assigned stations by the OTC.

(d) The guide will be the center of the carrier task group occupying station No. 1.

(e) Any rotation of the fleet axis will be performed about the fleet center. The formation axis of the task group need not coincide with the fleet axis.

(f) Each task group commander will dispose the ships of his task group at discretion employing Cruising Dispositions in USF 10, or dispositions prescribed by himself. When oilers are present with a task group, the task group commander will station them in the center of his disposition. The oilers' escorts will be stationed with the destroyers of the carrier task group.

(g) (1) Carrier task groups in stations 4 and 5 (or the downwind groups if the fleet axis is not into the wind) move out prior to flight operations (Method ABLE) if necessary. Maintain visual and TBS communication with task force commander by linking vessel.

  (2) Each carrier task group will maintain its own combat air patrol and antisubmarine patrol, unless task force antisubmarine patrol is specifically prescribed. In addition, the carrier task group in station no. 1 will provide antisubmarine patrols for the support group in station no. 6.

  (3) Special air searches, scouting missions and air pickets will be established on orders of the OTC.

(h) In the event of surface radar contact in low visibility, or submarine contact, or actual or threatened air attack, the task group commander will maneuver his task group as required by the situation. He will keep the OTC and the other task group commanders in the disposition informed of his movements. The other task group commanders will maneuver their groups as necessary. Stations in the disposition, fleet course and speed will be resumed as soon as practicable.

(i) (1) Task group commanders are authorized to increase the distance from the fleet center to attain freedom of movement, bearing in mind the necessity for maintaining visual communication with the fleet flagship.

  (2) All sonar equipped ships except screening ships shall stand continuous listening watch. Screening ships will utilize sonar equipment in accordance with current doctrine.

  (3) Radar guard and identification guard ships will be designated and radar sectors will be assigned by each task group commander so as to give all around coverage for each task group.

(j) ———.

CRUISING DISPOSITION 6R

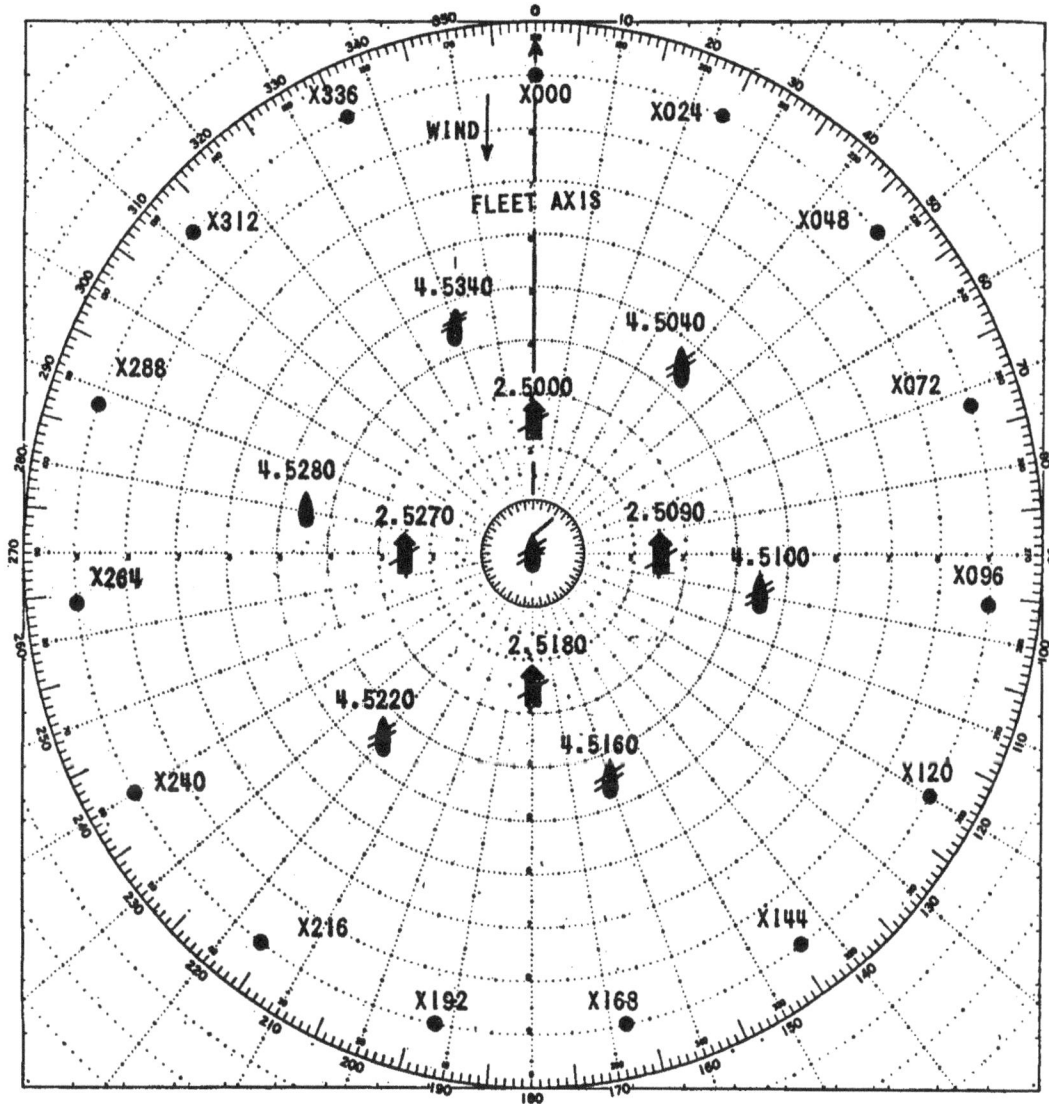

4 CARRIERS
7 HEAVY SHIPS BB, CA, CL
15 DESTROYERS

Figure 32.

(a) Cruising Disposition 6–R is a normal carrier force day or night high visibility disposition.

(b) It is suitable for use of a carrier force for defense against both aircraft and submarines. It permits a rapid shift to cruising disposition 5–V, the air defense disposition. Surface attack not probable.

(c) _____.

(d) The fleet guide is normally in the ship at the center. With a carrier in center of disposition, and independent carrier air operations contemplated, the guide will be shifted to the leading heavy ship along the fleet course. When the disposition is maneuvered into the wind for air operations, the guide will be as designated by OTC.

(e) Any rotation of the axis will be performed about the fleet center.

(f) Station assignments are as indicated in the diagram.

    (1) The carriers normally taking stations equally spaced.

    (2) Heavy ships equally spaced on circle 3. They should be alternated with the carriers to provide an alternate heavy ship—carrier—heavy ship.

    (3) Station assignments are indicated on the diagram, but may be varied by the officer in tactical command to suit existing conditions. The screening ships will be stationed in accordance with the instructions contained in part III.

    (4) When an AO is present, it will take station in center of disposition.

(g) Searches, patrols, and offensive air operations as ordered by OTC.

(h) Deployment from this disposition is unlikely. However, if emergency deployment is ordered, heavy ships will deploy on the heavy ship in the van on deployment course. Carriers and AO retiring towards disengaged side. Screen divide as previously designated by screen commander.

(i) Communications as prescribed in USF 70, unless other instructions are issued.

(j) All sonar equipped ships stand continuous echo-ranging watch unless otherwise directed. Sonar screen utilize supersonics in accordance with current doctrine. Radar sectors as ordered.

CRUISING DISPOSITION 6-S

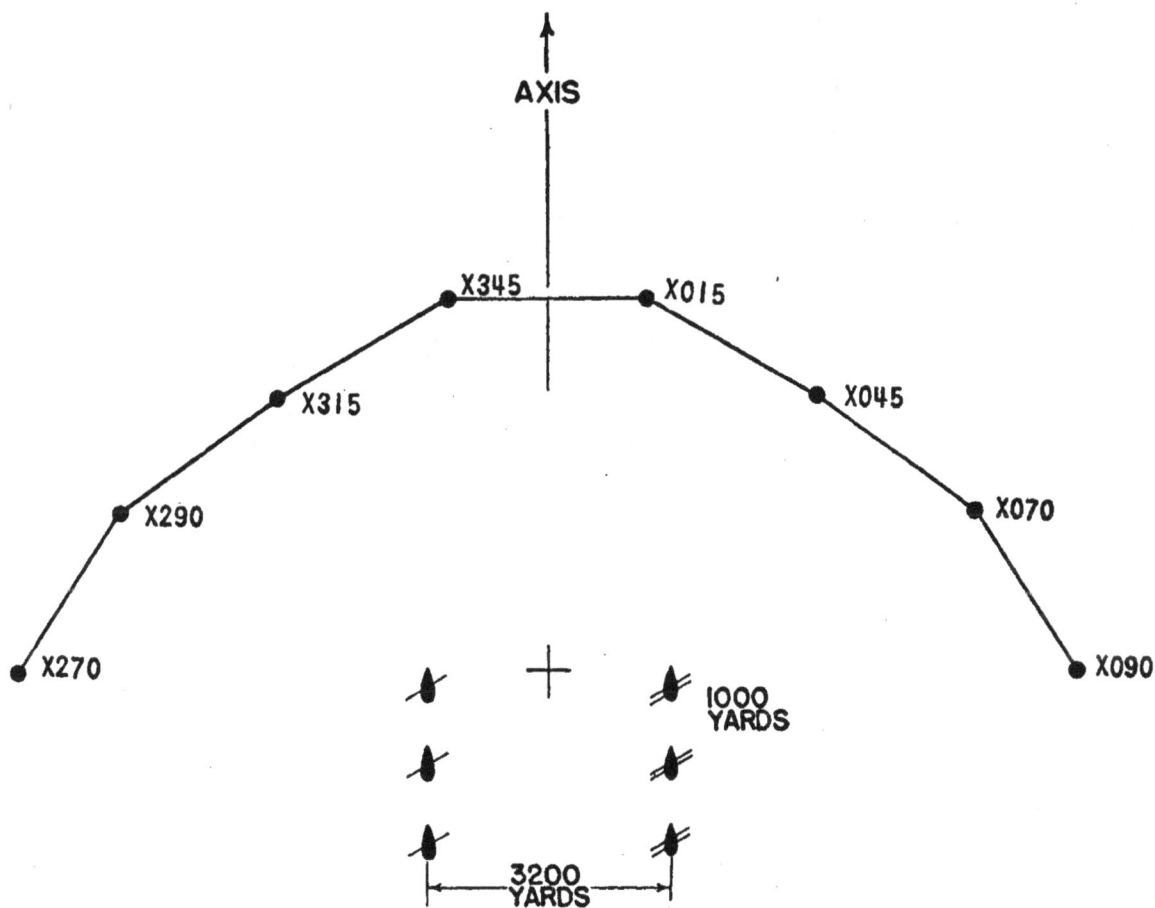

↑
AXIS

X345   X015

X315   X045

X290   X070

X270   X090

+   1000
                YARDS

3200
YARDS

Figure 33.

CRUISING DISPOSITION 6–S.

(a) Cruising Disposition 6–S is an antisubmarine disposition.

(b) It is suitable for the use of a small force without carriers. Although devised primarily as an antisubmarine disposition it is readily adaptable in the described form as a low-visibility or night-cruising disposition.

(c) _____

(d) The guide is normally in the leading cruiser of either column.

(e) Any rotation of the axis will be performed about the fleet center.

(f) Station assignments are indicated on the diagram, but may be varied by the officer in tactical command to suit existing conditions. In the interest of quick deployment, the interval in the screened body should always be maintained at a figure 1,200 yards greater than the length of the longer column. The screening ships will be stationed in accordance with the instructions contained in part III.

(g) Patrols and searches will be established in accordance with instructions from the OTC.

(h) Emergency deployment is practicable at any time.

(i) Communications as prescribed by USF 70, unless other specific instructions are issued.

(j) All sonar equipped ships stand continuous echo-ranging watch unless otherwise directed. Sonar screen utilize supersonics in accordance with current doctrine.

APPENDIX II TO USF 10B
ZIGZAG PLANS

ZIGZAG PLAN NO. 1

FOR USE IN AREAS WHERE SUBMARINES HAVE NOT PREVIOUSLY
BEEN OPERATING, BUT WHERE THEY MAY APPEAR.

SUITABLE FOR SINGLE SHIP, FOR A FORMATION OR
DISPOSITION WITH SPEED OF 7 TO 20 KNOTS.

DISTANCE MADE GOOD = 90% OF DISTANCE RUN.

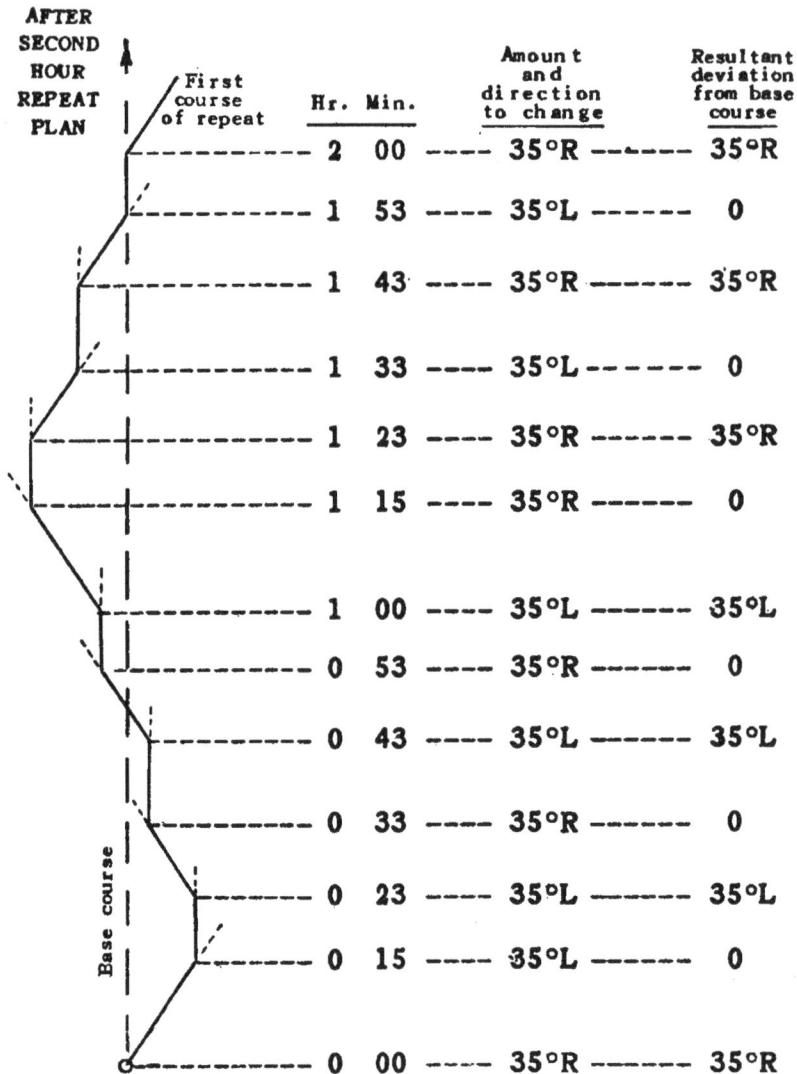

AFTER SECOND HOUR REPEAT PLAN	First course of repeat	Hr.	Min.	Amount and direction to change	Resultant deviation from base course
		2	00	35°R	35°R
		1	53	35°L	0
		1	43	35°R	35°R
		1	33	35°L	0
		1	23	35°R	35°R
		1	15	35°R	0
		1	00	35°L	35°L
		0	53	35°R	0
		0	43	35°L	35°L
		0	33	35°R	0
		0	23	35°L	35°L
		0	15	35°L	0
		0	00	35°R	35°R

Base course

Ap. 2–3

ZIGZAG PLAN NO. 3

FOR USE IN AREAS WHERE SUBMARINES HAVE NOT PREVIOUSLY
BEEN OPERATING, BUT WHERE THEY MAY APPEAR.

SUITABLE FOR A SINGLE SHIP OR A SMALL FORMATION
WITH SPEED OF 15 TO 20 KNOTS.

DISTANCE MADE GOOD = 90% OF DISTANCE RUN.

AFTER SECOND HOUR REPEAT PLAN — First course of repeat is base course	Hr. Min.	Amount and direction to change	Resultant deviation from base course
	2 00	10°R	0
	1 51	10°R	10°L
	1 45	10°R	20°L
	1 36	10°R	30°L
	1 30	10°L	40°L
	1 21	10°L	30°L
	1 15	10°L	20°L
	1 06	10°L	10°L
	1 00	10°L	0
	0 51	10°L	10°R
	0 45	10°L	20°R
	0 36	10°L	30°R
	0 30	10°R	40°R
	0 21	10°R	30°R
	0 15	10°R	20°R
	0 06	10°R	10°R
	0 00	0	0

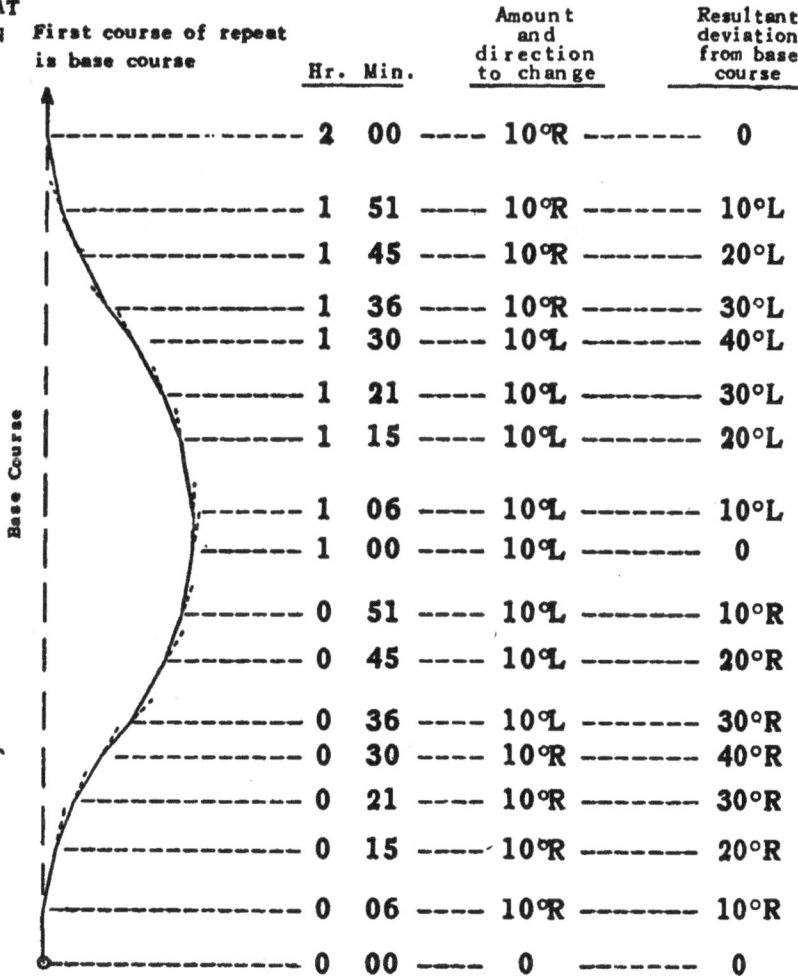

Base Course

ZIGZAG PLAN NO. 4

FOR USE IN AREAS WHERE SUBMARINES ARE DEFINITELY KNOWN TO BE PRESENT.

SUITABLE FOR USE BY SINGLE SHIPS
WITH SPEEDS OF 7 TO 12 KNOTS.

DISTANCE MADE GOOD = 69% OF DISTANCE RUN.

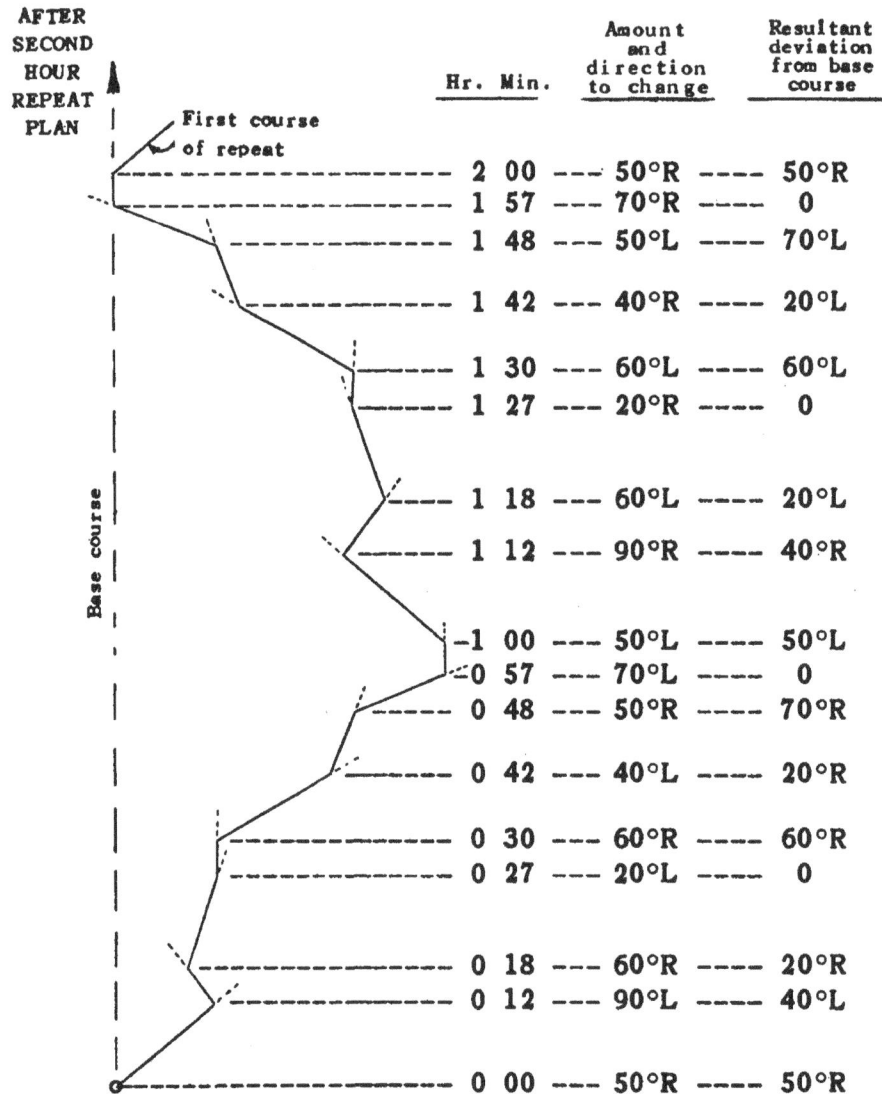

AFTER
SECOND
HOUR
REPEAT
PLAN

First course
of repeat

Hr. Min.	Amount and direction to change	Resultant deviation from base course
2 00	50°R	50°R
1 57	70°R	0
1 48	50°L	70°L
1 42	40°R	20°L
1 30	60°L	60°L
1 27	20°R	0
1 18	60°L	20°L
1 12	90°R	40°R
1 00	50°L	50°L
0 57	70°L	0
0 48	50°R	70°R
0 42	40°L	20°R
0 30	60°R	60°R
0 27	20°L	0
0 18	60°R	20°R
0 12	90°L	40°L
0 00	50°R	50°R

Base course

ORIGINAL

ZIGZAG PLAN NO. 5

FOR GENERAL USE IN SUBMARINE AREAS

SUITABLE FOR A SINGLE SHIP, FOR A FORMATION
OR DISPOSITION WITH SPEEDS UP TO 15 KNOTS.

DISTANCE MADE GOOD = 91.5% OF DISTANCE RUN.

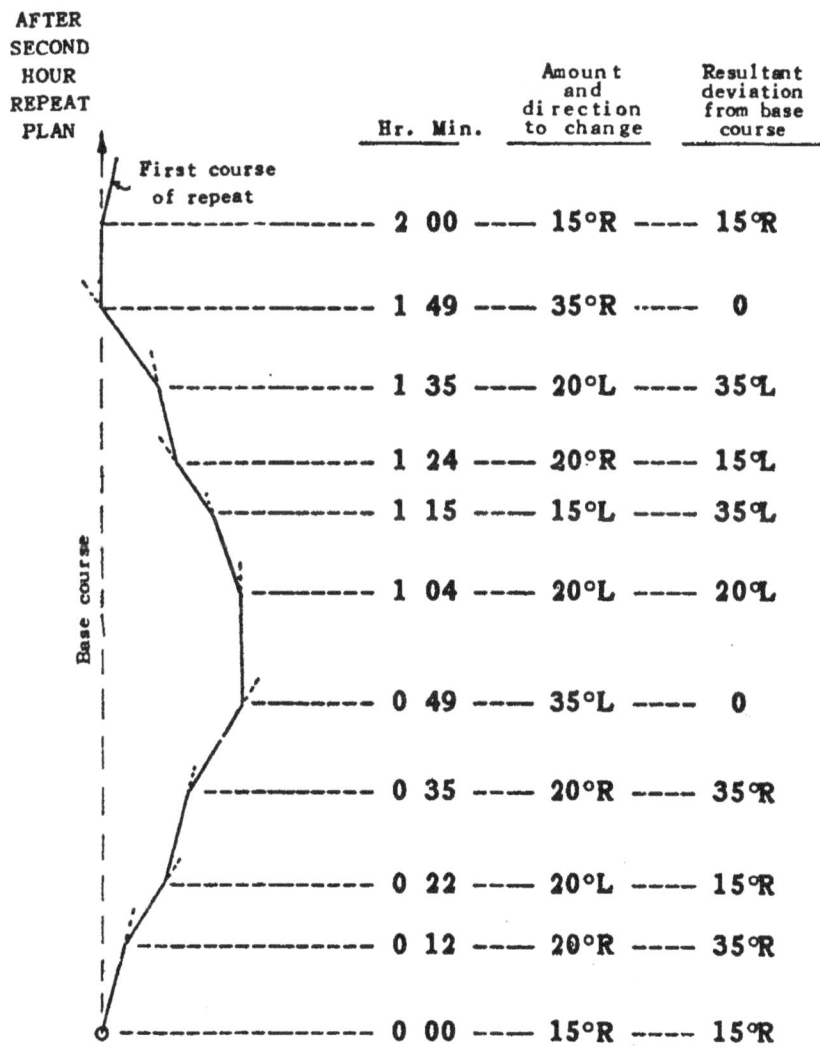

	Hr. Min.	Amount and direction to change	Resultant deviation from base course
AFTER SECOND HOUR REPEAT PLAN			
First course of repeat	2 00	15°R	15°R
	1 49	35°R	0
	1 35	20°L	35°L
	1 24	20°R	15°L
	1 15	15°L	35°L
	1 04	20°L	20°L
	0 49	35°L	0
	0 35	20°R	35°R
	0 22	20°L	15°R
	0 12	20°R	35°R
	0 00	15°R	15°R

Base course

Ap. 2-6

ZIGZAG PLAN NO. 6

FOR GENERAL USE IN SUBMARINE AREAS

SUITABLE FOR A SINGLE SHIP, FOR A FORMATION
OR DISPOSITION WITH SPEEDS OF 7 TO 30 KNOTS.

DISTANCE MADE GOOD = 9.4% OF DISTANCE RUN.

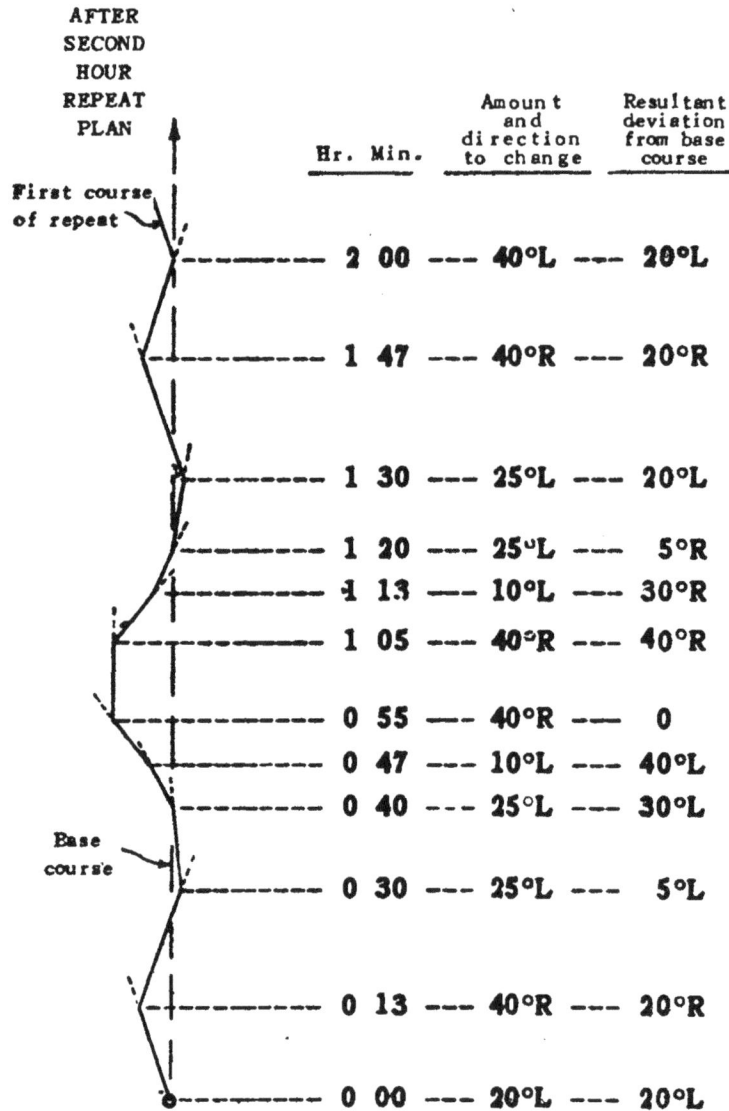

	Hr. Min.	Amount and direction to change	Resultant deviation from base course
AFTER SECOND HOUR REPEAT PLAN			
First course of repeat	2 00	40°L	20°L
	1 47	40°R	20°R
	1 30	25°L	20°L
	1 20	25°L	5°R
	1 13	10°L	30°R
	1 05	40°R	40°R
	0 55	40°R	0
	0 47	10°L	40°L
	0 40	25°L	30°L
Base course	0 30	25°L	5°L
	0 13	40°R	20°R
	0 00	20°L	20°L

DECLASSIFIED ORIGINAL

ZIGZAG PLAN NO. 7

FOR GENERAL USE IN SUBMARINE AREAS

SUITABLE FOR A SINGLE SHIP, FOR A FORMATION
OR DISPOSITION WITH SPEEDS OF 7 TO 30 KNOTS.

DISTANCE MADE GOOD = 90% OF DISTANCE RUN.

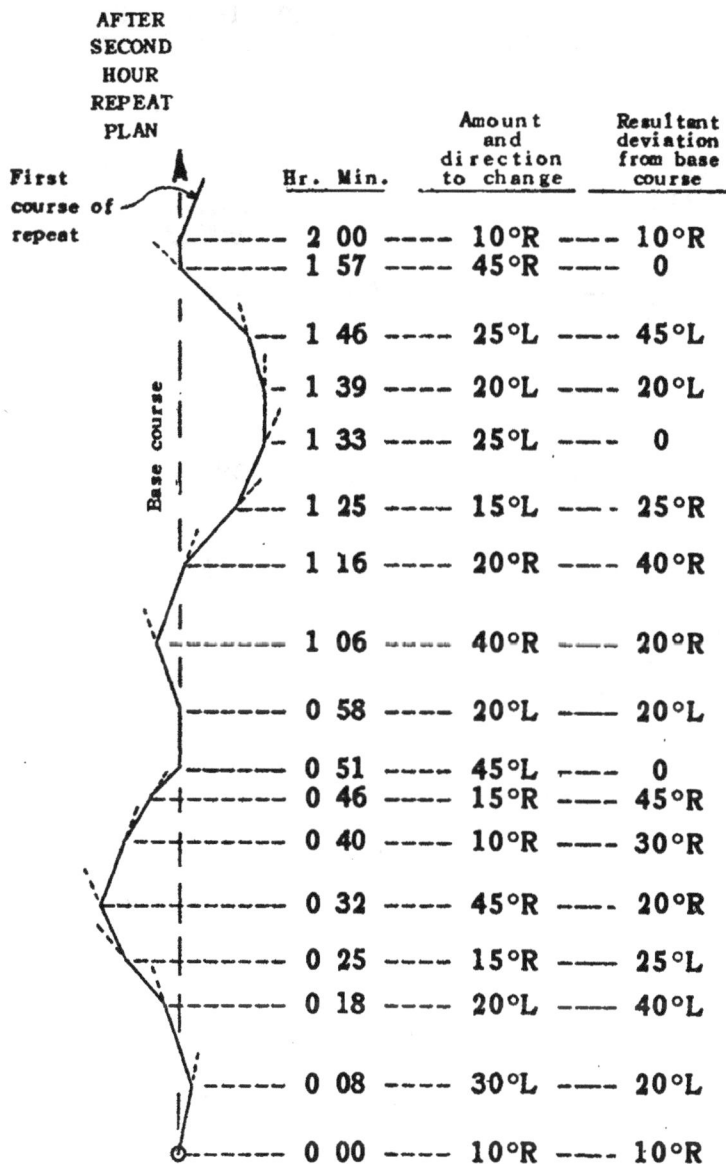

	Hr. Min.	Amount and direction to change	Resultant deviation from base course
	2 00	10°R	10°R
	1 57	45°R	0
	1 46	25°L	45°L
	1 39	20°L	20°L
	1 33	25°L	0
	1 25	15°L	25°R
	1 16	20°R	40°R
	1 06	40°R	20°R
	0 58	20°L	20°L
	0 51	45°L	0
	0 46	15°R	45°R
	0 40	10°R	30°R
	0 32	45°R	20°R
	0 25	15°R	25°L
	0 18	20°L	40°L
	0 08	30°L	20°L
	0 00	10°R	10°R

AFTER SECOND HOUR REPEAT PLAN

First course of repeat

Base course

ZIGZAG PLAN NO. 8

FOR GENERAL USE IN SUBMARINE AREAS

SUITABLE FOR A SINGLE SHIP, FOR A FORMATION
OR DISPOSITION WITH SPEEDS OF 20 TO 30 KNOTS.

DISTANCE MADE GOOD = 94% OF DISTANCE RUN.

MAXIMUM DISTANCE FROM TRACK OF
BASE COURSE = 9% OF DISTANCE RUN.

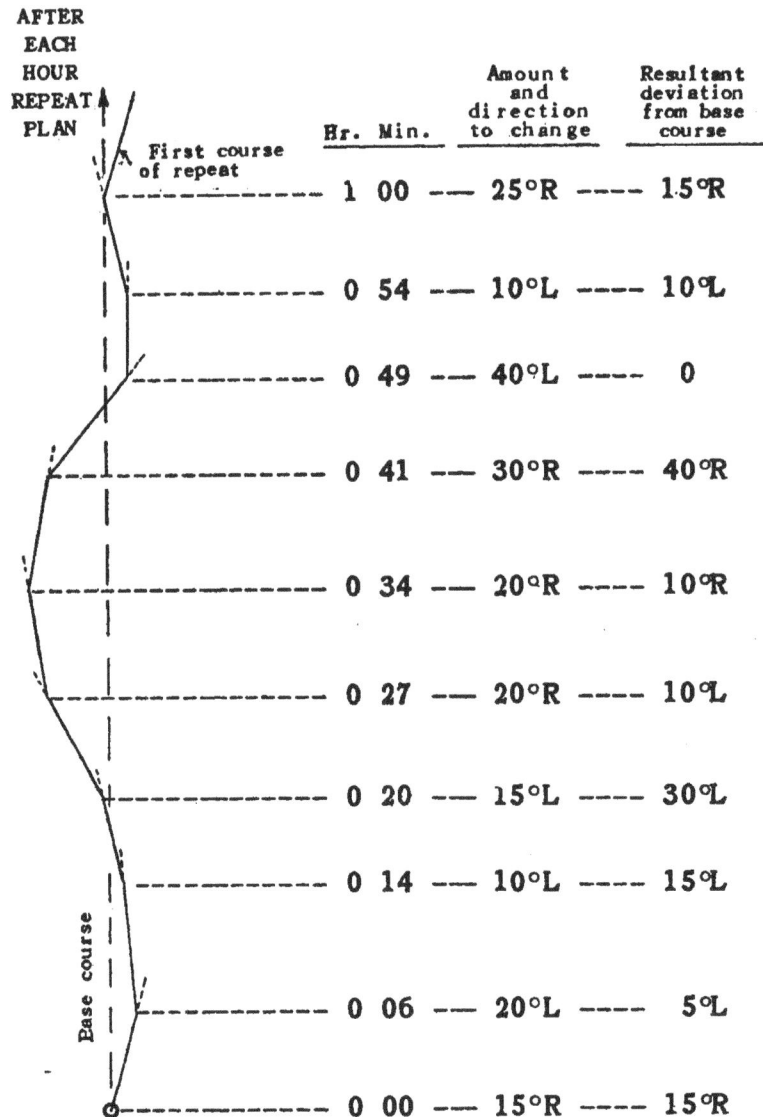

AFTER
EACH
HOUR
REPEAT
PLAN

First course
of repeat

	Hr. Min.	Amount and direction to change	Resultant deviation from base course
	1 00	25°R	15°R
	0 54	10°L	10°L
	0 49	40°L	0
	0 41	30°R	40°R
	0 34	20°R	10°R
	0 27	20°R	10°L
	0 20	15°L	30°L
	0 14	10°L	15°L
	0 06	20°L	5°L
	0 00	15°R	15°R

Base course

ZIGZAG PLAN NO. 9

FOR USE IN AREAS WHERE SUBMARINES ARE DEFINITELY KNOWN
TO BE PRESENT AND CIRCUMSTANCES REQUIRE PASSING
THROUGH THE AREA AS QUICKLY AS POSSIBLE.

SUITABLE FOR A SINGLE SHIP, FOR A FORMATION
OR DISPOSITION WITH SPEEDS OF 20 TO 30 KNOTS.

DISTANCE MADE GOOD = 93% OF DISTANCE RUN.
MAXIMUM DISTANCE FROM BASE COURSE 7% OF DISTANCE RUN.

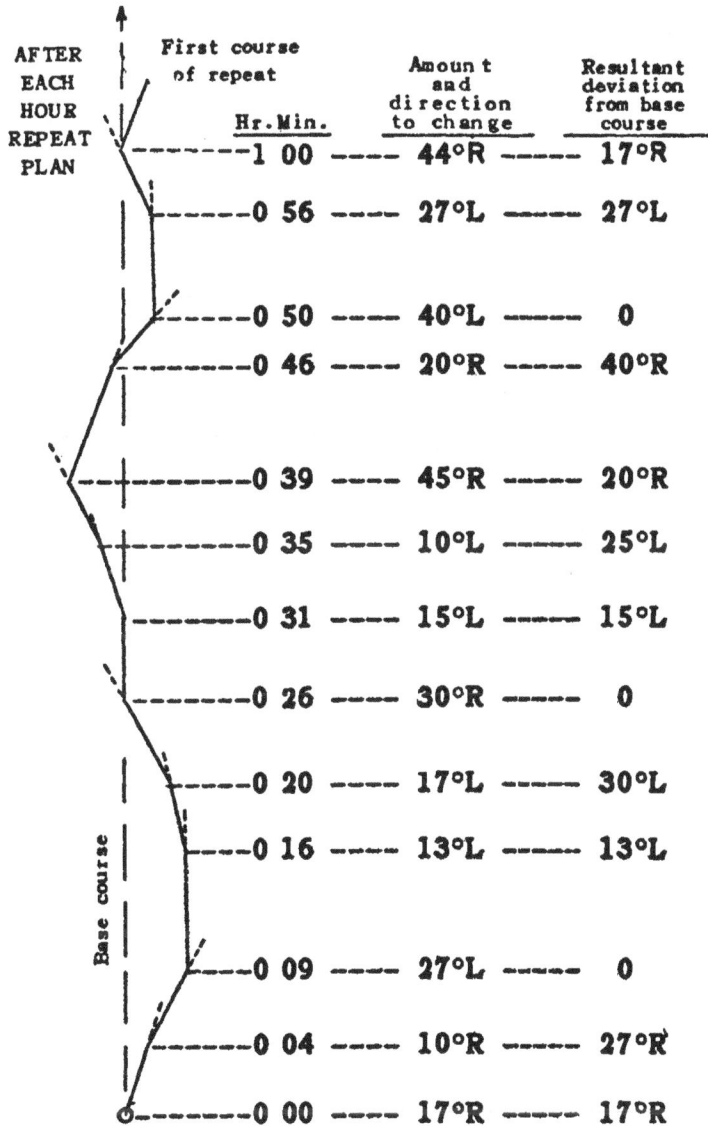

AFTER EACH HOUR REPEAT PLAN	First course of repeat Hr.Min.	Amount and direction to change	Resultant deviation from base course
	1 00	44°R	17°R
	0 56	27°L	27°L
	0 50	40°L	0
	0 46	20°R	40°R
	0 39	45°R	20°R
	0 35	10°L	25°L
	0 31	15°L	15°L
	0 26	30°R	0
	0 20	17°L	30°L
	0 16	13°L	13°L
	0 09	27°L	0
	0 04	10°R	27°R
	0 00	17°R	17°R

Base course

ZIGZAG PLAN NO. 10

FOR USE IN AREAS WHERE SUBMARINES ARE DEFINITELY KNOWN
TO BE PRESENT AND CIRCUMSTANCES DO NOT REQUIRE PASSING
THROUGH THE AREA AS QUICKLY AS POSSIBLE.

SUITABLE FOR A SINGLE SHIP, FOR A FORMATION
OR DISPOSITION WITH SPEEDS OF 20 TO 30 KNOTS.

DISTANCE MADE GOOD = 70% OF DISTANCE RUN WITHOUT
TAKING INTO CONSIDERATION SLOWING ON TURNS.

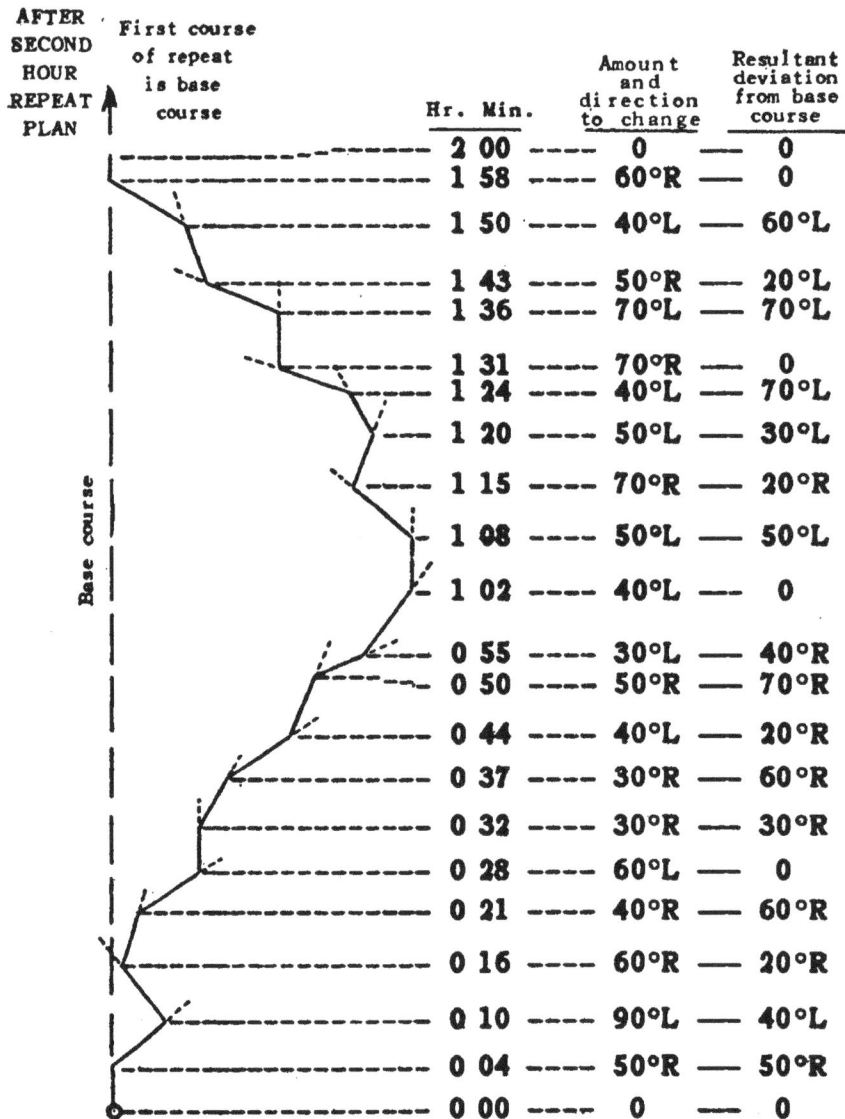

		Hr. Min.	Amount and direction to change	Resultant deviation from base course
		2 00	0	0
		1 58	60°R	0
		1 50	40°L	60°L
		1 43	50°R	20°L
		1 36	70°L	70°L
		1 31	70°R	0
		1 24	40°L	70°L
		1 20	50°L	30°L
		1 15	70°R	20°R
		1 08	50°L	50°L
		1 02	40°L	0
		0 55	30°L	40°R
		0 50	50°R	70°R
		0 44	40°L	20°R
		0 37	30°R	60°R
		0 32	30°R	30°R
		0 28	60°L	0
		0 21	40°R	60°R
		0 16	60°R	20°R
		0 10	90°L	40°L
		0 04	50°R	50°R
		0 00	0	0

AFTER SECOND HOUR REPEAT PLAN

First course of repeat is base course

Base course

ORIGINAL

ZIGZAG PLAN NO. 19

FOR GENERAL USE IN SUBMARINE AREAS.
SUITABLE FOR SHIPS OF SPEED IN EXCESS OF 10 KNOTS.
DISTANCE MADE GOOD = 86% OF DISTANCE RUN.

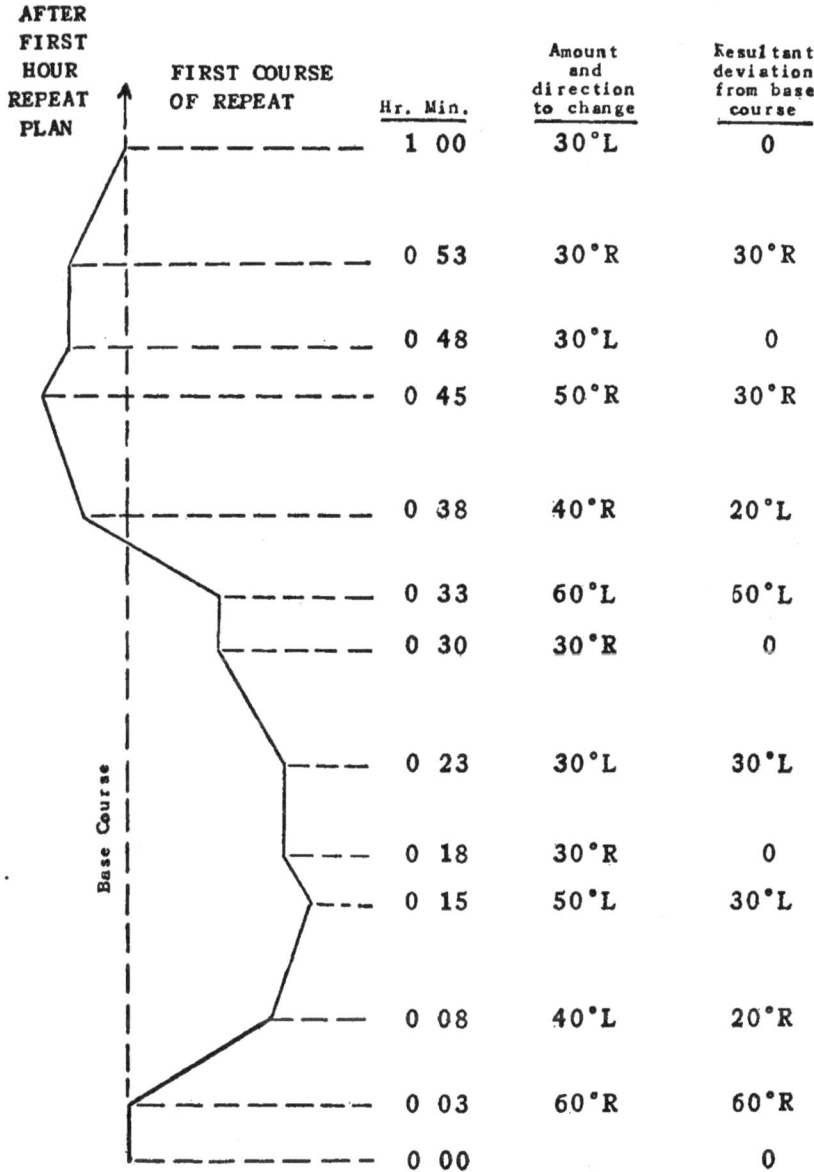

AFTER FIRST HOUR REPEAT PLAN	FIRST COURSE OF REPEAT	Hr. Min.	Amount and direction to change	Resultant deviation from base course
		1 00	30°L	0
		0 53	30°R	30°R
		0 48	30°L	0
		0 45	50°R	30°R
		0 38	40°R	20°L
		0 33	60°L	50°L
		0 30	30°R	0
		0 23	30°L	30°L
		0 18	30°R	0
		0 15	50°L	30°L
		0 08	40°L	20°R
		0 03	60°R	60°R
		0 00		0

Base Course

ZIGZAG PLAN NO. 20

FOR USE IN ESPECIALLY DANGEROUS WATERS BY A SINGLE SHIP,
OR FOR A FORMATION OR DISPOSITION WITH A FULL CIRCULAR SCREEN
OR WITH SUFFICIENT SCREEN TO COVER FLANKS ON WIDE DEPARTURES
FROM BASE COURSE TO BE USED WHEN SPEED OF ADVANCE IS OF
SECONDARY IMPORTANCE TO SECURITY.

SUITABLE FOR SHIPS OF ALL SPEEDS.

DISTANCE MADE GOOD = 70% OF DISTANCE RUN.

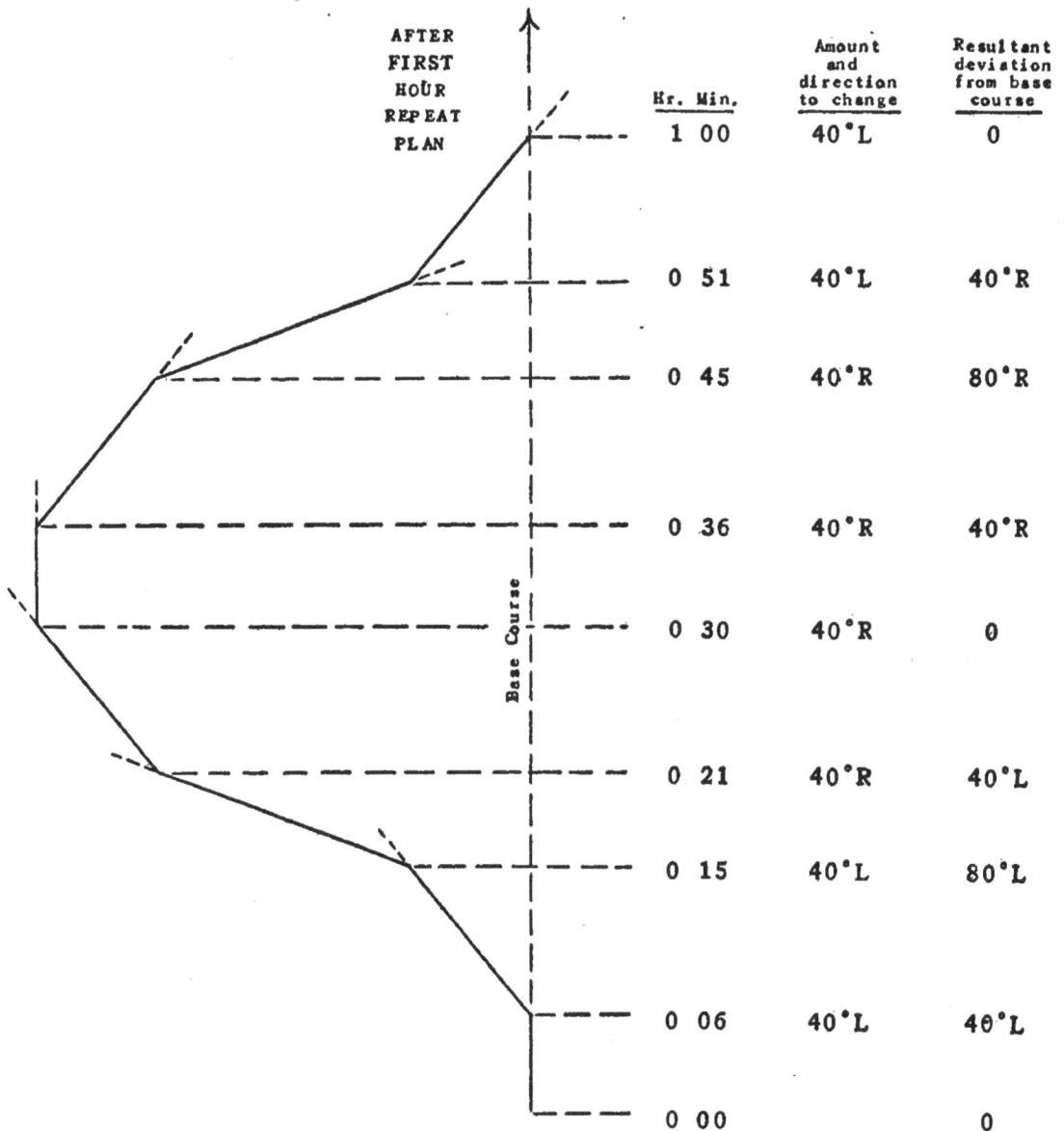

Hr. Min.	Amount and direction to change	Resultant deviation from base course
1 00	40°L	0
0 51	40°L	40°R
0 45	40°R	80°R
0 36	40°R	40°R
0 30	40°R	0
0 21	40°R	40°L
0 15	40°L	80°L
0 06	40°L	40°L
0 00		0

AFTER FIRST HOUR REPEAT PLAN

Base Course

Ap. 2-13

ORIGINAL

ZIGZAG PLAN NO. 21

FOR USE IN ESPECIALLY DANGEROUS WATERS BY A SINGLE SHIP,
OR BY A FORMATION OR DISPOSITION WITH A FULL CIRCULAR SCREEN
OR WITH SUFFICIENT SCREEN TO COVER FLANKS ON WIDE DEPARTURES
FROM BASE COURSE TO BE USED WHEN SPEED OF ADVANCE IS OF
SECONDARY IMPORTANCE TO SECURITY.

SUITABLE FOR SHIPS OF ALL SPEEDS.

DISTANCE MADE GOOD = 70% OF DISTANCE RUN.

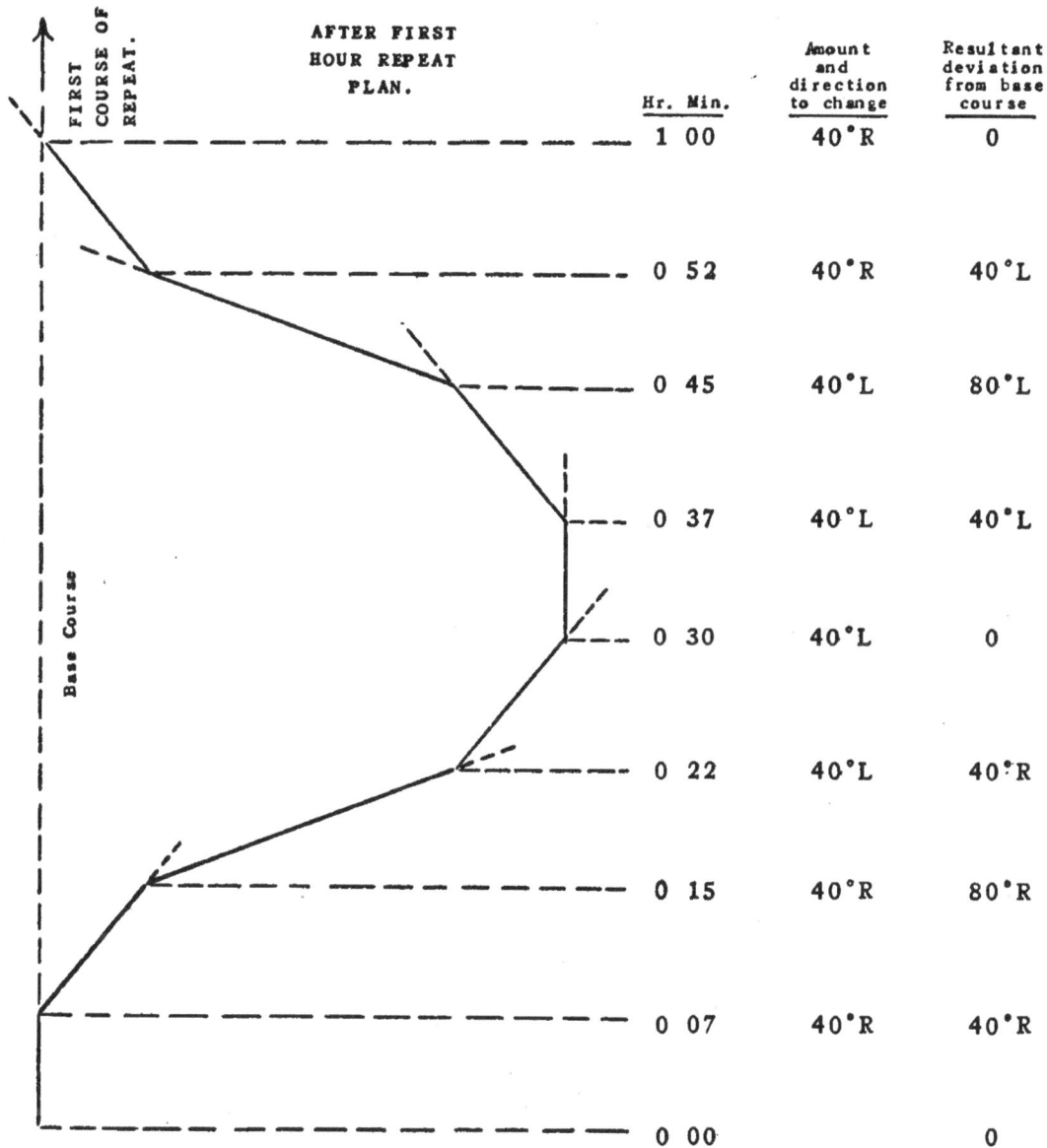

Hr. Min.	Amount and direction to change	Resultant deviation from base course
1 00	40°R	0
0 52	40°R	40°L
0 45	40°L	80°L
0 37	40°L	40°L
0 30	40°L	0
0 22	40°L	40°R
0 15	40°R	80°R
0 07	40°R	40°R
0 00		0

ZIGZAG PLAN NO. 22

CONSTANT HELM SWINGING 10° PER MINUTE

FOR USE IN ESPECIALLY DANGEROUS WATERS DURING GOOD VISIBILITY.
SUITABLE FOR SHIPS, FORMATIONS AND DISPOSITIONS OF ALL SPEEDS.

DISTANCE MADE GOOD = 87.5% OF DISTANCE RUN.

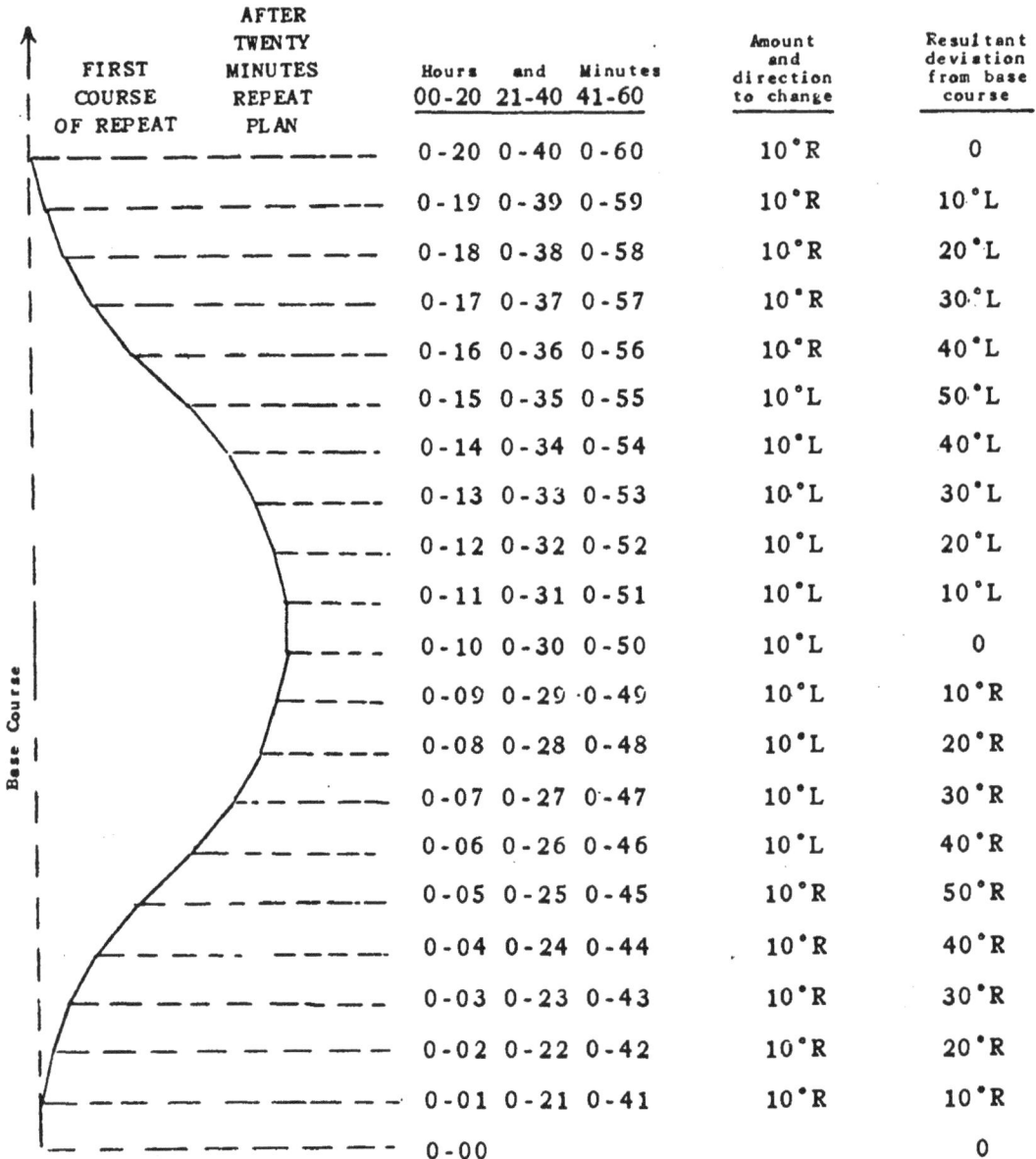

FIRST COURSE OF REPEAT	AFTER TWENTY MINUTES REPEAT PLAN	Hours and Minutes 00-20 21-40 41-60			Amount and direction to change	Resultant deviation from base course
		0-20	0-40	0-60	10°R	0
		0-19	0-39	0-59	10°R	10°L
		0-18	0-38	0-58	10°R	20°L
		0-17	0-37	0-57	10°R	30°L
		0-16	0-36	0-56	10°R	40°L
		0-15	0-35	0-55	10°L	50°L
		0-14	0-34	0-54	10°L	40°L
		0-13	0-33	0-53	10°L	30°L
		0-12	0-32	0-52	10°L	20°L
		0-11	0-31	0-51	10°L	10°L
		0-10	0-30	0-50	10°L	0
		0-09	0-29	0-49	10°L	10°R
		0-08	0-28	0-48	10°L	20°R
		0-07	0-27	0-47	10°L	30°R
		0-06	0-26	0-46	10°L	40°R
		0-05	0-25	0-45	10°R	50°R
		0-04	0-24	0-44	10°R	40°R
		0-03	0-23	0-43	10°R	30°R
		0-02	0-22	0-42	10°R	20°R
		0-01	0-21	0-41	10°R	10°R
		0-00				0

Base Course

ZIGZAG PLAN NO. 23

FOR GENERAL USE IN SUBMARINE AREAS.
SUITABLE FOR SHIPS, FORMATIONS AND DISPOSITIONS OF ALL SPEEDS.

DISTANCE MADE GOOD = 94% OF DISTANCE RUN.

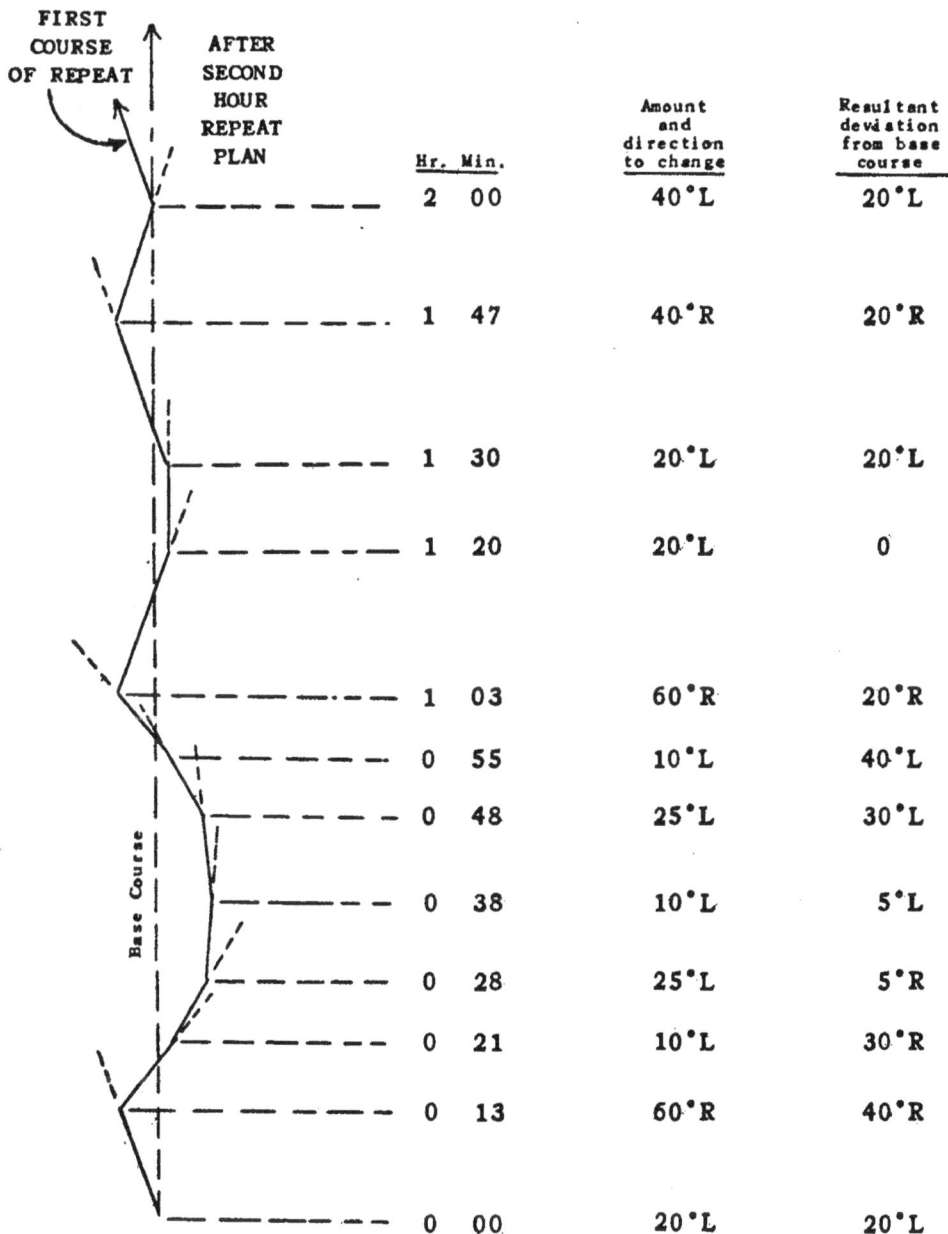

Hr. Min.	Amount and direction to change	Resultant deviation from base course
2 00	40°L	20°L
1 47	40°R	20°R
1 30	20°L	20°L
1 20	20°L	0
1 03	60°R	20°R
0 55	10°L	40°L
0 48	25°L	30°L
0 38	10°L	5°L
0 28	25°L	5°R
0 21	10°L	30°R
0 13	60°R	40°R
0 00	20°L	20°L

FIRST COURSE OF REPEAT

AFTER SECOND HOUR REPEAT PLAN

Base Course

ORIGINAL

ZIGZAG PLAN NO. 24

NOT SUITABLE FOR GENERAL USE.
FOR USE DURING ENTRY, SORTIE, OR WHILE IN RESTRICTED WATERS.

DISTANCE MADE GOOD - 97% OF DISTANCE RUN.

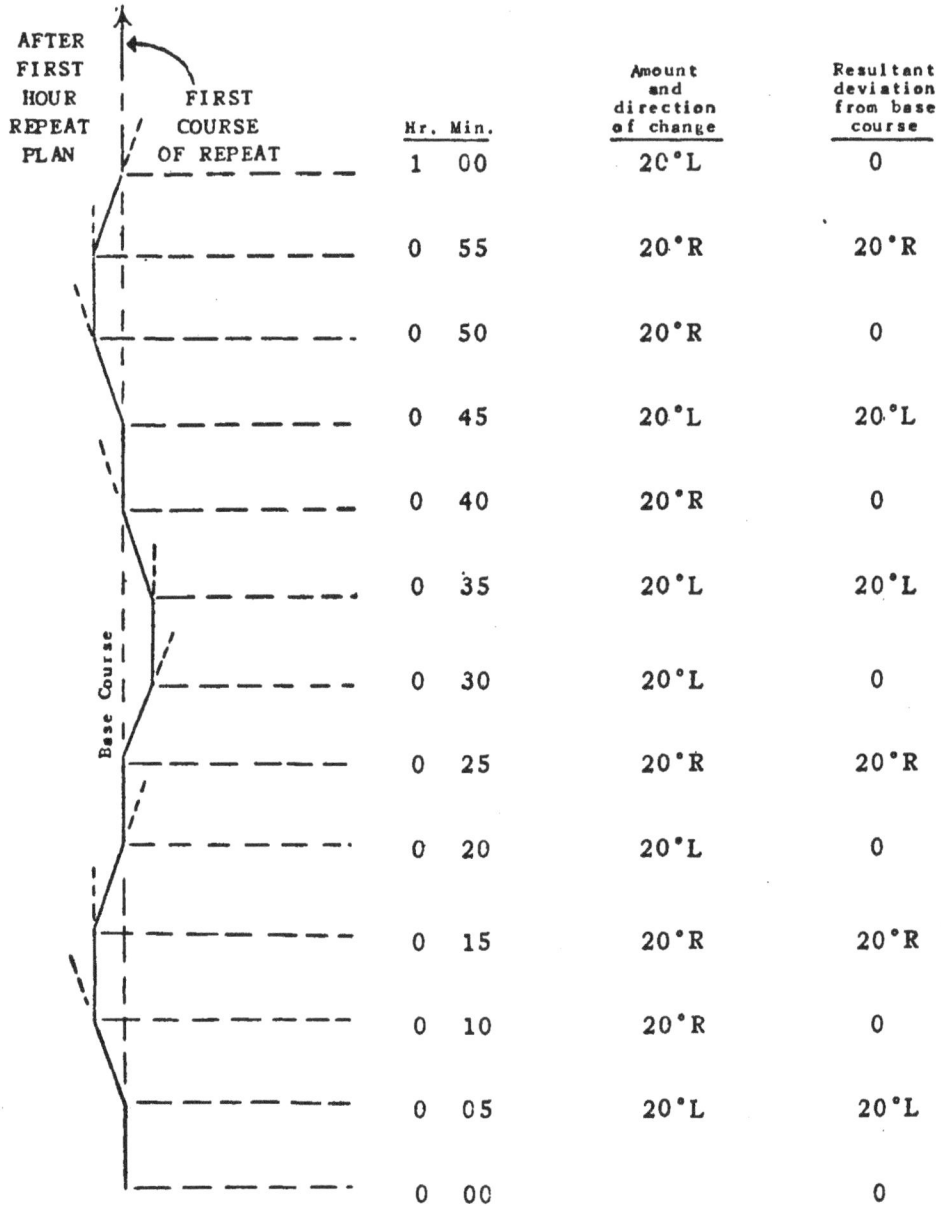

Hr. Min.	Amount and direction of change	Resultant deviation from base course
1 00	20°L	0
0 55	20°R	20°R
0 50	20°R	0
0 45	20°L	20°L
0 40	20°R	0
0 35	20°L	20°L
0 30	20°L	0
0 25	20°R	20°R
0 20	20°L	0
0 15	20°R	20°R
0 10	20°R	0
0 05	20°L	20°L
0 00		0

AFTER FIRST HOUR REPEAT PLAN

FIRST COURSE OF REPEAT

Base Course

ORIGINAL

ZIGZAG PLAN NO. 25

FOR GENERAL USE IN SUBMARINE AREAS.
SUITABLE FOR SHIPS, FORMATIONS AND DISPOSITIONS OF ALL SPEEDS.

DISTANCE MADE GOOD = 95% OF DISTANCE RUN.

*NOTE: This plan always starts on an hour divisible
by four (i.e., 0000, 0400, 0800, etc.)*

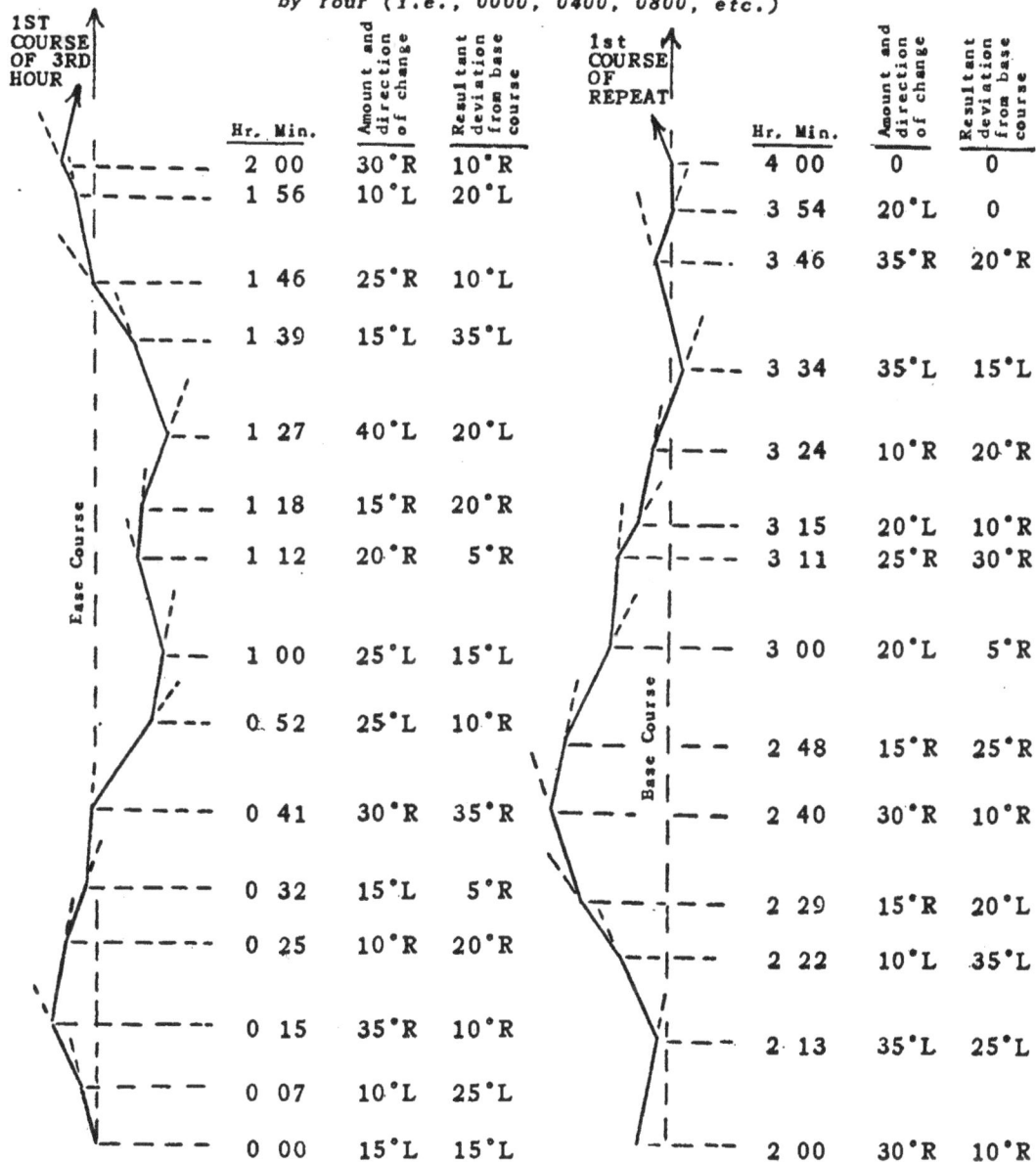

Hr. Min.	Amount and direction of change	Resultant deviation from base course
2 00	30°R	10°R
1 56	10°L	20°L
1 46	25°R	10°L
1 39	15°L	35°L
1 27	40°L	20°L
1 18	15°R	20°R
1 12	20°R	5°R
1 00	25°L	15°L
0 52	25°L	10°R
0 41	30°R	35°R
0 32	15°L	5°R
0 25	10°R	20°R
0 15	35°R	10°R
0 07	10°L	25°L
0 00	15°L	15°L

1ST COURSE OF 3RD HOUR

Base Course

Hr. Min.	Amount and direction of change	Resultant deviation from base course
4 00	0	0
3 54	20°L	0
3 46	35°R	20°R
3 34	35°L	15°L
3 24	10°R	20°R
3 15	20°L	10°R
3 11	25°R	30°R
3 00	20°L	5°R
2 48	15°R	25°R
2 40	30°R	10°R
2 29	15°R	20°L
2 22	10°L	35°L
2 13	35°L	25°L
2 00	30°R	10°R

1st COURSE OF REPEAT

Base Course

ORIGINAL   Ap. 2-18

USF 10B

ZIGZAG PLAN NO. 26

FOR GENERAL USE IN SUBMARINE AREAS.
SUITABLE FOR SHIPS, FORMATIONS AND DISPOSITIONS OF ALL SPEEDS.

DISTANCE MADE GOOD = 88% OF DISTANCE RUN.

*NOTE: This plan always starts on an hour divisible
by four (i.e., 0000, 0400, 0800, etc.)*

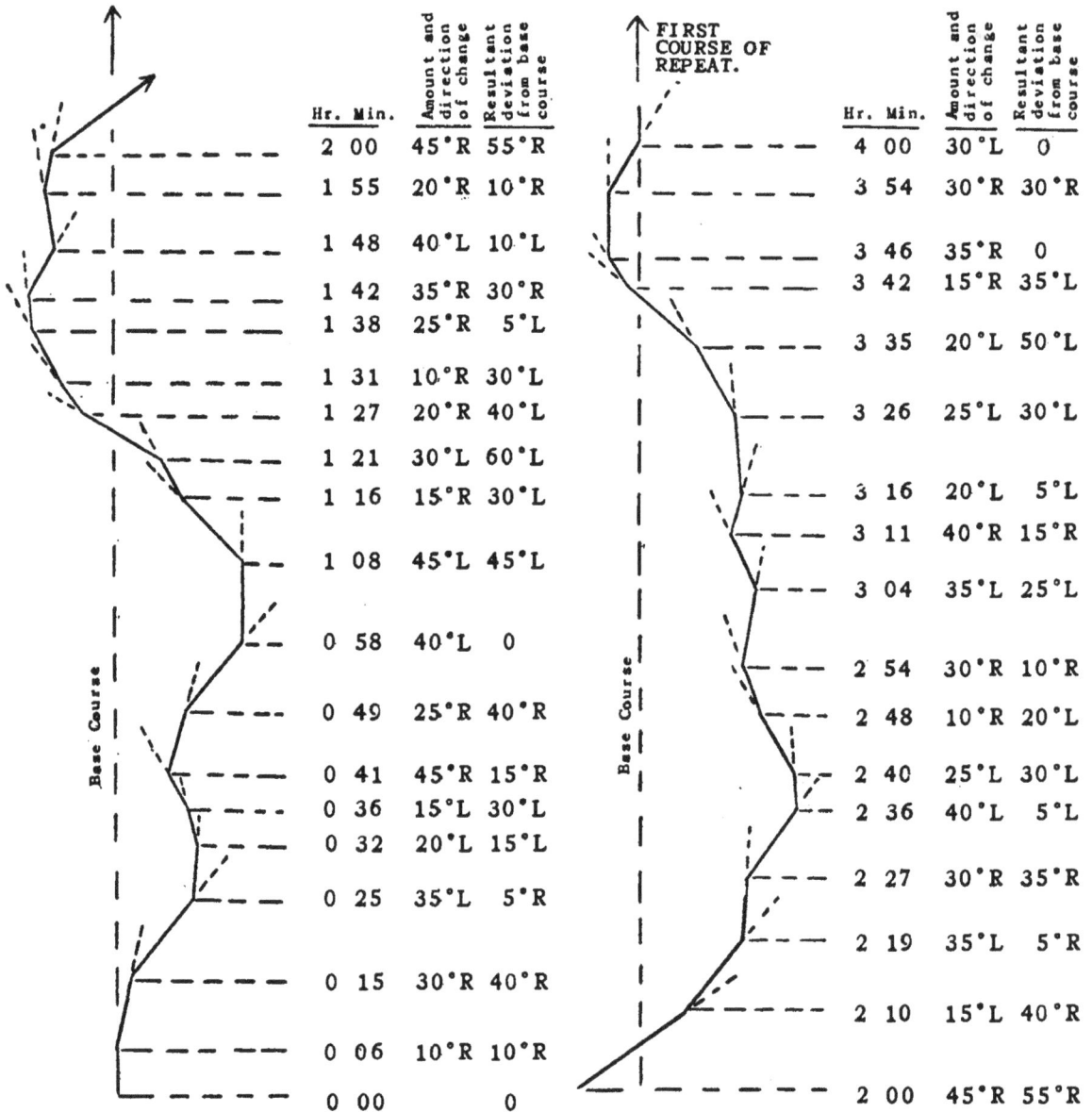

Hr. Min.	Amount and direction of change	Resultant deviation from base course
2 00	45°R	55°R
1 55	20°R	10°R
1 48	40°L	10°L
1 42	35°R	30°R
1 38	25°R	5°L
1 31	10°R	30°L
1 27	20°R	40°L
1 21	30°L	60°L
1 16	15°R	30°L
1 08	45°L	45°L
0 58	40°L	0
0 49	25°R	40°R
0 41	45°R	15°R
0 36	15°L	30°L
0 32	20°L	15°L
0 25	35°L	5°R
0 15	30°R	40°R
0 06	10°R	10°R
0 00		0

FIRST COURSE OF REPEAT.

Hr. Min.	Amount and direction of change	Resultant deviation from base course
4 00	30°L	0
3 54	30°R	30°R
3 46	35°R	0
3 42	15°R	35°L
3 35	20°L	50°L
3 26	25°L	30°L
3 16	20°L	5°L
3 11	40°R	15°R
3 04	35°L	25°L
2 54	30°R	10°R
2 48	10°R	20°L
2 40	25°L	30°L
2 36	40°L	5°L
2 27	30°R	35°R
2 19	35°L	5°R
2 10	15°L	40°R
2 00	45°R	55°R

Base Course

APPENDIX III TO USF 10B
LIGHT FORCES IN NIGHT SEARCH AND ATTACK

LIGHT FORCES IN NIGHT SEARCH AND ATTACK

GENERAL

101. This appendix covers the use of light forces in night search and attack. The ultimate task is the attack and destruction of the enemy objective. The search and contact scouting necessary to the success of the attack are contributory tasks. Since every search and attack problem will require a separate estimate of the situation, this appendix is intended only as a guide to present certain principles believed to be sound. These precepts are based on maximum use of radar both during the search and for the attack, and on the assumption that the enemy is also equipped with radar.

102. While this appendix is based on the assumption that radar will permit economy of scouts in search and will require a separation of forces to insure success for the attack, nothing in these instructions shall be construed in violation of the fundamental principles of surprise and concentration. Any dispersal of groups available for attack is based on the assumption that with prior warning the enemy may turn away and thereby reduce the effectiveness of the attack. If the enemy is assumed to have radar the advantage of land background for own forces should be sought. This may so reduce enemy radar efficiency that our attack may be a complete surprise. In this case a concentrated attack may be desirable, since the enemy will not have time to evade by a turn-away. If our radar is reliable, search units should avoid visual contact with the enemy until the attack starts.

FUNDAMENTALS

201. When a task force composed of light forces is ordered to inflict maximum damage upon the enemy objective during darkness (or during a period of low visibility), the operation is defined as night search and attack, light forces. — DEFINITIONS

202. There will usually be a search phase; there will always be an attack phase; preceding the attack phase, there may be a contact phase. — PHASES

203. The effective and proper use of radar with search permits wide dispersal and economy of scouts. Under favorable conditions scouts as such may be eliminated, permitting maximum initial concentration of all forces for the attack. When this condition obtains, the search will be conducted by the separate attack groups disposed initially as scouting groups. — SEARCH PHASE

CONTACT **204.** The contact phase is almost certain to begin with a properly evaluated radar contact and merges into the attack phase as additional information regarding the enemy objective is gained.

ATTACK PHASE **205.** Probable elimination of the surprise element with consequent evasive action by the enemy indicates that multiple attacks from separate sectors will insure greatest prospect of success. However, to exploit the element of surprise to the fullest extent, and prevent evasive action, all attacks should be launched as soon as offensive action by the separate attack groups may be coordinated.

TASK ORGANIZATION

ATTACK GROUPS **301.** The task force is divided into attack groups.

SCOUTS **302.** For the search, each attack group may have one or more of its units advanced as scouts, normally disposed as a scouting line. If early radar contact permits, these separate scouts will normally be joined by their attack groups. The task force then becomes an attack force composed of multiple attack groups, these groups being disposed on a scouting line. The task force commander may also act as an attack group commander.

CONCENTRATION **303.** As adequate contact information becomes available, attack groups should close their scouts, concentrate, and attack with them if possible. If cruisers are present, they should be assigned to support the separate destroyer attack groups insofar as the expected strength of enemy opposition will allow. Normally, cruisers should form with or as scouts in advance of the destroyer attack groups, and circumstances may demand that they attack at once.

THE SEARCH

LIMITS OF PHASE **401.** The extent of the search will depend upon how accurately the position and intentions of the enemy are known at the time the search is ordered. Search operations shall include those from the initial formation of the disposition up to the time the enemy is located either by radar or by sight contact.

RADAR **402.** Radar makes possible the approximation of day search formations at night. However, before this can be effectively accomplished the OTC must have definite knowledge of the proper method of using, and the limitations of, the types of radar installed in vessels composing the force. To this end individual ships must know what performance to expect from their radar in the particular area and the circumstances in which it is to be used, and advise the OTC accordingly.

There is no general rule; you must know your individual units. The weakest is your yardstick. While with the present radar equipment we can detect at night surface targets at approximately the same range as in daylight, we cannot in all cases distinguish the number of units, their type or formation. Under certain weather or land echo conditions the target may not even be detected. An indication of a large individual unit may turn into a group of ships as the range closes. Since a relatively wide dispersion of units in the scouting line is possible, we can maintain greater strength in each attack group and may employ a greater number of attack groups. This is most important as wide dispersal of our attack forces is necessary should the enemy attempt evasive tactics as soon as his first radar contact is made.

403. Initial search dispositions are dependent upon the following factors: **FACTORS DETER- MINING SEARCH DISPOSITION**

(a) Last known position of the enemy.

(b) Enemy intentions: Is the enemy committed by force of circumstances to a certain general direction of advance?

(c) Enemy disposition, speed, strength of screen, etc.

(d) Time available for search and attack. Under this time factor, we must consider the situation of our own forces after the attack; viz, distance from our own supports, whether or not dawn air coverage will be available and similar factors.

(e) Logistics.

404. The initial disposition of our forces should be such as to insure locating the enemy in the shortest possible time, and still permit the grouping of our maximum strength in as many widely separated sectors as possible for the attack if desired. The number of units upon the advanced scouting line should be kept at a minimum. **INITIAL DISPOSI- TION**

405. The scouting distance should be as great as possible consistent with the reliable range of radar and communication links. If, due to the tactical situation, it is not desired to use the normal high-frequency communication links, then an additional limitation is the reliable range of the superfrequency communication link available. Under normal circumstances a scouting distance of about 8 to 10 miles should fulfill these requirements and permit sufficient separation of attack groups. Scouting distances should be reduced or increased depending upon the reliable range of radar and the communication link in use in the operations. It is desirable that adjacent scouts or attack groups acting as scouts keep within positive radar and radio contact with each other to permit continuous and positive **SCOUTING DIS- TANCE**

mutual identification. It may be desirable to direct adjacent units or groups to scout at maximum distance at which radar contact can be maintained providing such distance will be consistent with the desired tactical concentration. Thus all units will be in positive touch with each other and the widest practicable front will be covered. If circumstances demand greater scouting distances, consideration may be given to using scouting distance equal to the sum of probably reliable radar range to adjacent units. In such cases the expeditious use of IFF with the proper code setting will assist in identification of various units but will not replace mutual understanding between units given by a sound understandable plan and pre-operation conference (if practicable).

SCOUTING INTERVAL

406. Scouts should be disposed sufficiently in advance of their attack groups to permit them to maneuver while tracking first contacts and reporting them. This interval must be great enough to insure that our attack groups do not charge into sight contact with the enemy before favorable attack positions can be reached, yet should allow rapid concentration of these groups with their scouts. Obviously this scouting interval will vary from a maximum when approaching at high speeds from ahead to a minimum when scouts are concentrated with their attack groups.

AIR SCOUTING

407. When the position of the enemy has been accurately determined by air reconnaissance shortly before nightfall and his general direction of advance may be predicted, the scouting line may be dispensed with, allowing the attack groups to proceed directly with the search and attack. The proper use of radar equipped aircraft will greatly aid the problems of night scouting and may eliminate its necessity. Due caution must be exercised regarding limitation and reliability of equipment. Mutual use of IFF will greatly assist the difficult identification problem.

METHOD OF SEARCH

408. Search will almost invariably be by the direct method, either from ahead, from the flank, or from the rear. Search from the rear may develop into a pursuit.

CONTACT SCOUTING

LIMITS OF PHASE

501. Contact scouting immediately follows initial contact and continues until all attacks are driven home. The scout making first contact with the enemy objective must scout this contact and hold it, assisted by adjacent scouts. Initial contacts are almost certain to be by radar. A properly functioning CIC will furnish the command valuable information on the enemy not otherwise available.

502. During this phase, the enemy objective must be located and essential information disseminated to the attack groups in order that the attack may be pushed home rapidly and effectively. It is imperative that the units first making contact, develop the track, giving information as rapidly as possible to the other units.

TRACK BY RADAR PLOT

503. Although the primary task of a destroyer in the scouting line is to gain information undetected, destroyer scouts will continue to attempt to gain information of the enemy objective even if assured, by being taken under fire, that their presence is detected. In these circumstances self-preservation, together with the principle of inflicting maximum damage upon the enemy, may require use of maximum speed, gunfire, and torpedoes. The use of smoke by a detected destroyer scout may assist it to break away from opposition in continuance of its primary task, but smoke shall not be used if it will interfere with the operation of the force as a whole.

PRIMARY TASK OF DESTROYER IN THE SCOUTING LINE

504. The primary task of a cruiser in the scouting line is to assist the service of information, directly as a scout and radar ship, and indirectly by using its full fire effect to inflict maximum damage upon, and create confusion among, enemy units which oppose the search, in order to enable scouts to penetrate the screen and in order to relieve the pressure on beset scouts.

PRIMARY TASK OF CRUISER IN THE SCOUTING LINE

505. Cruisers in the scouting line will not attempt to penetrate a screen except in the special case where they are later to attack a suitable enemy objective.

CRUISERS

506. Both cruiser and destroyer scouts should remain completely darkened as long as possible. When gunfire is indicated, the element of surprise should be exploited to the fullest by opening fire under full radar control.

GUNFIRE

THE ATTACK

601. The attack phase may be said to begin when one or more attack groups, following closely in the track of their scouts or concentrated with them, have located the enemy objective and are ready to start the attack.

LIMITS OF PHASE

602. The composition and disposition of own forces for the attack must depend primarily upon the type of the enemy objective, and the most suitable type for delivering the attack may range from cruisers alone against light forces to destroyers alone against battleships, with cruisers and destroyers in combination against carriers, train, or convoy. Even though no direct attack by cruisers upon the actual objective be contemplated, it may be essential for the

DISPOSITION OF OWN FORCES

attack groups to include cruisers; for example, to assure reduction of the screen at the points of entry of the attack.

ENEMY RADAR **603.** We must assume that the enemy possesses radar and will use it as effectively as we do unless the OTC has definite information to the contrary. It is possible by use of standard radar intercept receivers to determine whether or not the particular enemy objective is using radar and whether or not he has detected you. We must anticipate evasive action by the enemy objective by his using radar to determine our presence. Here the earliest concentration into multiple attack groups is mandatory. Rapidity of attack is necessary to insure contact with the objective and to prevent enemy retirement before maximum damage is inflicted. Ensuing attacks should follow in immediate succession to take full advantage of any confusion resulting from previous attacks.

ATTACK DOC-TRINE **604.** Attack doctrine requires that all destroyers remain completely dark as long as possible. Until certain that the enemy has made radar or sight contact, there is always the possibility of surprise coupled with the chance that our attack groups may close, track by radar, and launch torpedoes before they are observed. Consequently, attacking ships must develop every contact by CIC and keep the fire-control problem set up ready to open fire at a moment's notice using full radar control. Perfect coordination of CIC with torpedo control is also necessary in order that the torpedo directors may be kept set up and torpedoes launched at any moment using radar data to the fullest in solving the problem.

ATTACK BY THREE EQUALLY NUM-BERED GROUPS **605.** The ideal attack by a squadron would call for three equally numbered groups coming in from widely separated sectors, being able to find and track the enemy objective and to hit with torpedoes before being detected. Likewise, a successful penetration of the screen by destroyers or by cruisers followed by destroyers, should envisage the ideal of being able to open fire with guns and hit the enemy before being seen.

ATTACK BY SQUADRONS **606.** Should more than one squadron be available, the squadrons may be formed separately in closer attack formations and make attacks in succession from their respective sectors. Each squadron should normally be formed in groups that will afford the best sector coverage and greatest tactical flexibility.

CRUISERS AND DE-STROYERS IN VEE FORMATION **607.** For attacks upon strong forces of the enemy well screened by both cruisers and destroyers, particularly when the destroyer objective is enemy heavy ships, concentrations in greater strength are essential. In these cases, cruiser support for the destroyer attack is necessary, the cruisers preceding the destroyers to the attack. A concentration of at least one squadron of destroyers and at least two cruisers is considered the minimum force for such a case. The destroyer squadron shall be organized into three-ship units and formed with the division leaders of the two flank divisions about 1,000 yards on each quarter of the rear ship of the center division. Cruisers will be divided into two formations on both bows of the center division and 2,000 to 3,000 yards ahead. This formation is known as the Vee formation and is used when the cruisers are to attack and disorganize the screen without penetrating it. Upon reaching and subjecting the screen to heavy fire, the right and left flank cruisers turn to the right and left respectively and retire, allowing the destroyer squadron to penetrate the screen and launch their torpedoes against the enemy heavy ships.

608. A similar formation called the wedge formation is used when the cruisers themselves penetrate the screen and attack the enemy objective with gunfire. The wedge formation is particularly applicable when the objectives are carriers, transports, etc. In the wedge formation, the cruisers form in advance of the center destroyer division using their heavy fire power to disrupt the screen thus allowing the destroyer squadron to follow them through the objective. **CRUISERS AND DESTROYERS IN WEDGE FORMATION**

609. Should the movements of the enemy or the intelligence furnished by CIC indicate that he has radar contact on our attack groups, it is advisable for attack groups to employ proper evasive tactics during the approach in order to render tracking by the enemy more difficult. **ATTACK COURSE**

610. Night attack in pursuit usually implies action against an enemy force previously damaged in a day action. Normally every risk should be incurred in a pursuit action in order to make victory complete; but should radar search disclose strong forces disposed to cover the retirement, our best course of action may be to envelope the flanks and attack from ahead. This action is obvious when delaying tactics or cutting off a line of retreat is desired. **NIGHT ACTION IN PURSUIT**

611. Under normal conditions with radar installed, illumination should not be necessary. Whether or not illumination is desirable is dependent upon type of enemy objective and the disposition of his forces. Against a screened carrier group or troop convoy, surprise star-shell illumination of the objective might well be employed. The time and method for illumination should be prescribed by the operation order. Standard star-shell doctrine should be employed; viz, successive star-shell spreads from all groups. Flashless powder should be used. Flare illumination by planes may be used both to illuminate the objectives and to create confusion. Current doctrine for both cruisers and destroyers requires that searchlights when used be turned on for brief intervals to allow for accuracy in control of **ILLUMINATION**

fire without affording the enemy time to utilize our beams as a point of aim.

COUNTER-ILLUMINATION

612. Attack groups illuminated and taken under fire by the enemy should use both star shell and searchlights for counterillumination in an effort to confuse and blind the enemy.

SMOKE

613. The attack doctrine calls for the use of smoke when necessary during retirement to defeat illumination by the enemy.

COMMUNICATIONS

701. To organize and to dispose of units of the task force in their initial position by executive signal, the following elements must be indicated:

TASK ORGANIZATION AND INITIAL POSITION

(a) Type of scouting line.

(b) Method of search.

(c) Type of attack groups.

Signal: "CONDUCT NIGHT SEARCH AND ATTACK IN ACCORDANCE WITH PLAN INDICATED."

702. Then follow three numerals which indicate the three elements in the sequence mentioned above. The following table gives the meaning of each numeral. The table covers what are considered the combinations most likely to be employed. Simplicity requires a limit to combinations; no limit on the initiative of the commander is implied.

First Numeral Type of Scouting Line	Second Numeral Method of Search	Third Numeral Type of Attack Group (Includes Scouts on Line)
0. None.		
1. Destroyers, single ship units.	1. Direct from ahead.	1. Single destroyer.
2. Cruisers, single ship units.	2. Direct from flank.	2. Destroyer section.
3. Cruisers and destroyers in ship units.	3. Direct from rear.	3. Destroyer in 3-ship units.
4. Destroyers, section units.	4. Patrol method from flank.	4. Destroyer division.
5. Destroyers in section units, cruisers in single-ship units.		5. Destroyer squadron.
6. Destroyers, 3 ship units.		6. Destroyer squadron plus cruisers (Vee formation).
7. Destroyers in 3 ship units, cruisers in single-ship units.		7. Destroyer squadron plus cruisers (wedge formation).
8. Other combinations of destroyers and/or cruisers.		

DECLASSIFIED

DECLASSIFIED

www.ingramcontent.com/pod-product-compliance
Lightning Source LLC
Chambersburg PA
CBHW082147150426
42812CB00076B/2446